the Sustainable 🌿 Business

Fatum aut libatis?

© 2015 Jackson, Carter & Figg

The rights of Jackson, Carter & Figg
to be identified as the authors of this work have been asserted by them in accordance with the Copyright, Designs and Patents Act 1988.

All rights reserved. No part of this publication may be reproduced, stored in a retrieval system, or transmitted in any form or by any means, electronic, mechanical, photocopying, recording, or otherwise without prior permission of Cambridge Academic at:
The Studio, High Green, Gt. Shelford, Cambridge. CB22 5EG

ISBN 1-903-499-81-X
978-1-903499-81-8

The contents of this publication are provided in good faith and neither The Authors nor The Publisher can be held responsible for any errors or omissions contained herein. Any person relying upon the information must independently satisfy himself or herself as to the safety or any other implications of acting upon such information and no liability shall be accepted either by The Author or The Publisher in the event of reliance upon such information nor for any damage or injury arising from any interpretation of its contents. This publication may not be used in any process of risk assessment.

Printed and bound in the United Kingdom by 4edge Ltd, 7a Eldon Way Industrial Estate, Hockley, Essex, SS5 4AD.

Profit Through Change contact details
Email: info@profitthroughchange.com

"A sustainable business has no lasting impact on the global, national or local environment; commits to the rights and contribution of the employees across the whole supply chain and in the wider community whilst recognising its own need to generate a robust commercial structure to deliver on-going value to its stakeholders."

Contents

Preface 1
Acknowledgements 3
About the Authors 4
Introduction 5

1: The Sustainable Vision 9
Case Study: Easter Island

2: The Corporate Social Responsibility Policy – The People Pillar 39
Case Study: Tengizchevroil

3: The Corporate Social Responsibility Policy – The Profit Pillar 59
Case Study: Telemechanique

4: The Corporate Social Responsibility Policy – The Planet Pillar ... 95
Case Study: Freecycle

5: Sustainability in the Business Context 123
Case Study: Healthcare

6: Sustainable Procurement and Supplier Management 145
Case Study: Metal Conduit and Fittings Market Segment

7: Sustainability across the Supply Chain 173
Case Study: Dell

8: The Sustainable Sales Team 225
Case Study: Chubb Fire, Océ, & Trend Control Systems

9: Sustainable Operations Management 259
Case Study: Toyota

10: Sustainable Quality and Design 285
Case Study: Aviation Design Innovations

11: Sustainable Project Management................................319
Case Study: Wembley Stadium

12: Sustainable Risk..331
Case Study: Datacentres

13: Sustainable Legal and Finance................................347
Case Study: Enron

14: Measurement of Sustainability................................355
Case Study: Philips Lighting

15: A Sustainable Strategy...387
Case Study: Unilever

16: Conclusion..421
Case Study: Wiremold

Appendix i: List of Illustrations......................................435
Appendix ii: List of Abbreviations...................................441
Appendix iii: Sustainable Rules......................................447

Bibliography..449
Index..451

Preface

"You're too late", "We've run out", "There's nobody available"!

A difficult situation to manage in our personal lives, but what if you are running a business and your employees, customers and suppliers are relying on your actions?

Sustainability is about more than just going green or switching a few lights off. It's about building a profitable, low risk, stable organisation that operates with a responsible approach to its inputs, outputs and its people whilst being conscious about its impact on the environment and community in which it operates.

The Sustainable Business anticipates all eventualities, not from a risk management perspective, but from a desire to be fulfilling customer demand tomorrow, next year, and beyond; it has a focus on longevity – *The Sustainable Business* has three objectives:

1. To identify opportunities to increase profitability;
2. To help improve the welfare of the people involved with the business both inside and out;
3. And to act conscientiously about the environment and the natural world in which we live.

From a student's perspective – whether on the CIPS programme or any other similar scheme or course – the issue of sustainability should not be constrained to the "Sustainability Module" alone. Sustainability should flow throughout the business and across the syllabus, and is an excellent source of added value and extra marks within most units of assessment.

This book generates ideas, provokes comment and will hopefully instigate change. It is aimed at supporting the concept of sustainability as an academic work across university fields of study, and many of the current institute syllabi, with a particular emphasis on the Chartered Institute of Purchasing and Supply.

The chapters are broadly aligned to the typical organisational departments, with guidance, models and ideas for generating change.

Each chapter adopts a consistent structure commencing with a chapter summary and statement of key learning points and concluding with a case study relevant to the ideas and subject matter. The chapters contain numerous models and ideas – some old some new – aimed at reinforcing the concepts discussed in the text, text which is intended to be both readable and stimulating.

Commencing with *the Three Pillar* Model, the introduction and first three chapters look at the impact of people, the planet and the essential need to make money within an organisation, as well as the requirement for a clear corporate vision. These are the foundation of *the Sustainable Business*, without these the business will fail with its longevity mandate.

Subsequent chapters address various facets of the typical business. These include: the operating environment and structure of the business; the procurement function; the Supply Chain; the sales team; the operating processes; the quality and design activities; project spectrums; the risk function; the legal and finance activity; and concluding with how we might measure sustainability.

These individual assessments address the individual needs of the department or function whilst remaining cognitive of the wider organisational goals. In the concluding chapters the drawing together of the individual efforts as part of an organisation-wide sustainable strategy concludes the analysis and identifies tangible benefit and processes to enable the organisation to fulfil its sustainable ambitions.

At the end of the book, the reader will appreciate the overall importance and contribution a sustainable approach within a business can have, and will be able to clearly develop strategy to enable that goal to be reached. It is hoped that the reader will also have developed an understanding about the contributions and successes that a sustainable approach is having within organisations throughout the world, showing that anything and everything is possible.

In conclusion, we sincerely hope that this work adds value to the reader, the organisation, and the world in which we live. *The Sustainable Business* recognises that its actions have an impact, and that this impact must be managed, planned and balanced.

Acknowledgements

This book is intended to be both readable and informative, but importantly make a difference to the way a company might think, plan and operate, and influence how a student may entrench sustainability into his or her overall learning.

I would like to thank all the people who have contributed directly to the writing of this book: the co-authors Jason Figg and Ray Carter for their contributions; and the proof readers – especially my mother and mother-in-law – who painstakingly corrected my grammar and punctuation.

In addition, thanks must also be paid to my previous employers, clients and business partners who have peppered my career with sufficient experience and examples to hopefully *colour* the text throughout this work. When teaching, I have found that examples make the subject more tolerable, more memorable and more likely to make a difference; this book endeavours to entwine those practical examples with conceptual theory and academic research.

Where examples are used, specific company names have only been included where there has been a positive contribution to society or the planet. It is felt that credit should be given where credit is due, and it is evident that throughout the globe, organisations have started to wake up to the realisation that change is essential to the future of the planet. All specific references are made in good faith and entirely positively. Thank you to those companies for making a start.

Furthermore, whilst too numerous to list, as with all modern publications, the Worldwide Web played an important role in the research and validation of information, statistics and hearsay; without it, this work would have taken a lifetime.

And finally, a thank you to my long suffering wife and children who have heard about *the Sustainable Business* for months if not years, your support and encouragement has been fantastic.

About the Authors

Collectively, the three authors provide a varied and extensive mix of expertise gleaned within the highest level of business over many years. They possess experience ranging from small fledgling organisations to large multinational conglomerates and within the public sector, and are well placed to understand the issues facing any organisation looking to become more sustainable.

They regularly undertake consultancy projects, corporate roles and training activities through their various business interests in locations across the globe. Many of the insights within this book have been witnessed during projects carried out over the years.

This book follows numerous articles, books, blogs and other works published by the authors on a plethora of subjects.

Introduction

"Smart organisations ensure cross-business collaboration, to safeguard the social and environmental impacts that are vital to sustainability." –Tim Cummins, CEO IACCM

Once upon a time, we lived in a world without *man-made* climate change....it was something that would happen way in the future.... something to think about in years to come; we are now in that future, these are the years when we need to think, plan and do – now! What is the impact on the planet of our business, its structures, activities, processes and behaviours - what is our business impact? If we fail to preserve our vital resources it will affect our people, our planet and most definitely our profitability.

The "Credit Crunch" raised concerns globally about the on-going profitability of some of the world's largest organisations. Questions were asked as to how profits were generated, how long could they last, and what were their underlying processes, structures and ethics. Many organisations of course failed, profit was essential to their on-going success and survival.

For a number of years now, the heightened importance of people in business has been realised. People are the lifeblood of the organisation, it is essential that they are valued, nurtured, and developed. Recruiting the right employees into the organisation has never been more critical, but creating the right environment for them to flourish, operate effectively and to feel motivated is now more highly recognised. They will be responsible for generating the business profit today, tomorrow and in the future.

These are the hallmark of *The Sustainable Business*, its Profit, its People and the Planet. Sustainability must start now.

Politicians of all persuasions make noise around election time about the need to think and act green, but riding a bicycle to work or hosting a "green summit" is not enough. Trade restrictions, import agreements, and setting regulations should not be the excuse for why we can't encompass change, but a motivation to more passionately drive the sustainable agenda. Kyoto must not be something we talk about and confine to history; it must be something we deliver, for this and future generations.

This book will help guide the organisation, but it is not intended to merely suggest endless ways of being greener, such as switching out the lights or turning off the tap. Sustainability must be an intrinsic component of all that we do for the sake of our business, the decisions we make, and the actions we take. It need not constrain, but merely balance our choices. By making business truly sustainable, we will be on our way to a tolerable equilibrium.

The purpose of this book therefore, is to explore the impact of sustainability upon all components of business. The word *Impact* is used extensively throughout this book as it so eloquently reflects the concept of sustainability. Each of the typical parts of an organisation are examined to understand what each can do to help deliver change, add value and improve sustainability.

Furthermore, the term "Adding Value" is used frequently as, in order to succeed, it is essential that we focus on net value rather than cost. Cost is something we avoid, the term investment is more palatable, however value is what *the Sustainable Business* must cherish and strive to deliver.

Organisations tend to focus on their shareholders and on "this year's bottom line" as their primary goal. They see sustainability as a nominally desirable extra, not as a key part of the strategy. They produce elaborate CSR policy and then generate the corporate strategy in isolation, neglecting the defining features of the *Triple Bottom Line*, but perhaps ticking the box on a tender document or bulking out the web-site.

Our Mission details why we exist as a business, our *raison d'etre*. What is needed is a "Vision", a long-term plan, a clear goal. This Corporate Vision statement is critical. Without a clear vision it is difficult for the numerous business stakeholders to understand the strategy, or embrace the way forward.

To succeed, *the Sustainable Business* needs to understand what it wants to be and where it wants to go; it needs a Mission and a Vision:

Mission   Vision

The inspiration for this book is born out of frustration:

- Frustration that we know what is needed, but our perspective is for the here and now: it's short sighted, it's for the current financial year, for the political term, or for the duration of the prevailing business cycle.

- Frustration that we invest time and effort producing a Corporate Sustainability Policy, but then do little about implementing it.

- Frustration that politicians of all persuasions talk big on what they plan to do, but then fail to deliver once in power, claiming it will take longer than the current electoral period to deliver.

- Frustration that we have the technology, the innovation and the ideas, but not the inclination to invest and utilise what we know.

- Frustration that we have competent and effective business managers who can do, but don't do.

- Frustration that as a planet, we lack "Sustainable Conviction"!

To achieve change communication is vital. The structure of the text is therefore intended to be both readable, and hopefully useful. It aims to balance the academic perspective with useful tools and process, intermingled with examples of best practice or thought provoking ideas. Each chapter highlights the key learning points, useful models and tools, and includes a relevant case study.

The text is intended to be both informative and thought provoking. Whilst written for both the conscientious business leader and the academic, the structure and content is intended to reflect the Chartered Institute of Purchasing and Supply syllabus across all levels. It is the view of the authors that the concept of sustainability should form part of all modules in the CIPS and indeed other Chartered programmes and university courses.

Finally, it is hoped that this text might help stimulate ideas, innovation and some "Sustainable Conviction". *The Sustainable Business* has Sustainable Conviction: it has confidence of its future, confidence of its longevity, and confidence of its positive contribution to society and its stakeholders.

Examples of best practice and opportunities to make a difference are included throughout, and may help organisations make the investment. Many of the ideas add net value, albeit often in relatively small numbers or over a long period.

Should we spend a moment of our time to turn off a dripping tap, or just ignore it as the impact is so small?

Many organisations find reasons why they should **not** adopt a new idea, with most unwilling to take the leap of faith, to be the trailblazer, or to think outside the box – ideas and innovation **must** be implemented to allow them to add value to the business, to the employees, and to the planet.

We need to change!

Summary Chapter 1
The Sustainable Vision

Key Learning Points

- The need for a corporate vision to help determine the strategy
- The importance of thinking longer term
- Sustainability as part of the corporate culture
- Sustainability should be part of the senior management philosophy
- Understanding the current status of the organisation is critical
- Analysis of the prevailing status of internal and external issues affecting the organisation
- Assessment of the forces applying within the organisation's market
- Product Life Cycle & Boston Consulting Group Matrix
- Product contributions and strategy to maximise value achieved
- Ensuring product set meets the customer expectation
- Measuring the Company: Community relationship
- Understanding our business IMPACT
- Forecasting and predicting where we want to get to

Tool Summary

- Current Status Model
- SWOT Analysis
- PESTLE Analysis
- Porter's Five Force Model
- Product Life Cycle
- Boston Consulting Group
- IMPACT Model

CIPS Syllabus Reference

- All CIPS Modules

Chapter 1: The Sustainable Vision

"Vision without action is a dream. Action without vision is simply passing the time. Action with vision is making a positive difference" – Joel Barker

As with many business activities, the basis of success is in the planning, communication and of course the strategy. A failure at the corporate level to recognise the importance and benefit of a truly sustainable organisation, and *the Sustainable Vision* will remain just that, a vision.

The emergence of the Corporate Social Responsibility (CSR) policy in recent years is evidence of the prevailing trend towards sustainability. It is however interesting to determine whether the CSR has been introduced for genuine reasons or, as mentioned previously, merely to satisfy the political aspirations of the organisation's stakeholders, the small print in a tender return, or to fill space on the corporate web-site.

Evidence suggests that, at a managerial level, organisations pursue a sustainable agenda, but at a sub-ordinate level there is more scepticism.

The suggestion that a company should be looking at the long term picture may seem obvious, however rarely in SME organisations does this actually appear to be the case – especially in a recession or market slow-down. A vision of the future should form an underpinning component of the risk profile and of the strategy, but how often does this actually occur?

The importance of establishing sustainability as an integral part of the business culture is one of the key modern day business issues. When setting up or developing a business, it is critical to appreciate the business context in which it is to operate. Many factors affect the business context and it is necessary to identify those which are "Sustainable Drivers".

Sustainable Drivers are the keys to a truly sustainable business. They determine how success is achieved; the contributors to the success should form the focus of the strategy and the business efforts to achieve sustainability in all its operations.

The Corporate Vision

Corporate Vision is a high level statement of the organisation's primary goals, where is it trying to get to; who are its target customers; what are its core markets; and so on. Without a clear idea of where you want to go, planning the *route* can be difficult and ultimately doomed to failure.

But this is often confused with its Mission and there is a clear difference: The Mission tells us what we want to be, the Vision details where we want to go. Take for example Sodexho, their two statements read as follows:

Sodexho mission
- Improve the Quality of Daily Life of our clients and employees.
- Contribute to the economic, social and environmental development of the cities, regions and countries in which we operate.

Sodexho vision
- To become the premier global outsourcing expert in the Quality of Life services.
- To be recognized nationwide and worldwide as the best solution provider for benefits, motivation and gift programs in the corporate, individual and public-sector markets, with service excellence and innovation as the driving force.

The Vision is the organisation's destination; it needs to be where the organisation is aiming, yet sadly the typical organisation often only plans for the next financial period or two, rarely any longer. There are of course a few exceptions: accountants projecting payback schedules, research and development personnel with product planning and testing, lawyers looking at long business leases, or project managers looking after projects with a very long development time are but a few.

There are however organisations where extensive planning is undertaken, but failure to perform is addressed, with little compassion, as soon as the dark clouds start amassing. High level football managers are a case in point. Four (20%) of the twenty English Premier League clubs had changed their managers in the first four months of the 2010/11 season, with less than twenty games played. Only three (15%) of the twenty clubs had a manager who has served more than five years, and thirteen (65%) of the clubs had a manager with less than two years service. One club (Chelsea) had had six managers in five years. In contrast, the manager of one of the largest clubs (Sir Alex Ferguson of Manchester United) had managed the club for twenty six years before his retiring, keeping it at the highest level, consistently rebuilding the team, nurturing new talent, establishing effective training and exploring new management techniques. (Source: Football Association) This raises a critical dilemma for such organisations: much has been made of the then Alex Ferguson being one game away from the sack before an unexpected one-nil away victory at Nottingham Forest in the 3rd round of the 1990 FA Cup four years into his tenure. Yet the Manchester United board had faith, Manchester United had a vision.

Likewise, Bill Shankley had a vision as he built a similar dynasty, his "Bastion of Invincibility" at Liverpool. Albeit with several likeminded managers, this led to years of success with a trophy haul, commensurate with that of Manchester United, though superior at the European level.

Recognising the need to be sustainable must be embraced at the highest level in the organisation for it to succeed. Senior management need to manage for the future, build effective foundations, establish robust policy, create a positive culture, and so on.

Long term thinking does not come easily to many individuals however. Twelve large public and private companies were asked what long term (10 years plus) economic forecasting they undertook – whilst having a long term vision, none admitted to any form of long term economic planning, despite stating that the credit crunch had raised the risk rating on economic stability. In the event that any projections did occur, they were effectively quarantined, with nobody wanting to have their name associated with such a prediction, to buck the trend or stand-out as a pioneer.

Food for Thought: Does your organisation plan to be in business in ten years time? If it does, what provisions are in place for the development of employees, financial investment, currency fluctuations, prediction of market changes, strategy for new product

> development, market management, and so on. The Sustainable Business plans for today, and for tomorrow.

Equally, in the 2009 Staples National Business Survey, of 300 companies surveyed, over 75% suggested that they had yet to achieve their vision for the company in question.

In 2007, few would have predicted the turmoil that 2008 and 2009 would hold, however economic history predicted those events. Build-up and collapse of debt can be tracked back over centuries as explored by the 1930s economist Kondratieff among others. Long wave forecasts help us understand economic, social, innovation, political and even happiness trends.

But action is necessary. Change should not be overwhelmed within a wider corporate strategy, it can occur incrementally: less is sometimes more. The expression "eat the elephant" is appropriate – don't be overwhelmed at the enormity of the task we face, start one mouthful at a time.

It is a common held belief that "past performance is best predictor"; in business strategy and planning too, this has some truth. Understanding the organisation's history, the market's history, and the history of the competitive activity in the market is essential to effectively plan for the future, essential to creating our business vision and to creating *The Sustainable Business*.

So what should our Sustainable Vision look like?

In order to plan our sustainable journey, we need to know firstly where we are now and then where we need or want to get to. Once we have the start and the end points, we have some chance of producing the strategy that can get the organisation from *now* to the *then*.

But where the vision is some way off, effective implementation is often enhanced with an incremental approach; eating the elephant is easier mouthful by mouthful.

Essentially, there are four main areas that should be considered when looking at our "Current Status", or "where we are today" – see figure 1.1.

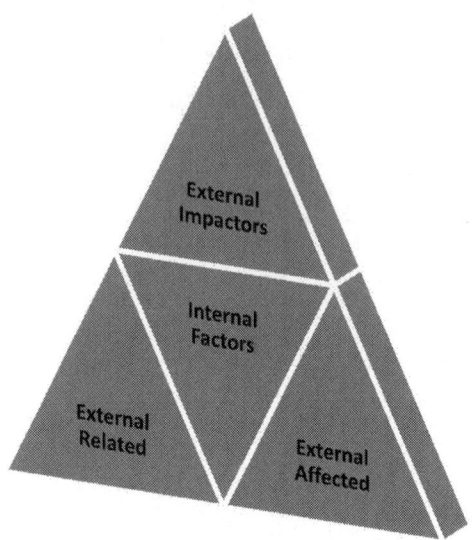

Figure 1.1 – Current Status Model

Internal Factors

Firstly we need to consider ourselves and our business, the part we can directly affect. We need to understand our structure, processes, assets and people, these are the foundations of a solid business, and take time to develop and blend. We also need to recognise the technology we employ. Most technology can change rapidly, and without vigilant monitoring an organisation can quickly become stale and left behind. Equally, it is critical that an organisation constantly reviews and refreshes its product offering, reflecting changes in demand, new innovations, competitor offerings and substitute products.

The development of new products through research and development is core to the success of *the Sustainable Business.* Consider the relative size of the investment made by Germany, France and the UK in Research and Development over the past few years. Whilst all are showing increased investment, both France and the UK lag the German investment by some considerable margin, and this contributes to the German dominance in Europe over the past decades – see figure 1.2. If there is any direct correlation between Research and Development and innovation, then this is a worrying trend for countries and companies who do not invest accordingly. (Source: OECD)

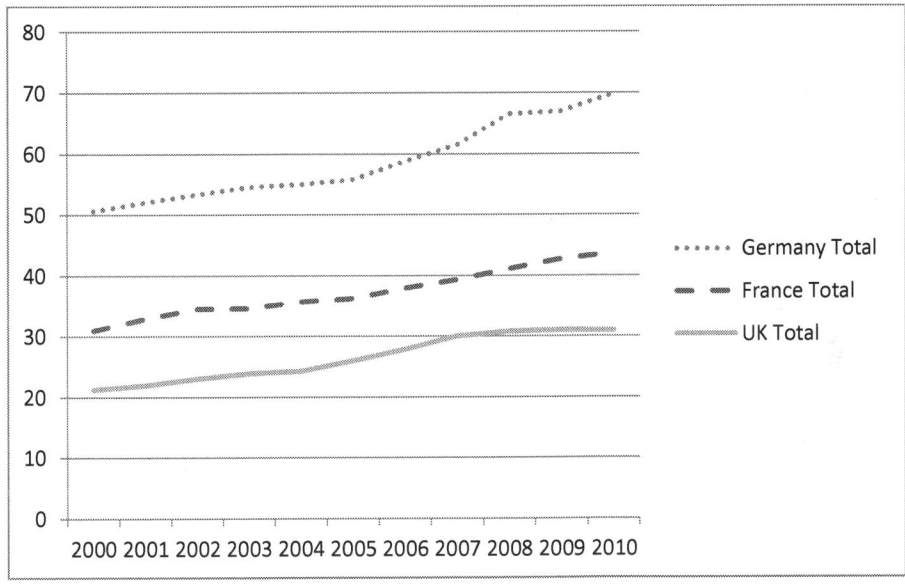

Figure 1.2 – Relative investment in Research & Development (M€)

Food for Thought: According to McKinsey, return on investment in R&D for drug companies has fallen in recent years from around 12% in the 1990s to around 7.5% since 2001. Whilst on the face of it, these may seem attractive margins, the cost estimates for the development of these drugs is now estimated at over 8.5%, i.e. it appears no longer worth the companies seeking new remedies.

An alternative approach can be to simply review the internal strengths and weaknesses of the organisation, perhaps using a SWOT analysis – see figure 1.3. This traditional four box model looks at internal perspective of the business, the strengths and the weaknesses of an organisation, as well as reviewing the opportunities that are open to the organisation, and any potential threats in the external markets in which it operates. Using this simple model, the organisation can develop strategy to use its strengths to exploit the opportunities and protect against any threats, whilst focusing resources to remedy the weaknesses. This helps develop both internal and external strategy as well as its risk policy, all aspects explored later.

It is also sensible for an organisation to constantly assess its capital and operational locations, as for example with Boeing moving from Seattle to Chicago in 2001, Microsoft from Albuquerque to Bellevue and then onto Redmond in 1987, or the BBC's decision to move out of London in 2010. In Boeing's case, the move followed a strategic review of the current operation, and what it felt it required to add value and create organic growth. The review critically highlighted the limitations of its geographic location, and the need to create autonomy across its different divisional operations.

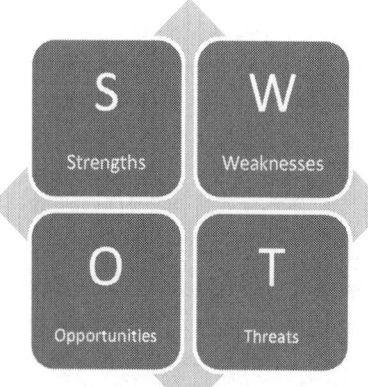

Figure 1.3 – SWOT analysis

However a significant percentage of organisations shy clear of any attempt to change the geographical location of its managerial operations, with many preferring to establish a clear base in one town or city, with satellite operations elsewhere as required. The important issue is that there are sufficient resources in the chosen location to fulfil future demand. Persevering with a corporate location with insufficient capacity of a resource will only cause cost inefficiency and uncompetitiveness in the future, ultimately leading to a loss of corporate value and potential failure.

To complicate matters further, Government policy of preserving society, the community and jobs actually motivates organisations to move to areas in need of regeneration, with incentive grants, development allowances, tax havens, etc. Albeit well intended, this acts as a market distortion and skews the dynamics of a competitive market. It encourages organisations to locate based on short term financial inducements, rather than its longer term sustainable needs. Indeed, in such circumstances, it could be argued that there is a direct conflict between the sustainable needs of the organisation and the sustainable needs of the nation.

This approach of steering corporate location policy can only be endorsed where there is a larger strategic aim as was the case in the 1800s in the UK. At that time, there was a need to develop the UK economy and wider industrial base for the good of the British Empire. Queen Victoria, in response to a financial collapse at that time, invested very heavily in regional centres of excellence – Stoke for the pottery industry, Sheffield for steel, Lancashire for cotton, Dudley for forging, etc. This was supported with capital intensive projects, such as the Manchester Ship Canal, and resulted with many of these areas assuming global recognition. This contrasts the 2011 UK initiative of "Enterprise Zones" which may end up being little more than cheap accommodation for start-ups and SME organisations.

In defence of such policies however, the decisions to develop run down areas can be extremely beneficial. Consider the redevelopment projects in Aden in the Yemen, the London Docklands in the UK, the Bangalore region of India, the Prijedor Municipality in Bosnia or Incheon Free Economic Zone in the Republic of Korea. These have all proven a success and delivered real economic prosperity to their communities.

Wider, it is recognised that a corporate relocation often coincides with a review of the business operating structure, a topic covered later.

> **Food for Thought:** How would the development of a sustainable future in the UK have been affected if Quantitative Easing – the printing of money – had been used to fund specialist universities - £1billion to form: The "University of Wind Generation" in Aberdeen, "University of Fisheries" in Grimsby, "University of Farming" in Salisbury and the "University of Low Carbon Transport" on the old Rover site in Birmingham?

Finally, the current financial status of the organisation needs to be assessed. The debtor and creditor ratios, financing terms, credit periods, loan stipulations, employee bonus schemes and shareholder requirements are all elements reflecting the current status and health of the organisation. Companies can legitimately manipulate these financial indicators to some degree but understanding the starting points is a prerequisite to establishing the true financial health of the organisation. If, for example, the organisation is carrying too much debt, this may lead to its inability to raise additional investment going forward, or lead to excessive interest rates being charged by the lender seeking to offset its risk. Equally, if an organisation has excessive monies owed to it, it is not making best use of its financial resources and is increasing its risk of bad debts. These areas are explored in greater depth in later chapters.

External Impactors

As important to where we are today is the need to consider the external forces that directly impact on our organisation and its market.

Porter's Five Force model – see figure 1.4 – highlights the forces that are present in a competitive market place and attempts to measure the relative power of each. This competitive rivalry is often the strongest External Impactor.

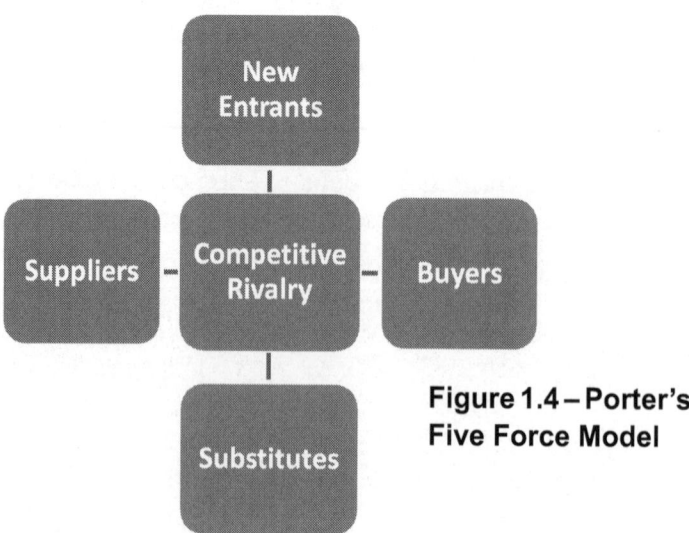

Figure 1.4 – Porter's Five Force Model

Arguably the most important force Porter identified for the average organisation is the buyer or customer base. Having a balanced customer mix is vital to a stable organisation. Understanding who your customers are, what they want, and having products to meet their needs is fundamental to *the Sustainable Business*. Recognition of changes to the equilibrium needs to be swift to ensure strategic actions can be implemented to counter or exploit any movement. Anticipation or foresight is a trait of the great organisations, a subject we will address in later chapters however an awareness that any of the organisations customers could fail tomorrow must sadly remain a possibility

The suppliers into the organisation and the related supply chains which feed the organisation with the resources to enable it to satisfy this customer base are important External Impactors. Effective selection of suppliers coupled with good supplier management leads to a maximisation of these resources. In recent years, the move from a Win-Lose mandate to a Win-Win approach has enabled many organisations to form stronger and more resilient relationships with their suppliers, thereby increasing the service levels and mitigating some of the related risk. Selection and management of suppliers and the supply chain is again addressed in later chapters.

Porter recognised the importance of substitute products and the risk of new entrants into the market. Both pose real risks to the on-going revenue streams enjoyed by the organisation, and thus affect its health as a profitable business. Quantifying and assessing the risk may help generate an appropriate strategy that may include the development of new market segments, consolidating and protecting existing business, new product design, or the cashing in of a product that may be facing an imminent decline. In this latter case, a number of the different business functions may, as a consequence, need to review their activity. For example, inventory levels may need to be amended, the business may need to reduce its manufacturing capacity, its personnel may need to be trimmed, or it may need to retrain its staff.

Furthermore, of late a sixth force has entered the reckoning, that of the complementary product; this will be explored more extensively in chapter 3.

To combat the threat from substitutes and new entrants, *The Sustainable Business* needs to guarantee the health of its product set. Products have a finite life as shown by the Product Life Cycle (PLC) – see figure 1.5.

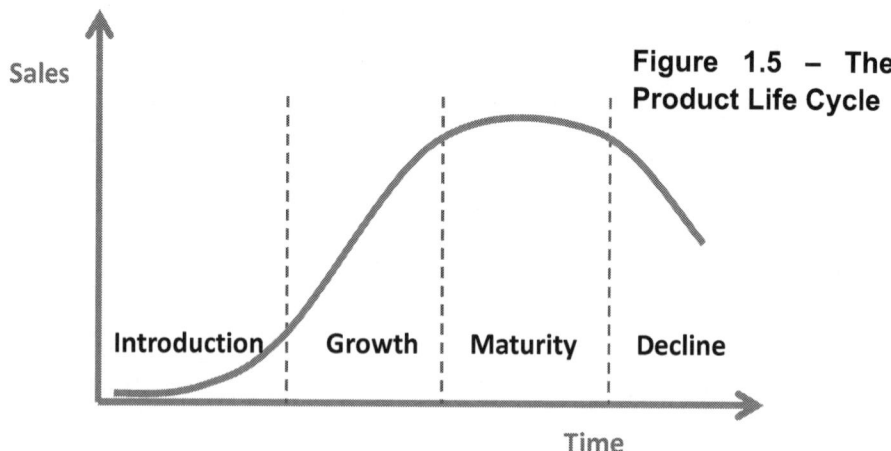

Figure 1.5 – The Product Life Cycle

Managing the product set to reflect the prevailing state is a very necessary activity. The length of the product life cycle is often relatively consistent between different products in the same market, thus giving some indication of the duration of a product's contribution, and giving time to find a replacement.

The Boston Consulting Group (BCG) Matrix – see figure 1.6 – takes this a step further categorising products into four distinct groups: Question Marks, Stars, Cash Cows, and Dogs. This helps clarify the products' status, and establish a strategy for both the product in question and the wider market requirements.

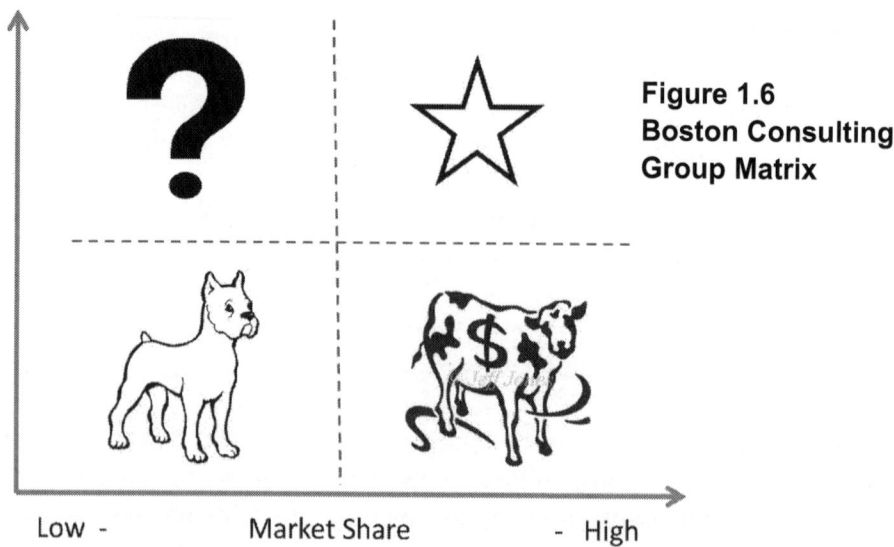

Figure 1.6
Boston Consulting Group Matrix

Each category warrants its own approach within the overall strategy. When we look at the new products entering the market, they start off as "Question Marks", with low market share but potentially high earnings prospects. This aligns with the "Introduction Phase" of the Product Life Cycle. In this phase we should be looking to divest products for which we do not see a future, to cut the investment in that product.

As the product is adopted and starts to gain market stature, we enter the "Growth phase". These products are referred to in the BCG Matrix as the "Stars". Here we need to invest in the product to ensure it maximises its potential across as broad a market as is feasible.

Next the product enters the "Maturity phase" when growth slows. Having invested in the product over the months or years, the organisation should now consider harvesting, i.e. getting as much profit out of the product as quickly as possible. Its days may be numbered, so extracting the last dregs is the strategic aim. These are the "Cash Cows".

> **Food for Thought:** Why does an organisation introduce new products? Is it:
> a) to satisfy customer requests,
> b) to compete with a competitor's product;
> c) because the Research and Development department produced them;
> d) because of an entrepreneurial gut feeling?

Finally the product enters the "Decline Phase" and becomes what the BCG Matrix calls a "Dog". Early appreciation of a product's senility gives *The Sustainable Business* the opportunity to replace the failing item and thus maintain customer loyalty, or develop some sort or relaunch, rebirth or evolution. No investment should be made on a product with a limited life expectancy, and the organisation should either be looking to its replacement and towards liquidating the product from its profile.

When liquidating a product however, a strategy is still required to ensure a suitable replacement has been anticipated and is available to maintain customer loyalty and, if applicable, to ensure that the product is supported with spares and maintenance support for the following few years. This maintenance and spares business can often be very lucrative, so it is worth assessing even if it is outsourced or divested. Generating a reputation of a responsible aftermarket has a positive impact on the sales cycle at the front end of the business.

> **Food for Thought:** Blue Ocean Strategy is a systematic process that focuses on finding the empty space within a market enabling an organisation's effort to exploit a competitor free environment and generate a market where the competition is irrelevant on the development and outcomes within. The strategy incorporates six core principles: 1) the redefinition of the boundaries and rules that are present in the market, 2) identifying the big picture, 3) the development of new sources of demand, 4) recognition of the optimal sequence of activities, 5) establishing methods to overcome market obstacles, and 6) helping establish strategy from market success and processes.

The competition in a market is also clearly affected by the other organisations supplying the goods or services, the organisation's competitors. These organisations may try and do things cheaper, quicker, the better; the Virgin Group of companies is a prime example. Recognising who the other protagonists are in the market is an obvious requirement of determining the current state of the organisation. It is useful to understand these competitors and the other characteristics displayed by the market. In a later chapter, process for a more detailed assessment of a market is discussed however knowing the strengths and weaknesses of your rivals is a primary determinant of an effective and sustainable sales strategy, and an obvious *External Impactor*.

Finally, it is worth mentioned in the concept of "Super-normal Profit". *Normal Profit* is defined as the point at which the profit earned by an organisation equals the minimum amount of profit necessary to keep the organisation operating in that market. Whereas, *Supernormal Profit* is the profit which occurs above this *Normal Profit* in a market. Where this additional profit is evident, there becomes an additional incentive for other competitors to enter the market.

External Related

Aside from the External Impactors, other external factors need to be taken into consideration when assessing the prevailing state of the business. These can be numerous, however they tend not to have such a direct involvement with the market and are thus only **related** to the organisation's performance. To assess this, we can use the PESTLE model – See figure 1.7. This model reviews six areas of external influence: Political, Economic, Social, Technical, Legislative, and Environmental.

For example, how does the organisation's activity fit with the incumbent political regime? If in conflict, how could this impinge on the performance of the organisation going forward, and thus affect the longer term earnings potential. What is the prevailing attitude of the political regime towards taxation, market controls, or market intervention? In the same way we can review each of the other PESTLE areas to help identify issues with the External Related stakeholders; this helps us identify areas which may affect *the Sustainable Vision*.

Equally, the organisation's relationship in the community can in some circumstances be decisive to its on-going performance. Where communities cooperate with an organisation tremendous benefit can be achieved, contrasted with where there is contention. Organisations such as "cooperatives" started life as organisations focused on matching commercial needs with the community requirements. By way of an example, the Swedish-Danish cooperative dairy Arla is a case in point. Its 100+ year history as a cooperative organisation has seen it grow to the world's seventh largest dairy group, it has over 7000 members and manages global brands such as Lurpak™ and Castello™.

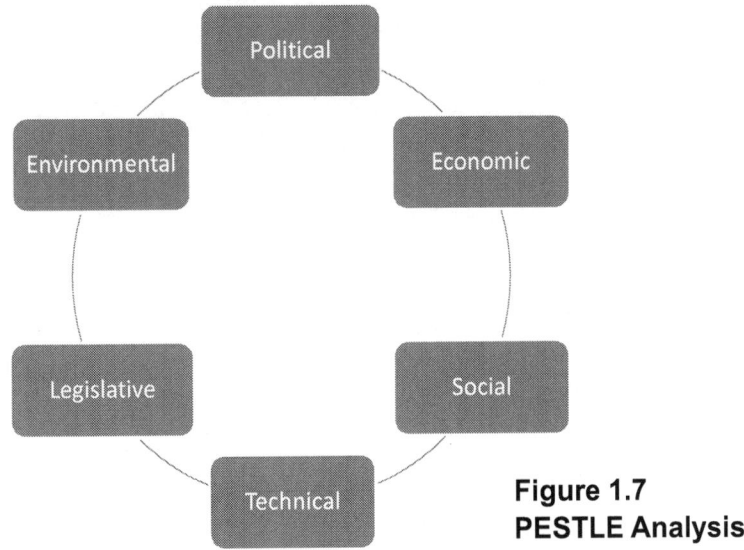

Figure 1.7
PESTLE Analysis

In contrast, consider the Richmond Dam Project on the South African/ Mozambique border; this has caused a major rift between the business needs and the local community over the disputed need for a dam in the Limpopo region. In this latter case, how much more successful would the project have been had it focused equally on the needs of the community, job creation, urban development, etc as opposed to big business and political pressures.

Looking further at the PESTLE model, monitoring related legislation and technical developments in a market are clearly related to our business success. Being a market leader for some product or service can enable the organisation to exploit this benefit, gaining commercial advantage and added profit. To achieve this, pricing and margin need to reflect the value being generated.

Technical expertise, patents or product innovation are other external factors that affects where the business is today. These can directly or indirectly affect the organisation, and the current status should, where possible, be considered. This may be easier said than done as competitors will often protect their research and development activities, and patents are by definition protected.

Equally, legislation and often more critically, changes in legislation, can affect the current status of the organisation. Clearly some markets and industries are more susceptible than others, but it is prudent to have an awareness of the consequences of this for the business.

Often, the most significant of the externally related factors is the economy. This, like the political characteristic, can quickly change and needs to be closely monitored. Particularly in times of economic turbulence, or where inflation and interest rates are fluid, recognising the criticality of externally related factors is key to the organisation's strategy.

Furthermore, the state of the economy influences the ability of the organisation to obtain additional funds when required. The ability to source credit has often been assumed in periods up to the 2007/8 turmoil in the credit markets, but increasingly proves more difficult, and may do so for the foreseeable future. As mentioned previously, this can lead to lenders seeking to offset this heightened level of risk with increased rates or reduced levels of loan values.

For *the Sustainable Business* looking to operate over a long period, the need to anticipate the economy and its fluctuations is essential. Economic forecasting is by no means easy, but whichever economic theorist is endorsed by the organisation, short, medium or long wave cycles will feature, and where there are cycles there are peaks and troughs, and usually with fairly predictable features. Recognising these can assist enormously in managing and directing the strategy of the organisation.

External Affected

Having examined the importance of the Internal Factors, External Impactors and Internal Related segments of the Current Status grid, the final element relates to the organisation's relationship with people or functions that are affected by its activities but have no direct input or control.

Typically, organisations view this segment as strategically the least critical, however there are many instances where organisations have neglected this group and regretted it. In most cases, the primary risk is with the bad publicity such conflict can generate. Examples can include contamination, anti-competitive behaviour, accidents, transport congestion generated by the business, and so on. Consider the impact of the 2010 Deepwater Horizon oil rig incident (Sea of Mexico) on the local community, and the cost thereafter to the business in fines and consequential damages. At the time of writing BP estimate that the total cost was in the region of $40bn, with business impact of $20bn and total payments paid at the start of 2012 already totalling nearly $8bn. In addition, over 1000 miles of shoreline was affected, a thick layer of dead creatures such as star fish strewn over 2900 square miles of sea bed (see Samantha Joye, University of Georgia) and a clean-up bill is estimated at around $2m per day.

Equally as catastrophic was the 1984 Union Carbide incident in Bhopal which resulted in over 500,000 injuries and resulted in perhaps as many as 20,000 deaths at the time and since, and cost the company around £470m at the time in compensation, albeit this sum was not considered as fair at the time or since. Other examples include the Amoco Cadiz, the Exxon Valdez, or the Ajka alumina sludge spill in Hungary.

Affected parties in such incidents may include the relatives of the employees of the organisation. These are the people who are affected by,

The Sustainable Business

for example, the high stress levels of the employees of a business, and for a variety of reasons may cause an employee to leave the organisation.

Whilst not all of the eventualities may be anticipated, it is worth *the Sustainable Business* adopting a considerate approach to all such facets, and an important part of understanding how the organisation is currently positioned.

So having now understood where we are as an organisation, before considering the future, it is useful to assess our current business impact.

What is the Sustainable IMPACT of the organisation?

When considering the sustainability of our business, it is necessary to consider the overall impact that the business activity and decisions have on the environment and our stakeholders. It is useful to review this alongside the assessment of where the business is currently.

The business impact can be split into three distinct areas: Impact from the choice of input sources; impact from the operation and associated strategic choices; and impact from the onward use of the goods or services further down the supply chain. These impacts can be split further into six areas of focus as shown within the IMPACT model, see figure 1.8

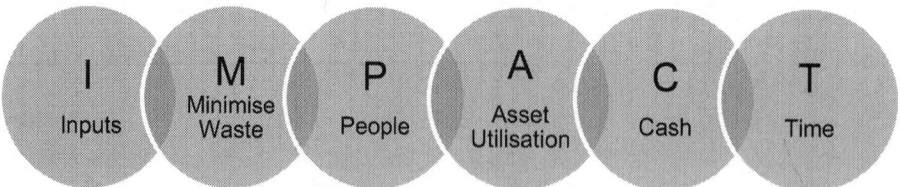

Figure 1.8 – IMPACT model

So how do we assess the business IMPACT?

I is for "Inputs"

Typically, procurement drives the acquisition of materials, services, finance and goodwill consumed by the organisation – these represent the key inputs needed to manage and operate a successful organisation.

Ensuring that a professional and responsible approach is adopted for the provision of these aspects is essential to limiting your IMPACT on the environment today, and with capital purchases, for an often considerable time into the future. Adoption of responsible procurement procedures and an effective measurement of the additional carbon emitted – possibly through using Activity Based Carbon Distribution – focuses attention on where consumption occurs and where sustainable improvements can be implemented to reduce your environmental IMPACT.

M is for "Minimise Waste"

For any given operation, there are inputs and outputs. "Desired outputs" are the primary focus of our business, they are what we are aiming to achieve to satisfy the customer; they are our core objective, our *raison d'etre*; it's how we *add value.*

However, from a sustainability perspective, it is critical for an organisation to measure and manage the "undesired outputs", its waste products. Wherever possible, waste must be eliminated or at least reduced, however a more proactive approach to the management of waste can be invaluable. For example, selection of materials which are either recycled, recyclable, or hopefully both, ensures that at least the waste produced has an afterlife. Use of technology which captures heat and transforms it into electricity, for example, has a clear mandate for adding corporate value through lower emissions, reduced power costs, and potentially community goodwill.

In respect of this latter point, a memorable example was a plastics factory situated on a previously arid mountain in the Altinekin region of Turkey. The factory had allowed the local villagers to use the clean hot water produced as a by-product of its production process, to wash and shower with. The balance of the water was used to irrigate the land immediately below the factory, transforming the previously desolate landscape into green, fertile and productive farm land for the community.

P is for "People"

Without people, commitment and experience, an organisation will flounder. As part of *the Sustainable Business*, there must be an ambition to develop and retain the workforce and generate a steady stream of future talent.

The provision of a sustainable HR policy, empowerment of management and staff, a coaching environment and an overwhelming desire to improve the welfare of the entire workforce, is crucial. An effective appraisal system helps formalise this, however more fundamental is the establishment of a "caring culture" and effective communication.

In all business areas, improvements in communication will pay dividends to those concerned. It will improve efficiency and effectiveness, reduce waste, lower stress levels, and raise employee morale, amongst many other tangible and intangible benefits. Although an employee's sense of well-being is difficult to measure, it is worth recognising the value it generates. Focus on happy employees and they will stay motivated, productive and loyal. Lower staff turnover will lead to a reduction in HR costs and thus improved profitability.

Wider, successful organisations aim to nurture links with people in the neighbouring community. This is the source of future generations of employees and helps establish a positive relationship with a stakeholder often overlooked. At a chance meeting at an Indonesian airport, an eight year old boy informed me that when he grew up he hoped to work for the Chevron, a major local employer who actively participate in community activities throughout their global operations.

Chevron's commitment to people both inside and outside its operations is admirable. The commitment to safety is second to none, their focus on training and development entrenched in the ethos of the organisation. In the longer term, they have strategic aims to migrate from ex-pat to the local workforce, thereby generating a sustainable solution to its manpower requirements in the future, and repaying the local community for sharing its prized asset, the oil.

However, Chevron does not stop here. It goes further by providing sanctuary and conservation areas for local wild-life, it supports critical local facilities such as logistics infrastructure, medical resources and the provision of utilities, and it encourages local business communities through, where possible, buying from local sources.

A is for "Asset utilisation"

Whilst financial considerations are important for an organisation, what is often overlooked is the need to ensure that assets already owned by the organisation are wherever possible used. There is often spare capacity which if not used is a waste to the organisation.

Understanding the breakdown of a cost is essential to generating value from this area. Cost is typically made up of a mix of fixed and variable costs. Fixed costs are incurred irrespective of whether the asset is used, variable costs are dependent upon the usage.

By way of an example, take a photo copier. A large part of the cost of leasing a machine is a fixed cost, it is incurred irrespective of whether any copies are taken. Additional costs are incurred when the machine is used, for example the paper, ink, power, and potentially a surcharge per sheet in the lease agreement, as well as the cost of the manpower needed to undertake the task.

Assuming that the machine is not already used 24/7, when comparing the costs of reproduction using this internal resource with using an external copy house, we should not directly compare the total cost of the internal resource with the total cost of the external option, as there is a clear difference in the cost structure. The fixed cost of the photocopier is by definition already incurred, the comparison must surely be between the variable costs of the internal solution and the total costs of the outsourced arrangement.

But from a sustainability point of view, the argument should not finish there. Having made the assumption that there is spare capacity on the existing photocopier machine, in the event of the outsourced solution being selected, the photo copier will by definition remain idle for a longer period, thereby introducing a "waste by-product" of the decision. As waste constitutes a manageable cost, this waste must therefore be added to the total cost of the outsourced solution to make the decision equitable.

Failure to utilise assets is a waste we MUST acknowledge and remedy if for no other reason than to validate the business cases that created them in the first place.

C is for "Cash"

Essential to the on-going success and continuation of an organisation is the need to create, or in the case of a public authority effectively consume, cash. A sustainable business needs to be healthy in both the creation and consumption of cash.

The measurement and targeting of both areas is a critical control for any organisation. Budgets, P&L accounts, and cash-flow forecasts are all measures commonly in use, but the impact of the role of the funds in the business goes to the very heart of the organisation:

At an individual, group, team, department and organisation level, the culture should be focused on the "adding of value". Effective value analysis and value engineering help identify the impact that each function or activity within the organisation has on the overall goals and contribution. We need to know which elements of the organisation have the biggest IMPACT in order to clearly establish our best strategy to maximise our stakeholder returns. This may be represented in the form of a financial figure or in the value created through the service offered. Either way, we need to understand either the cash generated or the return on the cash invested.

The sustainability of an organisation is intrinsically linked to the preparation and implementation of effective business cases which are clear, concise and inclusive of metrics aimed at establishing success. This success invariably reflects the cash invested and generated, or a combination of both - Cash underpins and is a key IMPACT on *the Sustainable Business*.

T is for Time

And finally, the concept of time must never be overlooked as a key determinant of sustainability; it goes to the very core of the concept.

Time is integral to our definition of *the Sustainable Business*:

*"A sustainable business has no **lasting** impact on the global, national or local environment, commits to the rights and contribution of the*

employees across the whole supply chain and in the wider community, whilst recognising its own need to generate a robust commercial structure to deliver **ongoing** *value to its stakeholders"*

From an IMPACT perspective, we need to appreciate the concept of time throughout our assessment.

We need to recognise that the effect of our actions now, as well as their IMPACT over time. Are the materials we consume reusable? What is the life of our product or service? When will the IMPACT of our actions be returned to nature? We need to consider our "Total Cost of Sustainable Ownership".

Time, by its very definition will outlast everything we do; our goal must surely be to make certain only the positive components contribute to our legacy, and that we pursue policies focused on eliminating the negative consequences of our existence.

Where do we want to go?

So having considered the current status of the organisation – the start of our sustainable journey – and the *Sustainable Impact* that the business is currently having on the environment, we now need to determine where we want to get to as an organisation, our *Sustainable Destination*.

The end goal is clearly affected by the future development of the organisation, of the External Impactors, the External Related factors, and to a lesser extent the External Affected parties. Some of these will have a relatively predictable future, however, foresight is clearly fraught with risk and danger of poor decisions. Included in any predictions must be some degree of probability, latency and flexibility to make the forecast as adaptable as possible.

There is also a need to temper probable with desirable, and to balance the realistic with the desires of the shareholders in the business. There is a tendency for shareholders to demand greater levels of profit year on year, irrespective of market conditions. It is not uncommon for organisations to base future plans, profit and sales forecasts on past performance with a percentage increase and not reflect the prevailing market or economic conditions, however this is not the way of *the Sustainable Business*; this is not the way to create achievable or realistic targets.

Business, sales and profit forecasts based on the last year's performance significantly increases the likelihood of failure or excessive over achievement. They fail to acknowledge issues in the marketplace, or with customer, production, cost, supplier or people associated with the business operation. Indeed, the oft heard management mantra of cut costs and raise prices is a common yet flawed and unsustainable approach to generating profit.

The Sustainable Business thinks further ahead than next year; it has confidence in its long term existence, and in its planning and implementation. It acknowledges that external forces may hamper its progress, but does not show the same reticence as traditional organisations to plan ahead for the future in which it believes. It takes a view on the economy, the market and other key variables, and sets itself a fluid long term plan. This fluidity allows the plan to be adjusted over the duration, and new operational decisions taken to ensured continued success.

Furthermore, *the Sustainable Business* avoids castigating individuals or groups who make the effort to forecast. They ensure that these parties are properly educated, coached and have the resources to support their endeavour, and then recognise that the art of forecasting is fallible.

As with all forecasting, the starting point is vital, but the underpinning parameters used to project and evaluate the possible outcomes are key to the success of the activity. In a later chapter we will look at measuring organisational performance and the success and accuracy of any forecast; measuring the success enables the organisation to evaluate its forecasting mechanisms, and improve its forecast delta – the difference between the forecast and the actual.

Central to most forecasts is a view of movements in the economy, market, customers and costs. Each will have its own unique characteristics which need to be examined and understood. Especially with external aspects such as the economy or the market, the organisation needs to educate itself and its management in these facets to ensure that forecasts are based on an educated perspective. Arguably the most influential – the economy – is explored more fully as part of the review into business contexts.

The need to plan ahead is clearly essential for *the Sustainable Business* and the management philosophy needs to reflect the longer term perspective. The risk profile is inevitably affected by adopting a vision, however with some fluidity and a recognition that *twenty:twenty foresight* is a commercial "holy grail", the business aspirations should accommodate some margin of error. Effective risk management, contingency planning and an ability to react quickly significantly help alleviate some of the potential losses that might occur, and indeed can, if managed well, lead to a more dynamic and service orientated business.

Once we have an understanding of the current status of the organisation, and a view of where the organisation is aimed, we can then explore how….This is *the Strategy* and vital to the organisation's success; this is examined over later chapters.

Case Study: Easter Island
A non-sustainable community

Sustainability requires a respect for the environment and the natural resources available in the community. There needs to be recognition of where resources come from, how they are consumed and the regeneration process and lead time.

There is ready recognition of the issues associated with the depletion of fossil fuel reserves, and the acknowledgement of the need to move to renewable sources of energy. So why do *we* continue to focus on developing elaborate carbon capture solutions to help hide the underpinning issue, i.e. that *we* are using a non-sustainable resource in an irresponsible manner. Catching the carbon dioxide and pumping it back underground to save it from entering the atmosphere is not dealing with the issue. It's a simple equation:

> **Replenishment Rate must be greater than Consumption Rate**
> If you cut down a tree, how long will it take to grow a replacement? And then you need to act, to plant the tree to make it happen.

Take for example the case of Easter Island in the South Pacific. This relatively small volcanic island of little over 140 square miles sits over a 1000 miles from its nearest inhabited island, and nearly 2000 miles from the South American mainland. Yet it has a long history and its population has in the past been over 5000 inhabitants.

Early explorers discovered the island in the 18th century, finding a relatively primitive population, supported by a fragile ecosystem producing barely enough food to support the then declining community. Several incursions by countries investigating the islands saw little reason to colonise, the remoteness and lack of obvious resources making such an activity unworthwhile.

However, explorers found evidence of a once thriving community, highlighted by the numerous stone statues, some over six metres in height, that are spread across the island.

Theories abound as to why and how the statues were produced, ranging from Inca involvement to far-fetched theories of *deliveries* from outer space. A more plausible explanation, however, is that the inhabitants had once been highly resourced and skilled yet had fallen on hard times with this as their "outlet" – so what happened?

The most common view is that the islanders, over their thousand year history, simply lived beyond their sustainable means.

The island was once heavily forested, however when the explorers arrived in the sixteenth century, they found no trees at all. Evidence suggests that these trees were cut and used for wood, without any strategy for their replacement. Much of the wood was used for housing, burning and to help transport and erect the massive statues. The source of this wood was not replenished, leaving the islanders unable to build boats, and thus trapping them on the island.

Housing on the island needed to change to reflect the lack of building materials, forcing the inhabitants into alternative cave dwellings. The lack of certain plant material inhibited the construction of canoes and fishing items cutting of an obvious alternative food source to that of animals, which were themselves limited in range and in short supply.

Furthermore, farming methods did not develop. Crop preservation methods, composting, manuring or soil management was not understood or applied, and the lack of land coverage increased soil degradation and erosion. The crops deteriorated until the base diet had reduced to little more than potato types and chicken, with evidence of cannibalism on the *menu* in the later periods.

In effect, the Islanders had destroyed the community they had created by simply living outside the sustainable scope of the island. They had exhausted all their resources, destroyed their habitat, and cut off their means of escape.

In contrast, issues with food demand and production drove the development of crop rotation during the seventeen century, and then fuelled the subsequent industrial revolution to maintain the demand for machinery required to continue the land development.

Crop rotation focused on land husbandry to make optimum use of the soil. It recognised the balance between using land to grow food and produce, with the need to feed the land itself, replenishing the minerals needed to maintain its effectiveness. This necessitated use of composting, manuring, and growing nitrogen intense plants merely to feed animals or mulch back into the soil.

Critically, the growing area was rotated with different plant types to balance the nutrients extracted with the replenishment regime. This was then supplemented with a portion of the land left fallow every fourth year to allow it to recover.

Crop rotation is a cycle that focuses on a simple principle: you have to replace what you take from an ecosystem to sustain it.

The philosophy of a sustainable community extends into other areas of society. Deforestation is an issue for the modern world, but what about short-sighted building projects? The Millennium Dome in London lay unused for many years with no clear use factored into its original business plan; the Cape Town Green Point stadium developed for the South Africa World Cup but now rarely used; the Marathon cricket venue in Australia now unused; or the Reims Formula One motor racing circuit in France, now rarely used.

Consider the Olympic villages and elaborate stadia in host cities across the globe that lay discarded after the event has come and gone - which of the historic Olympic stadiums are still in regular use? Beijing, Athens, Atlanta, Barcelona, Seoul?

And will we learn by the mistakes made previously? The London Olympic bid was based on the concept of legacy – will the legacy be that which was projected, or one of desolate venues, underutilised infrastructure and budget shortfalls? Sadly this is a reality of our societal short-termism, narrow horizons and unsustainable business philosophies.

The Sustainable Business

Notes Page | **Page Ref**

The Sustainable Business

Summary Chapter 2
The Corporate Social Responsibility Policy "The People Pillar"

Key Learning Points
- *The Three Pillar* model and the importance of *the People Pillar*
- Understanding the importance of people of the business operation
- Identification of the three dimensions of *the People Pillar*
- Recognition of the "character", the "corporate team", and the "community" in which the organisation operates
- The factors affecting the "character dimension" of the employee
- Teamwork issues within the organisational structure
- Theories of personality – Theory X, Theory Y and Theory Z
- Examination of the "Vulnerability Cycle"
- Understanding and nurturing community interaction

Tool Summary
- *The People Pillar Dimensions*: Character, Corporate & Community
- Belbin
- Tracom Four Styles
- Tuckman Team Development Cycle
- The RITE Way & The RITUAL recruitment cycle
- Theory X, Theory Y, Theory Z
- BARS – Behaviourally Anchored Rating System
- Five Vulnerabilities of People

CIPS Syllabus Reference
- Level 4 Managing Contracts and Relationships in Procurement and Supply
- Level 5 Sustainable Procurement
- Level 5 Management in Procurement and Supply
- Level 6 Leadership in Procurement and Supply

Chapter 2: The Corporate Social Responsibility Policy "The People Pillar"

Ancient Chinese Proverb
"If you want one year of prosperity, plant corn.
If you want ten years of prosperity, plant trees.
If you want one hundred years of prosperity, educate people."

The CSR Concept

The concept of a CSR policy is a well documented subject. The Chartered Institute of Purchasing and Supply refers to the "Triple Bottom Line", elsewhere it is referred to as "the three Ps – People, Profit and Planet" and the "Three Pillars of Social Responsibility". All focus on the three key components necessary to ensure sustainability in the organisation, invaluable in its simplicity – see figure 2.1.

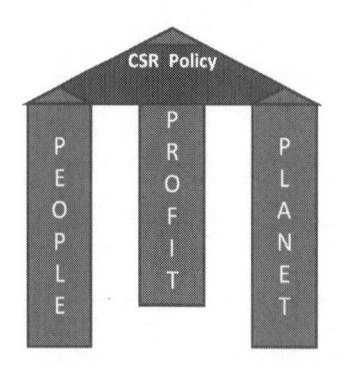

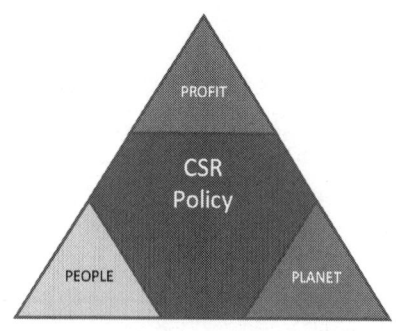

Figure 2.1

The People Pillar

Let's begin with the *People* in the business – See figure 2.2. The Human Resources function and establishing a strong personnel element is essential to sustainability and a successful CSR strategy.

The need to create a strong and effective team, with committed employees, low staff turnover, and harmonious relations is a prerequisite of a solid *People Pillar*, however *the Sustainable Business* needs to embrace the community in its sustainable vision. Without a source of future employees, educated and skilled to the necessary level, and of course willing to work, the organisation will struggle to maintain its business effectiveness. These are the foundations for a strong *People Pillar* and the driver of sustainable conviction within the organisation.

The Company

The first dimension of the *People Pillar*, is "the Company" and its role in developing an effective personnel management strategy.

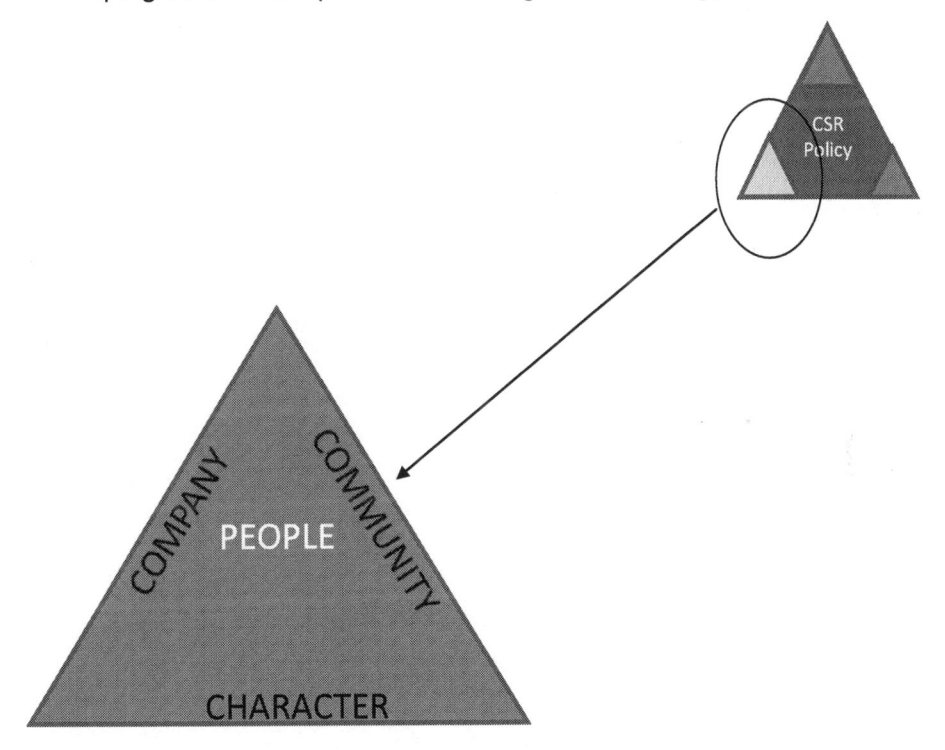

Figure 2.2

Creating a solid team was examined by a number of leading business authors however the Belbin team structure remains one of the pre-eminent views of the components of a successful team. Belbin identified a number of primary roles that team members can be seen to assume (see figure 2.3). Key to a sustainable team is the need for balance therein; attention to the roles that people play and the type of personalities makes a significance difference to the success, stability and endurance of the team.

Belbin Roles	Description
Plant	The creative and imaginative team member, who can often be relied upon to come up with the answer or special ideas
Resource Investigator	The team member who knows people and can get things the group requires. Usually a good net-worker with a list of useful contacts
Coordinator (Also known as Chairman)	The team member who controls the group, organises activity, ensures all members are heard, and that resources are used effectively
Specialist	The team member who brings the special expertise to the group, this is key for projects with a high technical content.
Completer	The team member who focuses on the detail and on finishing the project on time. They tend to be meticulous and painstaking.
Implementer	The team member who delivers what the team wants. He takes ideas and makes them work at a practical level, and has a realism that some lack.
Team Worker	The team member who bonds the group together. They are the first to notice atmospheres or interpersonal problems. They keep the team united.
Evaluator	The team member who can dispassionately and coolly assess and critique an idea rationally. His rational view can curb misplaced team enthusiasm and help prevent the production on a misguided solution.
Shaper	The team member who relishes the challenge, likes working under pressure. They tend to have drive, and are not afraid to take on risk.

Figure 2.3

Rarely is it feasible for corporate teams to be created with all the desirable personnel. Key individuals may well be employed on other projects, be unaffordable or merely wish not to be involved. In contrast, it has been seen that project teams have been used to "dump" troublesome or ineffective members of staff, or to assist with corporate restructuring or downsizing. Whilst employment legislation plays a role here, and employee rights need to be considered, a clear strategic decision needs to be taken as to which is the bigger priority – individual, team or corporate.

Ideally, to generate sustainable and highly effective teams, attention should not only be paid to the role types as described by Belbin, but also to the relative personalities of the individuals involved. Assessing the personalities of the perspective team candidates – perhaps using one of the numerous psychometric tests available in the market – coupled with a model such as the Tracom Four Styles (See figure 2.4) can help determine the most desirable mix of personalities in an effective, coordinated and balanced team.

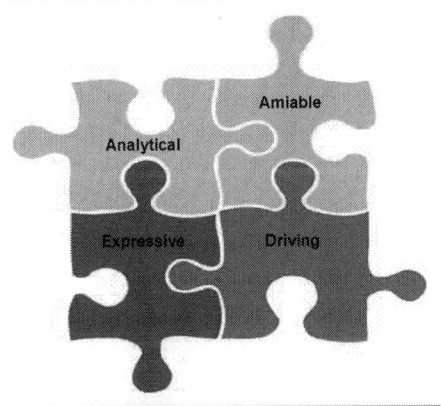

TRACOM Social Styles

Amiable - These individuals tend to be more preoccupied with relationships and are very people focused. The need to make friends and build relationships often has a greater focus than targets or goals.

Driving – In contrast, people who display driving tendencies are focused on the end goal. They are willing to take risks but like to understand the risk, weigh up the probabilities and be able to estimate the likelihood of success or failure, and the possible consequences. This type of person tends to be independent and usually very competitive, and likes to believe that they can control their own destiny. They are usually quite analytical giving clear direction and leadership, if not a little cold in their management style.

Expressive – These people like recognition for what they do. They tend to be open and transparent, are motivated by challenges, but may be eager to look at the next project, rather than complete the current one. They often get excited by risk taking, and may not always take a balanced rational or logical approach, but will be passionate about participating, certainly in the early stages.

Analytical – This type loves data, facts and figures. They like to compute, analyse model, and review, but communication may be difficult. Accuracy will usually be good, and they tend to be good time keepers. They tend to show a reserved approach to other team members, be cautious towards leaders and those with power, and may take time to show any trust.

This effort is an investment not a cost. The effective formation of a team will reduce conflict, improve efficiency, enhance communication, increase satisfaction levels and manage risk.

Sustainable teams, however, require more than just the right people in order to be effective. They also need to be managed correctly, and the team needs to bond. Tuckman's view of the development of the team process involves six steps: Forming, Storming, Norming, Performing and Dorming, Adjourning, Team Building – see figure 2.5. From a CSR perspective, *the Sustainable Business* needs to maintain a strong *People* element, and the role and functioning needs of the "team" cannot be underestimated. It can be shown, that to be truly successful, the team must be allowed to pursue this evolutionary route, however in many instances, managerial styles, team objectives or corporate goals frustrate the process.

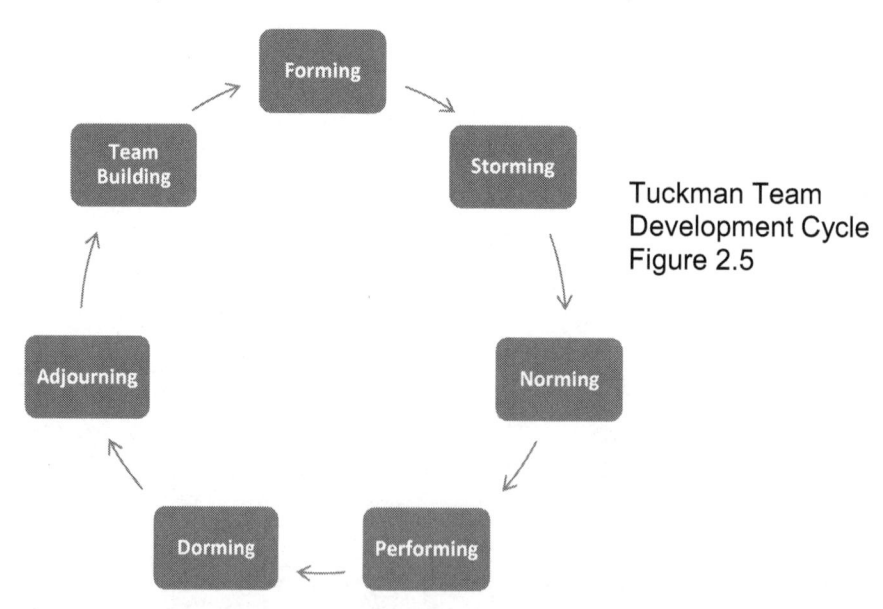

Tuckman Team Development Cycle
Figure 2.5

Equally important to the success of *the People Pillar* is the need to ensure that the employee's job design is both varied and fulfilling, often a tricky issue in the modern world of automation and factory production lines. "Job Enrichment", "Job Enlargement", and "Job Rotation" are hopefully now old news in terms of the design of an employee's role in Western societies, yet in developing countries this is less in evidence.

The concept of rotating workers has the benefit of enriching an employee's life at work, yet from *the Sustainable Business'* perspective there is a secondary benefit, diversity. Diversity in business skills reduces risk, increases flexibility, speeds up an organisation's ability to respond quickly and moves customer service – and the improvements in margin this can generate – to the forefront of its strategic thinking.

Boredom, in contrast is one of the most fundamental of business and society's wastes. It can be measured as a missed "opportunity cost", and in some cases a cost of poor quality (COPQ). In a process aimed at analysis of an organisation's ability to deliver quality – as with Six Sigma for example – this COPQ is of paramount importance and critical to business success.

> **Food for Thought:** Consider the game "Spider Solitaire" supplied free with Windows XP and later versions. Such is the addictive nature of the game, a group has been established to formally acknowledge the addiction. Whilst no estimate could be found for the number of hours of office time wasted each year by employees playing in work time, many organisations have decided to remove it from all business machines. What discernible benefit does the *Sustainable Business* gain from employees engaging in social networking sites in office time?

Diversity, in contrast, is a powerful competitive advantage. It allows an organisation to capitalise on opportunities it might otherwise have to forego; it can react where others may struggle.

Diversity may be illustrated in many forms and in many circumstances. It may simply be, for example, an organisation's ability to use a manager's car to make a delivery more quickly than its normal delivery channel, to use a neighbour's printer to quickly produce a business proposal in glossy colour, through training all warehouse individuals to drive the forklift truck or development of selling skills across product ranges. Investment in a strategy aimed at the diversification of employees and process will enhance both an organisation's ability to deliver outstanding service and improve productivity, whilst augmenting an employee's fulfilment and motivation.

What is needed is managerial understanding. Sustainability is a relatively modern business focus, it has evolved and become more prominent since perhaps the mid-nineties, however the true evolution of the managerial endorsement may arguably be lagging. Commitment to producing a CSR policy is not the same as actively adopting a balanced People-Profit-Planet corporate philosophy and a team needs to embrace its long term aims and sustainable ambitions into its operating procedures.

The Character

Having examined the role of the "Company" on the *People Pillar* we now need to consider the person or "Character". Key to this are two main dimensions: personality and ownership.

In most organisations and societies the person has ownership for his or her actions, they make a choice on how they behave, and the things they do and say. In contrast, the dimension of personality, relates to how the character integrates into the organisation, and acceptance into the group and relationship with colleagues. These two dimensions together can be used to suggest likely behaviours and corporate destiny.

Critical to *the Sustainable Business* is a strong understanding of the primary features of weak and non-sustainable personnel components in an organisation.

Evidence suggests (for example Zahhly & Tosi 1989) that one of the most important aspects leading to job-satisfaction and reduced conflict is having an effective new employee induction process. What is needed is a structured, planned and consistent approach, for example *The RITE way* – See figure 2.6.

> Recruit ▸ Induct ▸ Train ▸ Embed

Figure 2.6 – The RITE Way

The process can actually be seen to start with the initial **recruitment**, the impact that the process had on the individual, the professionalism, information passed, warmth of the recruitment person, and so on, through to job offer and acceptance. Even the welcome offered by the receptionist generates an impression.

Once appointed, on the first day, an **induction** into the business is required. This should **not** be merely an explanation of the fire drills and who you will be working with, but a comprehensive introduction to the business: what the business does, its goals and targets, its employee structure, how the individual fits into the overall picture and critically how they as an individual will add value to the organisation. This final statement is key, if the individual feels that they are important in the overall scheme, they are more likely to start with a feeling of worth; this feeling of worth is the bedrock of personal satisfaction.

Following their induction and commencement in the role, the employee will need **training**. This again is vital to the continued feeling of worth, to the management of stress and delivery in the workplace. Good training, whether technical, skills or knowledge, should be viewed as an investment. It motivates the employee whilst improving productivity, quality and value in the organisation.

Finally, the employee needs to be **embedded** into the organisation. This may take a while as the person gets to know their colleagues, the procedures, the norms, the rules both written and unwritten, and the overall organisational culture. The organisation can help facilitate this process with social events, networking, cross-functional activity, sport groups, etc, all of which help to make new employees feel part of the *team*.

The RITE Way is a philosophy focused on the needs of the employee, however this can be expanded to drive strategy and process within the Human Resources (HR) function. At the core of the process is the "cradle to grave" approach to employment, reflecting the underpinning concepts of The RITE Way. In this broader capacity, the employee lifecycle should become the HR department's RITUAL – see figure 2.7 – although this strategy needs to incorporate an appropriate measurement system as discussed in chapter 14.

As with the RITE Way, Recruitment, Induction and Training must be at the core of the HR processes, however from the organisation's perspective, utilisation of the individual and his or her skills is of paramount importance. The employee needs to perform his or her role in the manner and ability intended. This Utilisation is a key driver of the employee productivity and needs to be managed and reviewed by the HR function on an on-going basis.

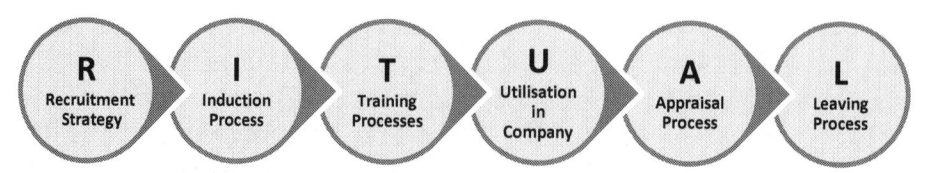

R	I	T	U	A	L
Recruitment Strategy	Induction Process	Training Processes	Utilisation in Company	Appraisal Process	Leaving Process

Figure 2.7 – The Jackson RITUAL

Regular reviews and interaction between an organisation's operating functions and the HR department are commonplace in many organisations, but by no means all; some HR functions operate an "as required" or reactive only service and this fails to maximise the employee contribution.

This links closely with the effectiveness of the "Appraisal Process". In circumstances where there is a regular and proactive interaction between HR and the operations, there exists a stronger commitment to a regular and structured appraisal process.

Furthermore, the HR function has a duty to ensure that there is alignment and fairness in the appraisal process, cross function and organisation wide. The implementation of BARS – Behaviourally Anchored Rating Scales (Ben Dattner 2010) – will help establish continuity.

Evidence can be shown that if fair and equitable, appraisals significantly improve both the motivation and commitment of the individual increasing the feeling of worth.

Finally, as with all things in life, consideration should be paid to the end of the relationship between employer and employee. This should be covered by a clear and documented Leaving process. Whether a forced dismissal for misconduct, as a result of a resignation, or through an agreed parting of ways, there should be some review of how the departure came to be. This review should then drive internal change as required to minimise the impact and ensure a better result in the future. Lessons learned through exit interviews, where acted upon, can be shown to have a major impact on future policy and success, thus improving an organisation's sustainability.

> **Food for Thought**: How much time effort and money goes into finding, recruiting and training staff. **This is lost** when an employee leaves the company.

As the US "Department of the Interior" guide on the subject reads:

Managing employee performance is an integral part of the work that all managers and rating officials perform throughout the year. It is as important as managing financial resources and program outcomes because employee performance, or the lack thereof, has a profound effect on both the financial and program components of any organisation.

Teamwork

Whilst team inclusion is crucial to the satisfaction and motivation of the employee, it can be seen that employing people does involve some issues and risks. In reality, all organisations have within, a myriad of different people characteristics, each person with their own personal, family and team objectives, with the majority prioritising these over corporate needs.

> **Food for Thought**: In 2007, a CIPD report showed that 84% of organisations who participated in the study stated that they had recruitment difficulties, with skills (65%), pay(46%) and experience(37%) all raised as problems with recruiting new staff. 70% of respondees stated they had where necessary adopted a strategy of recruiting people with potential and then investing time and resource in training the person. A later survey in 2010 shows labour turnover in the UK at 13.5%.

McGregor's Theory X & Theory Y assumptions (see figure 2.8) question whether employees are inherently lazy, or whether they seek work as a motivating and rewarding endeavour. *The Sustainable Business* however needs to look beyond this, deeper into what drives the employee. What motivates, how is it best to treat the team, what investments need to be made into their happiness and wellbeing.

Ouchi's Theory Z (1981) explores this with an alternative approach, focusing attention on the needs of the team members. It is recognised as a typically Japanese solution to people management: understanding what the individual is looking for from the relationship, and then fulfilling it as part of the corporate-employee commitment. Toyota has traditionally been a keen exponent of this approach in relation to its employees. In the JIT world, this approach is essential to combat the evidence of monotony associated with the repetitiveness of the tasks and structure.

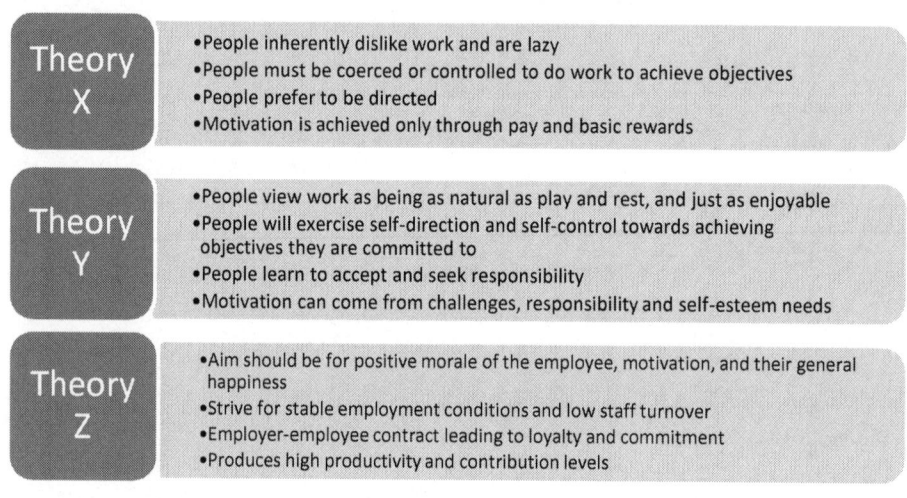

Theory X
- People inherently dislike work and are lazy
- People must be coerced or controlled to do work to achieve objectives
- People prefer to be directed
- Motivation is achieved only through pay and basic rewards

Theory Y
- People view work as being as natural as play and rest, and just as enjoyable
- People will exercise self-direction and self-control towards achieving objectives they are committed to
- People learn to accept and seek responsibility
- Motivation can come from challenges, responsibility and self-esteem needs

Theory Z
- Aim should be for positive morale of the employee, motivation, and their general happiness
- Strive for stable employment conditions and low staff turnover
- Employer-employee contract leading to loyalty and commitment
- Produces high productivity and contribution levels

Figure 2.8 McGregor & Ouchi Theory X, Theory Y, and Theory Z

To the organisation, people bring with them skills, but also risk. They can be seen to have inherent weaknesses, and this leads us to "the five vulnerabilities of people" – Figure 2.9 - if they are allowed to prevail, they will undermine the *People Pillar*, undermine *the Sustainable Business* and undermine its sustainable aspirations.

The aim must therefore be to produce strategy and disciplines to eliminate these vulnerabilities. Aspects such as truancy or unnecessary days off work are a key example of how an employee can directly affect the productivity of the organisation. Motivated staff and staff with a reward mechanism directly tied to achievement have been shown to take significantly less "days sick" than those who are more motivated. Measures such as the Bradford Index can be used to assess the willingness of a group of employees to work with ailments, though the Health and Safety and contagion consequences should always be considered. In one organisation, an employee's Bradford Rating was used within the appraisals and disciplinary processes to address such issues.

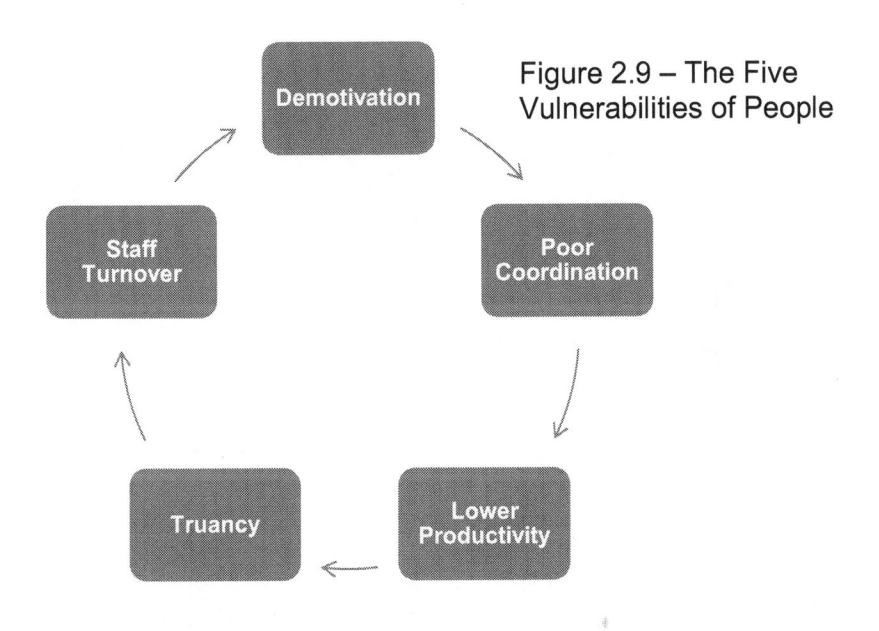

Figure 2.9 – The Five Vulnerabilities of People

- **Demotivated Staff** – Staff need to be motivated. In line with MacGregor's Theory X and Theory Y, Maslow's Hierachy of Needs and Herzberg's Hygiene motivation levels will vary depending on the type of personality.

- **Staff Turnover** – Staff consistency is essential to a stable organisation. The cost of recruiting, inducting, training, and embedding (*The RITE Way*) is substantial, however the consequence on the business continuity, organisational morale and public image is even more evident.

- **Truancy** – Staff can be employed however absenteeism, a low "illness threshold" or a belief in "your right to a few *sickies*" generates a cancerous sub-culture of ambivalence. An interesting counter to this is the relatively recent phenomenon of "duvet days", introduced to counter the employee who wakes up and "just can't be bothered to go into work". If so inclined, the employee can then phone in and take a "duvet day", i.e. a day when they can stay in bed. Is this a solution, or just papering over the underlying cracks? *As **Ruth Lea**, of Institute of Directors commented: "It panders to people's weaknesses."*

- **Low Productivity** – Poorly trained or ill-directed staff can often be the cause of low productivity. This in turn leads to a poor return on the investment made in the employee or function, may introduce a weakness in the organisational processes, or merely lead to a failure to meet deadlines. All have an undeniable impact on *the Sustainable Business*. Wider, low productivity can be as a result of poor systems or process. A culture that discourages employee input leaves the organisation failing to embrace a key asset, its people. The Six Sigma process adopts a simple concept of asking the employees for ideas in its Voice of the Customer process. See Chapter 10.

- **Poor coordination** – A failure to effectively coordinate and manage a team will lead to failure: failure to deliver on time, a failure in quality standards or consistency, a failure to hit budget or service targets. Poor coordination often goes hand in hand with the failure to plan! "Fail to Plan, Plan to Fail"

> **Food for Thought**: The Bradford Index can be used to analyse the sickness patterns of employees in the workplace. Based on a rolling year, the employee attains a Bradford Rating using the simple equation:
>
> **Bradford Rating = (number of occurrences)² x number of days off work**
>
> Accordingly, a person who has 1 period of sickness lasting 10 days would accrue a Bradford Rating of 1² x 10=10, as opposed to a person who had 10 single days would have a Bradford Rating of 10² x10=1000, the latter clearly having a more disruptive influence and impact on the business. This measure can then be used to manage the situation and to help identify demotivation or other issues.

The Community

The Company environment and the relative Characters are but two elements for a sustainable *People Pillar* in an organisation. The *people* must be coordinated, structured, coerced, targeted, and driven; they need to be managed, and they need to *want* to work. The *people* element is therefore, inextricably linked to the management philosophy and strategic approach.

The Sustainable Business, however, demands more. For a truly stable *People Pillar* there is a need for an integral involvement within the community. A strong *People Pillar* demands a strategic involvement with the community to ensure a future supply of employees; a loyal local and low carbon supply chain; and a local and a low carbon sales stream. This is of particular significance for organisations operating in remote, low-skilled or third-world communities where an organisation may engage in a strategy to make the regional operation self-sufficient. In such environments, the flow of suitably skilled personnel requires investment – a partnership with the local academic institutions, with the government, and with the local population.

In remote communities, key organisations can become more than just an employer. They can represent hope and development, a future for the younger members of the society, a key source of revenue, and an opportunity to develop the local infrastructure. Sports and transport are two key areas that are often most visible. Take for example the oil industry in Angola. After years of civil war, the oil is now bringing prosperity, development and growth to a downtrodden and war-torn society. Infrastructure such as schools, hospitals, roads and ports have been rebuilt, and this helped secure the hosting of the African Cup of Nations in 2010. Within there is a real feeling of optimism with a recent conversation with an Angolan national over the development of possible tourist possibilities.

Further, some notable organisations working in Angola such as Chevron and others have sought to create sanctuary areas where endangered species are allowed to maintain their natural habitat, free from poachers, away from the rigours of captivity, and without the commercial drivers that might underpin a traditional "national park".

Rule: Look after the People, and the Profit will look after itself

Whilst not without its issues, Chevron's work in Angola represents a fantastic example of where investment in the community has helped both the local population and the participant organisations to establish strong and lasting *People Pillars*.

Nurturing the "Community element" is perhaps a little more difficult than the Company and Character as it involves numerous external forces. There may be political pressures, trust, corruption and financial hurdles, and consideration needs to be paid to changes in the work-stress-family balance with its resulting social consequences. *The Sustainable Business* will however seek to overcome these obstacles, focused on the long term goals. Linking with the local education and giving work placements, playing in local sport leagues, simple sponsorship arrangements, community partnerships, openness with local residents over issues, participation in community events, utilisation of the local university for research and development work, and so on, all help the community relationship. From a wider perspective, nurturing a community critically helps establish a lower carbon cost of business and leads to improvements in local suppliers, shorter supply chains, reduced logistics, higher skill levels, etc.

> **Food for Thought:** Developing a relationship with global communities, markets and partners requires effective communication. The assumption that "everyone speaks English" fails to show due respect for the other party.
> From a usefulness perspective, why are French and German still taught in European schools? Greek and Latin were phased out in the 1950s after recognition that they had become redundant and now French and German must surely follow. Neither language features in the UN top ten most spoken languages, yet we persist in teaching it with the belief that once a first new language is learnt, others follow more easily; however unpalatable French and German have become "Non-Modern Languages".
> Irrespective of whether this second statement is agreed with, teaching a second language useful in twenty-first century commerce must surely be an ambition for all European governments going forward to help foster better international relationships and community interaction. Schools and teachers should be required to switch French for Spanish or Portuguese, and ensure all students have access to Mandarin, Urdu, Arabic Russian and other truly modern languages.

Case Study: Tengizchevroil

In 2008, Tengizchevroil was bestowed the prestigious Silver Paryz award by President Nazarbayev, President of the Republic of Kazakhstan. This award recognised the organisation's supreme efforts to establish a long term, meaningful and visionary approach to sustainability.

Tengizchevroil's vision is clear: look after the people in the organisation and the local community, look after the environment, and focus on delivering enhanced value to shareholders; it has four strategic intents:

- Be the leader in safety and environmental performance
- Develop the workforce
- Be respected in the Kazakhstan community
- Achieve superior operational performance

Kazakhstan is geographically the eighth largest country on the planet, lying in both Europe and Asia. It is the only country with known reserves of every element on the Periodic Table, has one of the largest, largely untapped, oilfields on the planet, yet has a population of just 16m people.

Tengizchevroil focuses on its employees as the core of its success. The Tengiz oilfield, where the organisation operates, is in a remote part of the Caspian Sea region and has had to overcome numerous problems with logistics, communication, resources, and people. Its stated core strategic objectives have helped make it both a desirable employer, and responsible neighbour to its Kazakh communities.

Since the organisation was founded in 1993, it has made every effort to focus on the "local". Understandably, a large proportion of its infrastructure has needed to come from further afield, yet it has invested over $30bn with local Kazakh entities, goods and services, as well as government tax payments and licences. In 2008, this figure reached over $8.5bn flowing directly into the national Kazakh economy and this will only increase with further expansion projected in the coming years.

The organisation is dedicated to its long term operational ambitions. Its commitment to both safety and the environment is at the heart of all its operational procedures with clearly stated aims which include:

- Have an injury free organisation
- Develop a healthy workplace
- Eliminate spills and environmental accidents
- Operate incident free
- Maximise the efficient use of resources and assets

These are measured, published and promoted relentlessly with investment in environmental projects exceeding $2bn in the last decade, and with notable successes which include, for example, an 80% reduction in flaring. (Flaring is the burning off of unused natural gas, a by-product of crude oil production – this is responsible for the flame often seen on oilfield chimneys. This flaring increases carbon emissions and is both a missed commercial opportunity and a wasted resource. Tengizchevroil has invested in gas capture and containment, and reuses or sells the gas to benefit the company.)

Furthermore, a secondary by-product is sulphur, produced in high quantities by the manufacturing process. This, too, is now sold to organisations in 26 different countries across the planet for, amongst other things, soil enhancement products, generating both a valuable revenue stream as well as a more environmentally responsible approach to resources and impact.

Yet it's the people content which makes Tengizchevroil special. It's the commitment to employees, their families and the local community that is so admirable. Its employees are paid more than ten times the Kazakh minimum wage, and where possible it engages Kazakh locals, who now make up over 78% of the managerial workforce and 85% of the total workforce. The organisation also supports the family ethos with support to local kindergartens, summer camps, internships and family scholarships.

And Tengizchevroil builds in the community, with over $450m spent since 1993 on schools, hospitals, roads and utility projects including waste treatment and water purification projects.

Tengizchevroil is focused on its corporate social responsibility and delivering the triple bottom line today, tomorrow and into the future.

Source: TengizChevroil Anniversary publication

The Sustainable Business

Notes Page　　　　　　　　　　　　　　　　　　　　**Page Ref**

The Sustainable Business

Summary Chapter 3
The Corporate Social Responsibility Policy "The Profit Pillar"

Key Learning Points

- Understanding of *the Profit Pillar*
- Recognition of the three *Profit Dimensions*
- The importance of a stable sales model
- Clients – credit worthiness, customer mix, debt levels etc
- Product Mix – Category management, product portfolio, R&D
- Market – Global versus local markets, Porter's Five Forces
- Margin – Cost models, customer mix, indirect/direct
- Cost allocation models
- Carbon allocation
- The Five Rights of purchasing
- Comparison between purchasing of goods and services
- Analysis of CRM concept
- Understanding the necessary steps to sustainable service

Tool Summary

- *The Profit Pillar* Dimensions: Sales, Service and Strategy
- Stable Sales Model
- Porter's Five Forces & Market Analysis
- Cost allocation models – Activity Based Costing, Activity based Carbon Distribution
- POINT & PREP models of communication
- Seven Steps to Sustainable Service
- QTC – Quality, Time & Cost

CIPS Syllabus Reference

- All Level 4,5 & 6 subjects are impacted by the need to make a profit.

Chapter 3: The Corporate Social Responsibility Policy "The Profit Pillar"

The purpose of business is to create and keep a customer.
– Peter F. Drucker

The CSR Concept

As stated in chapter 2, the concept of CSR policy is well documented. Using "the three Ps – People, Profit and Planet" concept, this chapter will explore the traits and opportunities associated with a strong *Profit Pillar* – See figure 3.1. This is the second CSR pillar, necessary to ensure sustainability in the organisation.

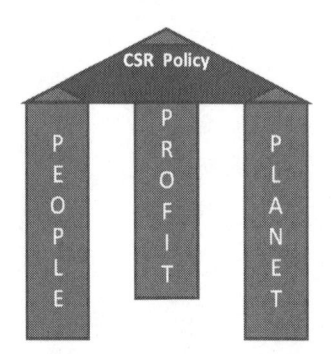

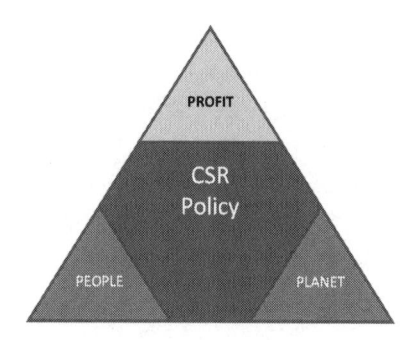

Figure 3.1 – The Profit Pillar

The Profit Pillar

The importance of *Profit* to the organisation cannot be understated. This *Profit* may be financial, or some other form of value depending upon the nature of the organisation and its goals.

Like the *People Pillar*, the *Profit Pillar* – See Figure 3.2 - can be broken into three core dimensions: Sales, Service and Strategy.

Profit is the value generated by the organisation's activities. To generate sustainable profit, it is essential that *the Sustainable Business;* has an effective sales stream; has a service that generates genuine value for which its customers are prepared to pay; has a strategy that ensures the highest possible return is attained for the sales; and a revenue that is greater than the total costs incurred.

> **Rule: Sales are Vanity, Profit is Sanity**

These three dimensions are the foundations for a strong *Profit Pillar*.

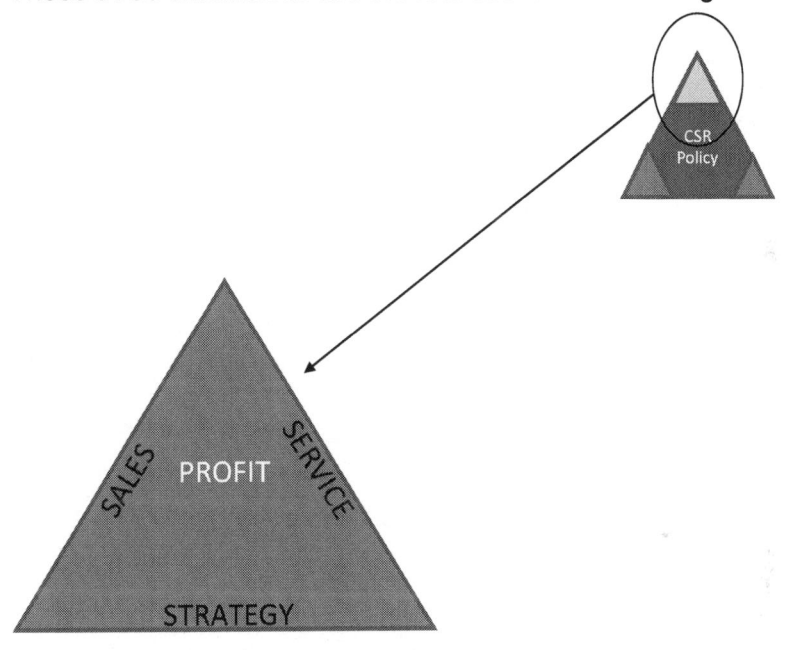

Figure 3.2 – The Profit Pillar Dimensions

The Sales

The first dimension of a strong *Profit Pillar* is "Sales". *The Sustainable Business* requires a steady flow of demand to ensure its future. This demand may be in the form of chargeable orders or activities that generate goodwill, but what factors can be developed to help create this sales pipeline?

Generating a sustainable sales function is explored in depth in chapter 8 however the need to have strong sales is a critical basis for a strong *Profit Pillar*. A stable sales dimension can be broken into four key areas: Client, Market, Margin and Product – See figure 3.3.

Figure 3.3 – The Stable Sales Dimension

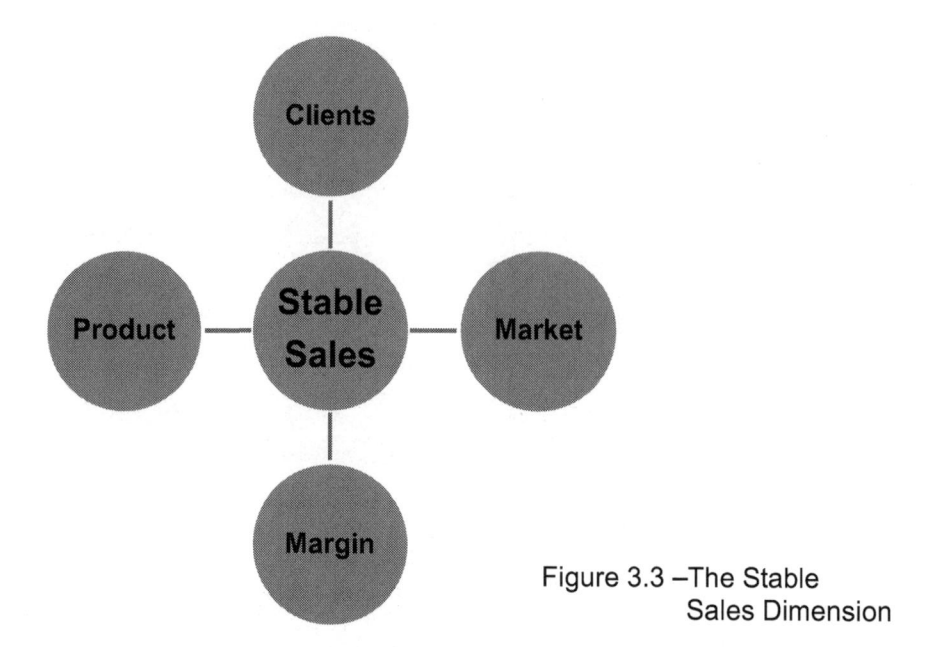

Clients – *The Sustainable Business* needs to have a strong client base, which is as diverse as possible: cross market, cross sector, cross industry, and cross border. Developing such breadth takes time, effort and investment. Reputation does not automatically flow through the market, it needs to be coerced and presented in such a way as to ensure the successes are visible and recognised.

The Sustainable Business nurtures client success, seeks referrals, recommendations and positive feedback. This forms the basis of successful sales development, with client loyalty underpinning sustainable sales. This helps when prospecting for new customers and to maintain the confidence of the incumbent relationships.

And *the Sustainable Business* needs to plan its customer demand. The sales pipeline is the classic tool used to plan sales over the period. It enables an organisation to identify what resources it will need in the coming weeks, months and possibly years as well as allowing the sales manager to project budget and revenue leading to a focus on trends and for reporting purposes.

Rule: Fail to Plan, Plan to fail

Never forget, a sale involves three components: negotiation, a transfer of assets and a payment. Without the payment we do not have a sale, we have a bad debt or a credit note; another organisation or person has grown in worth at our expense.

> **Food for Thought**: What level of sales are required to replace the money lost by a bad debt?
>
> Consider an organisation with an average margin of 10%. It sells some goods for $1000 and the customer takes the goods, however the customer never pays the invoice. This is a bad debt. To recoup the $900 cost of sale (the remaining 90% of the $1000), the organisation needs to make a **$9,000** sale – at the 10% margin – for the bad debt to be recovered.

The Sustainable Business checks the credit worthiness of its customers and monitors the time customers take to pay their invoices. An invoice with credit terms of thirty days which is paid after 90 days is not considered a bad-debt, but the impacted cash flow has eroded the margin and cost the organisation money. Projected margins generally assume that credit terms are achieved, a weak debt-collection policy leads to customers taking liberties and using this as a cheap line of credit.

Creditor days are an easy measure to appreciate. It reflects the average time customers are taking to pay their invoices. Comparing this with the standard credit terms, or on historical levels, shows how policy is affecting the trends. Ensuring that commercial queries are resolved quickly helps manage this issue.

A fresh commercial query is far easier to remedy than one that is several years old. Evidence becomes lost, the customer less ready to discuss the issues and people forget the history. Customers can use a commercial query to stall payment, reducing the cash-flow and increasing the risk that the invoice turns from query to a bad debt. Indeed, experience shows that a small percentage of customers even use bad debts as a commercial opportunity systematically rejecting invoices from peripheral suppliers with the sole objective of negotiating a settlement, confident in the knowledge that the supplier would not deem the sum worthy of court action.

It is however worth noting at this stage, any historic bad debts and commercial queries which have been written off previously that are resolved have a direct and often significant contribution to the bottom line.

But *the Sustainable Business* views a customer on a "Stop List" or trading with a competitor as a missed opportunity. One organisation examined, had adopted a culture that it would only pass credits as a last resort and only once the customer had chased for them three times, thereby holding on to the money for as long as possible, with many credits forgotten by the customer in the fullness of time. This is a somewhat naïve approach as it leaves unpaid invoices on the books unpaid increasing the risk of them becoming bad debts. It also inhibits cash-flow, reduces the customer's credit limit, and in many cases creates bad feeling. Said organisation had one customer which had huge levels of commercial queries – some dating back over five years – which could easily have been resolved, and the invoices paid, but which sank with the customer when it went bankrupt. This eradicated the company's entire trading profit for the 1994 and 1995 financial years, at the same time leaving a £1m sales black hole.

Statistically, outstanding invoices are not an unusual occurrence. According to the UK Government Department for Business, over 4000 UK businesses failed in 2008 as a direct result of late payments, with 73% of businesses surveyed citing issues with late payments. It showed average payment terms on invoices was around 39 days, with large corporates often the worst offenders seeking 90+ days payment terms, and, according to www.smallbiz.pod, by the end of 2008 there were over 1,000,000 businesses in the UK owed money in unpaid and overdue invoices.

Furthermore, in a separate piece of Natwest research, 71% of SME's had suffered from late payments, with UK companies having more than £15.7bn of invoices over 120 days in arrears, with less than half of the SME organisations having taken any steps to recover the money.

The Sustainable Business addresses commercial issues in the short term, maintaining clean ledgers and thus creating a platform upon which sales can flourish.

> **Rule: Deal with and clear commercial queries inside the first year**

Product (or service) – Having an effective product portfolio assists *the Sustainable Business* in obtaining profit through multiple channels and from a broad range of sources; understanding what the client is looking for and making sure that there is a product or service that meets their needs is key. A comprehensive product portfolio takes time to develop. Products can be designed and manufactured or alternatively bought-in, with both solutions requiring a corresponding and robust strategy.

Sourcing products necessitates resources, testing, and a procurement structure capable of maintaining Supply Chain security. Potential suppliers need to be reviewed by dedicated individuals focused on managing the market sector.

The use of "Category Management" structures the market segment enabling key suppliers, customers, products/services opportunities, capacity, risks, etc to be effectively managed. An experienced category manager will understand the segment, recognise the technology implications and ensure a balance between the customer needs and the supplier requirements: too many suppliers will dilute the volume benefit, too few will constrain customer choice and risk losing sales. Volume is a key procurement driver for which commercial value can be derived thus strengthening the *Profit Pillar*.

Alternatively, products can be developed internally. A dedicated "Research and Development" (R&D) department with adequate investment is a fantastic resource for *the Sustainable Business*. It generates the future product lines and sales solutions, and can be focused on the specific strategic requirements of the organisation, but this can be very expensive.

Products evolve: the Boston Consulting Group Matrix – see figure 1.5 – looks at how products mature and recognises how the investment, commitment and profit contribution from the products change over time. It is commercially useful to manage the impact and strategy relating to each product, to generate optimum return from the investment and thus maximise the contribution to the bottom line.

Of more long term benefit is the need to ensure that the R&D department – if that is where future products are created (as opposed to from an external supplier) – produces ideas and solutions that meet the future needs of clients, hence ensuring sustainability of the sales function. This requires recognition of the importance of the creative side of such individuals and teams. Time, space, and investment are rare commodities in the 21st century however they are central to generating, nurturing and establishing creditable ideas.

What can be overlooked in R&D departments however is the link between ideas and commercial opportunities. R&D teams are often driven by a passion for innovation and new ideas, where prudence and reality can be swamped by enthusiasm and excitement. Credible options can be overlooked in favour of the glamorous design; minds can be blinkered in pursuit of the holy grail of patents or innovative new directions, and wider a philosophy of "cost is not an obstacle" may prevail. And how often have successful products been resurrected from the "cutting-room floor"?

Consider the research and development needs of organisations dependent solely on discovery and new innovations for their commercial existence. As highlighted in chapter 2, organisations such as drug companies spend millions trying to discover, invent or develop new products to remedy customer needs. This upfront investment needs to be recovered over the life of the product to both justify the expense and finance the unsuccessful ideas that went nowhere, without this revenue stream such business seek to be commercially viable and thus unsustainable. And without such business endeavours the development of society can stagnate.

What *the Sustainable Business* needs is direction and control of the R&D function. Be wary of generating unbalanced teams, of the "Group Think" concept where all the members think in unison without due regard for the alternative perspective, or teams lacking key skill sets. Record all ideas, good and bad, don't necessarily reject ideas, but prioritise to ensure focus, and demand an independent review of those that *missed the cut*.

It must be recognised that not all ideas will flourish into tomorrow's *Stars*, and that rejection is a reluctant necessity. If the strategy allows, be prepared to take a short term gain from those destined for disposal.

Significant, if potentially not a little risky, revenue can be generated from these *runt saplings* where suitable entrepreneurial outlets can be found.

Above all, *the Sustainable Business* needs a mixed product portfolio. It needs a selection of products to meet the various needs of all its customers. Not having what the customer wants leads to a lost sale, a disappointed customer, and value added to a competitor.

Market – Understanding market dynamics, market forces and importantly, how a market is changing, is core to strong sales and the *Profit Pillar*.

Exploiting a sustainable market involves understanding the key market participants, and how they interact; this is perhaps best understood using Porter's Five Force Model – see Figure 1.3. This powerful and long established model identifies the five forces that have influence in the market; utilising this model helps us produce strategy, manage risk and exploit opportunities in a market to help generate profitability.

In summary, the model highlights the interaction between the customer and the supplier through the market, with the impact that new entrants have on the market dynamics and the consequences in the market if an alternative solution is introduced. The model recognises the flow and satisfaction of demand by the market, and how capacity and risk are managed by the various participants.

Subsequently, however, a sixth force has been added to the model, that of complementary products in the market:

- Competitive Rivalry: Take for example the car market. The competitive rivalry in the market was historically dominated by a number of major brands globally, such as General Motors, Toyota, Ford, Renault, VW, etc.

- Buyers: The buyers ultimately are the users, members of the public, corporate car schemes, car hire companies, taxi firms, etc. They have choice, and this choice is often the dominant force in many markets.

- Suppliers: Equally important to the market are the forces exerted by the suppliers of manufacturing items such as steel, tyres, electronic components, etc. This is especially so in times of shortages, or crisis, such as the steel crisis in the 1990s, or the earthquake and Tsunami on the Toyota plant in Japan.

In the normal course of events the car companies would challenge for both the customers and in some cases the supply of raw materials and components, looking for the cheapest suppliers to enable the car company to offer cheaper vehicles to the end user.

- New Entrants: So what happens when a new company enters the market, for example Tata or before that Kia? It could be argued that they targeted specific, untapped market segments to get a foothold in the market and thus overcome some of the barriers to entry, but ultimately a new entrant in such a market dilutes the market and reduces the income of the other players. This can lead to a more competitive offering in the marketplace as the market participants up their game to preserve their income streams.

- Substitutes: And what happens when alternative products take market share? In the car market, consider the impact of an increase in the use of bicycles possibly encouraged by government policy, or an increase in the attractiveness of public transport.

- Complementary Products: In addition, the recently introduced sixth force relates to "complementary products" in the market; these are products which are related to and affect the demand for the core product. In the aforementioned example, the price of petrol has a clear impact on the demand and competitiveness in the market.

What the model does not overtly recognise are the other members of the wider Supply Chain acting alongside those represented. From a supplier's perspective, the upstream, raw material supply chain is evidently affected by the dynamics of this market and will have reciprocal influence in their market. *The Sustainable Business* recognises the influence of the wider Supply Chains on the market, on generating a stable sales environment, and on the corresponding profitability of the organisation. The strength of the *Profit Pillar* is manifestly affected by the strength of these underpinning Supply Chains, a subject reviewed in later chapters.

It is, therefore, essential that there is a clear understanding of the market as a whole to enable the organisation to fully exploit all profit opportunities in the short, medium and long term. To achieve this we need to understand the wider market in which we operate, recognise the dynamics at work in the market, and be aware of our competitors and their associated strategies.

To understand a market, a useful tool is to plot the main suppliers or components in the market based on their quality and cost. If we again consider the global car market, then we might paint a picture such as shown in figure 3.4.

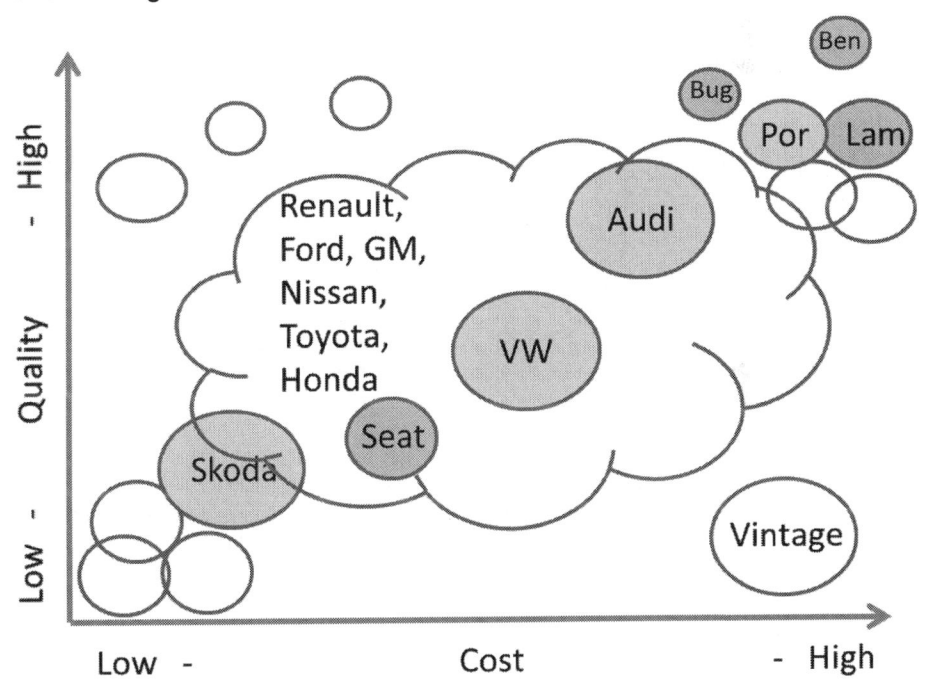

3.4 The Global Car Market

Clearly, in this market there are a large number of suppliers, each with their own specific product offering. Whilst a detailed assessment of some of the mainstream suppliers has been spared in the above diagram, there are a number of clear observations that can be seen.

Firstly, there are a number of manufacturers *perceived* as low-cost and low-frills suppliers such as Tata. Tata's early aim was to make a low cost vehicle that was affordable to all, however their global ambitions and product coverage has expanded and changed significantly with the takeover of the Jaguar and Landrover brands to form JLR.

We also have brands such as Rolls Royce (shown as RR), Ferrari, Porsche etc. which represent relatively small market shares, and sit in the high cost high quality area of the graph. These organisations – which of course include the aforementioned Jaguar and Landrover – generally adopt a strategy aimed at a specific market segment or customer type who can afford such products and services, making no apologies for the price charged for their products instead focusing on service and product quality.

Wider this model should also include products which are maybe a little niche, for example vintage cars. The definition for "Vintage" or "Classic" varies, however in this context, cars of say fifty years or more may be seen to have a certain mystique, an old fashioned class, or a heritage. This tag enables sellers to demand a high price, however here the definition of quality could potentially be called into question. Does a car built in 1930 have quality safety characteristics, air-conditioning as standard, or anti-lock brakes? And how economical or environmentally friendly are such cars?

What this model also shows are the relative market strategies of the main suppliers into a market. Using this, and looking specifically at the Volkswagen Audi Group (VAG), we can surmise an organisation's market and brand strategy – See figure 3.5.

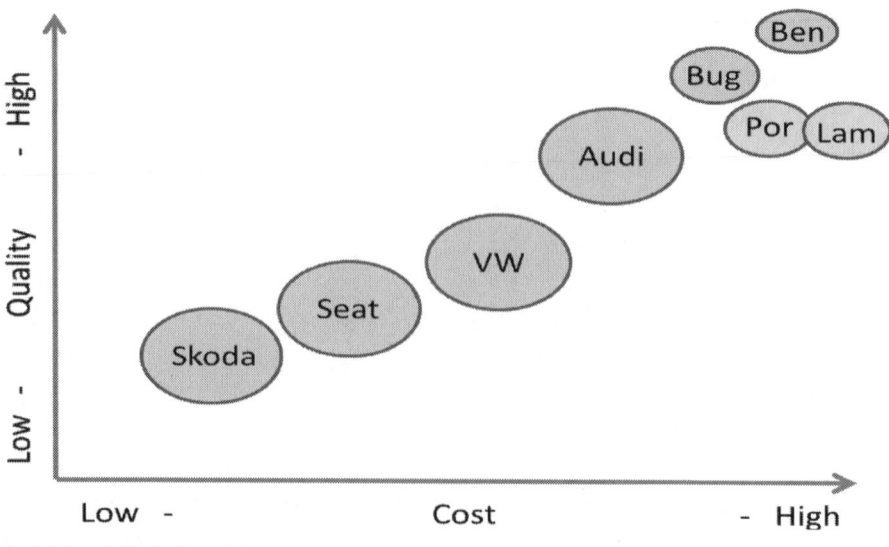

3.5 The VAG Car Market

Here it can be seen that VAG have developed a cross market range of products to capitalise on all market segments therein with limited internal conflict. This gives the VAG group a strength that its competitors may not have access to, as well as enabling manufacturing capacity to be shared between the brands to reduce costs and maximise procurement, design, manpower, etc. Optimising these costs leads to a lower total cost base, higher profits and a more profitable and sustainable business.

> **Food for Thought**: Tata undertakes its goals whilst still adopting a highly responsible approach to the environment at all times – from their CSR:
>
> *"Tata Motors' concern is manifested by a dual approach:*
> *Reduction of environmental pollution and regular pollution control drives restoration of ecological balance.*
> *Our endeavours towards environment protection are soil and water conservation programmes and extensive tree plantation drives. Tata Motors is committed to restoring and preserving environmental balance, by reducing waste and pollutants, conserving resources and recycling materials."*

Margin – Profit Margin is the reward and value added by the organisation, it is the foundation of the *Profit Pillar*. Understanding and planning margin begins with the interaction between the pricing policy and the cost base.

The evaluation of the cost of a product or service is vital to the management of the product margin which in itself determines how the sales pricing model is developed. What costs are associated with the product? Are they direct or indirect, fixed or variable? How much are costs likely to fluctuate? How is the cost of risk incorporated? And how will economic activity affect inflation or the exchange rate for our interaction with foreign sales or purchases?

To establish the true cost, we need to evaluate the direct costs, but also the indirect costs attributable to the product or service – see Table 3.6. Direct costs might include raw materials, the cost of labour related directly to the production, or any patents or copyrights for example, whilst indirect costs and more general costs in the business such as management overheads, head office costs, or administration support will be apportioned in some agreed manner.

	Direct	**Indirect**
Materials	Raw materials or goods for resale	Maintenance items, cleaning or office supplies
Labour	Personnel involved in the production process	Additional personnel, management, administration, purchasing
Overheads	Patent costs, copyright payments, licenses	Rent, rates, finance, general utility payments
Carbon Costs	Carbon generated in the production process, through the production of the raw materials or through any associated transport costs	Cost of carbon used in support functions, sales activities, personnel travel into work, etc

Table 3.6

How these indirect costs are allocated is a key strategic issue in the organisation's approach to cost management. They can be distributed in a number of different ways, looking at different facets of the business – see figure 3.7.

It is key to ensure that there is the right level of buy-in across the organisation for any cost allocation method, and that there is recognition that any change will have winners and losers.

Also included in table 3.7 is the concept of carbon costing. A relatively new concept in real terms, however understanding the carbon cost of a product, service or process is essential to reducing its impact. A significant number of organisations now measure their carbon impact, with a variety of differing approaches.

> **Rule: If you can't measure it, you can't manage it!**

Identifying the carbon impact accurately can lead to internal allocation of costs associated to the internal carbon output. Activity Based Carbon Distribution (ABCD Costing) takes the Activity Based Costing concept to the next level and introduces the needs and issues of the 21st Century.

For Activity Based Carbon Distribution to be truly effective, there must be a deep-rooted desire within the organisation to measure and constrain its environmental impact. Measurement of carbon emission needs to be established for all inputs including total net carbon content for all suppliers of raw materials, logistics and service industries and all suppliers within the Supply Chain up to and including raw material extraction.

Equitable allocation
Costs are distributed equally amongst all holders.

Easy calculation, penalises those who do not use an asset or function.

Allocation by usage
Costs allocated pro rata to the usage by a department. See Activity Based Costing (ABC).

Charging is based on usage. Can be difficult to measure or police.

Allocation by sales
Costs are allocated relative to the percentage of the total sales.

Assumes the largest sales area will have greatest usage or the largest ability to pay.

Allocation by geography
Costs are distributed equally across regions pro rata to regional size or similar factors.

Easy calculation, but often contested and political. Does not always reflect real usage.

Allocation by product
Costs are allocated relative to the product profile and contribution to the bottom line.

Charging based on usage of the product. Percentage of the split can fluctuate.

Allocation by carbon use
Costs are allocated relative to their carbon emissions or polution characteristics.

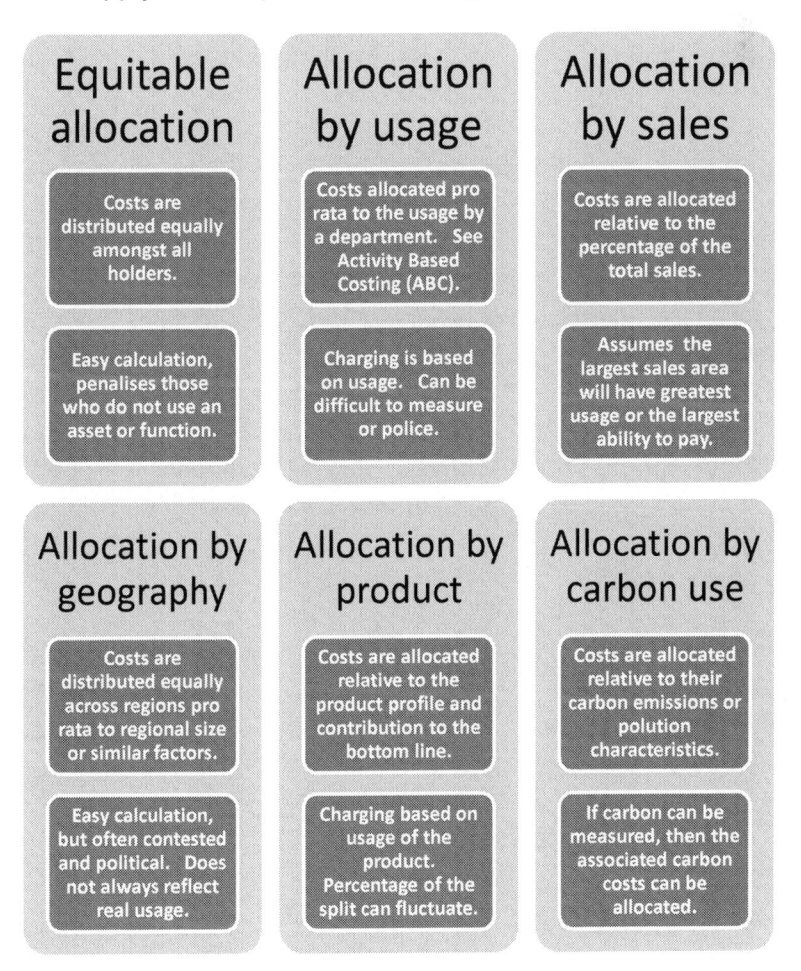

If carbon can be measured, then the associated carbon costs can be allocated.

Figure 3.7 – Cost Allocation examples

Furthermore, consideration needs to be given to forward carbon usage through to the next levels within the Supply Chain. This will include the carbon generated throughout the life of the product. This is explored in Chapter 10 with the design of goods and services examined to understand the impact of design choices on life cycle costs and carbon dioxide creation.

Whilst there is a generally stated desire to have carbon visibility throughout the Supply Chain, in practice society is some way from being able to accurately and consistently achieve this. Invariably, estimates and assumptions come into play, organisations fail to accurately collect data, and inconsistent approaches can taint the figures. These assumptions allow those with a vested interest, or those with poor statistics, to muddle through undetected or be allowed to hide in the shadows.

Furthermore, at a consumer level, a number of creditable efforts have been made by some organisations to highlight the carbon content of products through effective labelling. The European Union "Ecolabel" was launched in 1992 and has grown steadily over the years with over 17,000 products now covered. However, commitment and uptake of this labelling structure has been sporadic with Italy having the largest commitment to the Ecolabel, accounting for half of all products registered within the scheme. Although legislation in Europe, North America, Japan and other regions is increasing, the need to address this issue is clear, albeit that the auditing of such claims remains fragmented, inconsistent and subject to wide variation; use of ISO14000 and other such audit processes can help improve this situation.

Whilst it remains to be seen how such initiatives develop and whether they are maintained, of more concern is a general trend to passing the onus of responsibility for carbon decisions onto the ultimate consumer. This move makes several bold assumptions:

1. Firstly that the consumer cares more about CO_2 production than the implications on his or her purse (especially in times of hardship);
2. Secondly, it assumes that, with minimal training, the consumer understands the information;
3. Thirdly that the consumer actually believes what he or she is being told.

Accordingly, to be effective, it must therefore remain the responsibility of the producer to introduce measures for the constraint of carbon production. Understanding where the carbon is produced within the Supply Chain can only aid this endeavour.

When trying to establish a product cost, we need to be very mindful as to whether a cost is fixed or variable and what the organisation's overheads are: Is the cost affected by the number of units we produce or is it the same whether we deliver one, ten or a hundred?

So how do we determine what are fixed and what are variable costs, and what is our total cost of production – see figure 3.8.

Total Costs

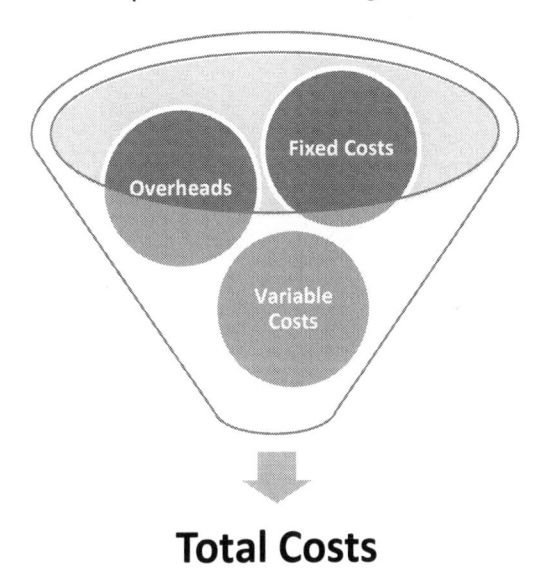

Figure 3.8 Establishing Total Costs

A fixed cost is by definition just that; a cost which is fixed and remains the same whatever the throughput. A fixed cost may be, for example, the cost of purchasing a wood lathe to produce a specific item. Within reason – assuming the lathe is able to fulfil the capacity required of it – irrespective of how much it is used, the costs of capital will remain fixed, i.e. the cost of buying the lathe.

In addition to the cost of the lathe, however, there is a requirement for electrical power and wood to produce the item. Clearly here we now have a variable cost. If we manufacture one widget, the quantity of wood or power required would be less than if ten or a hundred were produced.

And finally, we have the issue of the overheads needed to run the organisation. These may include management costs, head office, support functions, in some cases the property costs, etc. A high level of overheads on a business can be an unsustainable cost burden. *The Sustainable Business'* maintains a cost base which is affordable and prudent both for today and into the future. Planning of affordability is addressed in later chapters, and brings into play complex questions such as whether to "buy, lease or hire".

The Service

So what constitutes good service?

A good starting point when assessing the quality of a service is to look at the basic five rights of purchasing, and the QTC – Quality Time and Cost – concepts.

Good service is not just about securing the lowest cost possible, it's about fulfilling the five rights of purchasing:

Delivery of the right quantity of the right product, of the right quality, to the right place, at the right time.

The Chartered Institute of Purchasing and Supply defines these five rights as shown in table 3.9.

> **Rule: Happy Customers come back**

These represent the five basic requirements when placing a purchase order. Alternative thinking merely focuses on the QTC – Quality Time and Cost – see figure 3.10 – *Were the goods or service of the right quality available when it was needed and at a price in line with the customer's expectation?*

Customer expectation is the essence of good quality service. As mentioned earlier in this chapter, t*he Sustainable Business* needs to establish a flow of demand today, tomorrow and into the future. It needs customers to keep coming back, and the best way to achieve that is through meeting their expectations at a consistent level. Unfortunately, "quality" is a highly subjective concept, and not one that is easily challenged nor conquered.

Right Quality	• The right quality: quality as 'conformance to specification' and 'fitness for purpose', the costs of getting quality wrong, specifications and quality, approaches to managing supplier quality
Right Quantity	• The right quantity: determining the quantity required, factors influencing the choice of how much to buy, minimum order levels and values
Right Place	• The right place: in bound transportation of goods to the delivery point, issues arising from international transportation
Right Time	• The right time: internal, external and total lead time and factors that influence lead time, expediting, measuring supplier delivery performance
Right Price	• The right price: the different types of cost, and where purchase price fits in, factors affecting how a supplier prices their products or services

Table 3.9

The "Five Rights" should be central to *the Sustainable Business*' processes. They should underpin its every activity and be measured for effectiveness. Each should have its own specific metrics, and form part of the service assessment. For example, do we know how often "we" deliver the wrong products, or how often "we" deliver products which are faulty or broken? Without such evidence improvement of our systems and processes will never happen, and a percentage of customers will drift away.

> **Food for Thought**: Should we aim to exceed customer expectations? Recognising that all activities should add value, how does exceeding expectation, i.e. going the extra mile, add value? The value may be repeat orders or reputation, but the "extra" should not be done without some reward.

Figure 3.10 Quality, Time and Cost

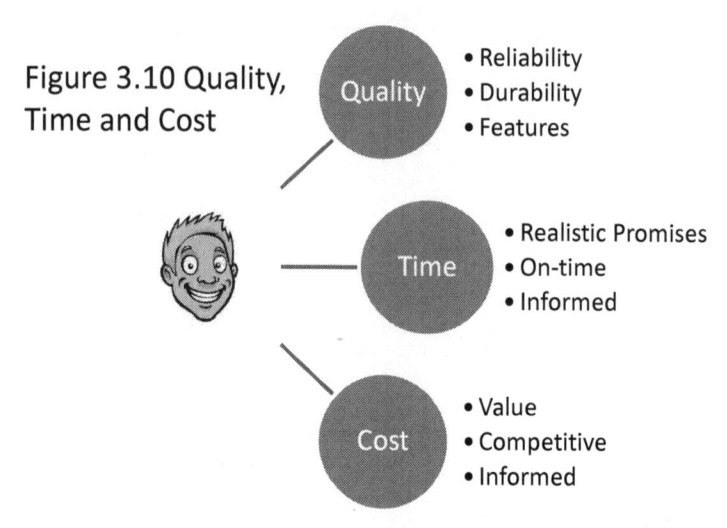

- Quality
  - Reliability
  - Durability
  - Features
- Time
  - Realistic Promises
  - On-time
  - Informed
- Cost
  - Value
  - Competitive
  - Informed

By way of example, consider the inventory held by an organisation. This may affect internal and/or external customers and is often critical to the success of an organisation. In many organisations having the right stock in the right place is essential to the delivery of a good service, however maintaining accurate inventory records, rotating stock, understanding usage trends, and recognising obsolescence all impact on the success of the inventory function.

Consider a retail outlet stocking golf equipment. An effective inventory will reflect size, age, gender and desires of its customers, but critically it must reflect left-hand or right-hand usage. Around 10% of the western population is left handed, so this should be reflected in the golf club inventory.

Similarly, a shoe shop would be advised to stock "pairs of shoes", and a ski-shop needs to ramp up its stocks of the latest designs shortly before the start of the new season. A business stocking snow shovels or desk fans needs to understand the weather forecast, and health services around the world need to reflect the potential epidemics – such as bird flu – that are prevalent at any one time.

> Rule: "At Air Canada, we are not happy until you are happy."

Good service needs to be instilled in the culture of the organisation – people need to care. Maintaining a strong *People Pillar* will help achieve this goal, however it needs management recognition, investment and above all belief in the organisation's goals. Training and communication underpin this to ensure all operatives think and act in a consistent manner. Good service is about fulfilling customer expectation.

Understanding the service provision of some of the world's preeminent companies is an excellent starting point. Recognition for great or consistent service has been the bedrock of many of the great global companies. See Table 3.11 for some commonplace examples.

Organisation	Competitive Advantage	Customer Value Added
MacDonald's, Burger King, KFC, etc	Consistent products and service	- Known and reliable Outcomes
Toyota, Honda, VAG, etc.	Reliability, quality and competitive pricing	- Product reliability
EDF (Électricité de France)	Market share through acquisition of regional market leaders	- European wide consolidation - Economies of scale - Commercial incentives
Starbucks, Café Nero, etc.	Location, brand and quality	- Right Quality - Right Time - Affordable cost
Chevron, Shell, Total, etc.	Global partnerships in emerging markets	- Security of supply - Diversity leads to lower reliance on volatile regions
DHL, UPS, Fedex, etc.	Highly established processes and networks	- Highly effective delivery solutions - Cost benefit from volume Operations
China Mobile, Vodafone, Airtel, MTN, T-Mobile, etc.	Telecommunication network coverage and capacity	- Cost benefits - Technical product advantages - Sole supply route

Table 3.11 Competitive Advantage and Customer Added Value

Is great service about doing things fastest, cheapest, or having the best product, or is it merely about meeting (or exceeding) the <u>expectations</u> of the customer? Organisations that recognise that it's the expectations of the customer that are the key, tend to steal the lead in their respective market.

The Virgin group of companies are particularly adept at this. They do not pretend to be the cheapest, and do not necessarily always reinvent the wheel, they just focus on what the customer expects, and on delivering it reliably every time.

> *The Virgin ethos is simple, take on the big boys and do it better. Richard Branson delights in upsetting the apple cart, and putting noses out of joint in stale boardrooms around the globe. "We look for opportunities where we can offer something better, fresher and more valuable, and we seize them. We often move into areas where the customer has traditionally received a poor deal, and where the competition is complacent."*

In contrast, organisations at the budget end of a market make no apologies for their focus on low cost even adopting branding such as "No Frills" or "Low Cost Airline". They endeavour to manage customer expectations to ensure that any delays, inconvenience or quality issues do not deter the customer from coming back.

Many of the organisations renowned for their service often focus on just one of quality, time or cost: Macdonald's, Burger King, etc focus on fast service, for example the drive through concept; Dell focus on delivering exactly what the customer wants in their specification; Coke have just one unique taste; DHL introduced package tracking to ensure that the customer expectations on delivery times are updated and met throughout the transit; and numerous organisations the world over commit to "match any price found cheaper on-line".

One organisation experienced had a goal to "always exceed customer expectations". Whilst noble, good customer service is all about **meeting** customer expectation; it is about making sure the customer gets what he or she expects, not necessarily surpassing those expectations. If the organisation has gone the extra mile, it will undoubtedly have cost it money. *The Sustainable Business* is focused on making profit, on making sure that each and every activity adds net value to the organisation through enhancement to the bottom line, improved goodwill or some other tangible or intangible benefit. Where an organisation exceeds the expectations of the customer, it needs to make certain that this value philosophy is maintained.

Rule: Adding extra value is fine if the customer recognises it.

Customer expectation is further enhanced with good communication. Customers like to be kept abreast of their "order". A broken promise or failure to meet schedules can to some extent be mitigated by merely keeping the customer informed. The parcel tracking implemented by some of the global parcel carriers helps customers understand at any point where their consignment is, allowing them to plan and amend plans to reflect the delivery schedule. Shops that employ numbering systems to enforce a visible FIFO system help communicate waiting time to customers, and organisations who publish "quality failure statistics" help manage customer quality expectations.

CRM (Customer Relationship Management) solutions are commonplace in today's organisations, recognising the importance of maintaining the relationship with the customer. Many of these systems, however, link directly into marketing and advertising portals to try and tempt the customer to spend more money. If the customer has experienced genuine delight they will generally come back anyway and over-exposure can often be detrimental to the customer's perspective of the supplier.

Effective communication is more than just the message; it needs to recognise the delivery and channels used to ensure optimum results. Publication in a quality newspaper, for example, will typically only hit a small proportion of a potential audience, an audience, in this example, diluted by numerous factors including: does the customer read the newspaper in question; did they get the newspaper on that day; did they read the appropriate page that day; were they attracted to the article; did they understand the content; were they motivated to read to the end; and so on. A newspaper will typically appeal to a limited section of society, a target audience. Society is often classified using the "A-B-C1-C2-D-E" metric, with many organisations focusing products, brands, price points, outlets, geographical distribution and many other elements of their business based on a specific target sector. This is addressed further in later chapters.

So how do we get our message heard? The POINT model endeavours to highlight five key areas of effective communication see figure 3.12.

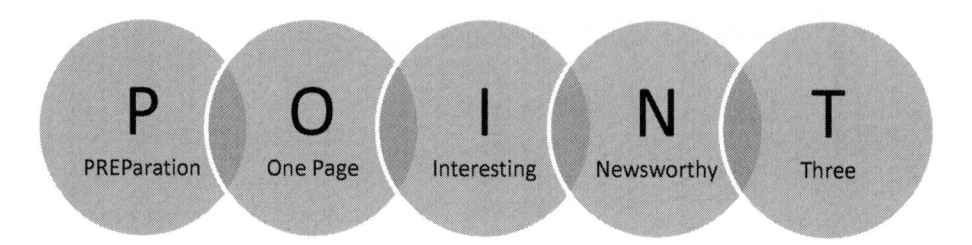

P PREParation **O** One Page **I** Interesting **N** Newsworthy **T** Three

3.12 The POINT Model

1.   P is for PREParation

Remember the old adage: Fail to Plan, Plan to Fail. Preparation is key to good communication. We need to prepare, structure and plan our approach. Using templates or standard structures can help, but what if you fail to plan? All is not lost, try the PREP approach – see figure 3.13.

Point ▸ Reason ▸ Example ▸ Point

3.13 The "PREP" Model

PREP works like this. Perhaps your boss asks you a question in a meeting that you have not prepared for. Start by buying a few seconds, by moving to the front to deliver your thoughts, by testing the sound system, or by being clumsy and dropping something (an approach often used by G W Bush!). These few seconds help you formulate your response in your mind.

Open with a line such as "Wow, that's a really big subject, but I think for me the most important point here is…." And make a POINT. Making the response personal with words like "I" and "Me" adds sincerity and gravitas.

Next give a REASON (just one reason) why you have made that specific POINT.

Then give an EXAMPLE to reiterate the importance of the POINT and to justify the REASON.

Then conclude by reiterating the POINT.

And finally sit down to avoid questions upon the subject you have just managed to convince everyone you are so well versed.

Tony Blair was great at this; he may not have sat down at the end, but merely beckoned for the next topic from the audience, critically never making eye contact with the original inquisitor. This effectively terminates the discussion at the moment when you might be cross examined. You control the audience, in Tony Blair's case usually the media, to ensure his key message was the last thing they remember being discussed in relation to the subject and thus often the next news headline. Statistically, being first, second or last is usually preferable, hence the significance of the expression "having the last word".

2. **O is for One Page Only**

   Where possible, strive to produce your message, business case proposal, etc, on ONE PAGE ONLY. One effective page will be read, a small book will be merely flicked through. Use diagrams, graphs, etc to highlight key points. In a business case, for example, try splitting the page into quarters, each containing one of: Cost, Benefits, Risks and Net contribution. The brain will focus on each quarter and find just one message therein, and remember it more easily. Make sure "Net contribution" is the last box. For the 90% of the population who are right handed, the brain will best remember the first, second and last boxes. – Remember, one page will be read!

3. **I is for Interesting**

   Make the content interesting to the key stakeholder. Interest will improve retention and aid the decision. If it is cost reduction, say so, give a percentage or value, and capture the INTEREST of the stakeholder. Show how value is added to the organisation.

Avoid lengthy tracts of text, this puts people off reading, use statistics or key words to add emphasis.

4.   **N is for Newsworthy**

Make the content NEWSWORTHY reflecting up-to-date issues, in line with the prevailing business or market focus. Follow the trend, catch the mood of the moment.

Use topical headlines, but don't regurgitate volumes of text. If it is truly NEWSWORTHY the reader will know about it.

5.   **T is for Three**

Make the "one page" stand out and be memorable. The human brain has trouble taking in complicated messages and retaining them in their entirety, so help it! Never more than THREE is the secret. The brain can take in up to THREE things well, after that it is confused and becomes inefficient at remembering the detail.

Strictly THREE colours only, for example. A white or light coloured background, and up to two others. No shades of a colour - a shade counts as a different colour to the brain.

Up to THREE types/sizes of text. Italics counts as an extra text type, so does going bold and underlining; use a maximum of THREE.

And don't right justify. This adds in variable spacing (more than THREE sizes of spacing usually) into the text, again making it difficult for your brain to take in the detail and can be shown to reduce reading speed.

Remember the old adage: Say what you're going to say, Say it, and then say what you've told them......Ah, THREE again! Help your brain remember the key message you're trying to portray.

When communicating, it is important to select a medium and language that the customer is likely to recognise. This is especially important when addressing the younger end of the market where texting and social media channels – such as Facebook, Twitter, etc – are prevalent.

Be aware of your body posture, facial expressions and tone. This can give a completely different message to the words spoken thus confusing the recipient. Equally, it is a good idea to watch the recipient. Their actions and posture may give a clue as to their thoughts and responses. Watch for signs of stress, anxiety or over confidence, it may change your delivery, approach or strategy. Frequent touching of the face, looking down and to the left, blushing or disparity between expression and the words can suggest a lack of truth.

Most critical of all to delivering a good service, however, is the motivation and support of the service providing team members. As highlighted in Chapter 2, the people in the organisation have a huge responsibility and impact on the performance of the business. Motivated staff care.

Looking after the staff in the organisation was covered in the previous chapter, however the need to deliver a good service reiterates the need for staff to come to work with a smile on their face, motivated to do a good job, and willing to go the extra mile needed for world class service provision.

In conclusion therefore, what are the key activities *the Sustainable Organisation* needs to undertake to ensure it delivers a great service – Great service today, tomorrow, next year and beyond? See the Seven Steps to Sustainable Service in figure 3.14:

The Strategy

The final dimension of the *Profit Pillar* looks at the need to have a strategic perspective with the business to link both the sales function and the service mandate of the organisation. Once again this is such a key part of the sustainable business that it warrants its own bespoke chapter and is addressed more fully in chapter 15.

It is however worth highlighting some of the key components necessary to ensure that the organisation optimises its sales function and maximises its profit return from its service offering.

Key to a successful strategy is a long term vision. The vision needs to be longer than the current financial period. It needs to embrace aspects such as stakeholder engagement, customer issues, long term funding, the development of people, procurement of capital assets, and so on. These can in some cases span many years and financial periods.

	Seven Steps to Sustainable Service
1	**Covet employees**: Coach, manage and nurture its staff to ensure that the good people stay and grow with the organisation. It's more than just about the financial remuneration; the desire and focus on giving good service takes time to instil in the culture of the organisation.
2	**Maintain competitiveness**: Product or service priced competitively in the marketplace. Price too high, and customers will expect more for their money or use a competitor, priced too low, and the organisation has undersold itself and missed a commercial opportunity.
3	**Meeting quality expectations**: Ensure customers know what they are getting, and get it every time. Consistency is key to customer feelings.
4	**React decisively to quality issues**: Customers recognise things go wrong but responding positively and promptly to resolve issues is imperative and will impress.
5	**Seek feedback and act on it**: All customers like to have a voice. Being asked for feedback shows a desire to improve, however actions are stronger than words.
6	**Meet not exceed expectations**: There is seldom any sustainable commercial benefit for exceeding expectations. Invest this effort on improving the percentage of times that you achieve the standards promised.
7	**Meet environmental commitments**: Failing to recognise and act responsibly with the environment has a detrimental impact on the expectations of customers.

Figure 3.14 The Seven Steps to Sustainable Service

What is vital is the on-going stability of the organisation. The vision takes into account the various long term commitments needed to be in place, and knits them together to formulate a strategy as well as short, medium and long term action plans.

To achieve success, the strategy needs to have buy-in from all the key stakeholders both inside and outside the organisation. If middle and even lower management are not "on-board", this will filter through and effect the staff commitment. If the banks or lenders are not engaged, sources of affordable funding will wither in time, or the risk strategies of the funding organisations may inhibit growth or force less optimal routes to raising capital investment.

Due to its complexity and the breadth of options available, raising capital is not covered in detail in this book. The myriad of institutions ready to offer venture capital options makes this a very personal issue to the structure, market, margin and ownership and invariably leads to a bespoke mix of solutions over the longer term; even mixing solutions has its issues and benefits. Diversity offers many benefits, and should reduce risk levels, however conflicts of interest, return on investment and the order in which the lenders might be paid in the event of a collapse affect the decisions.

Stability is central to a successful and sustainable strategy. The strategy should instil a feeling of planning and forward thinking, with stakeholders and staff alike encouraged that the management believe it worthy to produce a view into the future. Having a strategy can be shown to act as a corporate guidance for management.

And finally, a good cross market customer mix is desirable, incorporating where possible a mix of customers which are potentially:

- Large and small
- High project volume and steady on-going demand
- High margin and low margin
- Public and private sector
- Local and national

Turning the long term strategy into short term plans and tactics is a skill in itself, and may ultimately result in the strategy being amended. However, planning turns the strategy into the operational model against which the management and workforce can deliver the organisation's goals whether commercial or sustainable in nature.

Developing sales and expanding into new areas of business is a far from easy task, especially where the organisation has no history or anchor clients. Developing partnership plans helps leverage this, sharing risk, and generating a stable platform upon which to build. Use of commercial mechanisms and financial inducements - such as volume related discount structures, rebate schemes, settlement discounts, joint marketing funds, loyalty bonuses, etc - can all be effective.

In another former project in the electrical wholesaling market, strategic alliances with both customer and supplier were commonplace. Often through a combination of relationships, franchise arrangements and common end user demand, wholesale and manufacturer organisations would create close working relationships often promoting a vertical integration and working relationship to ensure price and quality of service were established. One of the pioneers of this approach was Telemechanique (now part of Legrand) – see case study 3.

Food for Thought: In one project undertaken by the authors, the organisation had aligned itself with a single tract of customer type where volume was very high but typical operating margin by customer was well below average, and the risk of bad debts exceeded the normal thresholds deemed acceptable by the head office management. This represented the worst possible mix of risk and reward. As remedy, a clear strategic focus was agreed to diversify the risk and margin portfolio, albeit at the expense of some sales volume. The phrase "Sales is Vanity, Profit is Sanity" was displayed around the office to reiterate the importance of a sound underpinning business model and numerous initiatives undertaken to develop other market sectors, customer types, as well as moving towards more accounts of a smaller individual turnover.

One measure implemented within this project was the "percentage of total spend covered by the top 20 and top 100 accounts". This percentage was monitored on a monthly basis in conjunction with

> the operating margin. As the percentage fell (i.e. the reliance on the top 20 accounts reduced) so a number of other impacts were seen:
> (i) the margin was seen to increase dramatically with the resulting impact on the bottom line;
> (ii) it led to the reduction in bad debts for the following year;
> (iii) it resulted in better utilisation of customer credit limits;
> (iv) and it improved the mix of product sold broadening the business scope and reach.

Such partnerships, whilst often constructed to generate sales benefit, can be used effectively to reduce costs and environmental impact. Many supermarket chains, Tesco and Walmart by way of example, now utilise the incoming delivery vehicles and suppliers to remove waste thereby reducing transport impact. Others have implemented refillable containers for shipping, reusable pallets, roller cages, and recycled packaging to establish a lower environmental footprint and reduce the high cost of packaging and the disposal of waste.

And Sainsbury in the UK have gone further, recycling out of date product as a bio-fuel to help claw back some of the investment, reduce the disposal costs, and mitigate some of the environmental impact of surplus demand. According to Alison Austin of Sainsbury, there are currently over 40 tonnes of waste a week in Scotland alone, all of which will be recycled at a Scottish biofuel plant, providing enough power to power 500 homes and save the equivalent of three tonnes of fossil fuel CO_2.

Wider, several importers from the far east now share container space, utilising surplus space for shipment of fast moving stock, rather than "shipping air" and several agents have set themselves up to facilitate this activity – see www.share-a-container.co.uk . Whilst such a move needs careful cost benefit assessment and a detailed inventory analysis, such a move shows the step change in logistics and space utilisation. The carbon footprint of shipped product is now a clearly recognised cost implication, which manufacturers, retailers and customers are actively taking into their strategic decision making model.

Strategic decisions within any business are underpinned by the need for a rigorous "Value Adding" business case with a supporting cost model or detailed financial projection. Use of Payback schemes, NPV calculations, discounted cash-flow analysis and other such approaches are invariably governed by the accounting function in the business. Change to these accounting rules is beset with issues and needs to be undertaken in a structured and predetermined manner which is outside the remit of this book. Notwithstanding this position, it is essential that the models and payback project decision period or payback assessment is mirrored by the financial planning, asset life projection, and the long term strategy.

In all too many cases organisations project lifecycles, leases, project cash-flows, etc over medium and longer term periods, whilst still maintaining an annual or short term business plan. This approach is inconsistent and fundamentally flawed. If an organisation commits to a lease agreement for a ten year office, it is by definition stating its belief that the business believes it will survive for that period, otherwise why not take out a short term tenancy and mitigate the risk. Conversely, few SME organisations state with conviction projected sales, profit and cash-flow further than at most 24 months in advance, and even fewer like to be drawn on financial markets, exchange rates, commodity prices, etc. Yet in many cases this is critical to the decisions being undertaken. *The Sustainable Business* acts and believes in its long term existence. It does project into the future albeit recognising that foresight and projections will change.

> **Food for Thought:** How is it possible for a business to make a truly considered decision over a long term project commitment such as a property lease or capital equipment purchase if it has no substantive underpinning cash flow, profit or cost projections?

Strategy, coupled with the Sales and Service mandate is essential to the strength of *the Profit Pillar*, to the composition and operation of *the Sustainable Business*, and to the long term sustainability of the business model. This will be explored further in chapter 15.

Case Study: Telemechnique

In the late 1980s and early 1990s Telemechnique were European market leader in electrical motor control equipment. They had developed an enviable position in the market through:

1. A clear strategic approach to franchising;
2. A focus on the product and service needs of the end user;
3. A respect for the business needs of its network of stockists across the regions supporting the day to day needs of the user;
4. A rigorously enforced geographical territory for each franchise;
5. A commitment to ensuring that all Supply Chain partners made a guaranteed margin;
6. Mandatory training attendance and support;
7. Set stock profiles and structured EOQ levels;
8. Fixed delivery days to ensure service and reliability;
9. A focus on packaging, and distribution alignment to reduce wastage;
10. Staged and reward based rebate structure to build a stronger and sustainable business partnership;
11. And a consistent, structured and reliable business process.

This strategy was put together following a detailed survey of stockists and customers. The product range was redesigned taking into account the user feedback, for example the introduction of captive screws, a specific response to engineers complaining that in harsh conditions terminal screws had been known to shake loose and become lost, and interchangeable coils to allow lower stock levels but higher service provision.

Above all Telemechanique focused on the quality and reliability of their product. This won favour with many of the large industrial clients wrestling with their own quality commitments. Organisations such as Toyota with their JIT and quality ethos adopted the product, thereby both endorsing the Telemechanique brand and strengthening the value of the franchise in the market.

Franchises became heavily sought after by stockists, with the mainstream electrical wholesalers in some cases clamouring for access to the product and in some cases taking actions such as acquiring competitor businesses.

Strict franchise agreements prohibited excess discounting of more than 37% to OEM customers or 30% to end user business, favouring the franchisee in their geographical area and guaranteeing them a margin in excess of 10% higher than a non-franchise holder. In return, the stockist needed to hold deep and broad stock levels, support business leads and Telemechanique driven specifications, as well as managing the administration and credit risks of user accounts.

In conclusion, the balanced approach taken by Telemechanique during this period made them a driving force in the development of long-term and sustainable business relationships in that market. The acknowledgement of the commercial needs for the partners up and down the supply chain was an underpinning core value which created long term and sustainable profits for both parties whilst delivering exceptional customer service to the users and clients further down the supply chain.

Latterly, however, European competition policy and legislation has to some extent fractured this model, albeit that the product range remains a dominant and very successful brand.

The Sustainable Business

Notes Page   **Page Ref**

The Sustainable Business

Summary Chapter 4
The Corporate Social Responsibility Policy "The Planet Pillar"

Key Learning Points
- Understanding of *the Planet Pillar*
- *The Three Planet Dimensions* – Reduce, Reuse, Recycle
- The Malthusian Trap and the concept of the Ecological Footprint
- The role of Mother Nature in recycling
- Introducing the Total Cost of Sustainable Ownership model
- The recycling hierarchy and different options to help reduce usage
- Lease driven supply reduction
- The "Eighth Waste"
- Understanding efforts which are made to reduce, reuse and recycle
- Recycling symbols, statistics and philosophy
- Planet focused design concepts

Tool Summary
- Reduce - Reuse - Recycle
- Total Cost of Sustainable Ownership
- The Eight Wastes
- The Eight Rs
- Freecycle

CIPS Syllabus Reference
- All Supply Chain modules
- Level 5 Operations Management in Supply Chains
- Level 5 Sustainable Procurement

Chapter 4: The Corporate Social Responsibility Policy "The Planet Pillar"

"As Mankind spends time consuming it forgets that Mother Nature has over the millennia become highly adept at self-renewal. Tapping Her ability and harnessing Her natural momentum is the missing link to sustainable recovery."
– Paul Jackson

The CSR Concept

As stated in the previous chapters, the concept of CSR policy is well documented. Again, using "the three Ps – People, Profit and Planet" concept, this chapter will explore the characteristics of a strong *Planet Pillar* – See figure 4.1. This is the third and final CSR pillar in the model focused on ensuring sustainability in the organisation.

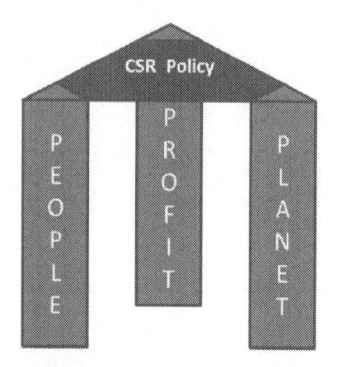

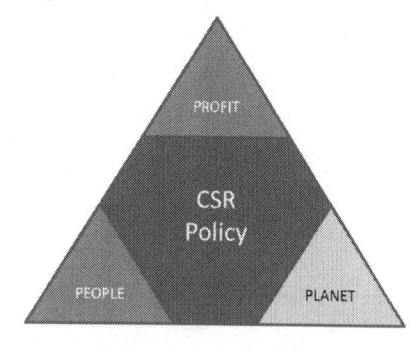

Figure 4.1

The Planet Pillar

The need to maintain and preserve our planet, our use of our resources and how we dispose of our waste has never been more publicised and never been more vital for the future of Mankind.

In 1778, Thomas Malthus suggested that the human race was expanding at a rate which the planet was unable to support – he proposed the Malthusian Trap, the point at which the Human race would exhaust its resources and cease to exist.

This is a notion that has been dismissed over the years in the manner he intended it, yet the concept still prevails, "The Ecological Footprint" is the modern day equivalent, defined as:

> "*The area of productive land and water ecosystems required to produce the resources that the population consumes and assimilate the wastes that the population produces*".

Since the 1980s this equation has been in deficit, i.e. we are using more than the planet can produce, clearly a non-sustainable scenario. Worse is the radical change needed to reverse and remedy. In addition, we have the added issues of carbon exchange from captured fossil fuel to harmful atmospheric CO_2 emissions and global warming.

Like the *People* and *Profit Pillars*, the *Planet Pillar* – See Figure 4.2 – can be broken into three core dimensions: Reduce, Reuse and Recycle yet the subject goes far deeper and is more entrenched, and will be explored in this chapter.

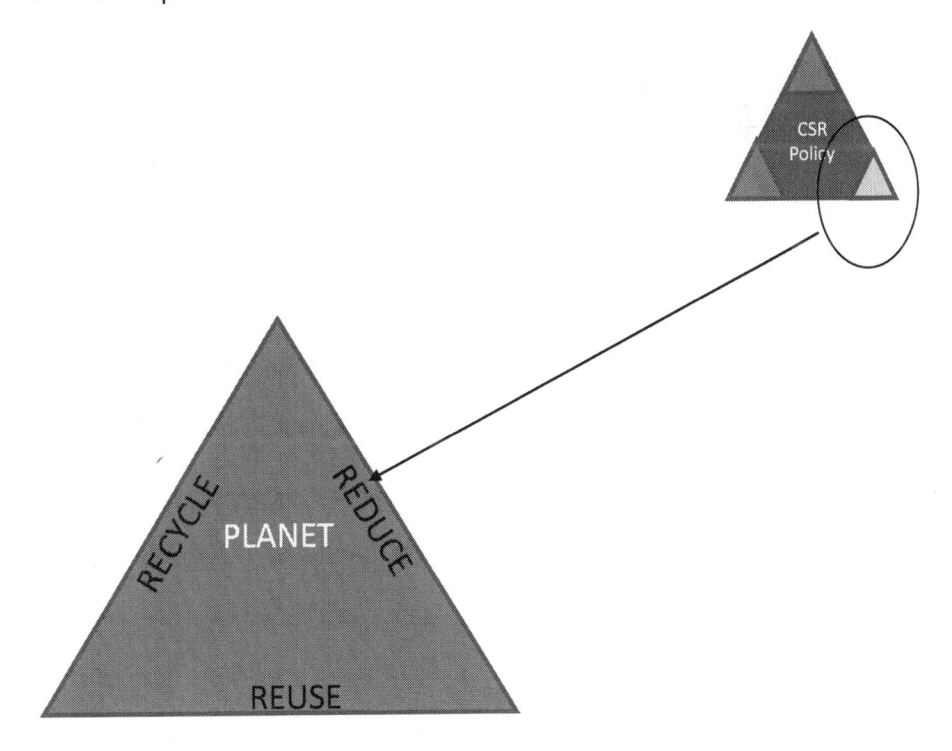

Figure 4.2

What the Ecological Footprint does not examine in enough depth however is the relative positioning of global renewable resources. As Mankind spends time consuming it forgets that Mother Nature has over the millennia become highly adept at self-renewal. Society has forgotten Her ability and this remains a widely under-utilised force; tapping Her ability and harnessing Her natural momentum is the missing link to sustainable recovery.

Take for example the little talked about issue of "Humanure" or "night soil" as it is often referred. Hardly an "over the dinner table" point of discussion, yet here lies a natural and highly sustainable solution to two of the world's issues: too much sewage from the burgeoning population and deteriorating soil from over farming to feed said masses. Indeed in 2003, it was estimated that over 670,000 Indians were involved in "night soil" collection for just this purpose, though social welfare organisations suggest that the true figure could indeed be over 1.3m.

Hardly a new phenomenon, this has been used since ancient times as a way of renewing the soil. Human excrement and especially urine are extremely high in nutrients and nitrogen making it far better than any shop bought organic fertiliser. Equally, in times gone by – for example the battle of Trafalgar – dead bodies were brought back from war not for burial but to manure the land, in that instance across Lincolnshire in the UK.

Unquestionably there are health issues to be addressed, with the transfer of illness, parasites and bacteria, yet no more so than with animal manure. Much of these are overcome with boiling, or easier still traditional composting where the heat generated inside the heap eliminates much of the harmful issues.

The use of Human waste is by no means simple nor without medical risk, yet with the appropriate caution, projects around the world have been shown to have managed this process successfully. These projects include the Rima River project in Nigeria where several hundred square miles of Sahara desert have been transformed back into fertile and highly productive land, and the Edmonton Composting Facility in Canada which incorporates the latest techniques to recycle both household recyclable compostable material with sewage product, reducing landfill and generating high nitrate soil enrichment product; the Edmonton project has forecast that it will have reduced its landfill waste by over 90% by 2013.

Development of combined waste treatment plant offers a real solution to many of the problems of central sub-Saharan Africa addressing the issues of waste management, crop production and recycling; and incorporation of natural recyclers like the voracious tiger worm can help fast track the process still further.

What society needs to do is to allow this alignment: allow the raw materials and processes of sustainable recovery to meet – in this case effluent and substandard soil, Mother Nature will then do the rest. This needs planning and motivation, but is by far the most efficient way of starting our planets recovery.

Total Cost of Sustainable Ownership

In addition, it is essential that sustainability is effectively costed and included in project cost analysis. It is wrong to take the view that just because Mother Nature will remedy our shortcomings, that we can turn a blind eye – history has done that for long enough.

The "Total Cost of Ownership" (TCO) model is a long standing concept. Rather than focusing on "just the price", Total Cost of Ownership highlights the different costs associated with the acquisition of goods, services and capital equipment, and is used to differentiate between suppliers, products or solutions; understanding the *true* and total cost of a solution has a dramatic impact on the profitability and return on investment derived from a procurement decision.

Throughout the many functions of business and across the supply chain, people are aware that the invoice price is not the only issue. There are costs which should be considered, from the initial identification of need through to the final disposal of the product. They include costs associated with the development of the business case, the design, formulation of the specification, costs pertaining to the tender and procurement activities, relating to the implementation, commissioning, maintenance, operation, storage and disposal. One popular definition of TCO reads:

> *'Total Cost of Ownership (TCO) is an assessment of all costs, both direct and indirect, involved with an item over its whole useful life. Most frequently, TCO is used at the beginning of the purchase process to evaluate which is the most cost-effective choice. When TCO is calculated at the time the choice is being made, many of the costs included will be estimates'. (Carter et al)*

However, with the increased focus on the "Triple Bottom Line", the modern world has a new concern to add to the issue of cost management and commercial woe: the concept of sustainability. To this end, the traditional model of TCO needs to be adjusted to highlight this new consideration, welcome the "**Total Cost of Sustainable Ownership**".

Consider the decision to purchase a new car. Factors assessed with the traditional TCO model may have included for example the cost of the time and effort researching the options (Internet costs), the selection of the best vehicle (time and expense visiting car show rooms), the daily cost of running the car (miles per gallon), and the cost of the annual maintenance and spare parts (service costs). Should we, however, now consider sustainability in this decision process? Do we ask if the car has been produced using recycled products, what is the carbon footprint of the production process, or whether any children were employed in any of the contributing supply chains? More importantly, what is the environmental impact going forward, emissions, fuel efficiency, etc, and how much of the raw materials are at the end of their useful life. In short what is the sustainability impact and contribution of this purchase on the "Total Cost" model.

Critics of this proposal might argue that the prevailing TCO model already includes for the idea of sustainability and the cost of sustainability is just included as an element of the component parts, however, rarely is there evidence of the sustainability issue having been raised with enough gravitas or conviction, commensurate with the importance of this aspect on our modern business environment. The TCO model incorporates costs over the entire life cycle of the product, however with sustainability this is no longer satisfactory. The decision is now dependent on the impact over a far greater period, the measure no longer concluded by the act of disposal, but bounded by the "**final point of impact**" see Figure 4.3:

So when is the "final point of impact"?

Planning Need & Spec	Purchase Price	Sourcing Costs	Installation	Operating Period	Disposal Process	Final Point of Impact

Figure 4.3 The Total Cost of Sustainable Ownership

Let us consider the life cycle of a nuclear power station. We establish a need, plan, construct and operate the power station over a number of years, before ultimate closure, decommissioning and disposal. But does our sustainable responsibility end there? Does our sustainable responsibility finish when we have cleaned up the site, or is it in several lifetimes hence when the last pulse of radiation is emitted from the toxic sludge produced, wherever we may have decided to *hide it*?

And this raises a further concern. Recognising that the primary purpose of the Total Cost concept is the comparison between projects, as we raise the influence of sustainability so we must also implement consistent and equitable measures across projects. Continuing our power station theme, how would we compare this project with the long term impact of a fossil fuel equivalent and the resulting CO_2 output; such analysis would inevitably make wind, wave, solar and hydro projects more competitive? And how would we factor in the positive contributions and social benefits of cheaper more reliable power?

> **Food for Thought**: Consider the USA/USSR initiative entitled "Megatons to Megawatts" which took old weapon grade uranium and recycled it into uranium power cells for commercial power production.
>
> Since 2009, Kazakhstan, the largest global supplier of uranium (30,000 tonnes per annum), incorporated this endeavour as an integral part of its production facilities, output thus producing an essential raw material whilst at the same time cleaning up a legacy of cold war politics.

To avoid any confusion, this approach does not advocate a "don't do anything which might harm the planet" policy. The view needs to be pragmatic and focused on the effective delivery of projects that add maximum value to business, to the community and to the planet; the *Triple Bottom Line*. It is however felt that we have an obligation to our children to act as responsibly as possible, within budget and the confines of society, but that environmental and sustainable issues should form an integral part of project cost assessments and of day to day business thinking.

So to conclude this observation, as discussed herein, it is merely suggested that the TCO concept is updated to reflect modern issues, namely the concept of sustainability. With the heightened need for attention to sustainability, it must be realised that a project impact "now" extends beyond the asset disposal process to the *final point of impact*, and that this should be considered when comparing projects.

Reduce-Reuse-Recycle

The concept of Reduce-Reuse-Recycle is in theory a simple one: we need to use less, reuse resources wherever possible, and recycle when a product ceases to be effective. But how do we realistically achieve this without sacrifice or detriment to lifestyle, and which is best to apply? – See Figure 4.4

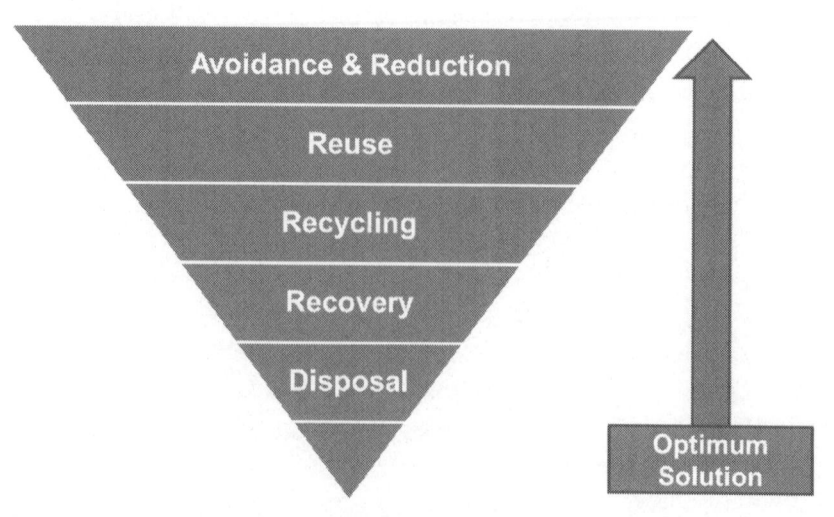

Figure 4.4 – Avoidance to Disposal

This proviso that "life may not get worse for society" is of course in many ways a misnomer: Life is already getting worse for a significant percentage of the global population, especially in sub-Saharan Africa and with worse to come if you subscribe to global warming predictions. Indeed, closer scrutiny would suggest that the level of living of this sector of the global populous has progressed little over history and is at best at the level of Europe in the Middle Ages.

And if we don't act, life will get worse for society in years to come anyway!

Reduce

So how can we begin reducing what we use? Society is not very good at saying "no", in fact it consistently "wants more for less", greater choice or "the latest model". So what are our options? – see figure 4.5.

Suppliers do not want to reduce supply, their responsibility is to their shareholders and optimal profits; the market has an obligation to its providers, customers and the classic supply and demand model; and governments – particularly those with more right wing policies – strive to avoid market intervention at all costs.

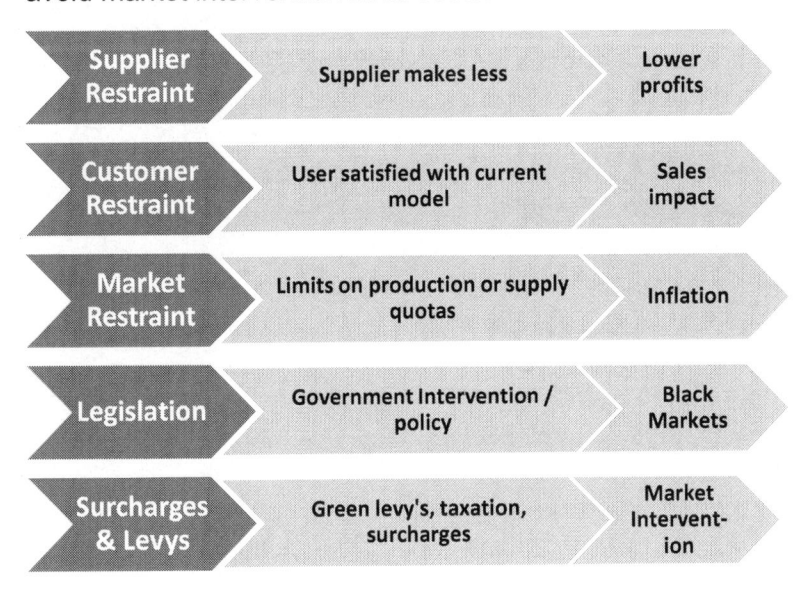

Option	Mechanism	Consequence
Supplier Restraint	Supplier makes less	Lower profits
Customer Restraint	User satisfied with current model	Sales impact
Market Restraint	Limits on production or supply quotas	Inflation
Legislation	Government Intervention / policy	Black Markets
Surcharges & Levys	Green levy's, taxation, surcharges	Market Intervention

Figure 4.5 – Reduce Options

There is a fundamental clash between "Reduce" and the traditional sales model of "More". In the words of one former sales manager – "What I want you to do is sell more at a higher margin". It is therefore essential that to be effective, any solution to drive the "reduce" agenda needs to carefully address the needs of all parties whilst simultaneously de-glamorising the product or demand.

Success will not be possible for all products, but we have to start somewhere. The media age coupled with PR profiles, image icons and celebrity make it nearly impossible to quash enthusiasm for consumer trend lines, however significant mileage can be achieved through managing other areas of the market.

One possible route is through Supplier Engaged Green Product Awareness (SEGPA). This, if coupled with detailed information about the Total Cost of Sustainable Ownership and product life cycle details, can lead to a slow change in consumer behaviour, along with the option for suppliers to enjoy a price premium for longevity.

Alternatively, a rise in the lease market can be seen to have occurred over recent years, most notably in the field of IT though it has of course been around for decades in the automobile industry where the leasing and second hand market have coexisted in harmony. This has a significant cost benefit to some organisations as it reduces their need to invest in capital equipment. Moving expenditure between CAPEX and OPEX can have major accounting and tax benefits in some circumstances. If this market could be adjusted to enable such benefits to facilitate better asset management it would benefit both suppliers and consumers alike and thereby extend the useful life of the products concerned, leading to a net reduction in product produced. See Figure 4.6.

We need however to start with the design of products and services. The prominence of "customer requirements" at the top of a design specification is understandable and from an environmental perspective entirely desirable: a key aim should be to produce product that the customer wants, the customer will use, and not something that the customer discards as not fulfilling their quality aspirations – see the Eighth Waste in chapter 7.

To help drive a reduction in product demand, we need to start by helping users to buy product for the long haul, and this often requires a shift in their view from a "purchasing cost" to a "purchasing investment", albeit a difficult shift to make. This needs to be paralleled with a softening of the sales focus with organisations tempering their sales forecasts and managing their sales ambition, again no mean feat.

If we consider traditional negotiation styles and approaches, the win-lose approach is steadily being replaced in some quarters with a more win-win philosophy leading to partnerships as opposed to adversarial relationships. In some larger and on-going projects at a business level, this can be seen to help facilitate both the suppression of greed and the "investment mantra, so perhaps some progress is slowly being made.

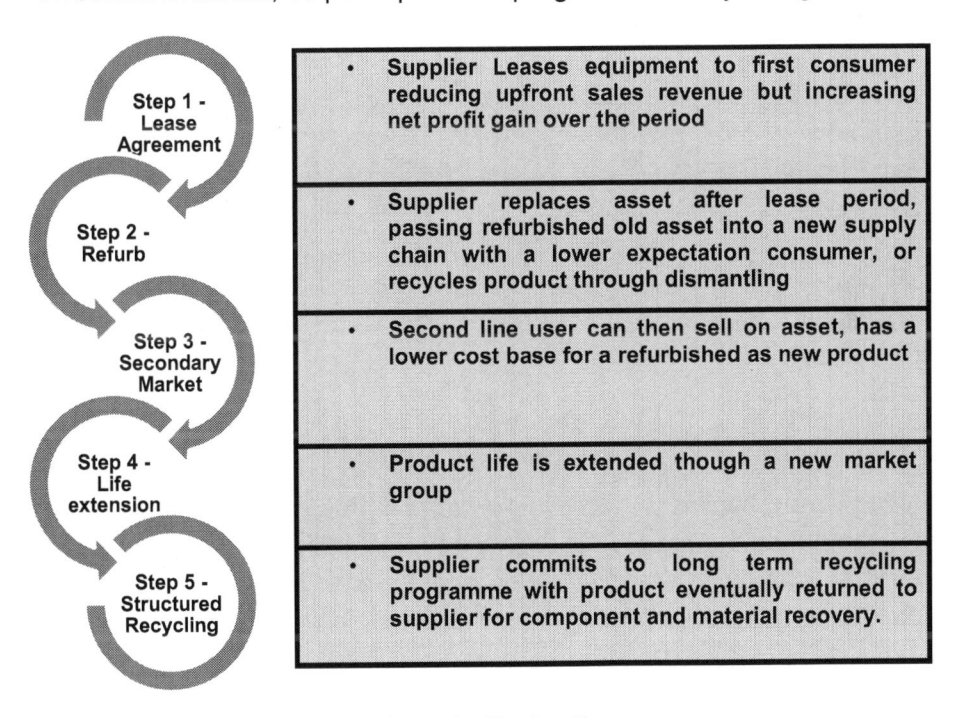

Step 1 - Lease Agreement	Supplier Leases equipment to first consumer reducing upfront sales revenue but increasing net profit gain over the period
Step 2 - Refurb	Supplier replaces asset after lease period, passing refurbished old asset into a new supply chain with a lower expectation consumer, or recycles product through dismantling
Step 3 - Secondary Market	Second line user can then sell on asset, has a lower cost base for a refurbished as new product
Step 4 - Life extension	Product life is extended though a new market group
Step 5 - Structured Recycling	Supplier commits to long term recycling programme with product eventually returned to supplier for component and material recovery.

Figure 4.6 – Lease Driven Supply Reduction

At the consumer and retail level however, exacerbated by the credit crunch and diminishing wealth in real-time, this approach is far more difficult to foster. It requires careful marketing and a process of "defashioning" coupled with a pragmatic approach to the business cost model to help encourage the consumer, however some products, the FMCG items, will inevitably take longer to address.

> **Defashioning – the art of deglamourising a product or service so as to reduce its fashion or iconic status**

But how often is longevity detailed as a key criterion on a specification? And how often does a user want the option to have *a new one* next year? A classic example of this is the mobile phone market where technology and fashion clash with delectable profit opportunities for the suppliers yet appalling consequences for the environment.

According to the US Government Environmental Protection Agency, the average life span of a cell phone is only 18 months, a view echoed by National Geographic who claim 14 months. The reasons for this can be debated, with fashion, latest technology and status undoubtedly a feature, however the prohibitive cost of repairs, the motivation of network operators to lure subscribers with the latest phone, and the spurious opportunity to believe you are "helping" by donating an old phone to charity only precipitates this issue – until we address these symptoms, we will not reduce the number of mobile phones we use. Free of charge software or operating system upgrades are however commendable first steps to achieving this, as are efforts to unify charging devices and connectors.

And so it is with so many of our day to day items, they have become disposable, with a belief that it remains acceptable to have a new "whatever" providing we recycle the old one. Recycling helps but only if it prevents a new one being brought into existence; recycling extends the life of the item being recycled but probably sends another phone – albeit an older model - into landfill somewhere else in the world.

What is really needed in the mobile phone market is a threefold solution:

1. Manufacturers need to make products that last longer or are viable to repair;
2. Network operators need to make contracts more attractive with incentives other than tangibles, and reducing their reliance on the financing of new phones from with the monthly contract fee.
3. And most powerful of all, what we really need to do is at some point

say "no, this one's fine" – try telling that to the average teenager! – possibly through cash back options or lower tariffs.

"Reducing" at a product level is not easy, and it needs sacrifice. Taxation has historically been used in some quarters either up front or at disposal however this often creates little impact. Take for the example the European efforts to reduce improve the recycling of tyres by charging a levy on new tyres, or the carbon tax to reduce carbon emissions. Barely before the ink was dry, industry and the market were devising ways to lessen the impact of such measures, so often through merely the addition of an inflationary increment in the price.

In contrast to products and services, reduction in the demand on utilities has a far more favour response from consumers. Perhaps due to the significant rises in utility prices in recent years, consumers appear far more willing to embrace a change in their usage patterns.

For example, initiatives to reduce power and water consumption within automatic washing machine cycles has been considerable over recent years with both technology of the machine, make-up of the detergent and publicity all united to the cause; moving the temperature of warm wash cycles from 40 degrees to 30 degrees, and moving from 3 x 1 to 4 x ½ fill of water for rinse cycles are two examples. Reducing the temperature on the office thermostat helps reduce power consumption during the winter, and raising the temperature in the summer keeps air-conditioning costs down, though be sure to keep windows shut to avoid heating or cooling the car park!

Similarly, the focus on low energy lighting has been highly publicised, supported by many facets of the industry, underpinned (albeit somewhat lately) by legislation and broadly embraced by the consumer, though this has not been without its issues. The user has had to temper the lower brightness levels, higher upfront costs, and a shortfall in lumen output of compact fluorescent lamps with longer life, lower running costs and a reduced CO_2 impact.

Furthermore, over publicised are the shortcomings with such lamps from frequent switching and dimming when it is suggested that the efficiency and cost-benefit curves plummet. It is agreed by eminent scholars that a fluorescent lamp power draw peaks at the point of ignition, however this only occurs for an instant making its impact negligible on the overall picture. The knowledgeable in such matters agree that it is a good idea to turn a lamp off if it is not going to be needed in the next five or so minutes. Frequent switching may nominally reduce its life time, but again the benefits of switching off outweigh this risk. Incorporating movement sensors rooms such as office canteens or domestic bathrooms could therefore mean a significant saving over time, albeit there will be an initial changeover cost which can be significant if electrical changes need to be undertaken. The development of LED lighting solutions also offers a potential solution that can complement the Compact Fluorescent solutions in these instances.

Equally as exciting for the reduction in utility consumption are innovations such as the shower water savers and "toilet hippo". The shower water saver is an extremely simple inline coupling device that has the effect of "pinching" the shower hose. This reduction in the diameter of the hose increases the pressure giving the water ejected more force, yet having a net reduction in flow. Perversely, this actually enhances the showering experience whilst reducing the water and heating power consumed.

Similarly, the "hippo" is usually a bag which is commonly available from water suppliers, which can be dropped in the cistern to reduce the amount of water per flush. This issue is also addressed with dual flush toilet systems and encouragement in some quarters to flush less: In one Eastern European company visited, there was a publicised policy which read "if its yellow, let it mellow, if its brown, flush it down"!

Similarly, in 2002, TeliaSonera, a Swedish global leader in the telecommunications and internet market, introduced a standardised datacentre design protocol focused on reducing the terawatts of power consumed at its global facilities. The policy recommended, for example, the use of plenum flooring to dramatically reduce leakage and drafts, improving the efficiency of the air-conditioning equipment, generating cool and warm air corridors, and reducing the need to cool all areas of the room. This had an additional impact as the sites were protected by an inert gas fire suppression system, the plenum floor enabled lower quantities of gas to be purchased and stored, which in itself had a major environmental and commercial benefit.

Furthermore, the datacentre specification recommended heat-recovery equipment which was incorporated into the design tackling the huge amount of heat produced by such facilities and transforming it back into electrical power for reuse – which (according to AFC) can give as much as a 20-30% saving on expelled heat. Sadly, the technical experts employed stopped short of allowing fresh air cooling, a decision which would have had significant additional environmental benefits.

And the same applies for the reduction in gas usage. Tengizchevroil of Kazakhstan focused on the issue of flaring – the burning of surplus gas on refinery chimney – reducing it to date by 94% through the introduction of new technology to allow the gas to be collected for use, for sale or for pumping back underground to increase the subterranean pressure pushing the oil out of the ground; this improves the production efficiency and effectively stores the gas in the natural underground cavities for a future generation to extract.

These later options show how important the issue of "reducing" can be on the planet and our impact however "Reducing" invariably needs to come from the heart of the user, or through the desire of the manufacturer. As neither is really conceivable in the case of FMCG goods, the prospect of either a Keynesian intervention in these markets – such as some financial recompense for a limit on production as used with farmers to encourage reduced production – or some prohibitive levy on manufacture or ownership is necessary. Both options remain politically unpalatable especially in governments who promote free markets; in such instances a reliance on Adam Smith's *invisible hand* appears the only hope.

Reuse

The concept of "Reuse" follows closely on from "Reduce". Instead of buying a new item, we should where possible encourage the concept of reusing the existing item.

The stigma of "second-hand" items can in some cases limit the appeal of the reuse concept, but here again an effective approach to the design of product can lead to more efficient refurbishment, repair and recovery of the product's former glory. Albeit incurring a CO_2 logistics footprint in the process. items such as IT equipment has for a number of years been systematically refurbished and shipped to less fortunate geographical locations to supplement educational efforts in those regions. Equally, clothes collected through charitable collections can be seen to have been laundered and redistributed again to aid less fortunate areas in poverty or crisis.

Addressing the aforementioned stigma is key. The Freecycle™ initiative is worthy of note – See case study 4. The concept is a simple one: stop putting items into landfill that someone else could use. Users simply raise an "offered" listing for an item they are looking to dispose of, and a would-be new owner can then simply collect the item free of charge, thereby extending the product life and reducing or at least delaying landfill. The Freecycle™ network alone has over 8.7million members worldwide across 58 countries, but has spawned similar concepts within other organisations such as Greencycle, Freemesa, Netcycler and Liberalestates amongst others.

Whilst the attraction of "something for free" reduces the objection to reuse, organisations such as Ebay, or even "the Classified Ads", play an important role in the extension of a products useable life. These second hand markets (recognising that Ebay also promotes sellers of new product) generate a viable outlet that both extends product life and enables the recovery of residual benefit for the user. Whilst relocating a product does have an incremental impact on the Total Cost of Sustainable Ownership, the benefit is clearly of advantage.

A final obstacle needs to be overcome to assist reuse – reparability. The issue of product design is essential once again to enable the product to be refurbished, repaired, updated or cleaned. It is an age old dilemma faced by manufacturers – do I make my item repairable?

There are manufacturers who deliberately make their products difficult to repair. Some incorporate mechanisms that prevent the item being put back together once repaired; some demand a special tool to facilitate a repair; some glue the body, so the only point of access is through breaking the "shell"; and some simply price the spare parts to the point that they become unaffordable. In any of these cases the manufacturer is irresponsibly or ignorantly preventing longevity of the product.

In IT and computer systems, the market has shifted somewhat to try and address this issue: Software is now upgraded to allow people to continue using old hardware; hardware is increasingly modular allowing easy replacement of parts, for example to help fit a new hard drive, or upgrade memory; and "drivers" or support software is generally available free of charge on-line. In contrast, moves by some leading printer manufacturers to make printer cartridges non-refillable, is a serious retrograde move.

In other consumer markets, life is changing as well. For example, many of the main baby-product companies – such as the brand "Mamas and Papas" – have user manuals online to help facilitate onward sale or use of prams, high-chairs, car-seats, etc, primarily to encourage the second hand market and elongate the product's life; they have realised that this move increases the resale value and attraction of their no-longer required product.

Wider, mobile telephone handset manufacturers, instead of changing the charger type for every other model, are now trying to standardise on voltage, power draw and connector. Following an agreement in 2009, most have pledged to unite behind just one charger type from 2012. This particular market understandably resisted the change for a long while, as the ancillary market for phones is so lucrative, but progress, consumer pressure and the environment needs won that battle.

Recycle

Finally, we have the concept of recycling, a now commonplace initiative in most towns and cities across the globe. The concept is a simple one: put the item that is no longer required through some form of reprocessing loop to bring it back to life either in its former role, or in some completely new guise.

Recycling in essence recognises that any deceased product has a residual value at either a product level, in its constituent parts, or at worst in recovered raw materials. Differentiating between "recycling" and "reusing" is at times vague and many of the aforementioned arguments are equally as applicable hereto, however the determination used by *the Sustainable Business* is that "Reuse" occurs where there is still some life in a product without any reprocessing, refurbishment, or residual investment.

There are in some cases a limited resource issue as well. Take for example rare earth metals. Whilst in many cases not that rare, they are typically spread very sparsely across the globe, making extraction unviable in most cases. Whilst there are several notable sources of rare-earth metals, nearly 50% (along with almost all of the world's rare heavy metal extractions) comes from the Inner Mongolian region of Bayan Obo. This region is therefore clearly of strategic interest to the rest of the world and the cause of some tension in recent years with China as the dominant player, imposing a quota system and a reduction of 35% on exports. It then halted production at 3 of its 8 production sites in September 2011, introducing some uncertainty of future supply.

Concern is therefore understandably high in relation to these commodities. The US Geological Survey has suggested that there is real concern that severe shortages of metals – both rare and otherwise – will be felt in the coming fifty year period, with some, including Antimony, Arsenic, Barium, Cadmium, Gold, Indium, Lead, Silver, Strontium, Tin, Zinc and Zirconium, likely to be an issue in the next decade. Iron is projected to be an issue around 2050: Shortages inevitably means price increases.

These concerns heighten the need for recycling now to capture and retain these valuable resources. Rare earth metals are present in some small degree in almost all electrical devices, so targeted retrieval prior to disposal make eminent sense to prevent these materials being spread even more sparsely, through landfill, than occurs under nature.

A further concern often raised relates to the effort and cost impact of recycling, and this needs to be factored into any recycling equation. Clearly it is environmentally inefficient to use more energy recycling a commodity than would otherwise occur, however costing future commodity price rises and increasing scarcity into the equation may be of some merit however this is not always the case. In the case of aluminium, recycling of aluminium takes barely 5% of the power required to produce new material from ore and clearly justifies the effort and expense.

The investment in recycling capacity undertaken across the world by governments and local authorities is extensive with refuse collection, processing and disposal issues all addressed. A move away from landfill has an immediate benefit, yet the recovery of precious raw materials reduces the need for mining, ore processing, logistics, and power consumption.

The Sustainable Business

In the middle of the 20th century, in Dudley in the UK, one particular factory dumped its waste into landfill within its factory boundary. Landfill at that time was widely recognised as a means of disposal, and the practise continued for many years until the organisation went bankrupt. A former employee bought the company from the liquidator, and started work excavating the grounds. He made hundreds of thousands of pounds selling the raw materials and repaying his investment many times over.

> **Rule: One man's rubbish is another man's treasure**

Examples of recycling successes are numerous, varied and often ingenious. For example, around the world, usually near to the coastline, you will see older buildings with slightly curved wooden beams. Typically in the 18th and 19th century there was a shortage of wood for construction, wrecked ships, or ships that were decommissioned became rich sources of seasoned yet sturdy wood. In more modern times US Navy has been known to deliberately scuttle ships to theoretically help regenerate and develop reef growth. (Note: this is considered by the author as a highly dubious choice of action, presumably it did not have anything to do with the high costs of disposal?)

In Victorian times in the Northern mill towns, collection of old clothing was commonplace, with rags shredded and mixed with new wool to produce "shoddy", with similar processes to recycle paper into a plethora of new materials.

In South Africa there is an organisation called "Scratch Patch and Mineral World". This organisation takes highly coloured, polished and relatively worthless stones, a waste product from the extraction of precious metals and gems, and puts them in a large room. It then allows parents to purchase a small bag for their children to roam the mountains of coloured stones looking for "the best ones to take home!" whilst the parents relax and drink expensive coffee in comfortable surroundings.

And also in South Africa, there is legislation that demands that restaurants and food producers who sell shell-fish must return the shells to the sea. Accordingly, on many beaches there can be found huge piles of shells waiting for the tide and environment to return them from whence they had come.

One former TV programme – Blue Peter – in the UK suggested taking old car wheels, and turning them inside out to make large plant containers;

The Sustainable Business

a 1980s Levi 501 advert suggested that old work-wear or ripped jeans were fashionable; and so on.

Yet still we tolerate non-refillable printer cartridges and non-recyclable plastics.

Placing the onus of responsibility on consumers has become the trend, with initiatives such as coloured bins for segregation, improved packaging and better material labelling, but more could be done.

At a recent school visit to a local environmental centre, effort was made to highlight the waste that was generated from the children's packed lunches. Plant matter such as apple cores and banana skins, and paper product were duly collected for composting, glass was entered into the glass recycling process, and plastics collected for landfill! Little was known about the symbols allowing differing plastics to be segregated for recycling, nor the processes undertaken by the local authority for sorting such waste. The local authority provides green bins for recyclables, yet consistently items are included that are non-recyclable.

In a survey of fifty local people in central England, it was found that little over half knew anything substantial about material markings on plastics – see figure 4.7 - with over half of those failing to correctly recognise the correct approach for the material identified. The survey did however show a significantly higher and more successful awareness of due process for metals, paper, cardboard and glass products. This was alas further exacerbated by only a nominal effort from the local authority to educate had allowed the initiative.

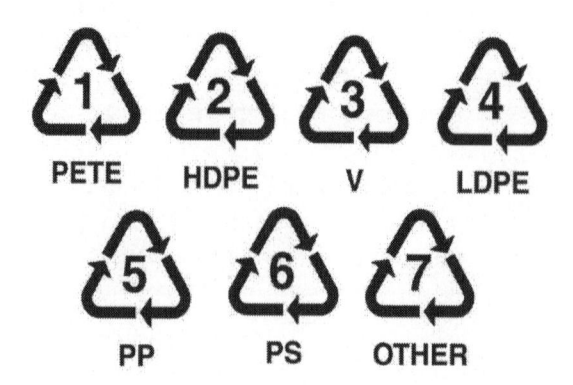

PETE	HDPE	V	LDPE
1	2	3	4

PP	PS	OTHER
5	6	7

Figure 4.7 – Recycling symbols and corresponding descriptions

Recycling rates vary considerably across the UK with recorded levels as shown in figure 4.8. Whilst only a cross section of figures, these can be shown to vary dramatically, with inner city rates often falling some way short of their rural counterparts. There are many possible reasons for this not least the ability of inner city households to store and waste over a longer period, and local authorities wrestling with the increasing costs of refuse collection at a time of financial austerity measures and council cutbacks.

These local authority rates pose an interesting question showing the difference between best and worst performers, with the UK average falling at around 34%. Evidence suggests that the best achievers have not only invested in resource to ensure recycling occurs, but have benefitted as a result through lower disposal costs.

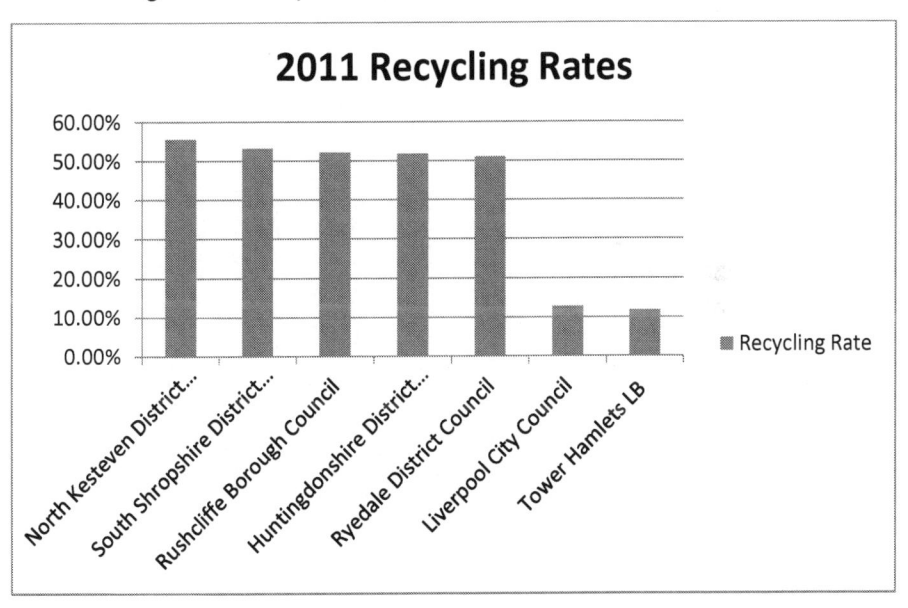

Figure 4.8 Recycling rates for top and bottom performers in UK local authorities. (www.recycle.co.uk)

Furthermore, the focus on composting globally receives a very mixed reaction. Whilst commonplace in many European communities, further afield it is rarely addressed. Albeit arguably not recycling but bio-regeneration, the extraction of all food and compostable waste significantly reduces the quantity of product sent to landfill, whilst generating soil enhancement product to reinvigorate Mother Nature's capacity to produce. When investigated, Atyrau in the Caspian Sea region on the boarder of Europe and Asia with a population of around 250,000, has no recognisable public recycling process in place, and an estimated 0.1% of the population had any form of composting facility. Yet this is an area with high salt ingression in the soil, and in desperate need of the essential nutrients such activity can produce. Likewise in many regions of sub-Saharan Africa, soil erosion seems to be accepted without any societal efforts to remedy.

In comparison with Europe, the figures in figure 4.8 compare poorly with the UK falling short of the EU average of 39%, and some considerable way short of the 60%+ level posted by Germany, Belgium and The Netherlands – see figure 4.9. Effort must be made to spread the success stories, to broaden this element of the environmental effort.

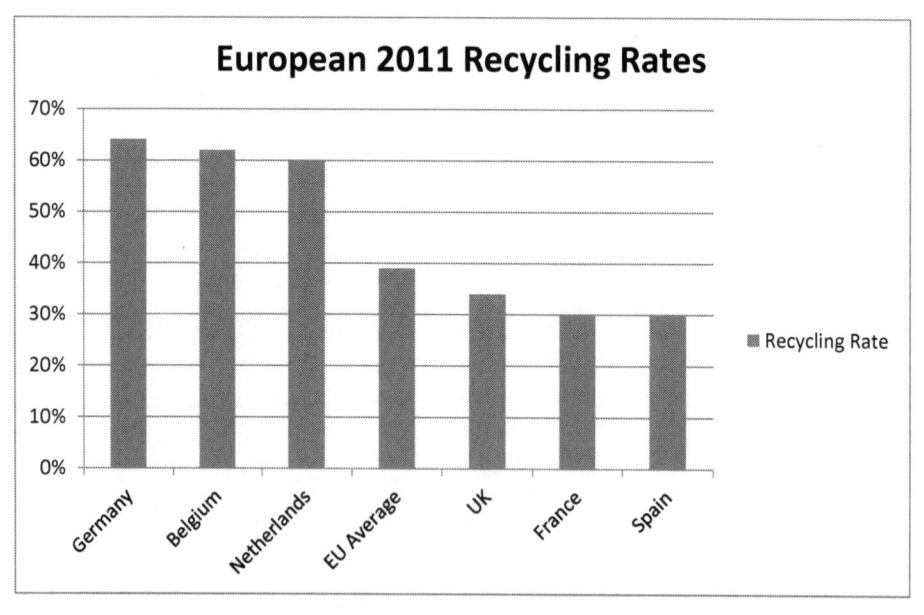

Figure 4.9 – European recycling rates (Reference www.recycle.com)

The 8Rs

Whilst Reduce, Reuse and Recycle are the commonly accepted terms for the management of waste, the 8R model expands the options available for the responsible treatment of waste – See figure 4.10.

Whether the recycling process use energy, chemical, time or labour intensive process, the concept of examining our waste for opportunities to address the on-going issue of raw materials is clear and should be incorporated in the business cases of all projects large and small.

	Description	Example
Reuse	Reuse the item for what it was intended for	Second hand items, e.g. clothes, cars, equipment
Resell	Resell the item for use by another	Ebay and other classified ad sales channels
Removal	Remove from the market for storage	
Remarket	Remarket the item in a new light	At a certain age an old car becomes a Vintage car, similarly with antiques
Return to Manufacturer	Return the item for dismantling and raw material recovery	Stock cleanse items, old equipment, project surplus materials
Reclaim	Extraction of components for use in other repairs or product ion	BAE Systems Reduce to Produce programme of taking serviceable parts out of old aircraft for continued use
Remanufacture	Re manufacture to extend the life of the raw materials	Car maintenance programmes, rereading of tyres, refilling of gas cylinders
Recycle	Recover raw materials from an end of life asset	Scrap metal dealers, rare earth metal recovery from electronic items

Figure 4.10 – 8R Model of responsible waste treatment

Planet Focused Design

The need for durability and a maintainable efficiency level is the final key for the long term usefulness of a product, and yet again the issue of product design becomes paramount. Environmental design is addressed in chapter 10, but it is nonetheless core to the success of the "Reduce-Reuse-Recycle" methodology.

Designs using both recycled product, and product that can be recycled in the future is essential, and in some cases becoming mandatory through legislation. Innovators, scientists, engineers and designers alike need to focus on what can be done with the responsible materials, moving from desirable to prudent in their selection. For example, whilst steel has been the product of choice in many construction designs, GRP may be a suitable alternative.

Visionary approaches to both design and innovation are required; reducing our demands of Mother Nature will neither be a quick nor easy journey. Nobody likes to be told no, too much, or accept less, but sadly that is the inevitable dilemma we have left ourselves.

Rethink

In conclusion to this chapter however, "rethinking" should remain an option. Within its procurement decision making process, *the Sustainable Business* should perhaps revaluate the whole business need, its precepts, or the basis upon which a decision is based. The organisational culture may suggest that a new "item" is the employees historical right – need this be the case? And alternative approaches can be overlooked, for example sharing with a supplier or customer, or dare it be said, a competitor.

Case Study 4: Freecycle™

"Our mission is to build a worldwide gifting movement that reduces waste, saves precious resources & eases the burden on our landfills while enabling our members to benefit from the strength of a larger community."

On May 1st, 2003, Deron Beal sent out the first e-mail announcing The Freecycle™ Network to about 30 or 40 friends and a handful of not-for-profit organisations in Tucson, Arizona. At the time Deron founded The Freecycle™ Network, he worked with a small not-for-profit organisation, RISE, which provides recycling services to downtown businesses and transitional employment to Tucsonans in need.

As the team recycled, rather than watching perfectly good items being thrown away, they found themselves calling or driving around to see if various local not-for profit organisations could use them. Thinking there had to be an easier way, Beal set up that first Freecycle™ e-mail group in a way that permitted everyone in Tucson to give and to get; Freecycle™ was off and running.

The Freecycle™ concept has since spread to over 85 countries, where there are nearly five thousand local groups representing over 8.7 million members, people helping people and 'changing the world one gift at a time.'

As a result, Freecycle™ is currently keeping over 500 tons a day out of landfills! This amounts to five times the height of Mt. Everest in the past year alone, when stacked in garbage trucks!

By giving freely with no strings attached, members of The Freecycle™ Network help instil a sense of generosity of spirit as they strengthen local community ties and promote environmental sustainability and reuse. People from all walks of life have joined together to turn trash into treasure.

"changing the world one gift at a time"

In just a few short years, Freecycle™ has generated a spectacular worldwide outpouring of generosity, changing the world one gift at a time.

People with extra, happily share with those who need gracefully receive, all without judgement – or any funds – passed.

Freecycle™ performs many wonderful functions: building bonds and community, keeping material items from the landfills, and redeeming the clutter that consumes us by moving it forward to a new, productive life.

Adapted from www.Freecycle.org

The Sustainable Business

Notes Page　　　　　　　　　　　　　　　　　　Page Ref

The Sustainable Business

Summary Chapter 5
Sustainability in the Business Context

Key Learning Points
- What is a Sustainable Economy?
- Long wave economic cycles and sustainable impact
- Kondratieff Theory
- The impact of Inflation on sustainability
- What is "Quantitative Easing"?
- Exchange rate management
- Geographic centres of excellence
- The use of utilities and raw commodities
- Innovation cycles and forecasting innovation needs
- Political and legislative pressures
- Changes in political structures and ruling parties
- Social needs
- The role of technology
- Business structure options
- Centralised versus Decentralised
- Types of business ownership
- Target and goal setting

Tool Summary
- Kondratieff Model
- The Technology Dilemma
- Business Structure analysis including Matrix, SCAN and CLAN
- SMART measures

CIPS Syllabus Reference
- Level 4 Business Needs in Procurement and Supply
- Level 4 Contexts of Purchasing and Supply
- Level 5 Category Management
- Level 5 Management in Procurement and Supply

Chapter 5: Sustainability in the Business Context

If you stand up and be counted, from time to time you may get yourself knocked down. But remember this: A man flattened by an opponent can get up again. A man flattened by conformity stays down for good.
– Thomas J. Watson

The Sustainable Business exists with vision and purpose and its "**need to generate a robust commercial structure to deliver on-going value to its stakeholders".** But the Sustainable Business has a further aim, it intends to be in business in many years to come; it has a long term vision.

The Sustainable Business exists within an external business environment which it needs to understand and take into account when determining its strategic decision making processes and its own internal behaviour. As mentioned previously, a common tool used to examine the external environment is the PEST or PESTLE analysis (see figure 1.6, chapter 1), and it needs to assess its response to the external position over a long term perspective.

The Sustainable Economy

Forecasting the economy in the short term is by no means an easy task let alone over a longer period. In 2008 the world experienced what was described by many political and economic commentators as the "Credit Crunch". The prevailing economic climate is one of the most influential factors affecting modern business and it is thus essential to understand, manage and forecast the impact that the economy will have on the business today, tomorrow and into the future. Yet, with the theories of Monetarism and Keynesian economics in disarray at such intersections there are few guides as to the best road ahead.

Fortunately, long term forecasting is more predictable and the global economy can be shown to have followed very predictable trends dating back several centuries. These are global trends, which local economies can resist in the short term, but they will eventually succumb to the wider pressures. The Credit Crunch is therefore not a new phenomenon; it has happened many times before at the end of what is termed a "long wave economic cycle", and it will happen again in the future.

Much has been made of the UK's Chancellor of the Exchequer - Gordon Brown's – "prudence" however this might now be viewed with some scepticism. Perhaps there was a little too much "living for today" and not enough focus on a sustainable economy for tomorrow. And then there was the sale of its "security blanket" – the bulk of the UK gold reserves. This was done in 1999, to raise £3.5bn for a spending spree which was not overly prudent – it would have been worth over £12bn had he waited until the proverbial *rainy day*.

> **Rule: Mend the roof while the sun is shining**

Furthermore whilst embracing the Keynesian perspective that government and fiscal policy needs to be structured to control the economy - for example increase interest rates and people will reign in their spending, and through elementary supply and demand theory, prices and thus inflation will fall – it soon became evident that national economies had lost the ability to operate in an insular manner. The issue shifted to the classic "global financial crisis" to try and draw attention away from the UK's and other's own specific shortcomings.

Whilst readers may harbour an alternative perspective depending on political persuasion, what can be shown is that the credit crunch was entirely predictable, the severity was of our own making, and the consequences – the 2010-20?? austerity measures – merely the payback for the good times enjoyed during the 1994-2008 period.

> **Rule: "What goes up, must come down!"**

So how does a long wave economic cycle work, and how can it affect the strategy of *the Sustainable Business*?

Exponents of long wave theory – most notably Kondratieff – suggest that the economy, over around 60-80 years, assumes a level of intrinsic debt which becomes unsustainable and which leads to a major financial collapse as was seen in 2008, some eighty years before in 1929, and on a number of occasions prior to that as well.

> **Food for Thought**: John Maynard Keynes described the situation in the 1930s as "a colossal muddle".

Once the crash has occurred, the financial institutions seize up, once "bitten" they shy clear of risky and uncertain investments; they become debt wary, anxious of default and keen not to repeat the recent calamities. The debt market clamps down on all but the most secure of debt, a situation prevalent from 2008 onwards.

Furthermore, as is often seen, during times of turbulence, banks resort to the safety of gold deposits, and invest in tangible raw materials that have a security in the longer term. This shift causes the inevitable rise in commodity prices, leading in turn to supply driven inflation for importers of such products.

The reluctance of the banks to lend exists for a considerable time, until the memories of the collapse wane – or greed takes over – and markets feel comfortable relaxing the stringent conditions imposed on it during the dark periods following a crash. In past downturns, this period has sometimes lasted for over ten years or more, and by the middle of 2012, a number of major economies had sunk back into recession – the so call double dip recession – making banking confidence even more fragile. Furthermore, it is quite likely that a number of further dips will be experienced before the return to genuine and sustainable growth possibly from around 2018.

The Kondratieff theory compares the 60-80m year cycle with the four seasons – Winter, Spring, Summer and Autumn – see figure 5.1.

During this "year", debt in the economy can be seen to grow steadily. At the start, still bruising from the crash that preceded it, banks and financial institutions are reluctant to trust lenders. Interest rates are low so their risk and reward balance would err on the side of caution. This lack of liquidity in the market is the biggest constraint on growth as organisations find it difficult to maintain their often fragile positions, and many fail as a result, only strengthening the banks' resolve and focus on safe investments.

At this time, demand inflation – inflation caused by people wanting more and having money to spend - tends to be somewhat subdued. Society is wary of turbulent times ahead, and whilst interest rates are low, will tend to try and preserve funds and resources, and cut back on the luxuries that prevailed a few years before; in many cases a period of deflation in such expenditure will be apparent through overall retail sales and profit margins. This deflationary pressure is only tempered by the inflationary pressures seen through the increase in prices of raw material imports caused by the rise in commodity prices and the expansion of the money supply as discussed later. *The Sustainable Business* needs to ensure that it manages any raw material requirements over this period whilst pragmatically adapting its business to changes in demand and product requirements. Long term fixing of prices is desirable to secure price surety and to maintain long term business cost models.

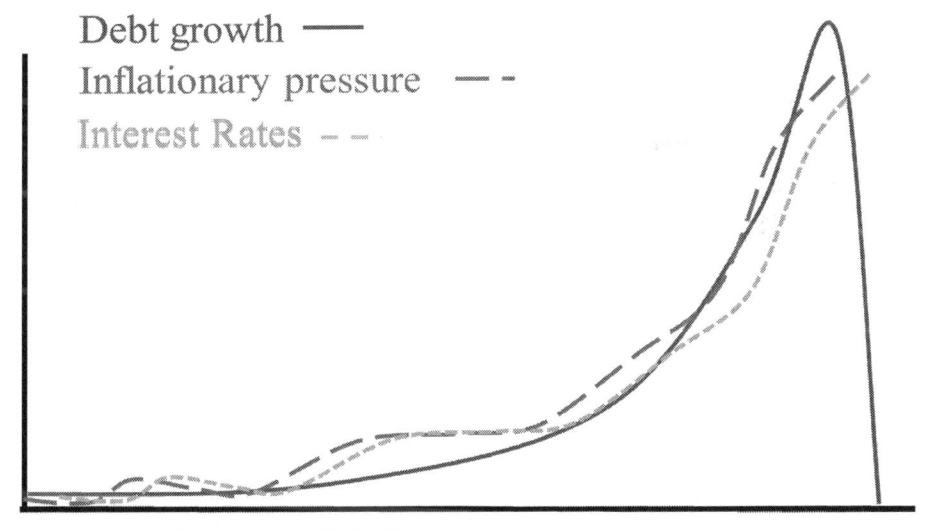

Figure 5.1 The Kondratieff Cycle

Utilities are also vulnerable at this time, with many pegged to commodity prices. For example, electricity prices directly track the price of oil which typically rises as the economy tries to claw its way from the recession. For large scale power users, for example, projecting oil movements is essential to help determine at which point to buy power on spot prices, and when to move to long term fixed price arrangements.

> **Rule: "Know your supply market, track prices and movement"**

During this early period in the Kondratieff cycle, a Keynesian approach is required to drive stability, growth and liquidity into the market; the market is irresponsible and needs *the guiding hand of government*. Quantitative Easing – the banking name for printing money – should be used to inject capital into the market at source. Successful nations in the subsequent years will have ensured that this money was active, circulating through the economy to generate activity, stimulate demand, and create employment. It should also have the effect of quashing some of the deep resentment and social dissatisfaction as society remembers the good times and comes to terms with a less affluent lifestyle.

Perhaps one of the greatest examples of successful use of Quantitative Easing was in the investments made in the UK during the Victorian period. At this time, *the printed money* was invested into the establishment of national infrastructure and critically the generation and development of centres of industrial excellence in geographic locations across the UK, such as Sheffield for steel, Stoke for ceramics, Oldham for textiles, and so on. Some of these became world renowned for their quality and technological success. This bred growth in those areas, attracted investment and the greatest minds of the age formed intellectual hotspots for industrial innovation, and so on. This established the impetus for the move out of the "winter" and formed the basis for growth through the subsequent cycle.

There was also significant investment during this time in infrastructure such as canal and rail networks. This generated employment, demand, growth and life after the "crash" driving cash into the economy at the bottom.

> **Food for Thought**: How different would the UK be if just £4bn from the £325bn of Quantitative Easing had been invested into four new "centres of excellence" (not just business parks) in strategic areas of the country each aimed at development of Sustainable resource, ideas, innovation and jobs. For example:

> £1bn to Grimsby to build: "The University of Sustainable Fisheries"
> £1bn to Aberdeen to build: "The University of Sustainable Power"
> £1bn to Salisbury to build: "The University of Sustainable Farming", and
> £1bn to Blackburn to build: "The University of Biofuels".

Whilst the core message from Michael Porter's "Competitive Advantage of Nations" is endorsed, diversity within the economy at such a time is of paramount importance – metaphorically, it's like deciding what seeds to plant in the spring. Investing the entire Quantitative Easing funds into the UK's primary industry – the financial markets – was both flawed and short-sighted.

It should however be noted that Quantitative Easing drives down the nation's exchange rate making imports more expensive to buy, but making exports more competitive, and combating the calamity of deflation. This is a great opportunity to increase demand for home grown goods on the world stage if the right strategy is employed. For *the Sustainable Business* an export strategy at this time in the cycle should be a key objective.

Key to the success of a nation, (and albeit on a smaller scale, *the Sustainable Business*) is the need to have innovations and new products to drive demand and develop its sales stream for the new cycle. Kondratieff highlighted the issue of innovations as the key to success of a nation and of an organisation, with those who could identify the key technology for the immediate future being in the best position.

Whilst hindsight is easy to commentate upon, Kondratieff and others identified how these cycles established themselves to resolve prevailing social and market issues. For example, the agricultural revolution occurred to increase food production to support the growth of the colonies and importantly the Americas. The Industrial revolution which came fifty or so years later was driven by the need for extra farm machinery required by the farmers now fulfilling the increasing demand for food. Next came an increased need to distribute raw materials, equipment and food around the country. This led to the development of canals and then rail network, and so on.

With each cycle came a pioneering innovation which was typically invented at the end of the preceding cycle. This innovation becomes the cause of the rapid increase in prosperity and growth seen at the end of that cycle, as it becomes commercially viable and demand increases. It is this unsustainable growth that then becomes responsible for the crash that follows – see figure 5.2. Also seen in this period of growth is an increase in global conflict. This is due to a surplus of funds to finance such forays, coupled with a desire to "help" in areas of "issue".

Organisations which become prevalent during this period are those that identify the opportunity and exploit it accordingly. This usually requires a dedicated business objective, or investment in R&D at the appropriate time and focused on the appropriate technology.

Take for example the invention of fibre optic technology in 1920 by John Logie Baird and Clarence W. Hansell and the patented fibre optic wire of Maurer, Keck and Schultz in 1970. This was developed slowly at first, but saw unprecedented growths as technologies aligned to create the internet and mobile telephony. Others include the steam turbine leading to rail networks, or the success of the Wright brothers and their first flight leading to jet engines and supersonic flight.

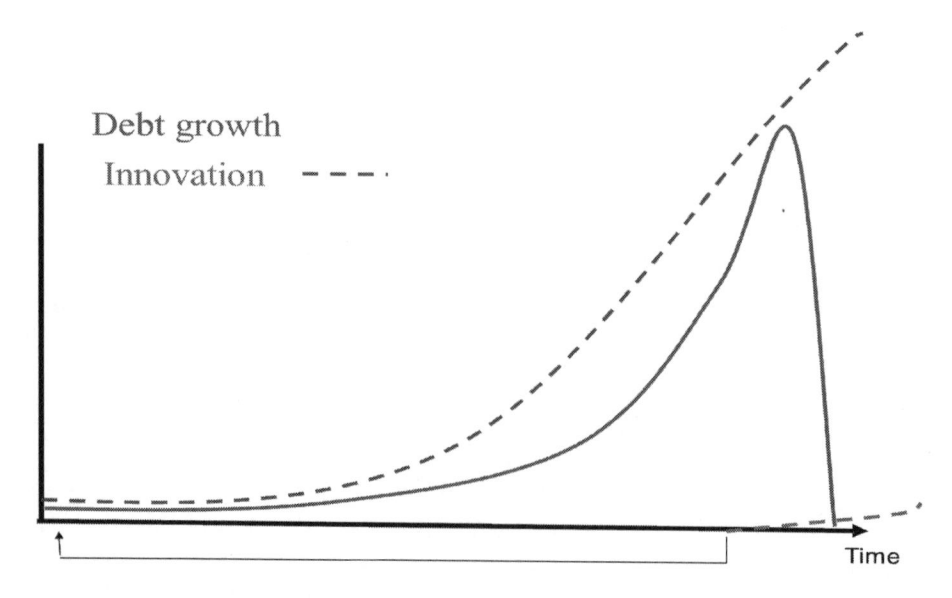

Figure 5.2 The Innovation Lag

Key in the early stages of the cycle is an awareness of the other issues which become prevalent in society. As mentioned hitherto, society can remember the good times, and undergoes a period of deep dissatisfaction, often highlighting itself with riots, social unrest, and revolutions, as has been seen with the Arab uprising, riots across the UK and in other parts of Europe. This in time can and has been seen to develop into increases in right wing extremist activity, with sections of society blamed for the crash and the prevailing issues in the economy and society – see figure 5.3. The rise of Hitler, Mussolini, Franco and others following the 1930 collapse is evidence of this, with such regimes often leading to revenge, seizure of assets to fuel recovery, and other such remedies that invariably lead to a second war.

During the years from 2012-2020 it would not be unsurprising to see a swing in the political focus in some countries – perhaps Italy, France, Greece, Spain, etc – towards harder right wing regimes, a scenario which will only be exacerbated with further recessionary pressure.

Whilst not necessarily directly impacting on *the Sustainable Business*, an understanding of the prevailing markets, economies and of global matters is essential for the management of risk and the formation of strategy. Risk is explored further in chapter 6 however it impacts across all areas of an organisation and needs to be a key driver on the structure and workings of the organisation.

The Sustainable Business needs to understand forecast, track and manage areas of the economy that affect its outcomes. Exchange rates, oil prices, commodity movements and inflation are all likely to have an impact and should as a minimum be measured, and strategy should be developed to accommodate the heightened risk of conflict. Depending on product, services or market, war can both positively and negatively affect the demand profile; *the Sustainable Business* will be ready.

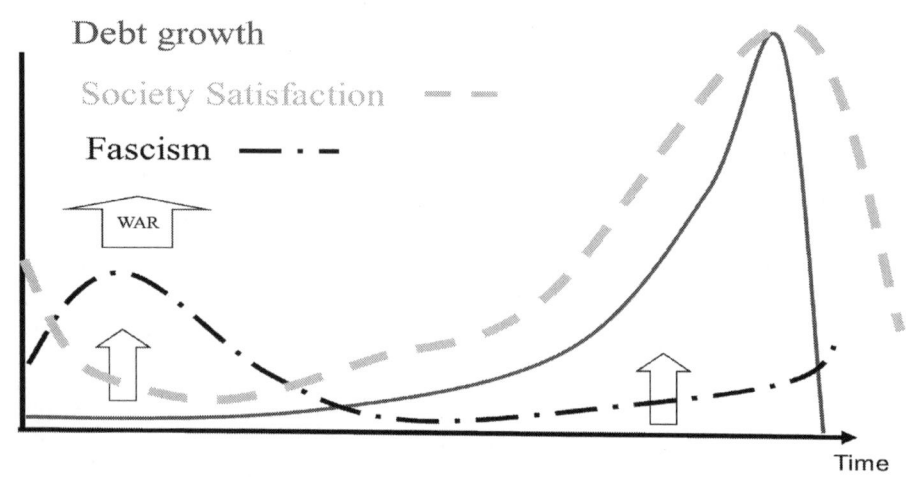

Figure 5.3 The Impact on Society

The Political, Legislative and Societal Angle

Whilst many governments claim to adopt a *laissez-faire* approach to markets, few can argue that policy does not change, nor impact on industry and with the renaissance in Keynesian economic intervention this is only set to increase. *The Sustainable Business* recognises this, and adapts accordingly.

Political allegiance is not an uncommon trait for individuals, with a significant proportion of the population fixed in their political leanings until death; the balance – the "swing voter" – arguably fickle and short-termist will move to the best offer on the table or be swayed by spin and dogma.

What is incontrovertible is the fact that following the fall of communism, bar a few rogue states, society now has freedom to choose; the Sustainable Business needs to recognise this and have flexibility to rapidly address changes in policy, taxation, fiscal policy and so on.

This flexibility aside, political diversity is vast – even inside a party – with coalition only complicating matters further. Evidence suggests that economic collapses can generate seismic changes in the political landscape, for example banishing the Liberal party to the boundaries of UK politics for a generation, sealing the end of the Whig party before that, potentially heralding the end of two party politics in the USA, and driving an axe through numerous dictatorship or monarchy regimes throughout the globe and particularly the Arabic nations.

The Sustainable Business

Like political structure, legislation is susceptible to changes on a frequent basis. Forecasting and managing change is far from easy and subject to time, regime and *force majeure*. *The Sustainable Business* needs to recognise the importance of politics and legislation on the economic landscape, and morph as necessary to reflect the prevailing climate.

Technology

In contrast, technology is a far more predictable facet of the modern commercial landscape. Research and development helps foster the improvements in available technology and aspects such as the internet heighten the awareness of options, developments and discoveries.

The speed of technological change is however unrelenting and accelerating, some would say out of control, but options are at hand to help such as leasing of technology, modular approaches to system configuration, software updates, and so on; yet there remains a dilemma betwixt future proofing and fit-for-purpose procurement.

The Sustainable Business needs to steer a careful path balancing its commitment to the environment and the planet, with its focus on long term survival. Key to this, are the following seven questions see figure 5.4:

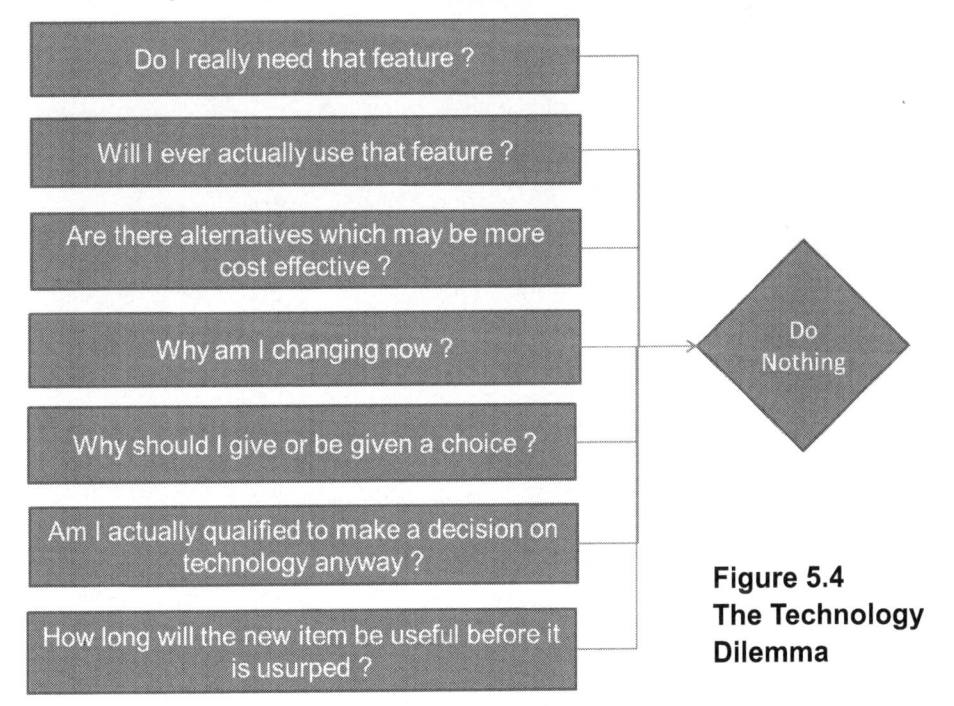

- Do I really need that feature ?
- Will I ever actually use that feature ?
- Are there alternatives which may be more cost effective ?
- Why am I changing now ?
- Why should I give or be given a choice ?
- Am I actually qualified to make a decision on technology anyway ?
- How long will the new item be useful before it is usurped ?

→ Do Nothing

**Figure 5.4
The Technology Dilemma**

> **Food for Thought**: A proportion of technology is purchased on a whim, a proportion of technological features are never used, and a proportion of technology is obsolete before it leaves its box, so why bother?

Business Structure

The structure of *the Sustainable Business* will be important over the life of the organisation and will have a significant impact on both its performance and its competitiveness in the market. It will also impact on the speed with which it can react to change whether implemented from within or enforced through external factors.

Organisations have over many years wrestled with the issues of whether to centralise or decentralise management of the day to day operations. This is an important strategic decision with advantages and disadvantages of each – see figure 5.5.

Whilst there are many exponents of both centralised and decentralised set-ups, the decision remains a very personal one to the organisation, market and service offering in question.

	Advantages	Disadvantages
Centralised	<ul><li>Cost tends to be lower</li><li>Coordination of resources</li><li>Consistency across all parts of the business</li><li>Communication improved</li><li>Economies of scale more attainable</li><li>Strategy easier to implement</li></ul>	<ul><li>Can be distanced from the activity</li><li>Can foster a them and us environment</li><li>Demotivates regional management</li></ul>
Decentralised	<ul><li>Closer to the customer</li><li>Increased reaction times</li><li>Often more flexible</li><li>Greater focus on local suppliers</li><li>Lower carbon footprint</li><li>Reactive to local needs</li></ul>	<ul><li>Unit costs tend to be higher</li><li>Less predictable margin</li><li>Corporate strategy less visible or effective</li><li>Renegade decisions often more risky</li></ul>

Figure 5.5 Centralised vs Decentralised

As a compromise, in recent years there has been a rise of a number of hybrid alternatives for example CLAN and SCAN.

CLAN – Centre Lead Action Network – is a relatively decentralised approach where procurement and commercial staff are located in the regions, reporting to the local management but with a responsibility to centralised function held at a central head office.

SCAN – Strategically Controlled Action Network – adopts a similar position to CLAN, but severs the local management link to focus the regional person on central strategy.

Added to this key strategic issue is the decision as to the management structure employed, and again there are a variety of different options commonly used.

The traditional hierarchical structure with a CEO at the top of the tree, underpinned by a board of directors each responsible for a different facet of the business – see figure 5.6 – remains very popular in many organisations especially the SME segment. Where the organisation originator remains involved, they would typically retain the CEO or MD role, however as the organisation grows so the introduction of a chairman to protect the shareholders and investors in the business is commonplace. This appointment helps add a balance in some key decisions on policy and process.

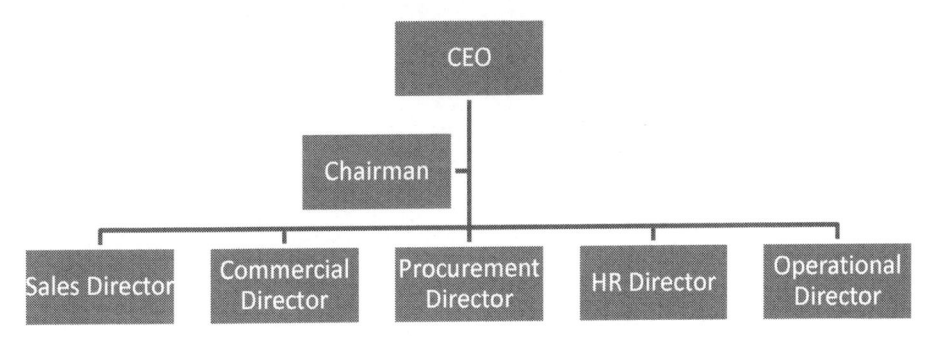

Figure 5.6 Hierarchical Structure

Similarly, instead of directorships by function, an alternative can be to have management by geographical regions – see figure 5.7. This has the benefit of allowing some regional control and decision making, whilst still reporting centrally under a consistent remit. The amount of responsibility divested can have a critical impact on the long term direction of the organisation and its ability to act decisively as one, and can lead to differences in culture, generating rifts through the business.

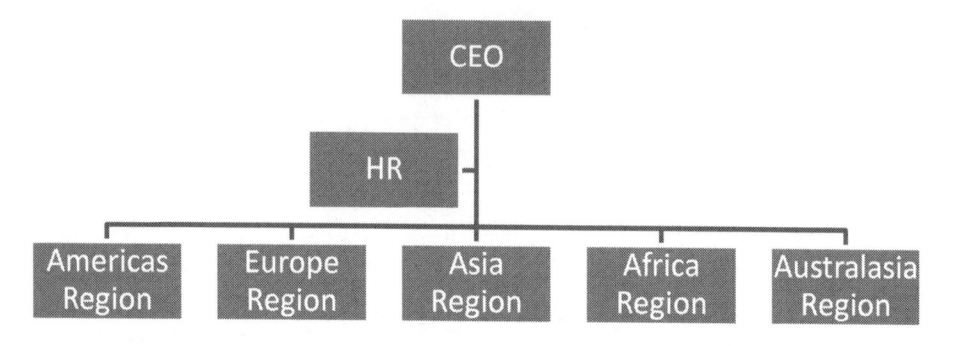

Figure 5.6 Hierarchical Structure

Where the organisation is of an appropriate size, more of a matrix approach might be adopted – see figure 5.8. This endeavours to blend dual responsibilities in larger organisations where staff members feel a split between their functional goals and their local geographical yearnings. They retain their policy and process driven responsibilities through their functional line, yet adopt a specific role within the regional activities.

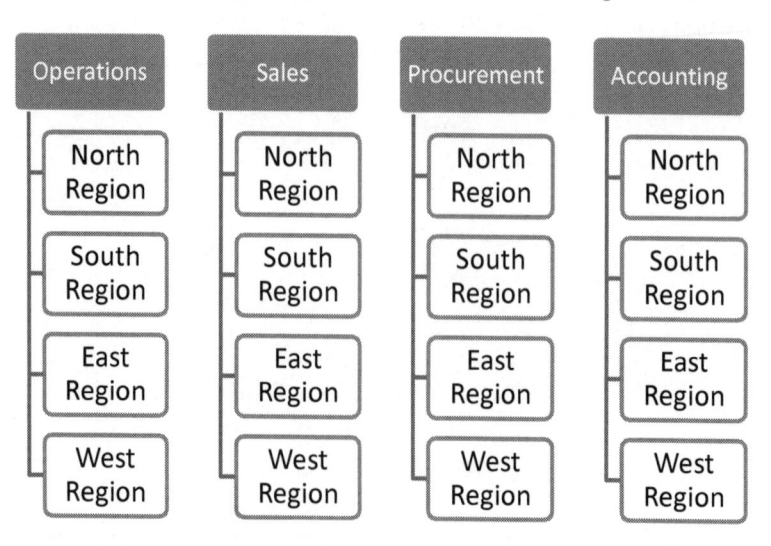

Figure 5.8 Matrix structure

Whilst perceived in its early days as a way to compromise central and regional differences, a major criticism of this is the fact that employees end up with effectively two bosses, one functional and one regional. This conflict can hamper activity, and cause untold stress on the individual. Equally, it can be seen to drive duplication of resource through a business with many tasks performed in solidarity.

Accordingly, for *the Sustainable Business,* it can be seen that there are a number of business structures and policies that may be adopted. The most suitable choice will depend on the organisation in question, its markets, customers and processes, and this may change over a period as the business grows or diversifies. Review of such matters is therefore highly recommended, with projections and strategy flexible enough to withstand changes as required.

Business Ownership and Legal Structure

Apart from the aforementioned structure, management and authority dilemmas, the issue of ownership and liability is vital to *the Sustainable Business* both from the perspective of optimum performance and most efficient use of resources, and the perspectives of longevity and legacy.

The Sustainable Business looks to the future; it has vision way beyond the current regime. It needs succession plans and the most appropriate, lowest risk ownership model possible.

Succession planning is by its very nature alien to human nature; it suggests that all things are finite. As leader, who will carry the baton when *you* fall? In centuries past, the standard bearer was key; if one fell, there was a designate to pick up the banner and maintain the drive, and in business it needs to be the same.

In one organisation experienced, succession planning was undertaken with post-it notes on a white board, it was both simple yet effective for that organisation. In another, a dearth of talent and enthusiasm drove immediate strategy towards training and recruitment, for each role a plan was in place to ensure that the service was maintained despite any eventuality. With headhunting embedded I the corporate culture, a book was kept of suitable replacements from both inside and outside the industry whom could be "approached" if necessary.

The Sustainable Business has a clear understanding of its people, their roles, and how their function can be preserved in the case of illness, departure or change.

Planning, cross-functional teams, job rotation, secondments, training programmes and so on can all be used to both develop and expand the individual, so every role is covered. An environment of progression, promotion and security helps lure new talent, whilst creating a feeling of worth within the organisation.

Inevitably, there will be plodders, stalwarts and blockers but they are often the bedrock of organisation not necessarily obstacles. The *Sustainable Business* blends this with ambition, enthusiasm, and sparkle and extracts the best from its resources.

> **Food for Thought**: Consider a slow flowing river. Removing some of the weed or increasing the sources of water supply will improve the flow, yet in the short and medium term you would hesitate to consider changing the banks, direction or bed of the river, and so it is with established and new employees.

Wider the liability and ownership of the organisation is important. Understanding the differences between a sole-trader, a partnership, a limited liability organisation, and so on is a minefield of jargon and confusion. Commercial, financial and operational differences occur for each, and careful attention should be paid when selecting the most suitable model. Thought and guidance at inception of a business helps future proof, and is less expensive in the longer term, when it is necessary to make strategic changes to ownership and governance. In short, all businesses will come to an end at some point; it may be through acquisition, bankruptcy, voluntary closure or merger, but having scope to do this quickly and efficiently will be an investment.

Targeting and Goal Setting

Finally, the essence of the corporate context is delivery of its business objectives, its goals. The vision clearly identifies what is required over the short medium and long term, and key to the success of the organisation is its ability to deliver these goals.

Setting targets and objectives, often linked to rewards and incentives, is an everyday part of life and one that *the Sustainable Business* endorses and supports. However this should be undertaken in a consistent, fair and equitable manner. Measurement of performance is discussed extensively in chapter 14, yet it equally warrants recognition at this point.

A number of ideas have been developed over the years to embrace target setting, yet few are as simple and effective as the SMART approach see figure 5.9.

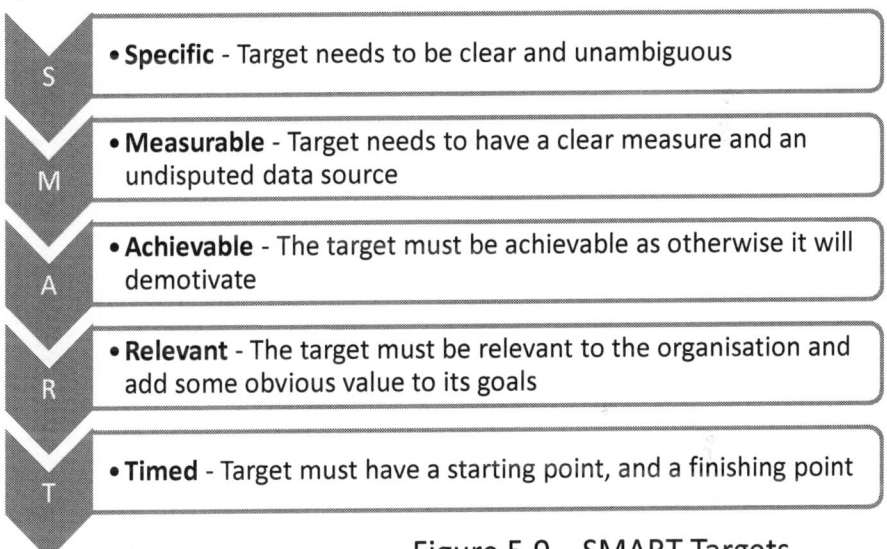

- **Specific** - Target needs to be clear and unambiguous
- **Measurable** - Target needs to have a clear measure and an undisputed data source
- **Achievable** - The target must be achievable as otherwise it will demotivate
- **Relevant** - The target must be relevant to the organisation and add some obvious value to its goals
- **Timed** - Target must have a starting point, and a finishing point

Figure 5.9   SMART Targets

This is the foundation of targeting, yet there are three further issues often overlooked – communication, visibility and review.

Setting targets are vital to the success of an organisation, yet so often they are lost in the melee of everyday life. They are not communicated effectively, they are not visible and they are oft forgotten. *The Sustainable Business* lives and breathes targets, it views them as part of the life-blood of the organisation, without them it is like going on a journey without a map.

Make sure staff understand the targets, use language that is recognised and check they appreciate the importance and impact of success, and make sure they are visible. In one organisation there was a complaint that there were *"too many references to targets in the office, saying it put* *pressure on the sales team to perform"....*success!

In Chevron the global oil company, targets are set globally, but locally every team member knows exactly where the organisation is in respect of its own targets. It even displays the current status in the toilet areas!

And review is vital. A target must be reviewed and as often as possible. A target that is reviewed daily is more likely to be achieved than one reviewed monthly or yearly.

The Sustainable Business does not lock away its targets it pins them to the wall and refers to them daily.

Case Study 5: Sustainable Healthcare

Nations around the world wrestle with the delivery of affordable and sustainable medical services for its inhabitants today and more worryingly for tomorrow.

The concept of the welfare state has evolved over the centuries from a concept originally introduced to encourage soldiers to participate in conflicts from as far back as Roman times. In the 20th century, the welfare state tended to be financed through tax or financial contributions made by society or an individual during their healthy years, with some aggregation to balance the healthy and the needy, but available to those when needed. What is incontrovertible is the fact that welfare systems have improved the average life of citizens through the developed world.

The model is however flawed in the longer term. The financing of a health service requires the persons currently in work to contribute in anticipation of their future needs, though these funds actually finance the current provision and investment. In circumstances where the working population is increasing this can be sustained however where the population is decreasing, the model implodes. This is of particular concern in China where the "one child policy" introduced in 1978 has according to authorities prevented over 400m births thereby skewing the population and causing a health funding time-bomb. Equally, in Japan, statistics suggest that society appears to have "lost the urge" to reproduce.

Post the second world-war, there was a significant increase in the population in many developed nations. The baby boom years as they were termed – typically between 1945 and 1960 – saw a huge increase in populations leading to many new workers and a significant injection of taxation into economies as a result. This taxation facilitated the development of health provision, however, based on a retirement age of 60, many of these baby-boomers are now retired or facing an imminent end to their working life; the taxation consequences of this are clear.

Worse still, statistically, the need for health provision increases as a person goes through life, and due to advances in medicine, health awareness, diet, technology and communications, the mortality rate has improved with people on average living longer.

Whilst it can be argued that a significant percentage of these former workers will hold pensions and savings with some residual taxable contribution, and secondary waves of population fluctuations have been seen since the primary baby-boom wave, the long term sustainability of a health service is in crisis. The US population aged over 65 years of age is set to increase from around 12% to over 20% in the next 40 years, with Japan having already exceeded this percentage and set to reach parity – i.e. as many workers in employment as those retired – before 2050.

At the current level of taxation, the workforce of many developed nations will not be able to work hard enough to generate sufficient taxation to maintain the current levels of health provision going forward leading to *welfare bankruptcy*. There is no political message here, there is no call for a review of policy; politicians on neither the left or right can overcome the problem with easy or *electable* answers.

So what can we do to make our health services sustainable and future proofed? Sadly there is no quick-fix and no palatable solutions:

1. Increase tax receipts to ensure that over a working life the employee generates enough to finance their own needs for the future.

2. Steadily increase the overall rates of taxation or the proportion of the tax receipts attributed to healthcare into the future, probably until circa 2050 assuming no new baby-booms are experienced.

3. Increase retirement ages significantly or reward working beyond the current retirement age with lower taxation levels.

4. Increase immigration levels to allow overseas workers to fill the taxation void. Allow people to work legitimately but remove all permanency entitlements for workers to remain once they stop working. *Alien workers* would contribute to the welfare solution and legitimacy would bring their taxable revenue into the public domain.

5. Reduce unemployment contributions for those not contributing positively to the national tax receipts and direct this into healthcare.

6. Rein in pharmaceutical research and development expenditure on "holy grail" cures or treatment.

The Sustainable Business

Notes Page | **Page Ref**

The Sustainable Business

Summary Chapter 6
Sustainable Procurement

Key Learning Points
- The Sustainable Procurement process
- The fulfilment of needs and managing Stakeholder expectations
- Value for money
- The concept of "Adding Value" and service levels
- Respect for the Three Pillars
- Win-Win relationships
- Sustainability in the tender process
- Sustainable business cases
- The impact of corruption
- Assessment and build-up of cost models
- Sustainable Supplier selection – location and evaluation
- Sustainable Supplier management
- Administrative tools and cash maintenance
- Sustainable negotiation – Process, preparation and tactics
- Generating procurement policy
- Sustainable specifications and measures

Tool Summary
- The Procurement Cycle
- Carter 10C model
- Reduce to Produce
- STOPWASTE
- Total Cost of Sustainable Ownership
- Critical Needs Analysis
- Training Needs Analysis
- Mendlow

CIPS Syllabus Reference
- Level 4 Negotiating and Contracting in Procurement and Supply
- Level 4 Sourcing in Procurement and Supply
- Level 4 Managing Contracts and Relationships in Procurement and Supply
- Level 5 Sustainable procurement
- Level 5 Management in Procurement and Supply
- Level 5 Managing Risk in Supply Chains

Chapter 6: Sustainable Procurement

"Sustainable Procurement is a process whereby organisations meet their needs for goods, services, works and utilities in a way that achieves value for money on a whole-life basis in terms of generating benefits not only to the organisation, but also to society and the economy, whilst minimising damage to the environment"
– Sustainable Procurement National Action Plan

Developing a truly sustainable mandate within an organisation is a long and involved process with many obstacles to be overcome. As discussed previously, the *Three Pillars* philosophy demands a commitment to the people in the business, to the on-going profitability of the business, and to the wider planet: it also demands a vision of longevity, a pragmatic approach to risk and a plan for the future.

Within the business operation there is a clear need to procure goods and services to fulfil its objectives. This process will involve generating a commercial relationship with suppliers throughout the Supply Chain, an activity which is one of the most critical areas for *the Sustainable Business* to manage, and right at the heart of organisation.

Yet the Sustainable Procurement function has other roles as shown in figure 6.1 which will be explored in this chapter.

A Sustainable Procurement function requires a detailed and clear process, underpinned by rigorous adherence to discipline, skill and character. The selection and management of third party organisations over potentially a long period of time – who will directly or indirectly represent or support the business – is a weighty responsibility and one which should not be underestimated in the overall pursuit of sustainable ambitions.

Sourcing Organisational Needs

The definition of Sustainable Procurement given at the head of this chapter outlines the role of the Sustainable Procurement function and its impact on the *Three Pillars*. Its aim is to fulfil the supply needs of the organisation whilst ensuring value for money to strengthen the *Profit*

Pillar, and adding value to people and the community whilst maintaining a continual focus on the green issues that affect our planet.

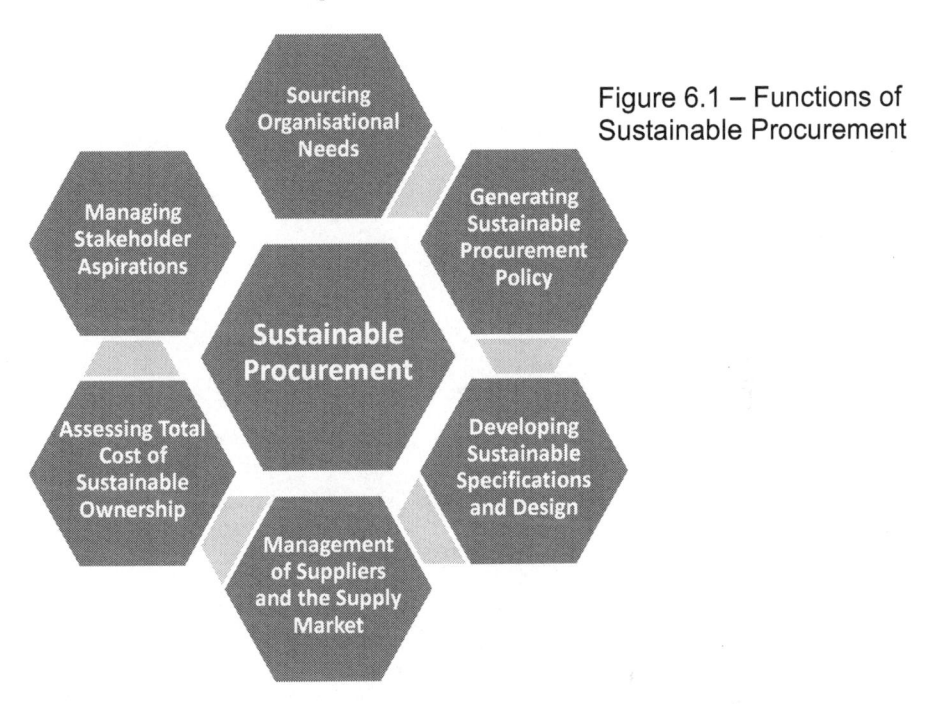

Figure 6.1 – Functions of Sustainable Procurement

Sustainability aside, the *raison d'etre* of any business must be to add value. Every activity within the organisation should make some contribution, either directly or indirectly, to the business objectives. If an activity isn't adding value, it should not be done. Some organisations lose sight of this very simple mandate, distracted by "the bigger picture", important deadlines, or fighting fires. This is a simple equation upon which all business should focus.

> **Rule: If total cost is more than the total contribution don't do "it"**

The Sustainable Procurement function has a focus on adding net value to the business, and this is at the core of all its decisions; it is its strongest procurement driver. It recognises that to achieve this objective it needs to fulfil some key roles in the organisation primarily to:
- Meet the demands of its stakeholders in an affordable and cost efficient manner;
- Recognise its Total Cost of Sustainable Ownership;

- Meet the quality and time expectations of its stakeholders;
- Minimise its impact on the environment.

The typical procurement process begins with the identification of "a need" from one of its stakeholders or a business unit, see figure 6.2. This need may be a specific item, or more commonly a problem statement. This initial request is the trigger for the procurement cycle.

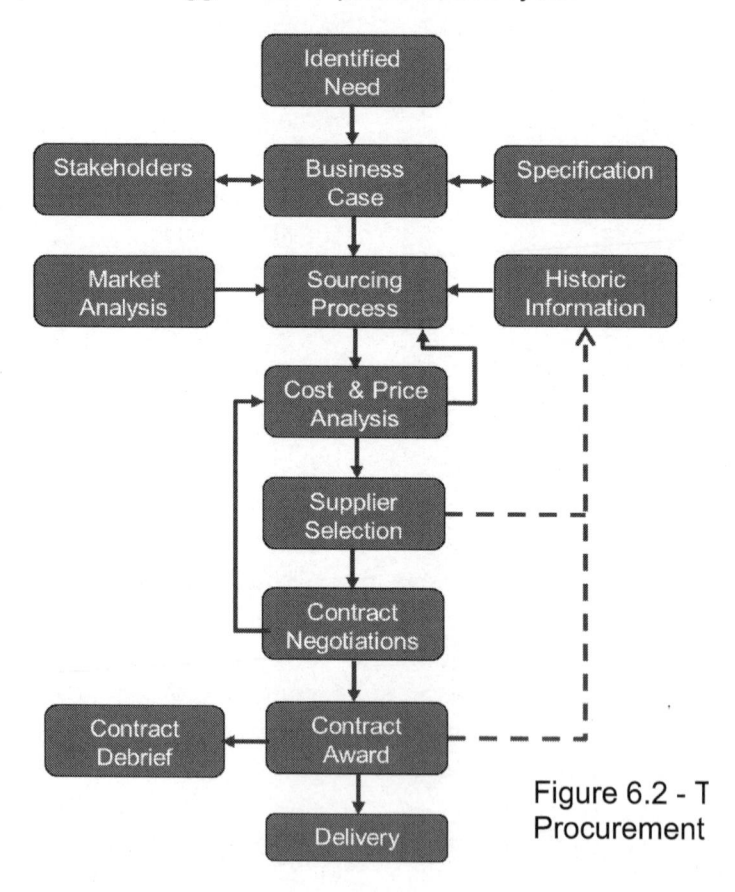

Figure 6.2 - T Procurement

The need may or may not be feasible, so following the request, further analysis is undertaken to formulate a business case. This analysis will involve input from relevant stakeholders, perhaps the finance team for a budget input, operations for a needs assessment, inventory management for a stock search or other departments as appropriate for the item or service sought.

Once identified, at either a formal or informal level, a decision is made as to whether the item or service is actually needed by the company, and more importantly will it add net value to the business. The business case assessment should primarily focus on just three aspects: How much will "it" cost, what will "it" give me in, and is "it" core to my business objectives.

This third requirement is core to the decision making process, yet often overlooked in the pursuit of the added value. Pursuing activities outside the corporate mandate, focused on something other than the company's mission statement, is indeed technically illegal for certain legal entities in some geographic locations.

Traditionally, the cost in procurement terms is a mix of fixed and variable costs which might include raw materials, utility payments, contractor fees, time, administration overheads, finance charges, legal expenses, and so on; it will also include the usage costs, maintenance, and disposal costs, see figure 6.3. This cost assessment is often the primary focus of the Sustainable Procurement function, with a core underpinning objective of prudent use of the limited resources made available to it.

Net Present Cost

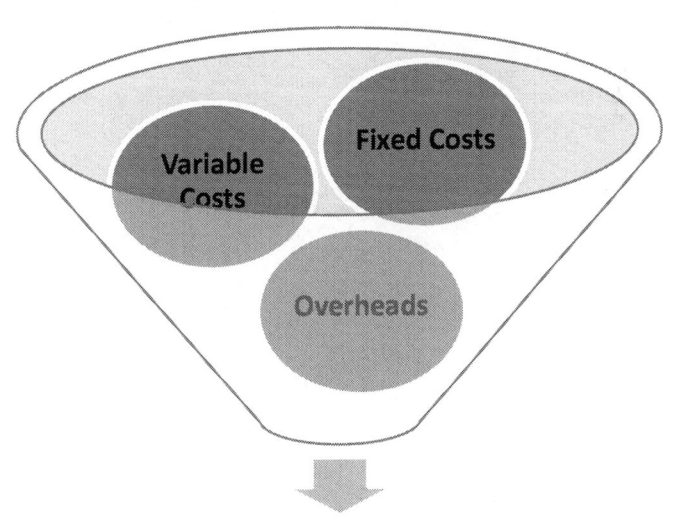

Figure 6.3 – Cost Collation

The Sustainable Procurement function will project the cost calculation into the future, in an attempt to understand the long term cost implications of the decision; it will look at the Total Sustainable Cost of Ownership – a concept explored in chapter 4 – to determine the total cost from need through to disposal and final impact.

To ensure a balanced assessment, it is equally as important to take a similar stance with respect to the value contribution of the asset. This will include the value contribution of the asset or service over its life cycle as well as considering any resale value or disposal. This resale value may come from any revenue secured if the item was sold, or any residual income if the product was disposed of for scrap or spare parts. This assessment should also try to ascertain whether recycling the product at the end of its life would prevent further raw-material being worked. In such an event, there would be a positive impact worthy of inclusion into the assessment.

> **Food for Thought**: An example of positive impact would be the recycling of aluminium. The commodity cost of the scrap does not represent a true reflection of the environmental impact saved from not reworking fresh ore: 1 tonne of newly produced aluminium uses 14,000kWh of power as opposed to 700kWh for the equivalent for recycled product, and not to mention the 1300 tonnes of water required, the 13 tonnes of CO_2 and the 5 tonnes of residue toxic waste produced from 1 tonne of new aluminium generated. (Source Resourcities)

Once the business case has been produced, and approved, the process needs to determine the best source for obtaining the goods or services specified, and here begins the sourcing element of the cycle.

The structure referred to in figure 6.2, represents the full tender route. *The Sustainable Business* recognises that there is a cost for all parties of undertaking such a process for every requirement, so alternative procedures and arrangements may work in parallel.

For example, in an effort to minimise administration and process costs, framework agreements and purchase cards are now commonplace in organisations to enable the prompt procurement of lower value items, or items where there is a regular or recognised source. This may allow the Sustainable Procurement team to identify a source quickly and efficiently. Such decisions would include an assessment of the cost of raising a purchase order, payment terms, rebate opportunities and other commercial benefits which may be available. In short, for all purchases the Sustainable Procurement will adopt and follow standard process to ensure that the lowest Total Cost of Sustainable Ownership is achieved.

Where the requirement is of a higher value, thresholds and corporate policy must be in place to determine the appropriate authority has been obtained before a formal tender or price investigation commences. Process which involves third parties invariably takes extra time and costs more to undertake both for the Sustainable Procurement team, and the wider market.

Many organisations demand that multiple quotations are obtained over a certain fiscal level, so by definition the decision will lead to some companies in the marketplace making an investment in time and effort without reward. The Sustainable Procurement team needs to respect this. As part of its *Three Pillars* commitment, it will recognise that it is in the long term interests of the *Profit Pillar*, and part of its *People* commitments that the potential supplier is well treated and receives due acknowledgement. This will at the very least demand a notice explaining the decision to place the business elsewhere. Effective debriefing is essential to the long term development and maintenance of a competitive marketplace.

The Sustainable Procurement department will have in place a structured team of incumbent suppliers with whom a working relationship and partnership agreement will exist. These tried and tested suppliers will in many cases form the starting point for any new requirement; they represent relatively low risk solutions, should have a lower administration cost level as credit checks, supplier assessments, etc will already have been undertaken, and will be familiar with the prevailing culture of *the Sustainable Business*. These circumstances can prove an overwhelming incentive to place business with the same few suppliers, yet this needs to be tempered.

The Sustainable Procurement function needs at all times to remember its sustainable mandate: obtaining best value, respecting the *Three Pillars* and longevity. As such, there is a need to constantly assess the market to review opportunities and new suppliers. As shown in other chapters, the Porter Five Force model illustrates that the market is a dynamic beast, changing all the time with new entrants and substitutes offering opportunities that the Sustainable Procurement department needs to consider.

Depending on the size and breadth of the demand profile, adoption of a Category Management approach can represent a good investment allowing market specialists to flourish and commercial opportunities to be identified more easily. As discussed in earlier chapters, having a subject expert generates extra margin from commodity purchases, helps nurture value in project spend, and establishes working relationships that add benefit throughout the Supply Chain.

Where there is a desire to introduce new suppliers a Pre Qualification Questionnaire (PQQ) is recommended to establish at relatively low cost, a potential supplier's interest and scope. Adoption of this approach ensures that the understanding of the market remains fresh and competitive, however the document should not be overly onerous, to encourage would-be suppliers to complete said enquiry.

Furthermore, it should be highlighted at this stage that in some circumstances there may be legislation specific requirements for some organisations to undertaken mandated process. OJEU directives would be one such example affecting public sector, public funded projects and utility organisations within the European Union.

The relative level of corruption in a country is highlighted by organisations such as Transparency International who compile corruption reports looking at the relative state of countries and their efforts to address corruption. In the 2011 report, New Zealand, Denmark, Finland, Sweden and Singapore occupied the top five spots, with Germany the highest G8 country at 14th, and USA appearing in 24th, somewhat surprisingly two places below Chile.

Countries such as Nigeria, whilst falling towards the bottom of the 183 countries surveyed, are making notable and significant efforts to remedy their shortcomings. In 2007, the Bureau of Public Procurement developed and implemented a Procurement Act to build on efforts made by the President Goodluck Jonathan to clean up the Nigerian image. This Act clearly identifies the requirements for corruption free public procurement, and whilst clearly still an entrenched issue, this has resulted in movement in the right direction with annual auditing of public authorities focused on removing nepotism and cronyism, and cleaning up the issues.

Statistics collated by Transparency International – see graph 6.4 – show that Nigerian corruption has improved steadily since 2001 when they were second to bottom of the countries surveyed, reaching 130th out of 184 in 2011, albeit other areas such as internet scams, bogus donations and fake inheritance emails have risen sharply over the same period.

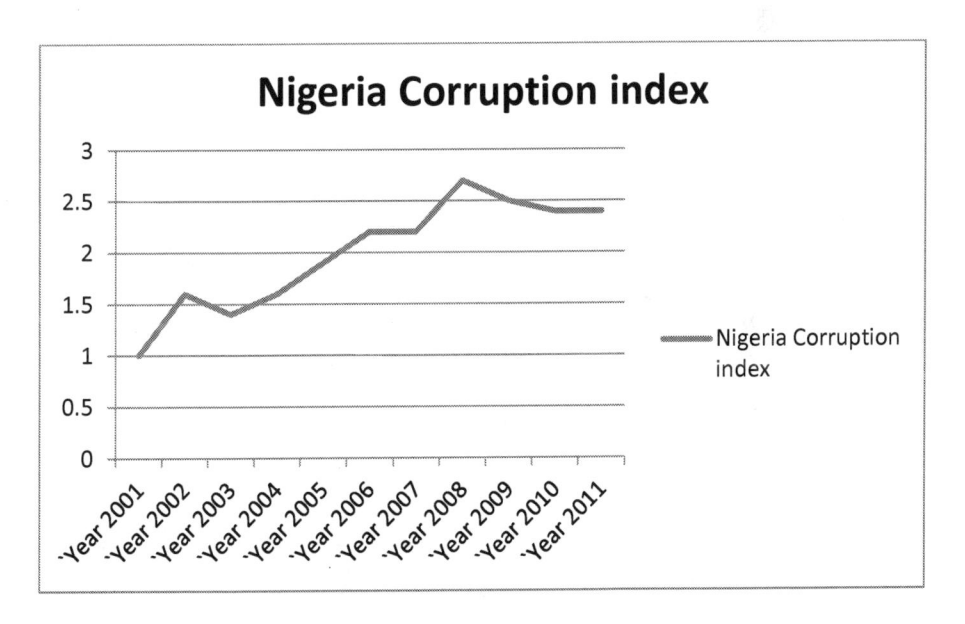

Graph 6.4 – Nigerian Corruption Index (improvement from a 2001 baseline)

The selection and inevitable elimination of potential suppliers is of course contentious with opinion often divided even within the selection team. To ensure fairness, *the Sustainable Business* will use a clear and published assessment structure to eliminate and select successful bidders. These criteria can be applied as early as the PQQ to minimise wasted effort for suppliers who will not meet said criteria.

Once a list of potential suppliers has been generated, the choice of information request becomes important. It can be shown that this choice can directly affect the response from the market, and the competitive nature of the negotiation thereafter; a balance is thus required between a large tender document and a short-form Request For Quotation (RFQ).

Further, the content of any market facing request needs to be carefully assessed and should be cognisant of confidentiality and commercial sensitivity. It also needs to meet any legislative needs such as those prescribed by OJEU, UNASUR and others, and should adhere to any timescale restrictions as appropriate. These are varied and complicated with local requirements researched to ensure compliance.

> **Food for Thought**: As a side note, be aware of other common adaptations of such documentation which include but are not limited to the following:
> EOI – Expression of Interest   BPF – Ball Park Figure
> RFP – Request for Proposal   LOI – Letter of Interest (or Intent)
> RFQ – Request for Quote   CBD – Competitive Bid Document
> RFI – Request for Information   RPL – Recommended Price List
> TSD – Tender Submission Document
> NISO – National Individual Standing Offer
> RFSO – Request for Standing Offer
> NMSO – National Master Standing Offer
> ROM – Rough Order of Magnitude
>
> Consider a balance with the use of acronyms which can discourage would be interested parties: a glossary should always be provided.

The process for bid opening and assessment of price proposals needs to be regulated as well. *The Sustainable Business* prides itself on equality, fairness and transparency at all times, and consistent with its ethical stance, clear process for this activity is advisable.

In many cases, as each tender is opened, attention inevitably focuses on the bottom line price. This is human nature yet detailed price analysis by an independent team is required. As with the other measurement criteria, the assessment must be uniform and fair for all bids received. Inclusion in the bid pack of a pricing matrix can help steer bidders to some sort

The Sustainable Business

of uniformity, but this is by no means certain. Rarely can a sales person be relied upon to feel that *his* offering fits in a standard box; *his* offer is unique, somewhat special!

Designing the pricing matrix is a skill in itself, as poor structure can inadvertently steer the supplier's thought process. The aim is to allow flexibility without introducing too many caveats or pricing options that may distort the analysis. Each matrix should be considered separately and reflect the relevant needs of that requirement.

Opened tenders need to be assessed and there are a number of ways in which this can be achieved. A note-worthy and market leading approach to supplier assessment is the Carter 10C model – see figure 6.4. This approach is widely regarded to address all the main issues surrounding the appointment of a supplier whether new or incumbent.

Capacity	Has the supplier got the physical resource to fulfil the requirement?
Consistency	Does the supplier deliver consistently to the same specification?
Culture	Will the supplier's core values complement our core values?
Clean	Is the supplier ethical, responsible, and "squeaky clean"?
Control of Process	Does the supplier have control of their operating processes?
Commitment to Quality	Does the supplier strive to deliver quality first time, every time?
Competency	Are the supplier's people and functions competent and well trained?
Cost	Is the product or service competitively priced?
Cash	Is the company financially stable, how strong are its accounts?
CSR	How strong is its Corporate and Social Responsibility?

Contractors Score from 5   Strength of Evidence Score out of 5   Weighting of facet being measured

Contractor A	Score out of 5	Weight	Evidence	Total
Competency	3	x3	x2	18
Capacity	2	x1	x2	4
Clean	4	x2	x1	8
Culture	4	x2	x1	8
CSR	3	x3	x3	27
10c Rating				65

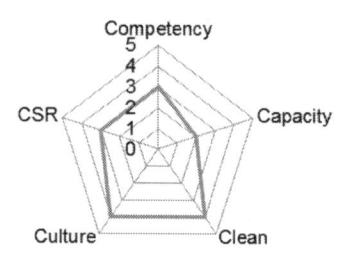

Figure 6.4 – Carter's 10C Model

It is not necessarily recommended that suppliers are assessed for every "C" characteristic, however factors which are central to the business strategy should be examined. These chosen criteria can be weighted to add further focus, with additional impact allocated as a result of the strength and integrity of the evidence underpinning the assessment.

The selection process is the ideal time to review all suppliers against the chosen criteria. Such policy will prevent a supplier from being contracted who is or may soon experience difficulties.

As mentioned in the last chapter, the need to forecast is essential for *the Sustainable Business*. As such, when assessing suppliers for long term contracts which might impact on its longevity aspirations, there may be a call for an assessment of three additional characteristics: future strategy, future finances, and approach to risk.

Albeit very difficult to do with any great certainty, an assessment of a supplier's future business strategy, its underpinning financial projections, and its perceived attitude to risk is highly advisable. With a mission critical supplier relationship, each of these characteristics has the potential to irreparably undermine *the Sustainable Business* with disastrous consequences. So how can this assessment be achieved?

In summary, there are no guarantees but the responsible approach is to at least try. Whilst suppliers may be reluctant to outwardly divulge their future strategic ambitions, in some circumstances – perhaps shrouded with appropriate due-diligence and non-disclosure protection – a chink of light may be forthcoming. Of more significance may be the openness or lack thereof – if they can't trust you at the start when no water has yet flowed under the metaphorical bridge, then when can they trust *you*?

Previous analysis may well have suggested that the supplier had a compatible approach in business. If this is the case, then would it not be unreasonable to surmise that the supplier would, like *you,* have a long term strategy? In the interests of mutual benefit would not the win-win partnership ethos benefit from alignment of these strategies at least over the duration of the contract period? Furthermore, understanding future target markets, segment developments, new product launches, etc would surely help strengthen the position of both companies, and precipitate mutual gain.

And would not the risk management activities of both companies benefit from shared resources, entwined latency, and leveraged risk? Both organisations could be holding contingency for the same eventualities, for example, or maintaining duplicated disaster recovery provision.

> **Rule: The essence of trust is not in its bind, but in its bond**

Once the preliminary selection of the supplier has been undertaken, in most cases the negotiation and bargaining can then begin. This is the period of the trade-offs, the negotiation tactics where clever manipulation can wriggle a price upwards or downwards depending on the end-game.

The Sustainable Business needs to be very wary during this phase. Establishing clear boundaries is the secret: have a fixed BATNA (Best Alternative to Negotiated Agreement), a clearly understood MDO (Most Desirable Outcome) and LDO (Least Desirable Outcome).

Salespeople are trained to win in negotiating so ensure the skill sets of the Sustainable Procurement *team* are equally matched. Negotiation training should be an established feature of all procurement staff. This should include how to identify and use negotiation tactics, and being able to combat them and negate them at source.

Tactics do not sit comfortably with a sustainable ethos. They do not promote win-win partnerships, or fair play or long term trusting relationships, so be very wary of entering into such tussles, or engaging organisations which "try it on". In one multi-million dollar negotiation witnessed, the supplier attempted to "hide" the contentious elements of the contract within a packed agenda, after a large lunch, in a warm, dimly lit meeting room; hardly the beginning of a beautiful relationship!

> **Food for Thought**: **The power of the pen** – The secret of negotiation is in the planning, but power and control play a big role. One tip, sit close to the whiteboard or flip chart. At the first opportunity, offer to scribe key points, stand up, you now hold the pen and you have a height advantage, everybody else is looking up to you. You control what goes on the whiteboard and what doesn't.

Once the negotiation phase has been completed, the negotiated position needs to be recorded in a formal contract. Arguably, the trusting relationships that are central to the sustainable ethos would suggest that a contract would be unnecessary. However, *the Sustainable Business*, whilst recognising partnerships and strong relationships, remains aware of the risk and the pitfalls that can entrap project based relationships.

And finally, before work commences on the delivery of the items or service, as mentioned previously, debriefing of the unsuccessful contractors will pay dividends. Maybe not in the short or medium term, and maybe not for every supplier, but one day you may want to have a further dialogue, so treat them all fairly.

> **Food for Thought**: In the USA the TINA – Trust In Negotiations Act – legislation makes it compulsory for public sector contractors to make known their cost levels in any bid situation.

Generating Sustainable Procurement Policy

Whilst existing sustainable procurement policy may be in place, it is necessary that this is reviewed and maintained at regular intervals. Policy should reflect the needs of the organisation over the foreseeable future, and the wider corporate mission objectives; it should consider both the internal and external risks and opportunities and the strategic direction of the organisation. The procurement activity represents just one of the cost-value business case assessment criteria, policy needs to reflect the magnitude of this responsibility.

In the high pressure of today's commercial environment it is easy to overlook the necessity of policy review, with reading all the legal policy documentation or the financial press rarely very high on even the most ardent of professional's "to-do list".

Yet failure to do exactly that can lead to a potentially critical "responsibility gap" developing, especially in fast moving policy generation regions, such as Europe and the Americas. Unknowingly, an organisation can miss changes that can significantly affect its management and earnings potential. For example, tax amendments are no longer confined to the annual national budget statement, but occur throughout the period, environmental legislation is developing all the time, import and export restrictions can change daily and commodities by the minute. In cross border transactions, currency differentials can affect the margins on contracts, and the cost base of the business assessment, making any decision vulnerable to fluctuation and change.

Whilst onerous and apparently not value adding, policy review must be a structured part of the Sustainable Procurement department's function. Daily digests, journal subscriptions, and contracting out of the responsibility of the on-going review are all options for the faint hearted, but the need to update policy remains ever present.

Developing Sustainable Specifications and Design

Although not always directly part of the Sustainable Procurement's remit, generation of sustainable specifications and design should at least be validated and reviewed prior to any procurement thereof.

Whilst discussed in depth in chapter 10, it is a subject worthy of comment at this point. A set of clearly agreed sustainable design parameters is a good underpinning discipline for *the Sustainable Business*. Having in place such criteria helps other parts of the business focus on a clear objective and helps drive unity, compatibility and cohesion as well as containing unauthorised choice by renegade operatives: the supplementary benefits are numerous across the organisation: lower inventory costs; simpler maintenance process; stronger warranty cover; supplier allegiance; reduced risk; and so on, to name but a few.

Food for Thought: How many purchases you have made where you have secured features that are never actually used: was this a good value decision ?

However, from the Sustainable Procurement department's perspective, such a decision is of unprecedented benefit helping it in almost every aspect of its activity – the exceptions being some of its adherence to competition policy and possibly some weakening in its stance against a supplier confident of its continued nomination. Capitalising upon such a decision can lead to significant commercial benefit and a major competitive advantage for which the Sustainable Procurement department is required to deliver.

Management of Suppliers and the Supply Market

In addition to the selection of suppliers, the Sustainable Procurement function should take responsibility for the on-going management of the engaged suppliers, and maintain an awareness of the supplier market as discussed earlier in the chapter with the comments on Category Management.

Whilst *the Sustainable Business* engages suppliers on a win-win partnership basis, and endeavours to foster a relationship based on trust, the on-going management of suppliers is vital to maintaining the service levels, for ensuring contractual compliance and for collating supplier performance data for future use – see figure 6.5.

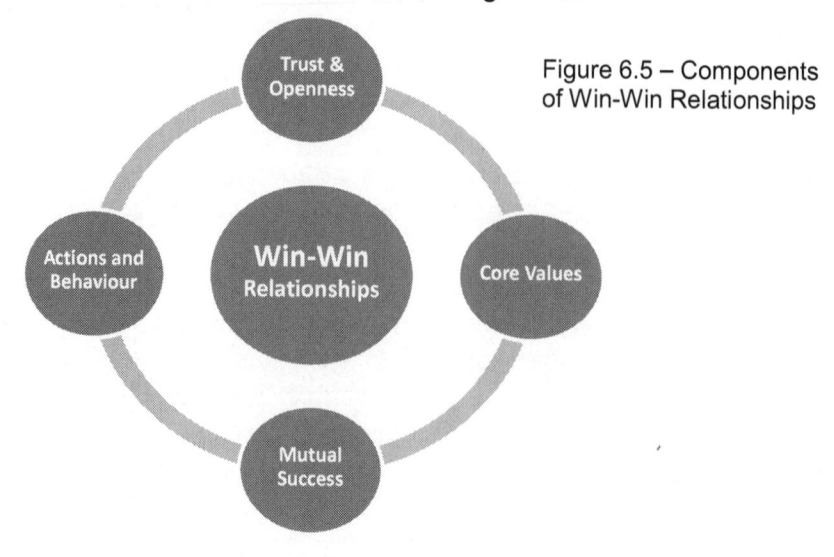

Figure 6.5 – Components of Win-Win Relationships

Developing an environment that is both conducive to measuring supplier performance and produces effective and meaningful results is sometimes easier in theory than in practice. As discussed in chapter 14, measurement systems need to be structured in a way that identifies the metric, allows data to be captured easily and reliably, and is a process which adds net value to the profitability of the organisation.

The collection and analysis of the data is however only the initial phase of the activity. The Sustainable Procurement team will then utilise the findings in constructive and on-going supplier development dialogue. These meetings help focus all the parties on the core objective of providing a particular product or service in a responsible manner, in line with *the Sustainable Business* stated objectives.

Where long term contracts are in place with a focus on service levels, problem solving and joint initiatives, meeting schedules can often occur on a weekly, monthly or quarterly basis. For example, within some of the UK military contracts, suppliers are required to enter into gain-share and pain-share agreements allowing contract opportunities to be investigated with a shared reward programme. This motivates both parties to seek and implement cost reduction and service enhancement ideas; ideas and project plans are discussed in what are referred to as Joint Quarterly Review Meetings, where they are measured against a SOAR (Supplier Opportunities Assessment Review) to establish success and savings achieved. Where initiatives prove exceptionally beneficial, they are then extended across other suppliers, other vehicles, or other parts of the operational fleet.

One particular example of this involved some suppliers when the UK Tornado F3 fleet were taken out of service. With so many of the parts inter- changeable between the different Tornado variants, suppliers were encouraged to participate in a programme entitled "Reduce to Produce" (RTP). In this initiative, the decommissioned F3 aircraft were stripped of any interchangeable parts. These recovered assets then went through a quality and serviceability assessment before being fed back into the supply chain servicing the remaining GR4 fleet. This both reduced cost for GR4 repairs, as well as prolonging the life of the serviceable assets and minimising carbon and raw material impact of buying new assets – see figure 6.6. As the GR4 fleet approaches retirement, this highly successful philosophy looks to be reutilised to generate repair holidays and reduce maintenance costs.

Furthermore, as part of the endeavour to make best use of the resources, the supplier is closely involved with the management of spare parts required for the military vehicles. By generating this engagement, the supplier can help reduce the inventory levels, enabling surplus assets to be returned or recycled through the supplier's networks. This both reduces the supplier's cost (through lower manufacturing costs) and the user's costs (through lower disposal rates, better use of financial resources and improvements in inventory costs) as well as enhancing *the Planet* impact by allowing better use of raw materials and extended product life cycles.

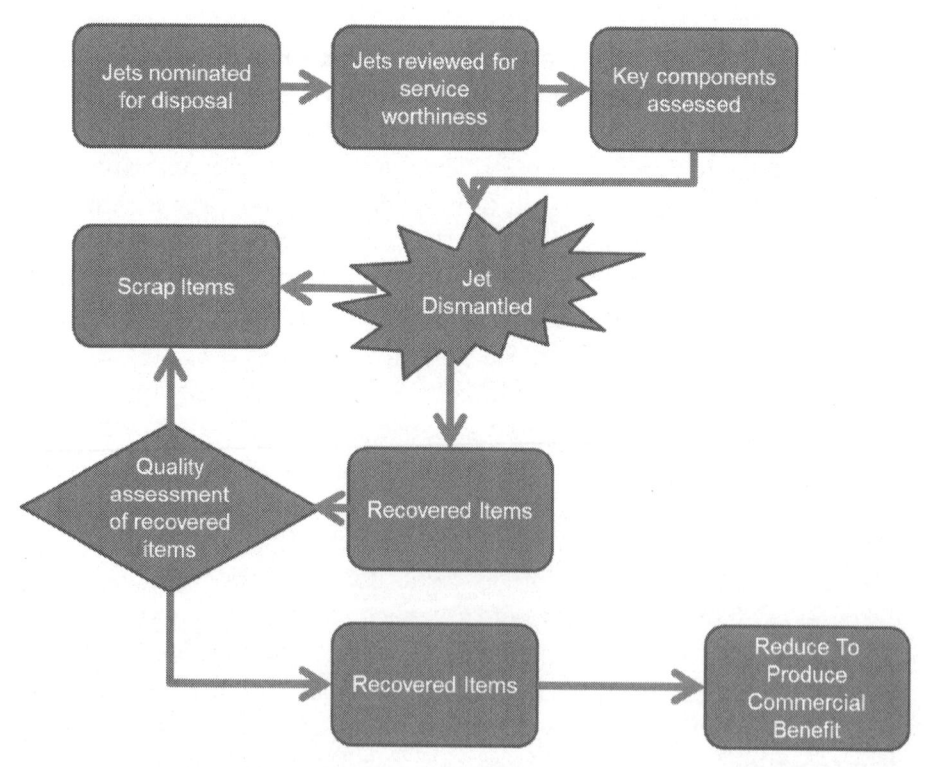

Figure 6.6 – RTP Process

Design of measurement systems is discussed in more depth in chapter 14, however producing an agreed and sustainable measurement structure will help in the development and on-going support of the relationship.

Where such measures are tied into contractual obligations and reward schemes, the supplier, in return for his extended effort enjoys real benefit in either recognition or financial returns, providing added motivation to the win-win partnership.

On-going supplier management may not relate purely to direct performance but also to the wider "health" of the supplier. Recalling the Carter 10C model, this model can be adapted to allow on-going measurement of supplier's suitability. By adopting this model for supplier management, the organisation can continue the assessment of 10 "C" characteristics, improving supplier continuity and reducing risk in the organisation; both features of *the Sustainable Business*. The analysis is undertaken to make sure, for example, that capacity does not become an issue, to show when the financial health of the supplier deteriorates, to highlight where the supplier's commitment to quality wanes, or where the supplier's cost moves out of line with the market.

The issue of the supplier's cost becoming uncompetitive is an age-old concern of contract management so how can we future proof the contract price to ensure we are always getting a great deal? This is a key commercial consideration for the Sustainable Procurement team, and if adopted the Category Management function as well.

Category Management focuses nominated team members on a specific segment of a market, on a particular product, customer type or some other supply or demand facet. This enables the organisation to develop a product or service offering to directly and competitively address a particular market or area of customer demand – see case study 6.

A key role for the Category Manager, therefore, is to maintain a supplier and competitor price file. This price file will record prevailing market prices, demand options, product types, and the dynamics of the market including mergers and takeovers, failures, new entrants etc. A good Category Manager lives and breathes his category: he is the company expert on that product line; he knows all the suppliers; he constantly looks for innovation, competitive advantage, new products or suppliers and complementary products that could increase the volume or margin quotient.

Assessing the Total Cost of Sustainable Ownership

As mentioned in earlier chapters, cost is a key driver of both profit and the success of *the Sustainable Business*. Cost is however more than the amount of money charged on the invoice; it is the total cost of the transaction including all the ancillary charges for the product from identifying the need through to the disposal, and thereafter until the final point of impact. Hitherto – see Chapter 4 – this has been defined as the Total Cost of Sustainable Ownership.

The Sustainable Procurement team is focused on the total cost at all times. It recognises the need to understand the mix between operational and capital costs, and the long term sustainability costs, as well as the need to fulfil the sales ambitions of the company

Analysis of the costs over the life of a product is by no means easy, and will involve some degree of trust in the supplier, as well as accuracy in the forecast of use, cost movements, contribution to the business case, maintenance, consumables, resale values, etc. It will however also need to address the issue of impact, recyclability, longevity of use, use of end of life materials, etc; it will also need to challenge the issue of waste.

Over the course of the life of an asset, and business in general, there is a call to minimise the waste that occurs. The STOPWASTE model identifies the various causes of waste to help *the Sustainable Business* reduce waste wherever possible, see figure 6.7:

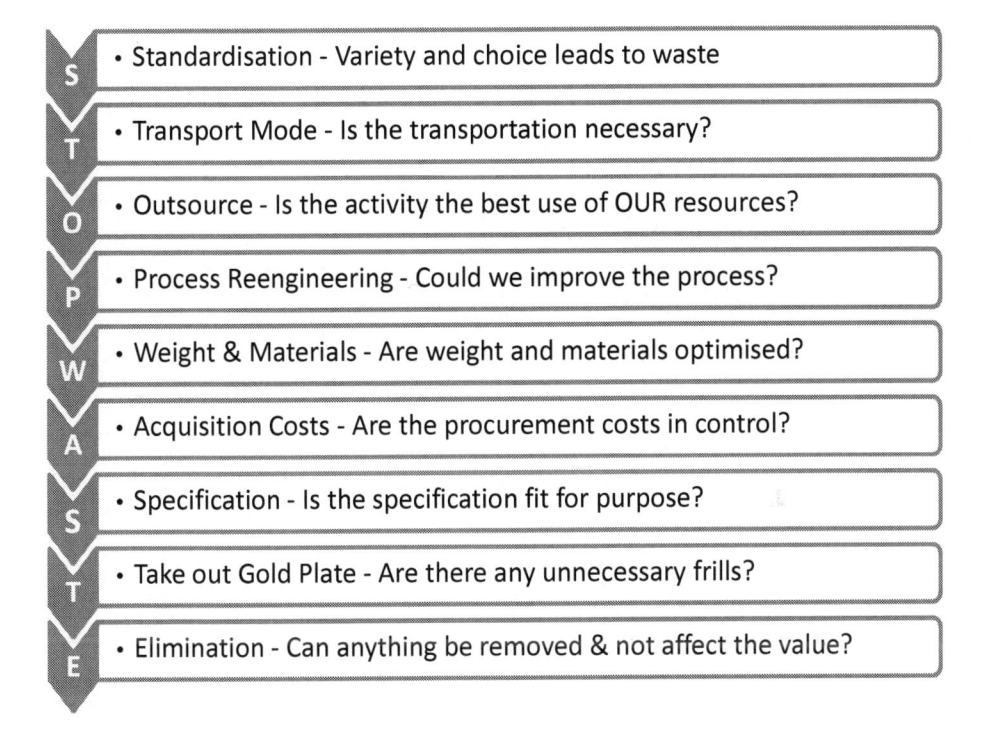

- **S** • Standardisation - Variety and choice leads to waste
- **T** • Transport Mode - Is the transportation necessary?
- **O** • Outsource - Is the activity the best use of OUR resources?
- **P** • Process Reengineering - Could we improve the process?
- **W** • Weight & Materials - Are weight and materials optimised?
- **A** • Acquisition Costs - Are the procurement costs in control?
- **S** • Specification - Is the specification fit for purpose?
- **T** • Take out Gold Plate - Are there any unnecessary frills?
- **E** • Elimination - Can anything be removed & not affect the value?

Figure 6.7 – STOPWASTE Model

As part of the Sustainable Procurement's activities therefore, careful consideration should be paid to what this ultimate cost might be, both for *the Sustainable Business*, and for the wider planet.

Managing Stakeholder Aspirations

And finally, arguably the most important issue for the Sustainable Procurement function is fulfilling Stakeholder aspirations.

At the start of any sourcing activity is a "need", identified by a stakeholder in the organisation. In short, the Sustainable Procurement department is responsible for fulfilling this need and satisfying the stakeholders who are affected. Using Mendlow (see figure 6.9) and others' research we can identify the importance and strength of stakeholders, allowing a better categorisation and management of the respective affairs of each individual stakeholder.

Stakeholder Strategy Matrix

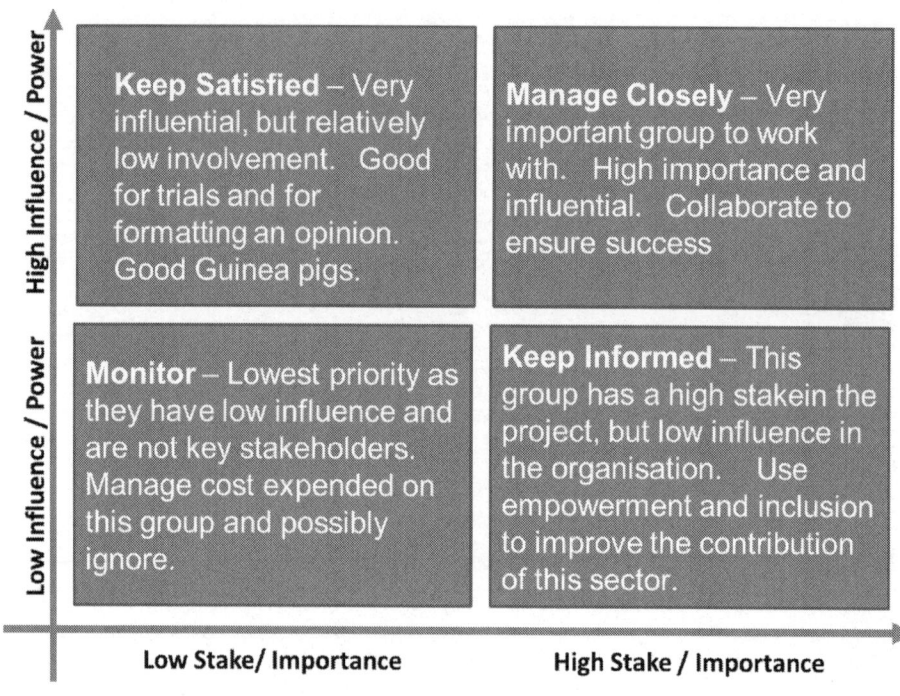

High Influence / Power, Low Stake / Importance:
Keep Satisfied – Very influential, but relatively low involvement. Good for trials and for formatting an opinion. Good Guinea pigs.

High Influence / Power, High Stake / Importance:
Manage Closely – Very important group to work with. High importance and influential. Collaborate to ensure success

Low Influence / Power, Low Stake / Importance:
Monitor – Lowest priority as they have low influence and are not key stakeholders. Manage cost expended on this group and possibly ignore.

Low Influence / Power, High Stake / Importance:
Keep Informed – This group has a high stake in the project, but low influence in the organisation. Use empowerment and inclusion to improve the contribution of this sector.

Figure 6.9 – Stakeholder Strategy

As mentioned previously, where there is a clear demand identified, an unambiguous specification should be generated and signed-off as fit for purpose. Producing a faulty item is one issue, producing an item that is functional but does not meet the needs of the user is inexcusable if it is as a result of poor communication.

Sustainable Procurement conclusion

In conclusion, there is a difficult path to be walked between flexibility, added features, high service levels and future proofing, and over engineering a product or service.

What are important at all times are business continuity and a culture aiming at continuous improvement. Cost reduction is important, but so is the need to furnish the business stakeholders with the tools to develop the business, and to drive the organisation forward: as ever it's a balance.

People make the difference. Having commercially trained and competent employees within the Sustainable Procurement function is an investment.

Frequent Training Needs Analysis (TNA), succession planning, talent mapping, cross postings and secondments help facilitate this, however simple appreciation of a job well done often has an equally beneficial outcome.

The strategic decisions faced by the organisation can be many: to outsource or in-source, local or global, standard or differentiated, to name but a few. Deciding between the different strategic options is explored in later chapters however it remains the role of the Sustainable Procurement team to implement these strategic endeavours as effectively as possible.

Case Study 6 – Metal Conduit and Fittings Market Segment

Consider the market for steel electrical conduit and conduit fittings. A relatively benign and unexciting product sector incorporating tube and fittings generally made from steel and finished either in black enamel, galvanised metal or stainless steel.

In the 1990s, the UK had two main domestic conduit suppliers and around six domestic suppliers of fittings before a large influx of Chinese and Indian manufactured fittings flooded the market. These imports were of varying quality and often a poor finish. A UK campaign by the electrical press was launched to discourage the use of the inferior product, with many organisations banning all imported – particularly Chinese – conduit fittings.

Whilst the publicity affected volumes, these and other overseas sources – including Korean, Pakistani, Russian and others - sought to improve their quality and design, focusing on the features adopted by the brand leaders. Over time, the foreign suppliers developed their manufacturing resource, attained BS/EN quality acceptance, and slowly encroached on the UK market with prices as much as 80% lower than the home grown equivalent.

In response to these market movements, one of the suppliers elected in 1999 to move their production off-shore to the middle east to try and recoup some of their commercial edge. As a relatively low cost manufacturing location, this enabled the organisation to reduce prices significantly to try and maintain competitivity, and enabled them to remain as active market participants, albeit with margins and volumes dramatically lower than previously.

At this time, however the market was suffering from Chinese production capacity released from the newly completed Hong Kong Airport. As a UK colony, the new Airport had been designed by British architects to BS standards, with the local Chinese manufacturers had risen to the challenge developing facilities capable of producing BS standard products; once the airport was completed, these companies inevitably turned their attention to export business, and of course the UK was an obvious target.

From a category management perspective, such a development is of great significance as the market undergoes a radical transformation. This is the classic Porter "New Entrant" force in his five force model discussed in chapter 1. These new sources increased capacity, innovation and competition which saw prices fall by in excess of 40% over a three year period at a time when global steel prices were rising.

Early customer adoption of the new sources of supply, coupled with detailed assessments of quality, capacity, cost and consistency issues enabled organisations to engage these new supply sources, and, despite some early issues, many of the new sources came and became established at the expense of some of the old UK producers.

Conduit fittings, due to their relative small size, were however the easy segment of the market to crack. The wider issue of the conduit market was of more issue. Conduit was produced in 30 metre bundles, or 8 x 3.75m lengths. These bundles were both heavy, and cumbersome, and not ideally suited for shipping over long distances, however it was only a matter of time before this too would be addressed.

In 1999, in the UK there were two main conduit suppliers, each with book and net costs at a very similar level, and neither willing to fracture the market with any standout offers or deals to customers; yet the weight of steel to cost price suggested a significant margin for both companies.

In the absence of any commercial deals offered by either company, the Chinese market in Shenzhen near Hong Kong was scoured for sources of BS standard product. Research produced the names five or six suppliers, these were visited, assessed and the deal done. As a sole importer of Chinese conduit at 40% below the UK market price, one wholesaler gained a significant market advantage on projects for a number of months, both through use of the Chinese product, and from the immediate cut-price offers given in response by the two incumbent suppliers.

The Category Management function understood the market, the main players, the product and its features, as well as the options to develop supply sources, margin and a competitive advantage. The visits to China, the shipping costs, customs, letter of credit incoterms and other investments were notable however the first shipment generated a very significant profit and introduced invaluable leverage in the marketplace.

The Sustainable Business

Notes Page	**Page Ref**

The Sustainable Business

Summary Chapter 7
The Sustainable Supply Chain

Key Learning Points
- The philosophy and definition of a Sustainable Supply Chain
- The importance of the Supply Chain Strategy
- Flow of value and demand
- Identification of value adding activities
- Understanding the service mandate
- Avoidance of waste
- Features of Lean and Just-In-Time processes
- Inventory best practice
- Development of a detailed specification or service standard
- Recognition of the importance of good quality – Fit For Purpose
- Measurement of the COPQ (Cost of Poor Quality)
- Market and product influence of the Supply Chain
- Use of the SIPOC model
- Explanation of Six Sigma
- Causes of issues and use of the Fishbone diagram
- Fundamentals of Logistics & Warehousing
- Explanation of Standard Deviation and statistical techniques
- Managing a stock profile
- Inventory management decisions
- Import/Export processes and instruments
- Understanding of Letters of Credit, Escrow accounts, Incoterms, etc
- Distribution methods and structures
- Warehouse layout options
- Effective use of personnel and utilities
- Management and cross functional team techniques
- Brainstorming and communication

Tool Summary
- Value Chain
- 3 Pillar – 9 Dimensions Model
- SIPOC
- Toyota 7/8 wastes
- Value Analysis
- Fishbone diagram

- Kraljic
- Cost of Poor Quality (COPQ)
- Ansoff Planning tool
- As-Is To-Be
- Managing Risk Model
- Developing Sustainable Strategy
- Incoterms
- Critical Needs Analysis
- ERP Solutions – Enterprise Resource Planning
- Inventory Tools – EOQ, Safety Stock, reorder level, etc
- Standard Deviation

CIPS Syllabus Reference
- Level 4 Sourcing in Procurement and Supply
- Level 4 Negotiating and Contracting in Procurement and Supply
- Level 4 Managing Contracts and Relationships in Procurement and Supply
- Level 5 Sustainability in Supply Chains
- Level 5 Management in Procurement and Supply
- Level 5 Managing Risk in Supply Chains
- Level 5 Improving the competitiveness of Supply Chains
- Level 5 Category management in Procurement and Supply
- Level 5 Operations Management in Supply Chains
- Level 6 Strategic Supply Chain Management
- Level 6 Supply Chain Diligence

Chapter 7: The Sustainable Supply Chain

"A business which makes nothing but money is a poor kind of business" – Henry Ford

A Customer lies at the heart of every business; it is central to the organisation's *raison d'etre*. The organisation needs to take appropriate resources and "mould" them into whatever it is that the Customer wants from you. This input-to-output process is the Supply Chain.

The Supply Chain embodies the core values and is central to all of the organisation's activities. As such, *the Three Pillars* are inevitably entwined in everything that happens within the Supply Chain: its people run the Supply Chain activities; the planet provides many of the raw materials and utilities; and one of the outputs from the Supply Chain should be a profit for the organisation.

> *Having a Sustainable Supply Chain enables the Sustainable Business to deliver products or services to its customers and value to its shareholders, whilst fulfilling its Sustainable Vision.*

At the core of the Supply Chain there lies a strategy; this strategy should focus on its customers, and an overwhelming desire to deliver sublime customer service. As we have seen previously, great customer service is one of the underpinning foundations of *the Profit Pillar*.

Reason enough, therefore, that the Supply Chain is understood in its true context, and the impact that a well-managed Supply Chain can have on the *Three Pillars* is fully appreciated. As with so many other elements of *the Sustainable Business*, the basis of a successful Supply Chain is in the planning, communication and of course the strategy.

Definition of a Supply Chain

The Supply Chain is the process which takes resources, goods, services and information through the organisation, to enable the delivery of goods and services to the Customer. It is the process which fulfils, and hopefully, satisfies the Customer's demands.

The Supply Chain is a dynamic process which reflects the individual demands of the Customer – also known as the "order". It coordinates the inputs, it measures and transmits information through the Supply Chain and aligns activities to deliver a quality solution to the Customer, on time and for an accepted budget. In return, the Customer pays for the goods or services with funds passing back into the business as reward for the effort, and adding value to the bottom line, see figure 7.1.

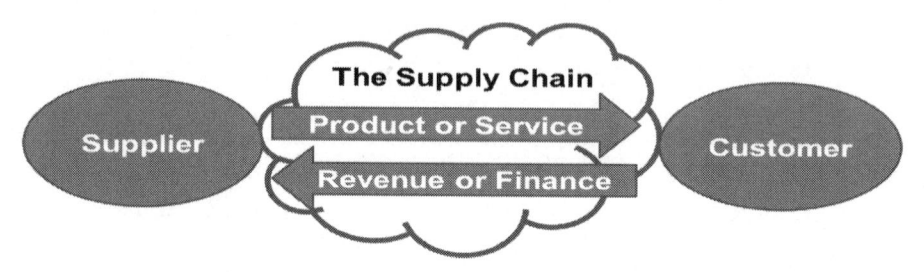

Figure 7.1 – The flow of value through the Supply Chain.

So what do we mean by the term "value"? The secret of a successful and sustainable Supply Chain is its ability to clearly define what it constitutes as "value". The core role of the Supply Chain is of course to Add Value, so it is a good starting point to define what true value is. It is also important to recognise that value will mean different things to different people, to different Supply Chains and to different organisations.

Success is best achieved with focus. Whether the value targeted is higher profit, improved employee relations, cost reduction, enhanced customer reputation, or lower carbon output, measuring and targeting these values will improve the chance of success.

Understanding where in the organisation value is created is key. Use of the Value Chain Model – see figure 7.2 – can help pinpoint the value adding activities which need to be nurtured, and the areas which need to be revised:

Identifying the functions and activities in the business which adds value is not always as easy as it sounds. Understanding where cost savings can be realised is perhaps achieved with scrutiny of the financial accounts, and the profit margin equation may give some of the answers, but what makes the customer smile? How important is Supply Chain continuity, and how does caring about the environment help the business?

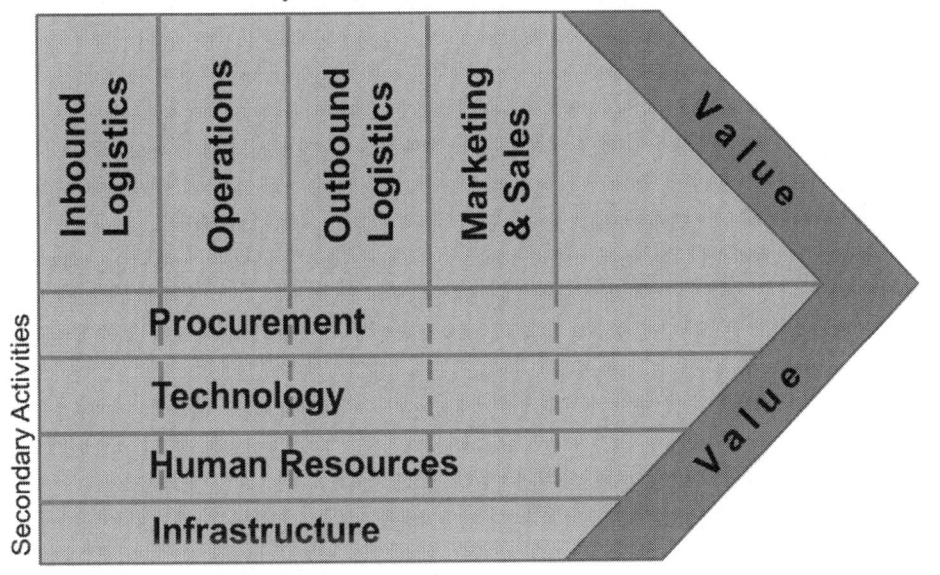

Figure 7.2 – The Value Chain

Within the organisation there exist business processes and procedures which are the foundations of the Supply Chain. These processes reflect the core building elements of a Supply Chain which include:
- A customer;
- A customer's demand;
- A business process
- Suppliers of raw materials or services;
- Coordinated activities and resources to fulfil the demand;
- Information and measurements of process;
- And value for the Stakeholders; the Suppliers; the Customer; and the organisation of which the Supply Chain is part.

Each of these needs to be considered when developing a sustainable Supply Chain strategy.

Coordination is the key to a successful Supply Chain. It ensures that goods, people, capital, finance, contractors, and so on, are all where they need to be, when they are required – not early and not late – to enable the seamless delivery of goods or services to the customer without any waste.

> **Rule: Value is the motivation for all the parties, all of the time, and is their motivation for taking risk**

Consider a restaurant delivering a service to a customer. We know that within *the Sustainable Business*, the *Profit Pillar* demands a quality service to develop a reputation which helps nurture a sustainable sales-stream. Accordingly, aspects which surround the diners such as the ambience are important, however the effectiveness of the kitchen and the waiter services will be the primary factor which determines the experience. The restaurant should meet the customer expectations. The way a luxury restaurant behaves will differ significantly to fast food establishments; for example, when was traditional dining etiquette mandatory in a burger bar?

Whilst easy to say, and without addressing the operational issues which are entailed, simple guidelines for a successful restaurant operation might look something like the following:

1. The Customer should be made to feel welcome;
2. The Customer will need to order some food, so in comfortable time they should receive a menu;
3. A drinks order helps enhance the experience, and provides additional revenue for the restaurant;
4. Once the order is taken, starters should be served first;
5. All diners should be served at the same time;
6. A short respite should be allowed between courses to allow diners to rest and socialise, to replenish drinks (increasing the revenue) and to allow the kitchen to finalise the second course; if the second course is served too quickly and the diners will feel rushed, left too long and they become impatient or some meals will become cold;
7. And so on....

And so it is with the Supply Chain: goods need to arrive in the right quantity, at the right place at the right time, and to the right quality. Failure in any single element will result in a diminished quality of output, poor service and a potentially tarnished reputation.

As mentioned previously, waste is the scourge of *the Sustainable Business*. Wherever possible, waste should be avoided, the astute business will be looking for waste every moment of every day, in everything they do. But waste also includes missed opportunities – for example in the restaurant scenario, missing the drinks order whilst the customer chooses their meal or failing to secure the coffee order at the end of the meal.

> **Food for Thought**: Within the Supply Chain, for most organisations, there is the greatest potential to generate and reduce waste.

Frustrating for the conscientious onlooker is the reticence of some organisations to address waste citing that "remedy of the issue is not the best use of resources", or "it's a necessary cost to the business", or worse still "the waste has been factored into the price to the customer". Possibly fuelled by envy, the Toyota and others focus on waste has been referred to by some as "obsessive". They measure vehicle output to the second, they measure process accuracy to the millimetre, and they investigate any differential however small. If a car was delivered 1 second early and of the right quality they ask "why and how can we capture and embed the benefit", yet they are equally wary as to whether any shortcuts have been taken which might compromise quality in the longer term.

The importance of quality has marched steadily up the corporate agenda over the past few decades and is now a customer given. Gone are the days of the consumer accepting poor performance, late delivery, or broken promises. Choice is ever present; if one supplier fails to deliver there will be another ready to step into the breach. Indeed, in some countries, legislation now protects against poor quality, for example The Sale of Goods Act in the UK.

> **Food for Thought**: If we can save a second per widget, and we manufacture 100 widgets per day, that is an annual equivalent to saving one working day.

Core to the success of the Supply Chain is its management. As discussed in chapter 14, measurement is the driver of management decision making. The effective Supply Chain is measured from start to finish, information is its lifeblood. Systems such as ERP solutions (Enterprise Resource Planning) or a WMS (Warehouse Management System) now steer the day to day operation of many a business, but it is still information that decides the direction and decisions taken within its operations.

Measurement and the results from these measures will affect the organisational targets, its KPI's business ratios, and consequently the motivation and support of many of its stakeholders. This is an important issue often overlooked by IT implementers, but considered outside the remit of this book, other than by acknowledging that a failure to recognise *the People Pillar* will undermine *the Sustainable Business* going forward. By way of an example, one of the authors' former employers lost its market leading status and saw a significant erosion of market share, profit and customer credibility through a single IT decision. The system and implementers began dictating strategy and future policy to make the organisation fit the computer system dynamics. This arguably started a cancerous erosion of its position and market image which it is still struggling to remedy.

The Supply Chain and the Three Pillars Principle

In the opening chapters of this book, *the Three Pillars* concept of sustainability was introduced: *People, Profit and Planet.* These were discussed in terms of their underpinning dimensions, see figure 7.3:
The Three Pillars represent the essence of sustainability, they are the foundation of *the Sustainable Business'* vision and its operations; equally, by definition, they are the bedrock of the Supply Chain therein.

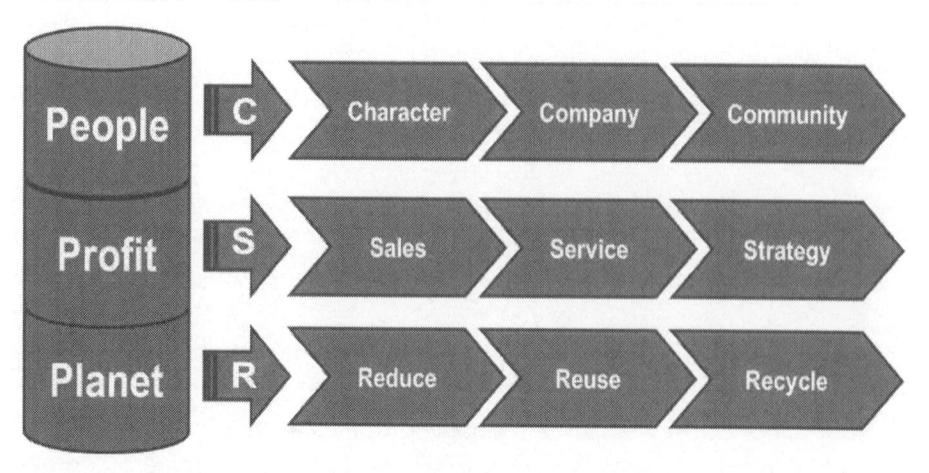

People — C → Character → Company → Community
Profit — S → Sales → Service → Strategy
Planet — R → Reduce → Reuse → Recycle

Figure 7.3 – The Three Pillars and their associated dimensions

People and process unite to drive the Supply Chain onwards, processing the inputs – of which people are one – in order to add value and **Profit** whilst limiting the impact on the **Planet**, and generating an output which satisfies customer demands. *The Sustainable Business* therefore recognises that once again *the Pillars* have a driving force in the achievement of its overarching sustainable aspirations.

Equally, each of the three people dimensions are sustainable stakeholders in the Supply Chain's activity: *the Character* will be employed in the Supply Chain; *the Company* will enjoy the fruits of the people in the Supply Chain; and *the Community* will suffer the impacts – which can be both positive (through improved employment prospects, community involvement, etc) as well as negative (such as traffic congestion, noise, inflationary pressures, etc).

> **Definition: A "Sustainable Stakeholder" is someone who affects or is affected by a sustainable issue**

Identifying the *Sustainable Stakeholders* will enable *the Sustainable Business* to develop strategy and managerial direction to help coach and nurture the affected parties throughout the Supply Chain. Incorporating external people initiatives helps bond the various elements.

Of primary importance to the success and purpose of the Supply Chain however is the *Profit Pillar*, with the three *Profit* dimensions: *Sales, Service and Strategy*. Each dimension clearly features in the Supply Chain, the ultimate goal of which is to fulfil demand from the customer and improve its commercial success. Ideally, through great service, this demand will lead to further orders (sales) either directly from the original customer or from other users via word of mouth or positive publicity, thereby generating a sustainable sales-stream.

Great businesses recognise that the best way to develop a healthy sales pipeline is to nurture existing customers; here the difficult work of "opening the door" has already been done. This is best achieved with the highest quality of customer service.

> **Food for Thought**: Why do companies battle to open new customer accounts when they are not maximising benefit from the accounts they already have?

Understanding the market is a major step on the road to determining the customer base and its needs, and to forming a sustainable Supply Chain strategy.

Companies such as Virgin have broken long established competitive equilibriums, with a deep understanding of the respective market and the prevailing Supply Chain infrastructure, challenging the *status quo* that exists and offering something different. They offer a service that is consumer driven, not supplier focused: for example Virgin records changed the music industry by signing niche performers and developed new channels to purchase product; Virgin Airways replicated the efforts of Laker airways but succeeded in developing a credible alternative to British Airways *et al*; Virgin Trains have shown that rail travel need not be a chore, and so on. This *status quo* is often protected by high barriers to entry, or closed networks preventing access from "outside the club".

Virgin State: "We believe in making a difference. Virgin stands for value for money, quality, innovation, fun and a sense of competitive challenge. We deliver a quality service by empowering our employees and we facilitate and monitor customer feedback to continually improve the customer's experience through innovation."

Throughout the 1980s and 1990s there was a global sea-change — albeit at different paces in different parts of the globe — with the aim of fostering market competition with even ex-communist regimes now enjoying *relatively* open markets and flexible supply chains. In parts of China such as Shanghai, relative freedom is now commonplace with global brands now in evidence and a softening in the traditional market pressures.

Food for Thought: Hong Kong retains top spot of the world's freest economy *(BBC Website 12th January 2012)*

These open markets have not been without their issues, and undoubtedly, in some sectors, and in some countries there have been mistakes. In others, some suppliers have played the game with outstanding success. Take for example the deregulation of the European electrical power networks. Here, countries such as Germany and the United Kingdom raced to embrace the free market philosophy, leading the charge for open competition, improved service and choice for the consumer. In contrast the French regime played a shrewd and tactically astute game of wait and pounce. By delaying deregulation of the French market, it enabled Electricité de France, through acquisition, to develop a market leading presence in other European markets, financed by government support and their monopoly profits in their home market. See Table 7.4. These acquisitions helped establish EDF as one of the pre-eminent power providers by market share around the world but especially in Europe (with 20%+ market share), granting them a critical mass that makes challenge extremely difficult. This fundamentally changed the dynamics of the market, introducing new barriers to entry.

Country	Trading Company
Austria	Vero
Belgium	Semobis,
Brazil	Lidil
China	Synergie
Germany	EDF Ostalbkreis & EDF Weinsberg
Hungary	Démász
Italy	EDF Energia Italia
Netherlands	Finelex
Spain	EDF Iberica
Sweden	Skandrenkraft
UK	EDF London Power, British Energy Group PLC
USA	EDF Inc, EnXco, EDF Trading

In many deregulated markets, however, change, progress and choice can be seen to have evolved. The Supply Chains that exist within markets such as the airline industry have changed dramatically with deregulation of the former flag carriers. Although airlines such as Lufthansa, Air France, BA, Liberia, etc, are still very major participants, others such as Ryanair, Virgin and Monarch have developed into major brands albeit focusing on being a success in specific segments of the market.

Ryanair for example, has established itself as one of the main low cost airlines with an extensive "no frills" service across Europe. They have built a product based on low cost with no extras built into the price. Extracting any element within the Supply Chain which can be shown to be a cost driver – for example the meal, checking in, administration and policing of aspects such as seat allocation, etc – has allowed Ryanair to reduce ticket prices significantly, albeit at the expense of some customers bemoaning the service gap between Ryanair and the traditional airlines.

> **Rule: You get what you pay for!**

The biggest differentiator however has been the development of smaller, often rural airports, rather than clogging the traditional hub airports of Frankfurt, Heathrow, Charles de Gaulle, etc. This has had the advantage of spreading the transport loading, and arguably reducing the environmental impact of flying through some of the congestion these other airports suffer from, with the consequential benefits of lower fuel usage, fewer delays and easier access.

Ryanair in Europe, Virgin Blue in Australia, Silkair in Indonesia, JetBlue or Southwest in the USA and many others are proof enough that customers want the choice of what they pay for and what they don't. Particularly in times of hardship and austerity measures, passengers and companies are choosing the no-frill option as an acceptable alternative to the mainstream carriers. The significant rise in the 2011 profits of Easyjet attributed to this change in sentiment. If the customer experience was so unacceptable, these businesses would not have survived and flourished to the extent they have. For the Southwestern Airline view on this subject, see figure 7.5.

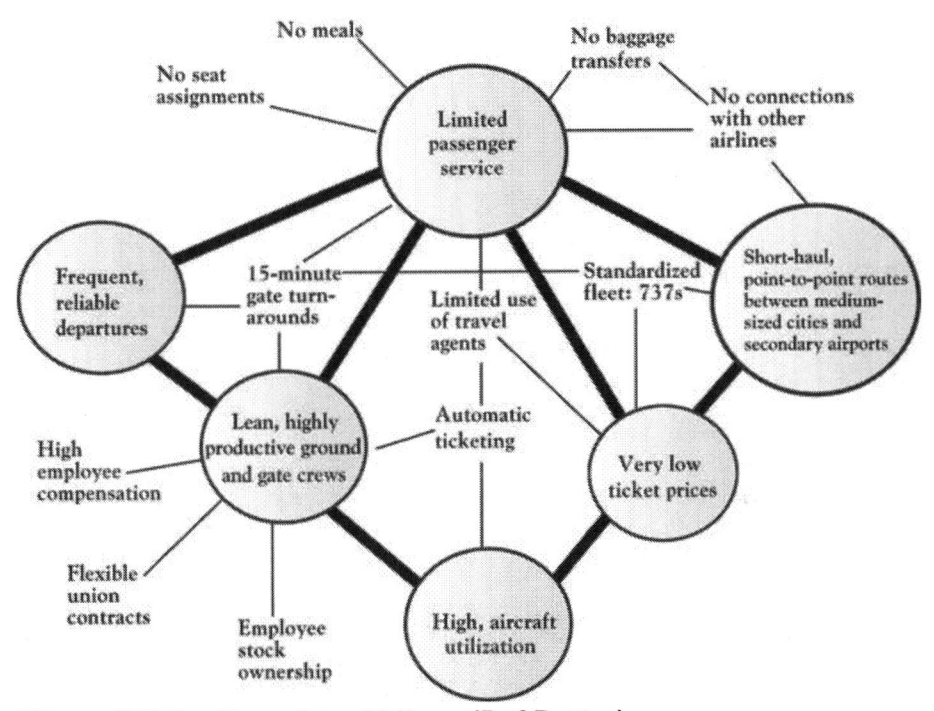

Figure 7.5 Southwestern Airlines (Ref Porter)

Diagram labels:
- No meals
- No seat assignments
- No baggage transfers
- No connections with other airlines
- Limited passenger service
- Frequent, reliable departures
- 15-minute gate turn-arounds
- Limited use of travel agents
- Standardized fleet: 737s
- Short-haul, point-to-point routes between medium-sized cities and secondary airports
- High employee compensation
- Lean, highly productive ground and gate crews
- Automatic ticketing
- Very low ticket prices
- Flexible union contracts
- Employee stock ownership
- High, aircraft utilization

> **Rule: Great service is not just about what is delivered, it is as much about value for money and meeting expectation**

But *the Profit Pillar* needs more in its sustainable Supply Chain strategy. It needs a cost strategy, a customer development strategy, and a marketing strategy amongst others.

> **Food for Thought**: Low cost airlines have moved air travel from a high class but expensive service experience to a functional activity and lower cost alternative to rail or road travel. The comparison with rail travel ironically seems more logical than with other airlines. Traditionally and on many rail routes, seats are not allocated, you sit where you want, you buy a ticket either on-line or from a machine, and no meal is included in the ticket. Customers buy the basic service, and top up where they want something extra, for example a meal.

Cost is central to the profit mechanism – See figure 7.6 – and hence imperative for *the Sustainable Business* to embrace. Understanding cost is addressed elsewhere in this book with dialogue on the Total Cost of Sustainable Ownership, by way of example, but this reiterates the need to manage and sustain an affordable and competitive cost base. This is done with: effective commercial dialogue by the Sustainable Procurement team; through discipline at a business case and managerial level to maintain responsible budget control; through the development of affordable design and production solutions; and with managed expectations of stakeholders.

Cost and restriction of budget invariably creates division and conflict, yet it is essential for the *Sustainable Business* to maintain a strong stance. Areas such as fuel, risk, time and inventory are very difficult to accurately establish and monitor in many Supply Chains, yet these can create a cancerous erosion of profit and capital.

Profit = Sales Revenue − Total Costs

Figure 7.6 – The sales and profit equation

> **Rule: Look after the pennies and the pounds will look after themselves**

Referring to the Toyota Seven Wastes in chapter 7 we recognise that Inventory, Transportation, Motion, Waiting, Over-production, Over-processing, and Defects in a business are all areas where waste can accumulate and fester. But there is now an eighth waste identified – the production of something the customer does not want or an item which involves a cost investment but which generates little or no value. Amalgamating this with concepts such as the STOPWASTE model (see figure 6.8), and Value Engineering we can generate a far more detailed picture of our Supply Chain waste profile, both corporately and personally. Managing and addressing these waste areas is a key responsibility of the Supply Chain Management team, albeit with other areas of the business undoubtedly wanting to have their say. Finance and Procurement amongst others, enjoy heavy involvement in cost cutting programmes or sanctioning of expenditure, partly as a way of easing their own respective business pressures, but also to some extent to enable them to revel in the kudos that comes with success. Cost saving analysis and cost management, as subjects, are covered on a number of occasions in this book and are a necessity for *the Sustainable Business* and for the responsible Supply Chain operation to consider.

> **Food for Thought**: There is a Chinese expression which can be translated as: *The busy man has time to blow out the flames, but doesn't douse the embers.* How much time and thus money would be saved by dealing with the underlying issues in the Supply Chain?

Supply Chain Analysis

Understanding the Supply Chain in its entirety is the basis of Strategic Supply Chain Analysis. *The Sustainable Business* needs to clearly understand where it is now, and where it wants to get to. Numerous tools mentioned hitherto assist us in understanding the Supply Chain and where included elsewhere in this volume, will only be recounted in summary here for reference.

The analysis overview is very simply highlighted by the SIPOC model. This endeavours to simplify the Supply Chain in terms of the suppliers who supply inputs to a process which generates outputs which feed through to the Customer – see figure 7.7. This helps breakdown the Supply Chain into clearly identifiable elements that have defined meaning within the overall focus.

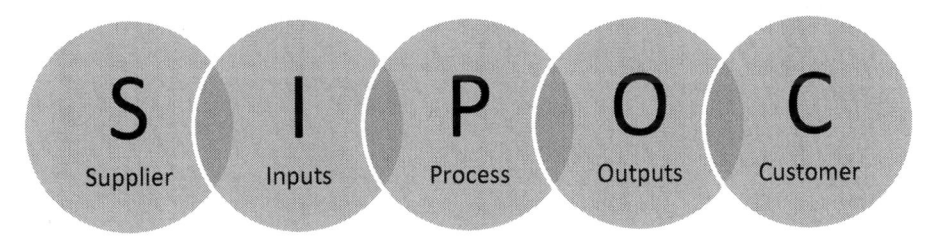

S Supplier **I** Inputs **P** Process **O** Outputs **C** Customer

Figure 7.7 – The SIPOC model

Consider a typical office cleaning company. They would have a number of different **suppliers** who provide the **inputs** into the process for example

raw materials such as cleaning chemicals, labour, vehicles, stationary, etc. The cleaning operatives would then go about their cleaning **process**, to achieve the desired **outputs** – for example empty bins, clean toilets, vacuumed carpets, washed cups, etc – with the sole purpose of fulfilling their contractual obligations and to satisfy the **customer** requirements.
The SIPOC model is especially useful for identifying where, in the Supply Chain, issues – particularly associated with quality – are being generated. This can be used in conjunction with a fishbone analysis – see figure 7.8 – to identify the possible root-causes of a quality issue or process problem.

These root causes generally fall into categories, for example – Machine, Man, Method, Mother Nature, Measurements or Materials. Using the cleaning example, if the customer raises a complaint about unclean cups (Quality issue) we can look back and check if the process (washing-up) is fit for purpose (Method), is the detergent satisfactory (Materials), is the operator (Man) performing as would be expected, and so on (although clearly some branches of the fishbone may not be populated in all circumstances). Brainstorming and "Voice of the Customer" techniques can help identify these core issues.

This could then lead us to consider the inputs, for example the detergent and then the respective supplier. Assessing whether a process or business operation is fit for purpose is examined further in chapter 9.

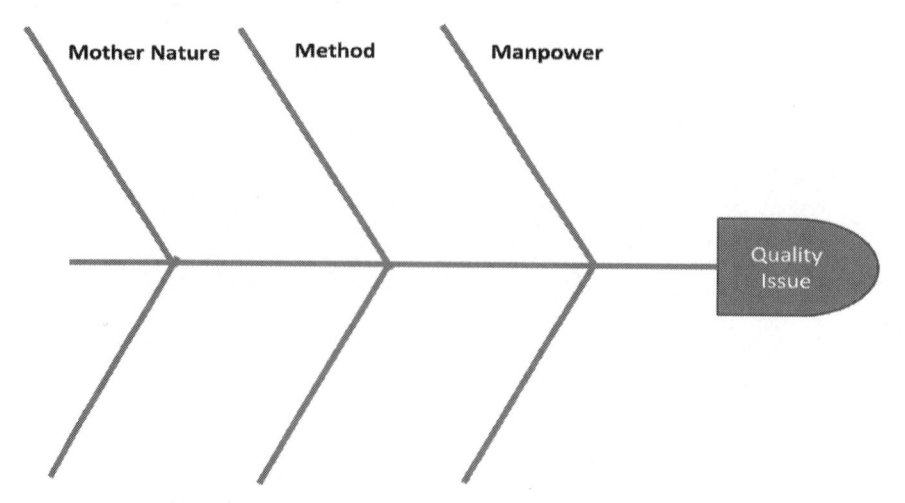

7.8 – Fishbone Diagram

> **Food for Thought**: Six Rules for Brainstorming:
> 1. Everybody is equal, there are no ranks, bosses, grades or any other differentiation of participants;
> 2. There are no bad ideas at the brainstorming stage, what is wanted is as many ideas as possible;
> 3. Encourage ideas which are as wacky and diverse as possible;
> 4. Manage dialogue making sure everyone can and does speak, and that only one conversation occurs at any one time – Participants need to concentrate as this may well spawn other ideas;
> 5. Develop ideas to try and delve deeper into a specific area;
> 6. All ideas are recorded with elimination happing after the Brainstorming has been concluded;

When we consider the current status of the Supply Chain it raises the inevitable question of where we need to be to achieve our goal, and to deliver customer needs. This is the "As-Is" / "To Be" question, and we can consider this from a number of different perspectives.

Furthermore, figure 7.9 highlights some of the common models – many discussed hitherto – that can be used both within the operation and the wider market to understand how the business is performing. This drives the strategic review and should identify the financial, resource, training and asset requirements needed to steer *the Sustainable Business* to its utopic destination.

Internal / External Environment	Costs / Waste Management	Market & Product Analysis
• SWOT Analysis • PESTLE Analysis	• Total Cost Of Sustainable Ownership • STOPWASTE • Activity Based Costing • 3E	• 5 Force Model • Market Analysis • BCG Matrix •

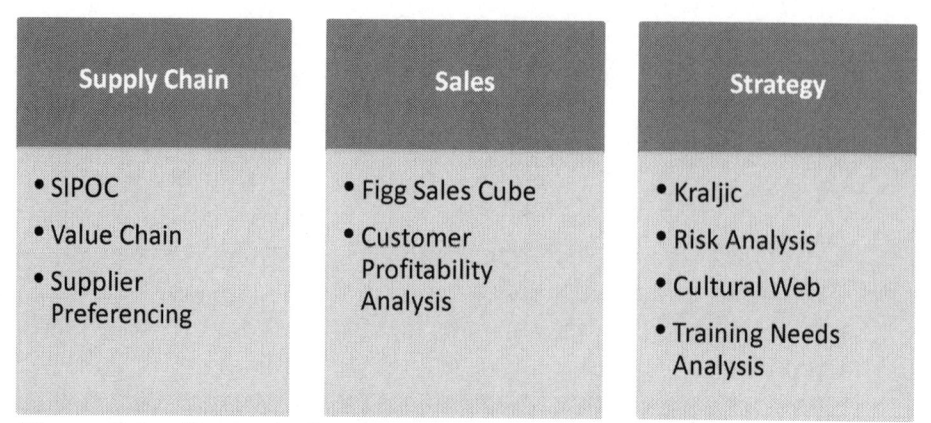

Supply Chain	Sales	Strategy
• SIPOC • Value Chain • Supplier Preferencing	• Figg Sales Cube • Customer Profitability Analysis	• Kraljic • Risk Analysis • Cultural Web • Training Needs Analysis

Figure 7.9 – Example Supply Chain Analysis Models

Clearly the outcome of any such analysis will be reflective of the organisation in question. Each model is intended to simplify and pinpoint the specific areas needing attention, i.e. those identified above or elsewhere in this book. For a full list see Annex 1.

Furthermore, these models will help the user recognise the key issues that will drive Supply Chain success with the identification of costs, waste, lead-time, CSFs (Critical Success Factors), customer requirements, opportunities, risk, etc. These tools will also help model and map the Supply Chain.

The As-is/To-Be review highlights a "strategic gap" which underpins the formation of the strategy. The Ansoff model – see figure 7.10 – addresses the need for a coherent strategy, breaking the planning process down into manageable and distinct steps, each with its accompanying assessment or management models intended to drive planning, budgets, process, project programming, etc.

In some circumstances the strategy may require a fundamental overhaul of process and policy. In such instances, a detailed project and change process would accompany the strategic initiatives identified: such a process is explored in more depth in chapter 11.

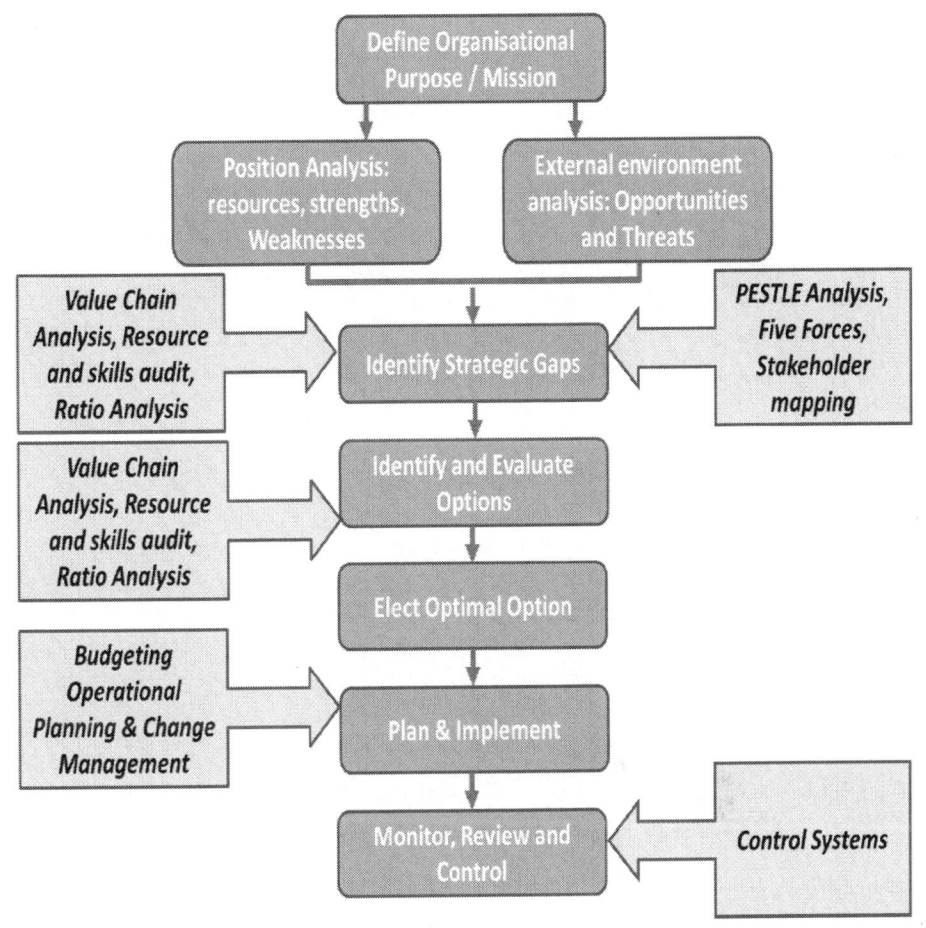

Figure 7.10 – Ansoff Planning Model

Development of a Sustainable Strategy is fundamentally interlinked with the People-Profit-Planet model at all times; in the Supply Chain instance, this will drive costs, resources and people engaged in the operation to ensure longevity. The cost needs to be realistically measured against true and real value, whilst reflecting risk and market trends. Prior to the 2008 credit crash this was evidently omitted, most notably within the USA mortgage operations Freddie Mac and Fannie Mae where a rational assessment of the true value of investments became distorted with targets and business momentum usurping reality.

> **Rule: What goes up, must come down**

The concepts of "Risk" and "Longevity" are not compatible bedfellows. By definition, "Risk" is a calculated gamble. Winning, as any bookmaker will tell you, will not last forever, thereby negating any ambition of longevity.

Yet all activities involve some element of risk; merely getting out of bed in the morning introduces risk into our lives. Reward is allocated in direct relation to how much risk is taken, without this reward nobody would ever take risks. Consider a spin on a roulette table: odds are measured relative to the risk taken. Ignoring the zero or green slot (which introduces the croupier's margin), red/black, high/low numbers or even/odd bets pay double; a specific number within the thirty six numbers pays odds of thirty six to one; and so on.

Probably the most important aspects of a Sustainable Supply Chain however are cost and the value added. If we recall our fundamental business case decision criteria – a project or operation should only occur in a business focused on longevity, if it adds net value, i.e. value added is greater than the cost incurred.

Specification

Identified earlier, the "Eighth Waste" is "producing something which the customer doesn't want". Establishing the customer aspirations is therefore essential to generating a sustainable outcome.

Producing a detailed and effective specification is however easier said than done. Consider a specification stating a colour. According to the RAL colour coding systems there are 36 different greens, so immediately use of the word "green" could cause an issue, especially where a customer's brand makes a clear distinction; the Pantone colour classification produces similar results.

> **Food for Thought**: The iconic Macdonald's "Golden Arches" are constructed using two colours: Yellow (Pantone ref 123) and Red (Pantone 485)

Getting detailed stakeholder or customer input is therefore essential. Use of effective questioning skills will help identify the core requirements, and enable an accurate specification to be produced. The more accurate the specification, the greater the likelihood of the output being deemed fit for purpose.

Understanding the proposed life expectancy of a product is an important consideration towards ensuring that the output is well received. If a product is anticipated to last a year and it lasts for just six months, then dissatisfaction will prevail. *The Profit Pillar* demands high levels of service to drive the sales pipeline onwards and into the future. Longevity demands preservation of the supplier's reputation.

> **Food for Thought**: Accurate and reliable asset life projections are essential for the analysis of many business cases. Indeed, with some organisations, a capital purchase will have a life expectancy, at the end of which the asset is removed from service and sold. This is in stark contrast to organisations which will push an asset way beyond its anticipated life, mending and patching to keep the asset in service – but how efficiently is the asset then performing and how much is the maintenance and repair process costing?

The specification should recognise aesthetic needs and consider the impact of the selection of material and process. Use of metals such as freshly extracted aluminium contain a significant extraction legacy, with recycled aluminium considerably less. Specifying recycled materials can make a huge difference and should always be considered by *the Sustainable Business*; choice of materials is explored further in chapter 10.

> **Food for Thought**: Recycled aluminium requires only 5 per cent of the energy required to make "new aluminium". Blending recycled metal with new metal allows considerable energy savings as well as the efficient use of process heat. There is no difference between primary and recycled aluminium in terms of quality or properties. (Reference International Aluminium Institute)

When specifying products, careful consideration should be given to the compatibility of the product with the existing solutions. Even at a micro-scale this can have implications. For example, when specifying nuts and bolts, exact matching of the metals is essential to prevent bimetallic corrosion i.e. corrosion that occurs when two metals are in direct contact. This is often the cause of nuts and bolts that become immovable; both nut, bolt and washer need to be made of exactly the same metal to prevent this occurring; merely saying "stainless steel" is not enough, it needs to be the exact grade that it cited.

> **Rule: Under promise and over deliver**

Furthermore, demanding specific components, product ranges or manufacturers can have dramatic service and inventory benefits for an organisation. This in turn can be used to extract improved commercial agreements (i.e. enhancing the *Profit Pillar*), reduce waste (through reduction in obsolescence or inventory levels), improve service levels (with better understanding and use of inventory), and so on.

More critical than anything else, however, is the way in which a specification is presented and how conformity is enforced by management. There are many different ways of presenting a specification see figure 7.11:

The Supplier

The selection and support of effective suppliers in the Supply Chain is of paramount importance. As mentioned previously in chapter 6, the supplier selection and tendering process along with the Carter 10C model strive to ensure that, notwithstanding competitiveness, the strongest and most sustainable suppliers are identified to support the organisation.

For example, suppliers need to have the capacity to deliver the volume of product required by the Supply Chain; the product or service supplied should be of a consistent type; the supplier should have a responsible approach to quality; have control of its process; and so on. Equally, attention should also be paid to protect against negative aspects such as the supplier's view of contamination, dubious sources of funding, support of less reputable causes, in short, verify that the supplier is "Clean". As stated previously, the Carter 10C model ensures suppliers are wherever possible sustainable and focused on longevity.

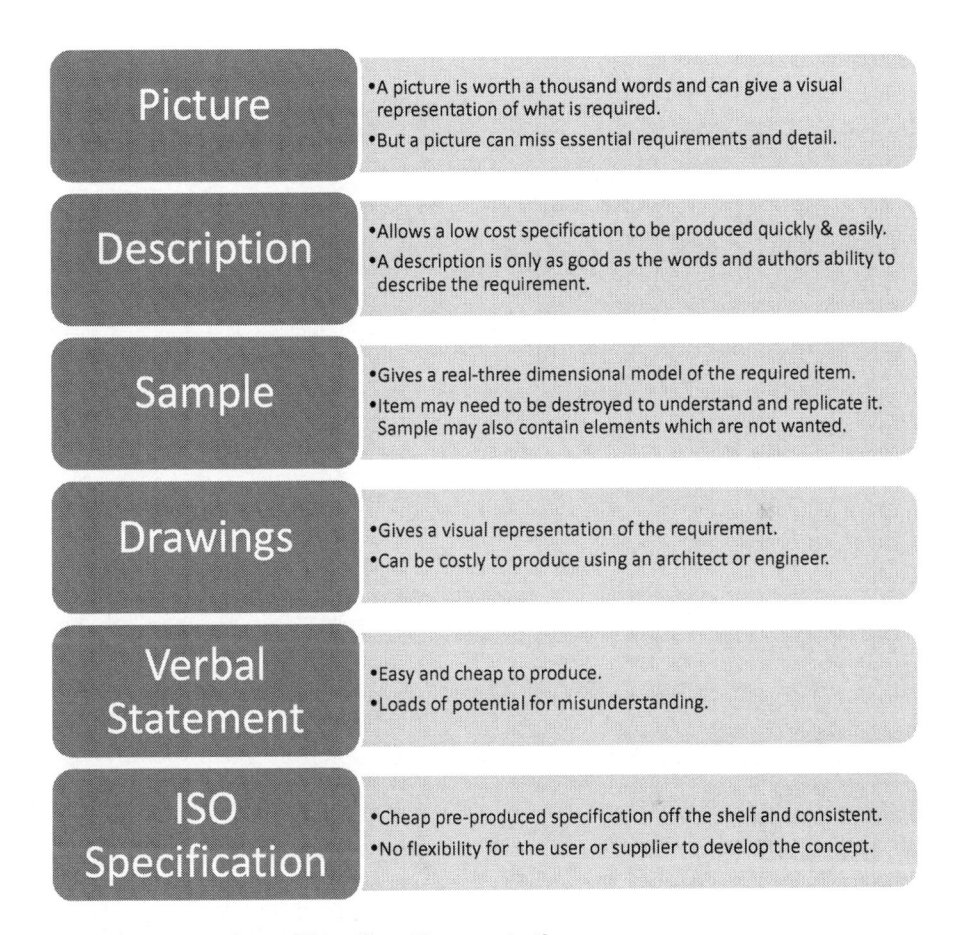

Picture
- A picture is worth a thousand words and can give a visual representation of what is required.
- But a picture can miss essential requirements and detail.

Description
- Allows a low cost specification to be produced quickly & easily.
- A description is only as good as the words and authors ability to describe the requirement.

Sample
- Gives a real-three dimensional model of the required item.
- Item may need to be destroyed to understand and replicate it. Sample may also contain elements which are not wanted.

Drawings
- Gives a visual representation of the requirement.
- Can be costly to produce using an architect or engineer.

Verbal Statement
- Easy and cheap to produce.
- Loads of potential for misunderstanding.

ISO Specification
- Cheap pre-produced specification off the shelf and consistent.
- No flexibility for the user or supplier to develop the concept.

Figure 7.11 – Specification Presentation

Whilst only a very small percentage of products supplied are generated from scratch by a customer with a new specification, where the supplier is engaged at the outset, great long term partnership benefits can be generated. Although not always possible – due, for example, to legislation such as OJEU stipulations in the European Public Sector, or where specification incorporates prescriptive licensed components – Early Supplier Involvement (ESI) should be encouraged wherever possible and is a foundation of a sustainable supplier-user relationship.

Food for Thought: The Forward Commitment Procurement (FCP) concept is used in European Public Sector to procure goods or services based on an outcome or vision. Procuring in this manner can motivate the market to invest and develop resources to enable the vision to become reality.

Equally, where resources are in limited supply, sharing research and development, equipment or knowledge with suppliers can foster beneficial interactions. The recognition of "mutual value" can lead to long term interactions, though licence and ownership criteria needs to be addressed at the outset, and a clear statement of the long term goals and ambitions of each of the organisations in the partnership should be explored and understood.

In most organisations, there will be a large number of suppliers, each with a different impact on the business in question. This impact should determine the amount of effort and time allocated to the management of the relationship and be commensurate with the value derived. Use of the Kraljic's matrix can help *the Sustainable Business* establish a supplier strategy accordingly – see figure 7.12.

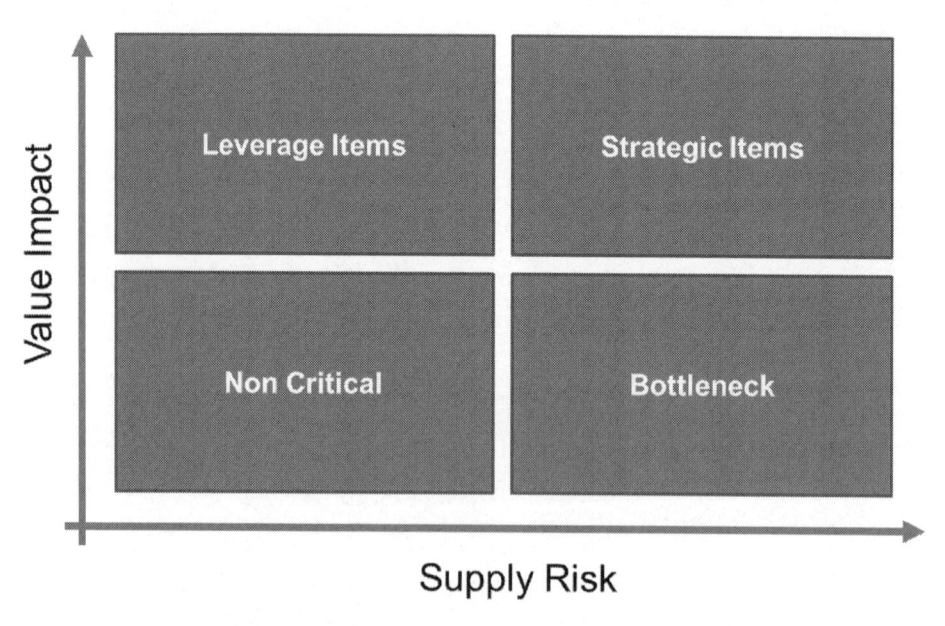

	Leverage Items	Strategic Items
Value Impact	Non Critical	Bottleneck

Supply Risk

Figure 7.12 – Kraljic Matrix

Once selected, the supplier becomes an intrinsic element of the Supply Chain and the operation of the business. Effective supplier management process then needs to measure and steer the supplier on a day to day, month to month basis. The Carter 10C model can then be modified to identify the key areas that need to be monitored over the longer period to ensure the continued ability of the supplier to meet the aspirations of *the*

Sustainable Business. Failure to monitor the supplier base increases risk and impacts on the organisations ability to promote its longevity agenda.

Entwined in the supplier management activity should be the measurement and targeting mandate explored in chapter 14. Use of KPIs, targets and measures helps capture the critical success factors (CSFs) and increases the probability of meeting and surpassing the aspirations of the business plan.

Quality

The importance of quality within the Supply Chain cannot be underestimated. It is at the core of the Supply Chain purpose; customer satisfaction is critical to a sustainable profit and to longevity.

The traditional definition of quality is that a product or service is "fit for purpose", yet in a Sustainable Supply Chain the quality of a product or service may encompass more than just a "fit for purpose" final output. In many ways, Sustainable Quality embraces all the features of the production process as well as the sources of supply and quality of the final outputs. It considers more than just the product or service itself, but also all the consequential outputs. Recalling the IMPACT model (Figure 1.7), the Sustainable Supply Chain is focused on the inputs into the process – for example the materials it uses – helping contain unnecessary costs and thus improve profitability. It also minimises wasted time, an intangible that some businesses take as a natural consequence of doing business.

Elimination of waste is at the core of Sustainability and central to the Six Sigma assessment of the Cost of Poor Quality (COPQ) explored further in chapter 10. In summary, COPQ is an excellent way of assessing the cost and impact of quality and to understand what would happen if the quality levels were to fall.

Take for example a simple metal bearings manufacturer with traditional inspection based quality processes – see figure 7.13. If raw material is allowed to enter the manufacturing process, a product could be produced which would fail the end of process quality inspection. This could lead to a replacement product needing to be made, thus delaying the delivery to the customer, taking up valuable machine time, occupying labour, and necessitating extra raw material to be consumed, amongst other things. Intercepting a faulty product is of course advisable from a customer satisfaction perception but also health and safety and cost angle, as well as to meet the potential litigation should something untoward occur. Yet a late delivery also has issues.

In inspection based quality processes, defects are expected with a visual and/or mechanical check made to ensure quality adherence.

The ultimate effect of a quality issue is to increase wastage; wastage of time, power, material, manpower, etc. These wastes feed straight through to the profitability of the organisation, reducing the shareholder return on investment or the money invested back into the business in future years. This shrinking of investment can ultimately lead to a reduction in the throughput for the business, leading ultimately, if not corrected, to a reduction in manpower and employment.

Figure 7.13 – The Cost of Poor Quality

Whilst this example is perhaps a little extreme, the effects of poor quality should never be under-estimated. Not mentioned is the fact that disenchanted customers will be more likely to tell someone else – another customer or a perspective customer – about his or her experience. In research relating to the impact of word of mouth referrals on the buying behaviour of over 3000 consumers by US firm Colloguy's, 58% stated that experience of a cohort, colleague, relative, etc, was their number one influence. Furthermore, 75% suggested that they would pass on negative experiences as opposed to only 42% who would pass on positive thoughts, with the average number of people told double that with a negative issue. This negative publicity is extremely hard to measure and yet is proven to have a detrimental effect over time. In a world of blogs, internet surveys, Twitter, social networking, etc, news of poor quality is made public very fast indeed and can ravage the hard earned reputation of an organisation.

In addition, the effort and resource needed to keep checking the quality of product is an unnecessary expense if the Supply Chain and production process is designed with quality at its core. Total Quality Management (TQM) is explored further in chapter 10.

The need to ensure quality is central to the Sustainable Supply Chain culture and ethos has never been higher. Whilst quality is clearly important in the Supply Chain and production process, the best way to ensure quality exists in *the Sustainable Business* is to design quality into the product (or service) and systems at the outset and to run quality processes that can easily and quickly identify issues that may occur.

Cost
Looking at the costs incurred across the Supply Chain can broadly be categorised and investigated as: inventory, logistics or movement of goods, time, personnel, waste, utilities and quality amongst others.

Inventory
Let's begin by considering the issue of inventory. As any JIT or Lean enthusiast will tell you, inventory is "evil" and should be eliminated wherever possible. Inventory is, however, sometimes seen as an investment within the business which in theory is not adding any value: a situation which immediately breaches our definition of an investment. Yet proponents of

inventory would argue that inventory is there to mitigate the risk of the operation coming to a standstill, a situation which – depending on the industry – could cost more than the cost of the inventory in question.

In this revised view, the value added is the mitigation of risk; as ever, life is about balance.

> **Food for Thought**: The inventory, in effect, decouples the demand and the supply sides of the Supply Chain.

Notwithstanding the arguments for and against inventory, in most businesses there is more inventory than is strictly necessary. Whether dead stock, safety stock, or cycle stock, many businesses – or more particularly their systems and Supply Chains – are just not responsive enough to facilitate a zero inventory policy.

Experience suggests that organisations actively avoid addressing inventory issues, instead justifying the situation with arguments such as "we will use it one day", "we've bought it now, if I sell it below cost, I will incur a loss", "it takes too much time and effort, when I could be doing other things", and so on. This short sighted view overlooks storage charges, opportunity costs, administration costs and so on. The issue is that inventory just sits there; it doesn't make any noise as it drip-drains profit from the bottom line. Profit, as we have stated on many occasions to date, is one of *the Sustainable Business' Three Pillars*; how can we let one of the foundations of our sustainable organisation be eroded in this way?

Some organisations attempt to highlight the issue of inventory excess through prohibitive charges (often 10%+) placed on inventory or on surplus/dead stock levels. Whilst this punitive measure does have an impact, decisions from the heart are more sustainable that those from the pocket. Consider a teenager, ensuring a consistently neat and tidy bedroom, with clothes put away, etc, needs to come from the heart. A rewards based system has a limited appeal.

> **Rule: Inventory decisions need to be driven from the pocket, not the heart**

Of equal concern is variety and choice. Introducing choice into an organisation will invariably lead to an expansion of inventory. Human nature relishes the freedom to make a personal choice. This choice is often considered essential so as not to undermine the responsibility of the manager or demoralise the individual.

Take for example the invariably passionate debate on the choice and allocation of corporate mobile phones. In many organisations, of varying shapes and sizes around the world, employees have come to believe that a new phone is their "right". Genuine excuses that have been heard include:
- "I need the latest phone as I'm a salesman and people expect me to have the latest…"
- "I can't have a second-hand phone as my doctor has told me it contains other people's germs and it will affect my allergies"
- And "I need a …..phone as it's the only one that fits the car kit in my wife's car".

Management needs to balance such decisions with the motivating or demotivating consequences, against the added cost of such decisions: it's a company phone, not a personal phone, the user always has the option of buying their own phone, and exchanging the SIM card! This has led increasingly to the decision being taken in some companies to assume that the employee will have their own phone anyway, and that corporate phones are not necessary.

The decision to introduce a new item into stock should be carefully considered. Many organisations live with virtually no stock at all. Undertaking a Critical Needs Analysis (CNA) can help determine whether an item is genuinely needed or merely the whim of an employee or as a result of an overly zealous salesman. Wider, simply asking the question as to whether the item is actually already in stock, or is there an alternative which can suffice, will help stem the growth of the inventory profile.

Increases in inventory escalation can be helped through the introduction of design policy aimed at limiting the use of new products, or focusing on preferred suppliers. By selecting a single manufacturer of a product type helps *the Sustainable Business* at many levels: lower spares stock, improved product knowledge, faster replacement, manufacturer support, compatibility improvements, etc.

Analysis from CIPS suggests that inventory costs account for between 25 and 33% of an item's total cost to business, a significant percentage compared to the actual purchase price – see figure 7.14. Sadly such figures are often lost inside other cost allocations, and direct allocation by item is thus avoided.

Considering the relative magnitude, it is somewhat surprising that such a burdensome element within Supply Chain is tolerated so readily by so many organisations. Of particular concern is the erratic approach to inventory taken by some wholesale and retail organisations. One might assume that an organisation whose sole purpose is buying stock in bulk and breaking it into smaller consignments would be highly focused on rapid stock turns, yet often average stock turns may only reach three or four times a year.

Whilst to some this may appear potentially tolerable, behind this average will be items that have been gathering dust for many years. Whilst process is often agreed, these items are hoarded, justified by virtue of their "service" nature. These items eventually sell or are disposed of, but with no clear "total" cost, the numbers fade into the aggregates and policy never changes.

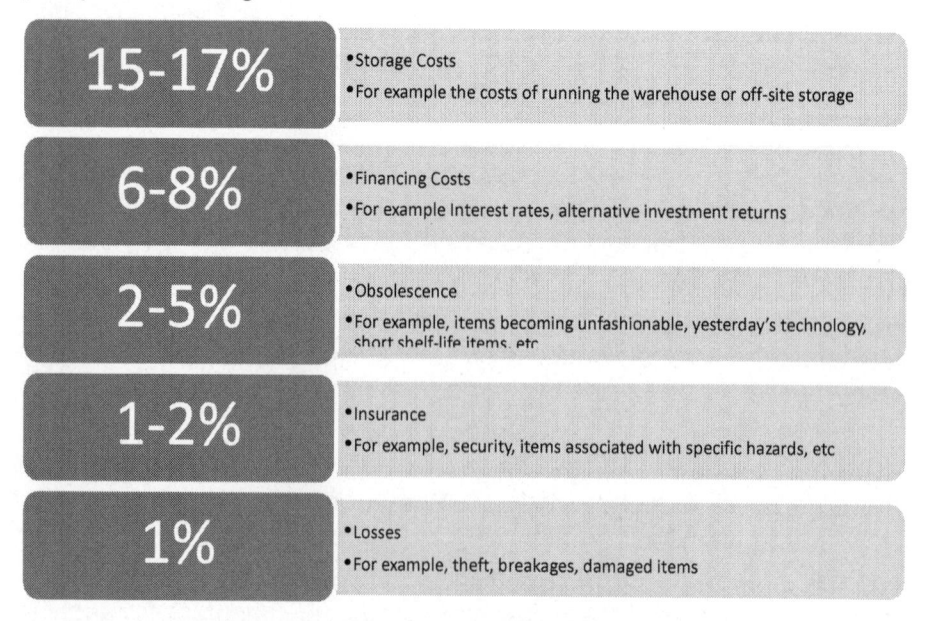

15-17%
- Storage Costs
- For example the costs of running the warehouse or off-site storage

6-8%
- Financing Costs
- For example Interest rates, alternative investment returns

2-5%
- Obsolescence
- For example, items becoming unfashionable, yesterday's technology, short shelf-life items, etc

1-2%
- Insurance
- For example, security, items associated with specific hazards, etc

1%
- Losses
- For example, theft, breakages, damaged items

Figure 7.14 – Costs associated with holding Inventory (Chartered Institute of Purchasing & Supply)

If we take the view that inventory is a necessary evil, the management of the inventory becomes an essential task to the preservation of the organisation and its sustainable ambitions. The significant costs detailed hitherto necessitate action.

The Inventory Management process balances the risk, cost and contribution that an inventory item makes to the Supply Chain. Using detailed statistical analysis – usually hidden deep within a software solution – stock levels, demand profiles, lead times, and usage patterns combine to generate an optimum stock level and criteria relating to the reorder frequency, the reorder size and the reorder process.

At the root of this process and its acronyms however is a forecast. As discussed within previous chapters – for example in relation to the economy – forecasting is by its very nature likely to have some level of inherent inaccuracy. This may be due to changes in usage patterns, for example changes in fashion, the weather, fluctuating production schedules, and so on. Understanding or predicting future requirements demands expertise either by product, by commodity, or by market, once again promoting the virtues of adopting dedicated inventory specialists or a category management concept.

The reordering models also rely on statistical analysis which needs various criteria to determine its recommendations. Standard Deviation – one of those statistical terms that send shivers through many a former pupil – drives much of this analysis.

In brief, Standard Deviation is simply the amount a collection of data fluctuates around an average, indicating how difficult or otherwise it is to predict an upper or lower limit or the extent of any such movements. See figure 7.15.

Looking at these data sets, both Product 1 and Product 2 have the same average represented by the centre line, however there is a marked difference in fluctuating monthly demand levels. This is a graphical representation of an item with a low standard deviation (product 1) and one with a high Standard Deviation (Product 2).

Where an item or facet fluctuates vigorously around an average – and thus having a high standard deviation – there is likely to be a much higher risk level. Both risk and forecasting impact on the Supply Chain and consequently both affect the performance of *the Sustainable Business*.

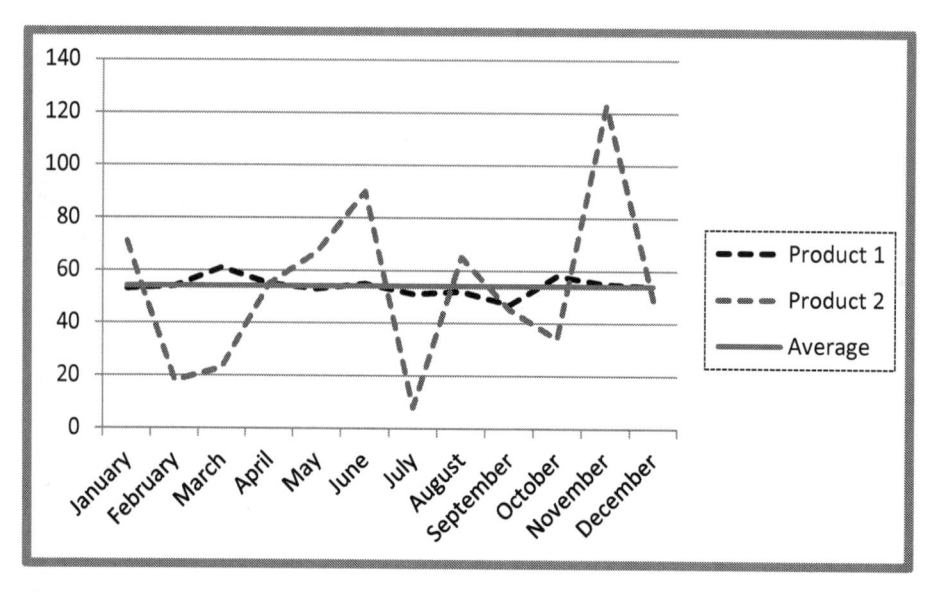

Figure 7.15 – Standard Deviation

Furthermore, on the supply side, accurate lead times are essential. Indeed, given the choice between short or reliable lead times, reliability will always come out on top. Having a very reliable order-to-shelf quotient goes a long way to enabling the computer software or inventory specialist to ensure the correct stock is on the shelf at all times. Equally, knowing what to order, how much to order and dealing promptly with inventory issues such as obsolescence, theft, breakages, etc, helps improve the effectiveness of the Inventory Management function.

The supply side lead time is however made from a number of elements some of which the Supplier has limited control over. Logistics scheduling, Customs and Excise, traffic issues, strikes, etc, can all conspire to frustrate Inventory Management function and the corresponding service levels. To this end the inventory system or operator introduces the dreaded "Safety Stock" component.

Safety Stock refers to the inventory in the system to prevent a stock-out in the event that some variable – often the order lead time or demand profile – changes or fluctuates unexpected: it's the inventory equivalent of a security blanket. Whilst not an overly complicated statistical concept, it has been deemed that specific Safety Stock and lead time calculations are beyond the scope of this work.

Further, in line with minimising the levels of inventory necessary to support demand in the business, Economic Order Quantities (EOQ) should be determined and adhered to at all times. Each and every inventory item will have an EOQ based on its specific demand pattern, the lead time from the supplier and of course its Standard Deviation to compensate for the item's predictability or otherwise. The EOQ may also take into consideration practical aspects such as the box or pack quantities. For example, shipping bottles of wine are best done in multiples of six as this is the optimum packing quantity, shipping bottles of wine in quantities of five or seven increases the risk of breakages, a consequential cost which will quickly find its way into the Supplier's selling price and User's safety stock.

Whilst Inventory Management is predominantly focused on the management of stock items that are required to enable the organisation to deliver the necessary customer service, the management of items that are not required is also important. Reducing unwanted stock helps release capital, space and other valuable resources. The processes for the disposal of items not required should be honed to ensure that the stock held will be used effectively to add genuine value. Where demand has waned – perhaps due to changes in fashion, product obsolescence, commercial decisions, supplier development, etc – profiles need to be updated to reflect the revised demand patterns. The *Sustainable Business* will schedule this activity to ensure that the inventory held is correct and liable to add value and contribute to its vision.

So how do lean organisations or companies mandating a Just-In-Time strategy survive? – see Wiremold case study 16.

In summary, they eradicate fluctuations either through robust planning and process, through a movement towards very short manufacturing lead times, or by using third-party suppliers who can deliver everything that is required, exactly when it is wanted.

Take for example the Kanban solution adopted by Toyota. For anyone who has seen a Kanban, it is somewhat disappointing: it appears as nothing more than a label in a pouch attached with a band. The label details the item, and specifies the exact 30 minute delivery slot when the item is to be delivered. It is the supplier's responsibility to ensure that the correct item is attached to the Kanban and delivered in the allocated window, with penalties incurred for both an early and late delivery (with no goods-inwards or warehousing, an early delivery will have no "home" and will generate a risk to either man, process or product). Contracts are relatively lucrative, awarded for life, or until the supplier fails to fulfil the necessary service levels on a regular basis. This builds a strong supplier-organisation loyalty and relationship.

Equally, where the Toyota model highlights a requirement for raw material – for example rolls of steel – order quantities reflect just that which is required for that manufacturing day. Steel is used to form specific items – for example door panels – as they are required; the forecast for doors being an easy calculation once the car throughput is established. The high quality mandate of the Toyota philosophy precludes items being produced in error based on a belief that if process is proven and followed to the letter, quality raw materials are used, and no external influences can intervene, then no defects should ever be seen. In such circumstances, the Six Sigma concept will prevail, i.e. less than 1part in a million will be defective.

Lean manufacturing follows a similar zero inventory mandate, but focuses on only making what the customer needs, when they order it. This is often achieved by ensuring that order-to-output times are as low as possible, forecasts are as accurate as possible, products use common components wherever possible and down-stream stockists take-up the slack in the wider Supply Chain. Wider, Lean manufacturing adopts a make-to-order or, at worst, a very small batch approach.

So recognising that inventory is an unwanted cost with nominal value contribution, what can we do to reduce inventory in *the Sustainable Business*?

Food for Thought: Consider sustainability in inventory management: How does the cost of holding stock, the tied up capital, stock losses, insurance costs, etc affect *the Profit Pillar*?

> Effective use of reorder mechanisms, minimum order levels, order discounts, etc can all help improve the efficiency of the inventory and enhance the profitability of the organisation. In contrast however, where inventory is kept, the risk of a breakage, theft, or obsolescence increases. Having a product in stock, which doesn't get used and is then disposed of simply *erodes the Planet Pillar* – worse still is when the cost of the disposal is dismissed with the suggestion that the product has been written down and will have no impact on the bottom line!

To begin with, stop having periodic purges, but adopt robust process to deal with issues as they arise, review lead times and stock levels, and dispose of items when they are deemed surplus.

Failing this utopia, here are the "Inventory Management Ten Commandments", some of which will appear obvious yet readily still occur in 21st century business. See figure 7.16:

In summary, inventory for many organisations is a reluctant necessity to aid the management of the risk that the business fails in its relentless pursuit of customer service, profit attainment, and future sales. The format of inventory and where it is in the Supply Chain is critical to all elements of the Supply Chain and must be investigated and examined.

	Rules
1	Only buy what you really need and consider every purchase for size and true need.
2	Wherever possible insist on a stock-cleanse agreement especially for project purchases.
3	Do not "top up" orders at the bequest of a supplier – a bulk, end of month deal benefits the supplier more than it will you.
4	Use Pareto to focus on the important items and those which will have the most impact, but this does not excuse looking at the wider picture.
5	Eliminate as far as possible any variety or choice in the business – variety is the inventory management's worst nightmare.

6	Balance stock – E.g. only stock pairs of shoes, 9-10% of a population is left handed so reflect this where applicable, etc.
7	Review your stock frequently and investigate all discrepancies to understand the cause and effect.
8	If a product is surplus, get rid of it sooner rather than later.
9	If a project has some items left over, DO NOT create them as a stock item, return them to the supplier while you still can.
10	Effective training, motivation and management of inventory staff is essential to drive day to day activity.

Figure 7.16 – Inventory Best Practice Rules

Logistics

Recalling the *7 Wastes*, movement and logistics are considered central to the success of a Supply Chain and the profit of the organisation.

Logistics typically refers to the movement of goods into and out of the organisation as part of the Supply Chain activity. Goods will be ordered as required recognising the lead time offered by the supplier. This supplier lead time is itself made up of a complex mix of component lead times both from its own business, its suppliers, and the communication medium over which the orders are transmitted.

For example, an order sent electronically will arrive considerably quicker than a printed order sent by post, leading to an extended lead time. Longer lead times mean higher stock levels held by the business, leading to higher costs incurred and the erosion of the organisations profit or a loss of competitiveness. In contrast, a pre-arranged call off relationship or rapid alignment of resources through strong relationship management will help minimise costs but maintain the service levels required by the customer.

Equally, the use of IT and Vendor Managed Inventory (VMI) helps suppliers monitor stock at their customers in real time.

Transporting goods to ensure on time delivery is an art in itself. The determination of delivery routes, scheduling, vehicle selection, fuel choice, traffic congestion, and packaging are just a few of the considerations, the specific details of which fall outside the scope of this book. Recognising, however, that measurement is required to drive the management process, technology both old (e.g. Tachometers) or new (e.g. satellite fleet monitoring) is invaluable to the management function.

Worthy of note however is the impact of off-shoring or buying from remote markets. Both lead to longer delivery times, higher inventory levels in transit and risk. These costs are offset by the benefits derived from the procurement decision, yet in many such cases witnessed, little attention is paid to these "hidden" aspects, with invoice costs invariably the primary driver.

Furthermore, in a world of globalisation and opening international markets, the need to transport goods around the world has become imperative to the delivery of customer satisfaction and low cost aspirations. Whilst transporting goods incurs carbon miles - the carbon dioxide emissions generated from the burning of fuel for each mile of the transportation – there are global and ethical benefits to society from development of third world or less developed communities.

> **Food for Thought**: Consider the risk and cost evaluations necessary for the shipment of goods from China to Europe: by sea, Suez Canal is shorter but passes very close to Somalia and the risk of attack from sea pirates (albeit that the levels of sea piracy can be seen to increase in times of high commodity prices and economic turbulence); Cape of Good Hope is a longer route which means more time at sea and cost implications in extra fuel and shipping costs but arguably has a lower risk level; the northern sea passage is only open for part of the year and is a relatively long and climatically challenging transit route; air freight is fast but an expensive option; by land, routes might include a trip via the troubled Kashmiri mountains, or through the Himalayas; or along the barren desert regions of the old silk routes in Kazakhstan; and so on. Indeed a proposed new rail route network in Kazakhstan may make this final option more viable.

The risk of international logistics on the Supply Chain can be considerable. Time and effort must be engaged to develop and maintain the relationship with overseas partners, with shipments and associated payments, as well as legal and insurance protection, managed carefully to prevent corruption or losses.

Commonly, Incoterms and a Letter of Credit are two instruments of international trade which protect the buyer and seller.
- A Letter of Credit establishes the point at which payment from the buyer passes to the seller. Funds are deposited with a reputable third party – often in a dedicated Escrow Account with a merchant bank or other similar financial institution – with criteria set for the money release. Typically this may include a list of evidence that the seller needs to lodge, for example a "bill of lading" from the shipper, a detailed invoice, packing list, customs notice, insurance details, etc.
- Incoterms determine at what point the responsibility for the goods in transit pass from the seller to the buyer – see figure 7.17. This point can vary depending on the negotiations and agreed terms. The responsibility could, for example, pass at the moment that the goods leave the supplier, or when the goods are loaded onto a ship. Incoterms also determine who pays for the transport, insurance and payment of duties and taxes.

The list of Incoterms are however revised every ten years or so to reflect changes in international trade, logistics issues and industry needs. Numerous other Incoterms have existed in the past - for example DDU(Delivery Duty Unpaid) or DAF (Deliver at Frontier) – making an up-to-date awareness of such matters imperative.

From an environmental perspective, location of a business close to its suppliers or customers makes eminent sustainable sense. Why ship goods half way round the world for processing, only to ship the goods back again? Take for example the arguably inhumane UK livestock market, where living creatures – for example sheep and pigs – are shipped to France for slaughter, only to be reimported back into the UK for sale. In a world "allegedly" concerned over carbon emissions and animal welfare, how can this be allowed to occur?

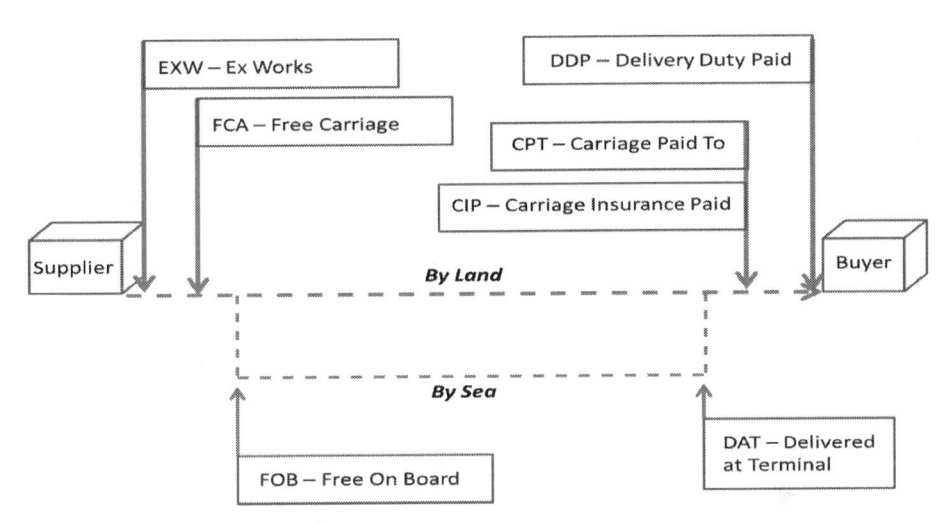

Figure 7.17 – Sample Incoterms

A list of the current Incoterms at the 2011 review is contained in figure 7.18.

The design of the logistic set-up has a dramatic impact on the environmental and *Planet* impact of the organisation. Decisions over the potential logistics structures are therefore critical, though far from easy to disseminate. hubs and spoke networks, regional or national distribution centres, "milk rounds", local delivery points, and so on. Within these structures positioning of the facilities, inventory, vehicle management, etc needs to be carefully located to minimise resources (such as fuel and manpower) and optimise the service delivered to the customer – see figure 7.19.

Reference	Description	Comments
CFR	Cost and Freight	Departure Pointt identified
CIF	Cost, Insurance and Freight	Destination Point identified
CIP	Carriage and Insurance Paid To	Destination Point identified
CPT	Carriage Paid To	Destination Point identified
DAP	Delivered At Piont	Exact point of delivery identified
DAT	Delivered At Terminal	Destination Terminal identified
DDP	Delivered Duty Paid	Destination Port identified
EXW	Ex Works	Location identified
FAS	Free Alongside Ship	Port identified
FCA	Free Carrier	Location identified
FOB	Free On Board	Departure Port identified

Figure 7.18 – 2011 Incoterms

So what criteria need to be taken into consideration? The elements that will dictate the most effective structure will vary from business to business. Every organisation will have its own set of customer product, service, cost and geographical issues that the distribution network needs to take into consideration. These may include any of the following as well as a plethora of other factors that *the Sustainable Business* deems as important in its pursuit of its *Three Pillar* mandate, and its longevity aspirations:
- Location of main business facilities
- Location of the Customer
- Service level requirements of the Customer
- Predictability of service requirements
- Geographical issues
- Cost of fuel
- Contract clauses
- Risk profile
- etc

World Class distribution networks have become an intrinsic part of global industry. Coordination of resources to deliver excellent customer service is now expected as the norm – See Case Study 7 – Dell Corporation.

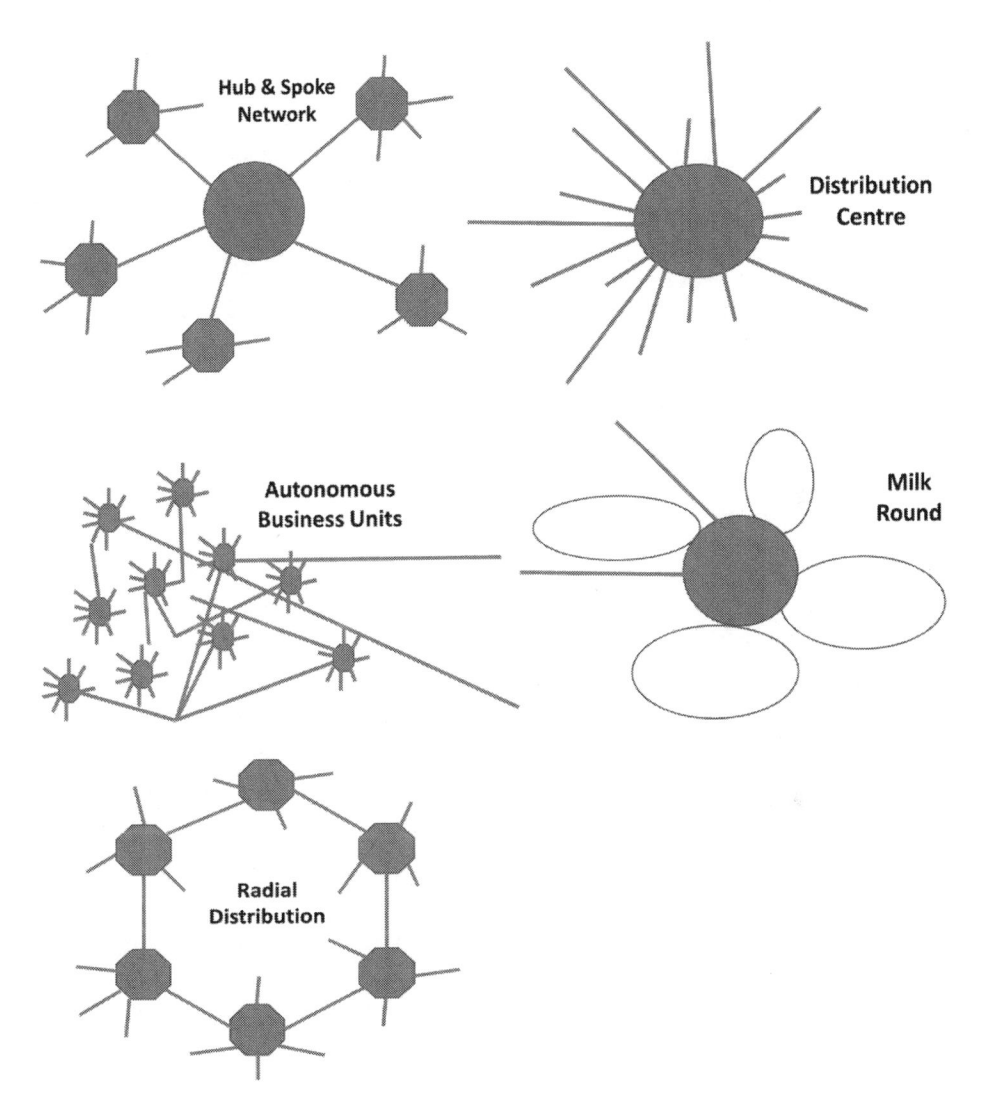

Figure 7.19 – Distribution Structures

Warehousing

For organisations where stock is a significant part of their business, the logistics function or structure is closely interlinked with the warehouses where goods are stored ready for use or onward shipment. In many organisations, these warehouses are a critical part of the infrastructure and must therefore be coordinated within the overall business activity model.

Notwithstanding the fact that *the Sustainable Business* often frowns on inventory as a concept, effective and sustainable management of warehouse facilities is nonetheless important. Warehouses represent a significant investment in most cases, with buildings, people, equipment and IT infrastructure involved. Each of these elements represents a cost driver, and therefore has an impact on the *Profit Pillar*.

As discussed elsewhere in this book, management of cost is necessary to develop *the Profit Pillar* but also to help ensure longevity. It is important to measure the effective use of space and resources within the warehouse operations to assess both the best use of resources as well as the service levels offered from that facility. Effectiveness of the warehouse network will often depend on the warehouse locations, but is also impacted by the logistics and communication links between them and other parts of the Supply Chain. As detailed earlier in this chapter, the Supply Chain and the wider business can be structured in a number of different ways, and this will drive the size and location of the warehouses required to support the business.

When determining the location of a warehouse, many factors may come into the assessment. These may include aspects such as cost of real estate, access to logistics networks, locality to the key customers, expansion potential, personnel issues and so on. There is a further dilemma between one mega distribution centre versus a small number of medium warehouses versus lots of smaller locations. This decision needs to be carefully modelled to assess the impact on inventory duplication and investment, service levels, and time.

Once the warehouse location has been established, it is necessary to equip the premises with appropriate layout, racking, equipment and inventory. The issue of the layout of a warehouse is important to its effectiveness and there are numerous possible layouts that can be adopted. For example, goods can be organised in the warehouse in accordance with their relative usage – see figure 7.20.

Here, fast moving goods will be at the front of the warehouse, medium movers in the middle, and slow movers at the rear. Inventory tends to follow traditional Pareto distribution, and Pareto can be used to assign stock categorisations within the Inventory Management function. In this set-up, order picking times are significantly reduced as time spent walking around the warehouse is minimised.

Warehouse structured by stock categorisation, with faster moving goods nearer to the customer

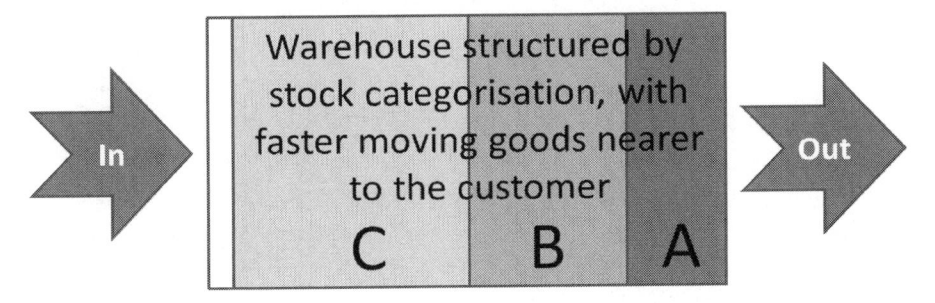

In → C B A → Out

Figure 7.20 – Goods organised by usage rates

Similarly, where there are changing product demand patterns, or ranges of product or franchises that warrant storage together, inventory can be racked according to other criteria – see figure 7.21. Typically this increases pick times but reduces the reliance on IT directed order picking and can allow untrained employees or customers to undertake the activity if required. This also makes it easier to manage product ranges as well as adding or deleting items from the profile – retail organisations may adopt this sort of layout.

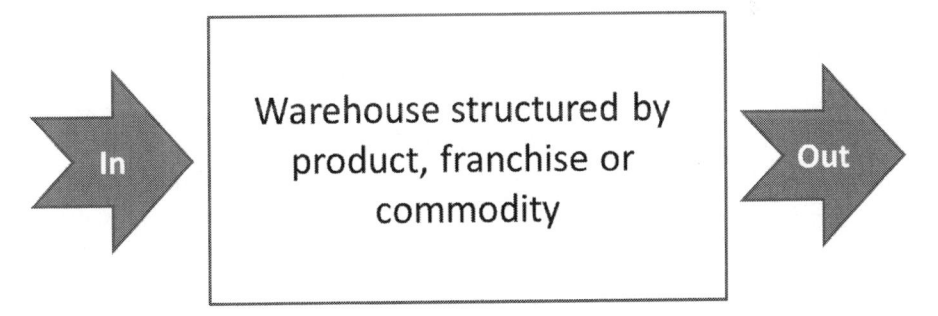

In → Warehouse structured by product, franchise or commodity → Out

Figure 7.21 – Goods organised by product range, type or franchise

Equally, in some circumstances, the warehouse may contain only slow moving items. In such a warehouse a common in/out door may be used with goods stored by commodity or product, often racked by part or inventory reference – see figure 7.22.

```
┌─────────────────────────────────┐
│  Slower moving warehouse –      │
│   Goods organised by            │      ┌──────┐
│  manufacturer or product        │ ───▶ │ In & │
│         type                    │      │ Out  │
│                                 │      └──────┘
└─────────────────────────────────┘
```

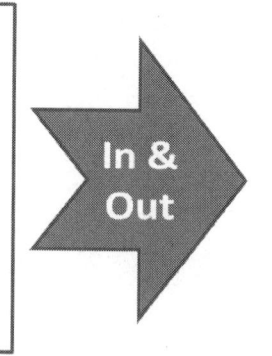

Figure 7.22 – Single In & Out

In addition to the warehouse and the layout, equipment and machinery requirements need to be considered. Equipment such as fork-lift trucks, conveyors, pallet trucks, and trolleys are all commonplace items in a warehouse, but when selecting such items *the Sustainable Business* should be mindful of the fuel and emission implications and its *Planet Pillar* aspirations.

Fork-lift trucks, for example, commonly use a number of different fuel types: battery, diesel, and gas amongst others. Each has their own issues. A diesel version, for example, should not be used inside a building without significant ventilation; depending on the climate, this can result in a very cold warehouse and disenchanted employees; a battery version has low emissions, and can be used in an enclosed warehouse, but requires downtime for charging as well as a number of health and safety considerations relating to acid and high voltage equipment amongst others.

Selection of fuel types is also relevant when considering heating and lighting in the warehouse. The type of light source can make a huge difference to the costs and efficacy of a lighting design, as well as the quality of the light. For example, older lighting schemes may use sodium light sources – similar to the old fashioned yellow street lamps – which are cheap to run, but give poor colour rendering and can in some warehouses lead to order picking errors. More modern solutions include metal halide or mercury vapour lamps which may overcome some of the issues with sodium sources, but what is the relative impact of using mercury for instance on *the Planet Pillar*?

Finally, locating a valuable inventory item into one location will inevitably attract attention from would-be thieves. In order to preserve the investment and the *Profit Pillar, the Sustainable Business* needs to provide effective security systems and trained personnel. Research suggests that providing effective remuneration for staff will significantly reduce the likelihood that this theft will originate from within. Initiatives that have been seen over the years are often ingenious and often difficult to foil.

> **Food for Thought**: One such scam involved the culprits putting good items out with the rubbish, before returning at night to retrieve said items. This was foiled by an ingenious security person who spent the night in the skip awaiting their return so as to capture the culprits red-handed – this individual later became known as "Billy the Skip"!

Utilities

Across the Supply Chain, a wide variety of utilities, fuels and resources are employed. These may include gas, fuel oils, electricity, water, telecommunications, and IP and internet connectivity; they represent a major element of the cost base, and their preservation needs to be considered both for the benefit of *the Sustainable Business* and the wider environment. In many parts of the world, water is a scarce and costly resource that can impact on both company and community in a large way.

Water collection and preservation remains a major issue for the planet of the 21st century. Construction of dams, water distribution systems and reservoirs helps ensure that water is available for a percentage of the global population, yet millions still do not enjoy the luxury of clean running water in their own home.

> **Food for Thought**: 97% of the world's water is salty, 2% is contained in frozen reserves such as the ice-caps, glaziers and permafrost, and only 1% is stored in a fresh water state.

What is arguably worse is seeing water wasted within the Supply Chain or in society and doing nothing to rectify the issue.

Yet in pockets of the world, society is doing something to remedy and reverse this trend. For example, in the Rima River Valley in Northern Nigeria, vast irrigation and soil enhancement has returned arid desert to fertile and highly productive land; in Gibraltar, where fresh water is in limited supply, buildings have two water feeds, fresh and salty, with all toilets flushed with salty water; in Saudi Arabia, large infrastructure has been employed to desalinate sea water, fuelled by waste oil product, and integrated into the electrical power production; in Turkey hot waste water from a factory producing plastic widgets, is supplied to a local village for washing, before being pumped into the fields to enhance crop production; and so on.

But equally, at the business or personal level everyone can make a difference: try fitting a toilet hippo as detailed in Chapter 4 to reduce the impact of a toilet flush; a water butt saves rainwater; turn off the tap when brushing teeth; mend dripping taps; and so on.

Food for Thought: Use of salt water for cooling should be used to generate fresh water as a by-product.

In terms of electricity, waste is also in abundance. Turning off lights is often cited as an issue, but it can be seen as a symptom of complacency. In one organisation, the author was informed that the gas used in the power generator was a free by-product of their business, and thus the electricity cost them nothing, vindicating the lights being left on all the time, day and night!

Telecommunications, IP network (Internet connectivity) and latterly aspects such as Wireless capacity, now form part of the modern utility portfolio. Their impact and cost within the Supply Chain is worthy of particular note and focus. Power, water, etc, have always been important to the effective running of a Supply Chain, however the rise of the Internet and mobile telecommunications has made this element mission critical – can a business survive in the twenty first century without mobile phones, the internet, or complicated IT solutions?

Personnel

As with all businesses, and as detailed in chapter 2, people are the essential lifeblood that forms the soul of the organisation, Understanding and managing this element of the business and the Supply Chain is critical to success.

> **Rule: Respect is the best reward**

Respect of an individual is the core of Human Resource Management. It underpins all other initiatives, especially in the Supply Chain, and most particularly in Customer facing scenarios. In many cases, this will be as important as delivering goods or services on time, or giving value for money. The human face is considered by many organisations as one of its primary competitive advantages, and responsible for percentage points in its margin.

> **Food for Thought**: Why do retail gurus focus so much on eye contact, acknowledging the customer, a smile, a quick response, and smart uniforms ?

Time

Time as an issue is ever present through the Supply Chain. It is like a metronome that keeps the business ticking. Almost every activity in a business and its Supply Chain are time orientated functions. Management of this element is therefore key to the success of the organisation, and thus its fulfilment of its *Three Pillars* mandate. Further, longevity, by its very definition, is time driven: time must be cherished and used effectively. Organisations that make every moment count go further.

> **Rule: Time is money, make every second count**

Utilisation of those spare moments in life can make a real difference. Everything *the Sustainable Business* does should be focused on adding value to the organisation, on fulfilling its *Three Pillar* objectives, and maintaining its existence long into the future.

Measurement of time is required to help the management of time itself. Audible and visual indicators help employees and systems appreciate time, and generates alignment and coordination. In ERP solutions, time is the primary coordinator. It ensures that the right items are at the right place at the right time.

> **Food for Thought**: Numerous clocks are of benefit in a motivated organisation but a distraction and detrimental in a demotivated organisation.

Customer & Service

The issue of good customer service is at the heart of the Sustainable Supply Chain. *The Sustainable Business* recognises that without a customer, they have no business, which will immediately affect *the Profit Pillar* as well as constricting the wider longevity mandate.

Many organisations claim impeccable customer service and pride themselves on the result of customer feedback surveys, yet this can sometimes be seen as preaching to the converted, with a proportion of society rarely likely to complain. Customer dissatisfaction is most evident by the simple decision to shop or buy from a competitor. Several times in this book, the importance of maintaining the existing Customer has been highlighted, and some customers may cite lowest price as the cause of a move elsewhere, yet often this is merely a smokescreen, a view qualified by the fact that the higher price organisations often survive by offering something extra that generates genuine loyalty.

So often, it's the little things that build customer loyalty: for example, the free cup of coffee while they are waiting. In one former employer, on the trade counter between 7.30 and 9.30 customers could get a free cup of coffee, make themselves some free toast and pick-up a free newspaper. This equated to a net cost of around £0.25 per customer yet generated an average of over £100 of extra profit per customer – competitors and sister businesses claimed that they could not or would not afford the extra cost!

Management & Cross Functional Teams

In the Sustainable Supply Chain, as with so many parts of *the Sustainable Business*, management and teamwork is crucial.

The Supply Chain coordinates a variety of resources within the organisation to produce a product or service to fulfil the demands of a customer. This Customer will then reimburse the organisation for the delivery of the product or service, this revenue leading hopefully to a profit and thus a stronger *Profit Pillar*.

Managing and improving a Supply Chain is far from easy. In many companies, the Supply Chain is home to some of the most entrenched processes and what Johnson and Scholes called "Paradigms". Motivating employees to change these habits or norms is not easy. Training and coaching helps highlight the importance of getting the Supply Chain right, and should be used to develop the team awareness. Using Cross Functional Teams (CFT) to investigate best practice and introduce Supply Chain improvements is highly recommended.

Extracting ideas from within the business is often an issue for organisations, however, if the employees or teams can generate their own ideas for Supply Chain Management and improvements, implementation of the ideas will be much easier. Use of "Voice of The Customer", Brainstorming and other idea generating techniques can help.

Generating ideas is of course only part of the process, with the implementation and project process critical to the overall success; Project process is explored in chapter 11.

Sustainable Supply Chain – Conclusion

In conclusion, the Supply Chain and the delivery of Customer demands are at the very heart of *the Sustainable Business*. Understanding what the Customer really wants will improve *the Profit Pillar*, effective management and motivation of the employees will improve the *People Pillar*, and the development of effective processes within the Supply Chain, and a resolute focus on the frugal use of resources and management of waste will improve *the Planet Pillar*.

Case Study 7: Dell Computing

"Making the Planet Greener for you is its own reward"

The Dell Supply Chain is recognised globally for its ability to deliver bespoke customer solutions quickly and reliably throughout the world at competitive prices.

The customer designs a computer to his or her specification with the Dell online order entry system, utilising common modular components that helps Dell manufacture, test and ship bespoke systems to order, efficiently and at the lowest Total Cost of Ownership (TCO).

Once the order has entered the system, it is sent to the manufacturing unit nearest to the customer "Ship-to" address. Each order is assigned a unique order number at the start of the process, which is printed in both man and machine-readable labels, and allows the system to track the order throughout the manufacturing process.

In terms of component and finished stock, Dell works on a near zero inventory, and has no inventory warehouses, with required components delivered from local supplier sources every two hours.

Dell incorporates what it calls "Custom Factory Integration" CFI to ensure that the customer requirements are the primary focus of the whole manufacturing process. To ensure that customers receive the computer system in a ready-to-go state, software is preinstalled and fully tested within the manufacturing process.

Once complete, the system is shipped to a "Dell Merge Centre" where it waits for other standard items – such as monitors - to arrive from their respective manufacturing unit. Standard and bespoke items are produced using the same manufacturing processes, yet still focused on the lowest Total Cost of Ownership and a zero inventory philosophy.

Once the order has been accumulated, all the items are packed as a single consignment so that the customer receives all elements of their order in one delivery. This boxing process, as with so many of the other elements of the Dell system, is fully robotic enabling a fast and efficient packing process with a low risk of breakage.

The whole manufacturing and distribution activity is managed by a dedicated production system, with orders and components tracked and measured at every stage of the process. Measures are consistent across all of the manufacturing units, measuring throughput, waste, lead-times, and customer satisfaction.

The production system also recognises the key wastes identified in the STOPWASTE model:
- Standardisation of components coupled with compatible and modular designs leads to near zero inventory;
- Transportation is minimised with manufacturing undertaken at the nearest factory to the Ship-To address;
- Outsource of component production with strong Supplier Management to ensure service levels are maintained at all times;
- Processes are monitored and where necessary reengineered to ensure they reflect best practice;
- Weight and materials are selected to give optimum performance whilst minimising the weight of the final product and packaging;
- Acquisition costs are maintained with strong supplier relationships, and competitive tendering;
- Specification of components enables up-to-date technology, compatibility and clear quality statements;
- Taken out gold plate to ensure that the customer buys what the customer wants, and not unnecessary frills;
- Elimination of Non Value Added (NVA) activities so that every element of the production contributes to the production of a high quality system at a competitive price.

Dell is committed to delivering products at the lowest Total Cost of Ownership, whilst honoured in 2011 as being the fifth greenest company in the USA, and 25th globally in the Newsweek Green Rankings. It is a copybook Supply Chain example.

For further details watch the "Dell Factory Tour" video on Youtube.

The Sustainable Business

Notes Page **Page Ref**

Summary Chapter 8
The Sustainable Sales Function

Key Learning Points
- The need for "Long Termism"
- The effect of departmental barriers and getting business buy-in
- Discounting and "Everything must go" philosophies
- Understanding the concept of "Sandbagging"
- Maintenance and structure of a salesteam
- Utilising Innovation
- "Greenwashing" and token gestures
- The concept of "Viewpoint Rankings"
- Avoiding past mistakes
- Identifying "Time Thieves"
- Producing Key Performance Indicators or Key Sales Objectives
- Incorporating CSR Policies into Sales process
- Recognising the perfect sales campaign
- Developing Contact Regimes
- Sustainable Canvas – Greenscreen

Tool Summary
- Figg Sales Ecocube
- Patron-Purveyor-Pitcher
- Pipeline-Proposal-Purchase Cycle
- Sales Process Recipe – Four Basic Ingredients
- Staple Range Model
- Herbs and Spices and Sales seasoning
- SUSTAIN Model
- MAN Model

CIPS Syllabus Reference
- Level 4 Managing Contracts and Relationships
- Level 5 Management in Procurement and Supply

Chapter 8: The Sustainable Sales Function

"Jam tomorrow and jam yesterday – but never jam today"
– Through the Looking Glass and What Alice Found There,
Lewis Carroll, 1871

Critical to the success and longevity of *the Sustainable Business*, is the need to generate and maintain a robust sales function. The significance of the sales operation was explored as part of its contribution towards a stable *Profit Pillar* in chapter 3, however, developing an effective and sustainable sales function is worthy of investigation in its own right.

The importance of a coordinated and united sales team, committed to an organisation's goals, and working in sync with other departments is often easier said than done. By their very nature salespeople – and indeed many procurement individuals – are extremely self-focused, often somewhat oblivious to the needs of sister parts of the organisation. Other departments will view this as inherently selfish, however it could be argued that salespeople thrive on personal targets and the thrill of success.

Departmental Barriers

Is there a disconnect between profitable progress and sustainable selling? How compatible are green and growth sales goals?

The Sustainable Business demands that you must both be in it for the duration and be innovative. So how are these requirements viewed in the Sales context?

Sales & Long-Termism

If long-term thinking is one facet of sustainability, then what kind of horizons bound a salesforce? On the surface, Sales can seem the most transitory focused of all business functions. There are a trio of mindsets at play here, "discounting", "maintenance" and "structure".

Discounting – The prevailing fixation is for the current period alone. Whether you report by week, month or quarter, the pressure is on to deliver 'now'; 'Yesterday', in fact. Usually to the exclusion of anything that may happen once the books are closed.

Buyers are of course wise to this. Whilst salespeople will dangle the seemingly huge carrot of period-end reductions to help create a sometimes false sense of urgency, procurement veterans realise that such offers will invariably remain in place past their supposed expiry date, often well into the next period - so no need to rush in to satisfy a vendor's forecast. Indeed buyers have been known to hold back orders at the bonus deadline seeking to ransom an extra per cent or two of discount.

> **Definition: "Everything Must Go!"** Period-end incentives come in many guises. A straight forward 'reward' for swiftly signing-up by way of time-limited reduced price is the most common. Then there is the avoidance of a threatened imminent price rise, or certain stock related movements (such as fresh or obsolete line replacement) or possible future delivery/resource scarcity.

Alternatively, salespeople – and indeed some tax accountants – are also alert to this. Many can adopt a tactic known as sandbagging. They elect to delay a sale rather than close it during the period.

> **Definition: Sandbagging** – Sandbagging is the practice of not declaring or chasing down a highly probable deal during " the period". Instead it is left untaken by the salesperson until early in the next period. The reasons for this can be twofold. Either the current period has gone so well for the seller they are keen to smooth sales over the year, or they have "taken a bath" (not sold anything) and think it's better to start the next period well. Both are usually the result of a payment plan judgement to maximise personal commissions. This is generally frowned upon by management unless they too have a vested interest.

> **Food for Thought**: End of season clothing sales generate sales volume but slashed margins: To what extent are margin reductions factored into the business model?

Maintenance

Investment in sales teams is universally low, indeed the sales training industry often use their own analysis on the paucity of training to promote their own services. Whether you recognise such figures as threadbare or just normal, the fact remains salespeople rarely receive classroom tuition. To compound matters, the amount of genuine coaching in the field is sparse.

If you were to buy plant and equipment to the same value as your sales force costs, then your company would probably insist on paying some kind of yearly maintenance. Whether this is 5, 10 or even 20 per cent, such a rate is hardly ever applied to the sales effort.

Structure

The turmoil many sales operations face often prevents extended vision. Management turnover can be high, and despite succession planning, a new broom has plenty of options to alter things in the Sales sphere. Changes can be frequent, with several variables to mix up. As discussed in Chapter 5, these include deployment by; sector or geography, account management or new business, product specialism or entire catalogue, solution or single focus, deal size/volumes, customer type, in- or outbound approaches.

> **Food for Thought**: How does the customer or the market react to such changes. Inevitably, radically altering a sales set-up destroys some highly productive relationships, but does it freshen up the sales force?

Sales & Innovation

Selling's track record when it comes to innovation is not great either. Like each vocation within commerce, Sales is subject to the allure of regular fads and onslaught from buzzwords. The latest such as Sales 2.0, builds upon a previous trend in CRM (the current three letter acronym that denotes software holding client interaction data) which itself provokes serious doubt as to whether any positive impact at all has accrued as result of efforts to innovate.

Another manifestation of this comes from the performance of selling new products. Most assessors find sales here to be below expectations. Many reasons contribute, but perhaps sales people have long known what Jim Collins refers to in "Good To Great", namely it is better to be second into a new market. 'First mover advantage' it seems may well prove a myth, with its license to the 'status quo champions' and the 'decision-averse'.

Traditional Behaviours

Tactical Lip-Service

Old school Sales-sages like to keep things simple. There's only two ways to increase your sales, they trumpet: either put more opportunities into the funnel, or close more deals at the bottom; preferably you'd do both.

Unless your *green drive* makes these happen, it is unlikely to be given due consideration by your sales force.

> **Definition Greenwashing** – Token gestures and actions that are erroneously thought to be Sustainability orientated can be a costly distraction. Several technologies exist for instance to reduce footprints of all manner. The telephone is one that's been around for over a century and still today it is underutilised, Web-conferencing is another example. How many laptops boast glitzy time and territory management software that helps, among other tasks, nail the eternally knotty "Travelling Salesman Problem"?
>
> Salespeople can all drive electric cars, only powered from renewables, or work from their spare bedrooms on Skype all day, and true Sustainability will be hardly affected.
>
> Such initiatives alone, although not without merit, tinker around the edges. A coherent sustainable sales strategy is needed. Otherwise, each such measure in isolation will be as triumphant as the world's best mousetrap – no path was beaten to its door.

Whenever a new edict comes from on high, if it is deemed potentially detrimental to these objectives, no matter how well intentioned, one of two situations will prevail: 1) salespeople will either get shown leniency by their own bosses who then cover for their non-compliance, or 2) the sales force can expend so much energy circumventing the rules that it can be detrimental to the winning of new business.

Triple Bottom Line - Adopting the Mindset

To fully appreciate the *Three Pillars*, it is possible to graft two extra dimensions onto the existing well-known framework. This makes it simpler to determine the steps specific to each entity within the Sales realm. See figure 8.1:

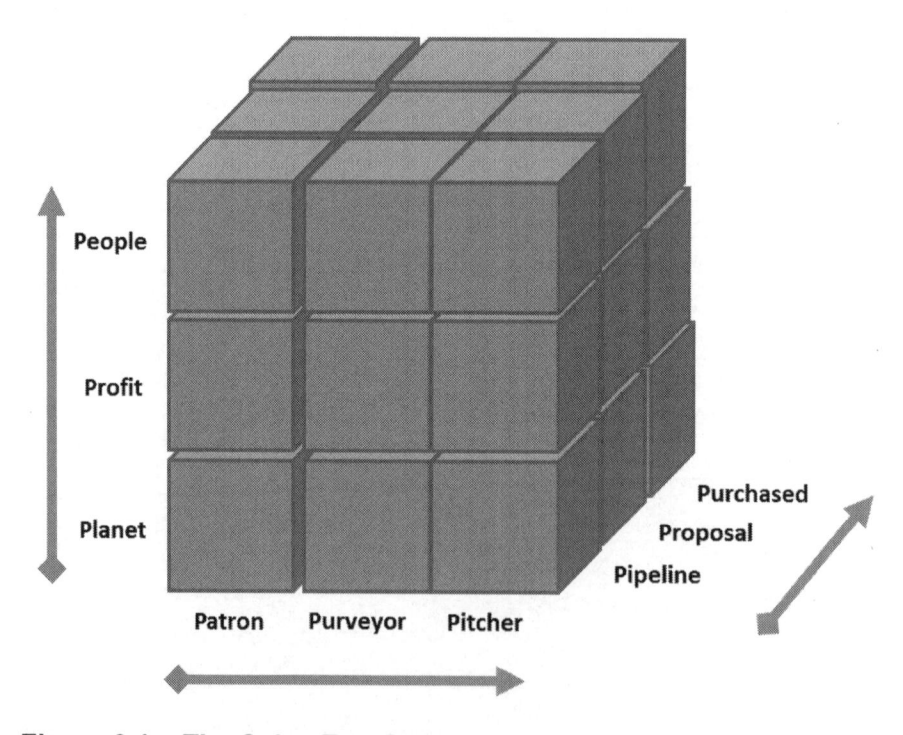

Figure 8.1 – The Sales Eco Cube

The Patron

The Patron is defined as the entity giving their patronage. This may refer to an organisation awarding "you" business, or a personal client you exclusively deal with. It can also mean someone not yet a customer, i.e. a prospect that you hope will take your wares.

The Purveyor

This applies to the umbrella organisation doing the actual selling. Whether a mere cog in the corporate machine, or someone with sole responsibility, the Purveyor will be aware of any allied efforts, such as with suppliers or associated parties.

The Pitcher

The single Sales individual most dependent upon the signatory. The 'deal owner', the quota-bearing rep, the person who's particular fortune or failure is most directly impacted by the sale that *they* alone are endeavouring to seal.

For each of the Patron, Purveyor and Pitcher, *the Three Pillars* will have a different bearing. From a sustainable perspective purpose, strategy and objectives need to be clearly established to ensure maximum impetus from the sales function.

Take by way of an example, the intersection of Pitcher, Planet and Pipeline, see figure 8.2. In this intersection, the person pitching for the order – the Saleperson, is anxious to maintain a sustainable pipeline of orders: orders which should be considerate of *the Planet Pillar* described in chapter 4.

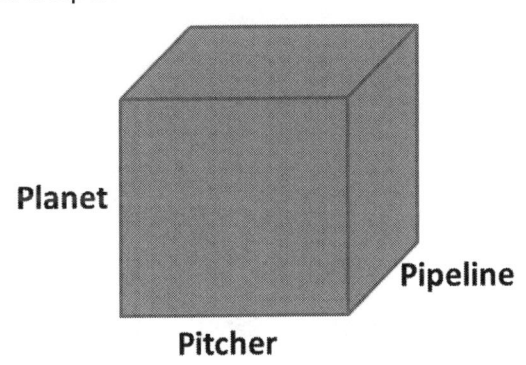

Figure 8.2 – Pitcher – Pipeline – Planet Intersect

There are obvious sustainability benefits to winning a customer over a long period covering hopefully many orders and populating the sales pipeline into the future. One-off sales are undoubtedly of some commercial benefit, but *the Sustainable Business* seeks on-going relationships wherever possible. Effort and investment needs to proportionally reflect the value and contribution that a customer makes to the business, if a sale is truly a one-off transaction, be cognoscente of the merits of a positive customer referral, and alternatively the danger of adverse publicity. And the sale needs, wherever possible, to remain "planet friendly" – as many companies have found to their cost, a sale which is environmentally un-friendly can have damaging and costly repercussions.

Viewpoint Rankings

A worthwhile and guiding principle to take to heart when selling, is the law of "viewpoint ranking". One solid observation that betrays inexperienced or struggling salespeople is that they pitch their standpoints in the wrong order. Most typically, you'll hear such salespeople talk predominantly about their product. Skilled sellers know that they must earn trust and sell themselves first, their company second, and product only as a distant third – See figure 8.3.

Salesperson First → Company Second → Product Third

Figure 8.3 The Sales Focus

Similar rules guide success here. Adopting a People-Profit-Planet mindset in part requires that salespeople follow potentially counter-intuitive stages. Rather than think first purely of themselves, to the dismissal of any other outlook, it is necessary to consider first the Patron, then the Purveyor. Only after should you reflect on your personal perspective as Pitcher. – See figure 8.4.

Patron → Purveyor → Pitcher

Figure 8.4 Patron – Purveyor – Pitcher

Next, it is possible to graft on the selling cycle stages. You can drill down into several layers here traditionally. The steps a deal can go through are manifold, the number of so-called Gateways (where you leap from one stage to the next) plentiful. So for model simplicity, consider the following three, see figure 8.5.

Pipeline → Proposal → Purchase

Figure 8.5 The Third Dimension

The word Pipeline in standard sales conversations, equates and is interchangeable with the funnel. Some feel that they're not strictly synonyms. Your pipeline is not necessarily your funnel. Funnel for sure refers to the entirety of what you've got on the go. When assessing what's in the pipeline, you're more likely to examine business hoped to come in the future. So in this context the term pipeline means opportunities that have not yet been fully opened or qualified. They are at the very mouth of your funnel, hopefully about to start their journey towards the spout. They are suspects as opposed to prospects.

Proposal – The Proposal is when a deal appears on your forecast. It is qualified and you are willing to put the resource in place to pursue it. It doesn't necessarily follow you've delivered a hand-crafted document outlining your proposition, but a formal outline of what you propose is in the offing.

Purchase – And then there's the signature. You have a (new) customer. Once they've purchased, a whole new slant on the funnel kicks in. Whether you're a dedicated new-business only salesperson or a hand-holding account manager, there are several post-sale consequences that follow on from the award of business.

Gaining Buy-In

To the outwardly ambivalent, at the very least, a sustainable focus should appeal as smoothing the notorious, and highly undesirable, wild swings of feast and famine. These are widely recognised as hastening the destruction of many an upward sales career. Sustainability offers the closest guarantee in selling to ending the stop-go, boom and bust cycles that so many in sales find frustrating and financially restricting.

There's both direct and circumspect ways of ensuring this framework permeates throughout a Sales department.

Take-up can be enhanced by conflating the *Three Pillars* mindset with Key Sales Objectives (KSOs). Criteria can be sculpted that guide salespeople placing the customer at the heart of the proposal and how they embrace and demonstrate application of 'People, Planet and Profit' ethos. These can also be made part of a tailored personal development plan for each salesperson as well as forming a basis for on-going one-on-one coaching.

KSO & KPI

These are sales monitoring siblings: Key Sales Objectives & Key Performance Indicators.

Most sales endeavours track KPIs, yet strangely only larger structures are inclined to formally involve KSOs. KPIs are readily measurable events. Classic examples include calls made, proposals delivered, quotes sent and presentations given, all within specific time periods. They highlight the numbers.

KSOs on the other hand, are concerned with less quantitative actions. Actions which are considered to support rather than signpost overall selling success. They are often related to training issues of the day, new behaviours or micro-marketing. Examples can include fresh skill development, expertise gained in a particular emerging arena or the population of a seminar. It is feasible to consider KPIs as addressing "hard" issues, KSOs the "soft" issues.

One further distinction is that sales teams can use the term 'key sales objective' in a generic context. Examples tend to arise surrounding customer retention or competitor lock-out measures. Such a non-specific heading is separate to the purpose defined above.

Other avenues are open to reinforce the message. Third-party endorsement is always worthwhile and this can be provided by actively engaging with customers and suppliers. Promising reciprocity through formal slots at sales conferences can help with this.

Then there's the most obvious way of trying to shape sales behaviour, a link to payment plans.

Incentives

The thrill of making more sales is alas not always enough to push a salesperson ever onwards. Despite a degree of academic protest – building on from Glucksberg's revision of Duncker's famed candle experiment to highlight the over justification effect, stating that performance related financial rewards do not in fact yield greater performance, and can actually diminish results – incentives continue to play a huge role in the recompense and motivation of salespeople. Indeed, it would take an extremely brave sales department head to eschew a backbone of formulised targets.

Conjuring the optimum incentive is a delicate operation. Too tough, and motivation will plummet faced with scaling an impossible summit; too soft, and a mutinous sales force will revolt from the perceived injustice of underperformer enrichment.

To succeed, attainment must be within the complete and sole control of the individual salesperson. Subjectivity must be removed, and the reward must be seen as commensurate with both effort required and ultimate achievement gained.

CSR Adoption

Sales Prevention Department

Sales functions are notorious for cultivating the perception that they deliberately operate in their own bubble. This can often be seen as both separate to the direction and outside the workings of the rest of the organisation.

Yet there is enlightened opinion that to truly succeed, a sales team must participate as a valued partner within the overall company framework and that mutual cooperation is necessary. This means that the highest levels of leadership must be intimate with their sales endeavours. You are, for example, more likely to be world-class if your Chief Exec is closely involved with your sales process.

This carries ramifications for Corporate Social Responsibility. All too frequently, diktats from on high suffer abrupt dismissal when they are perceived as having little relevance to Sales. Indeed in the past, published policies ranging from mission statements to carbon footprints were not just prone to Sales department indifference, but intentionally side-lined as a potential selling hindrance.

The phrase Sales Prevention Department has long been coined to describe any colleague(s) hampering selling. A label that at any time salespeople will happily and liberally apply to the likes of Marketing, Production, Customer Service and many centrally imposed edicts.

So how do we develop a CSR stance within the organisation? The textbook way to ensure take-up of any new way of thinking is to involve those required to implement it, from problem recognition to issue resolution. In this context, it would mean giving the sales force at all levels an opportunity to make an early input in the moulding the eventual CSR policy.

Seldom has any such inclusion of the sales force been seen when it comes to crafting such corporate thrust. One exception – where the mission emerged beginning with the desire to be seen as "the defining force" for their arena – the prevailing destructive sales culture jettisoned the outcome leaving the sales process suffocatingly unmoved.

So where CSR already exists, it is usually born without Sales assistance. It is then disseminated throughout the organisation via an array of events and messages. These are typically spearheaded by dedicated corporate communication resource or a brave lone sustainability warrior.

So the challenge must be to generate the acceptance and buy-in of the sales function; the question is how to ingrain the sales effort with something that they would ordinarily be disinclined to consider integral to their success?

Salespeople are not shy in asking the question internally that's forever on the lips of recipients of their pitches; what's in it for me?

One excellent way of gaining benefit acceptance by osmosis is to garner the power of the customer base. Where clients already have their own CSR aims, they should be uncovered (and documented) by the salesforce. This then provides a number of openings for the individual salesperson.

1. They can increase their footprint inside the client. They become both less reliant on just existing contacts and also move towards strengthening total contact spread.

2. They can unearth more reasons for continued purchase. The ability to align both party's CSR ambitions could introduce stand-out and unique reasons for continued and extra spend.

3. Further relationships across both organisations can be initiated. This lessens risk, with new exposure between both sides from departments and roles hitherto sheltered from one another.

These all help form the juiciest result of all. Client return on investment can rocket.

With more compelling reasons to maintain the buyer-vendor relationship and more people involved from both sides, all more closely tied to the prime sustainable goals of both firms, a fruitful relationship is more likely to stay in place and prosper.

Best-Practice & Process

Are Sustainable sales teams destined to prove elusive?

Remarkably, no. Whilst it is likely the odd skirmish may disrupt plans, the opposite ought to apply; the prognosis should in fact be rosy. This is because one fundamental force sways in its favour. For as long as everyone, from worthy practitioners and experts to dubious observers and chancers, have sought to codify sales the concept of sustainability has featured at the heart of selling best-practice.

Success Is A Process

The unequivocal evidence is that following a definable sales process sets the achievers apart. The intimacy with which senior management are involved with the sales process can also shape market leading results. If you know why you succeed on a sale, and try to replicate it, then you are more likely to reach the overall aim of any process; namely to generate and follow a sustainable, repeatable successful selling formula.

So what is a process? The English language reference, the Oxford English Dictionary defines 'process' as:

"A series of actions or steps taken in order to achieve a particular end".

It is this nuance of 'action or step' that is critical to a winning sales process. Those that embark on the process journey often do so from the starting point of the funnel. Assessing how you break down the journey from cold suspect to eventual client can produce a number of steps by which any deal will probably traverse.

Framing the bid progress by way of a series of discrete elements does have some merit. One good method of understanding the outline of your own potential best practice process is to investigate the steps that your target prospects go through in their vigilant buying processes.

Yet this approach can easily miss a crucial component; any difference between these 'steps' and required 'actions'. A sales process should acknowledge a sequential flow of events but what is also essential is to isolate other occurrences that significantly influence the sale and which can take place in a non-linear manner.

Examples where a huge improvement in the odds of an order following include:

- Pin-pointing key prospect individual buy-in (like CEO involvement or what is often called 'champion' identification. Securing support from an 'insider' with clout and will to sway opinion);
- Specific (possibly joint) activity (such as a piece of proofing or engagement with other parties), or;

- Vital (sometimes formally documented) intelligence (e.g. sign-off routine or agreeing the financial representation of pain resolution)

> **Rule: Nurture the pro, counter the anti**

Developing Your Culture

The Sustainable Business firmly believes that it is better to build on existing elements which work, rather than starting each time completely from scratch. The concept of "alpinism" can be used to evoke how difficult it is to carve a new path to a summit rather than follow the trail and use the ropes of someone that has already made the ascent.

There is no shortage of Sales strategy specialists that offer their own deciphered classification in this regard. For those with deep wallets, there are training companies that have expanded their global reach. Huthwaite with their Spin methodology and Miller Heiman's Solution Selling with their 'blue sheets' both contribute compelling ideas to the Sales oeuvre. Similar expenditure can secure the services of strategy consultants with heavy Sales arena affiliation. Names like Bain and Mercuri are inclined to be familiar with those having sold within FTSE100 structures.

In either case, much the same issues emerge. Someone else's concrete is poured over how *you* can do things. The path can indeed be valid. The remedy is derived with plenty of intelligent thought to herald it. Yet it is their process, not yours. It comes from a "plastic manual" as opposed to technique and strategy tailored to your business, your market, or your customers. Hence the cadre of any nascent sales process is best formed from the bones of what you do today that works. This will gain a head-start in terms of sales person adoption, when big ticket interventions bewilder sales people requiring too many new reporting and other skills they are rendered still-born.

Your Sales Process Recipe – Four Basic Ingredients

a)   Intent

The platform of any process is astonishingly overlooked in a majority of sales ambitions. The lack of any coherent mission or existence of a simple vision that each salesperson can readily articulate for their overall sales effort is astounding. Where such mantra might be found, it can be so shackled by vacuous, meaningless corporate-speak as to crush its usability, never to be applied beyond the ivory-towered walls from whence it came. Sales intent should be short and snappy, the less words the better. And preferably words from a customer's perspective, ideally in a way that eludes to the problem you resolve and parades the nature of your pursuit. Be careful though to avoid the style of a marketing strapline that could be misconstrued as glib.

b)   Qualification

A key facet of any process is rigorous qualification. Indeed, a process that keeps on delivering is one where at each stage the seller thinks of deals in terms of qualifying out, rather than trying to justify continued attention. A prime measure should be how closely the deal in question fits into the identified sweet spot. Target the zone in which you never lose, or never should lose, then deduce the extent to which the deal resembles such characteristics. If the characteristics fall outside this zone, then cull them from your activity. A sales process prone to fail is one in which deals are pursued that really ought not to be.

c)   Forecasting

Your view of where each deal in your pipeline is at, must follow the chosen process.

A forecast should be a living, breathing document. Whenever a snapshot is taken, you must be able to judge progress, and the inevitable likelihood of triumph, aligned to the actions and steps identified as necessary to signal success. Forecasting rituals often laser in on business written in the current time period.

d)   Post-sale

What happens once the contract is awarded can also suffer scant consideration.

Prevention is of course better than cure. All those things that can go wrong after an order is placed can be staved off with forethought. A stringent customer handover procedure is often seen as unnecessary extra work by a salesperson hunting down a signature, yet if the needs of post-sale resource are addressed pre-sale it can actually become a selling tool rather than obstacle.

> **Rule: Legendary customer service is the greatest deal closer**

Two Seasonings

If you're looking for inspiration on how your process could take shape, then take themes from the following pair.

i) Ideal Sales Campaign

This is usually based on a previous sale where the entire pursuit saw just about everything go well to such an extent that it is fondly recalled as the 'perfect' campaign. Each aspect can be extracted and dissected to form a basis of your budding process.

ii) Preferred Procurement Process

Many industries feature professional buyers who follow established purchasing rules. The rubric can be rigid, yet just about every supposed model can be influenced and tweaked as desired (by buyer and vendor). Whether selling into a specific sector or anywhere buyers share certain key traits, you can take their own recurring procurement routines and mould them into your sustainable sales process.

Staple Range

The Sustainable Business has a wide-range of staple ingredients to potentially draw upon

a) Impact of Change

It is long established that selling anything, where more than one person is involved in deciding, that will instigate a change, requires the seller to focus not on the change itself but the impact of that change. Any part of the process that brings this to the fore is welcome. Noteworthy events, challenge meetings, pre-proposal reviews, discussion with third-parties (for references) and any proofing and validation work can all warrant inclusion.

b)   Buying Criteria

To glean why people will buy, who has input, and on what timescales this should occur, is all fundamental buying insight.

c)   Role Players

Ensuring individuals are not neglected, blockers are overcome and a coach (or champion) is found.

d)   Vulnerability

Key security indicators, assessing stability factors and even documenting 'white space' (also known as gap analysis).

e)   Tempo

Monitoring how you gauge urgency, spot 'red flags' and other deal alerts such as escalation procedures.

Herbs And Spice

Finally, here are some "herbs and spice" to flavour any effective sales process.

1. Don't destabilise your efforts by a reliance on activity, focus should rather be on outcomes. Great golfers do not think about the putt, they focus on picking the ball out of the hole.

2. Seek a continuous improvement element. Place measurement value on actionable metrics over vanity.

3. Give your process a name. With a special identity, Project Process can develop a winning personality all of its own. Where possible

adopt a title that follows a desired image, or create a mnemonic from a selection of values. Either way, your succinct label will then be at the heart of your success story.

4. And understand the Critical Success Drivers (CSD) – the key reasons why the deal was won. Understanding the CSD's from winning bids, if used effectively will drive sales onwards and upwards.

> **Rule: Focus on why you succeeded and do it again!**

Avoiding Past Mistakes

It is indisputable that the largest determinant of sales success is the creation and following of a repeatable successful sales process. Indeed, if nothing separates the flush quota-busting rep from their sleepless underperforming colleagues more than the adherence to their finely honed sales process, then what mistakes are to be avoided when putting down a process?

Frequent surveys suggest that it almost doesn't matter what that process is, the fact that it is in place alone helps propel achievement. What matters more is that it evolves; adapting to change and applying what you've learned is required.

> **Rule: Continuous Improvement and learning = Higher sales**

Time Thieves

Anecdotally, you will hear salespeople tell you that excessive and spurious reporting is the bane of their lives. At the other end, there are salespeople that embrace the demands of forensic reporting. I've heard a sales leader of a 320-strong sales force bemoan such as "Laptop Larries".

It is obvious that any reporting, whether on expensively assembled software, cloud-based systems, or any assorted parallel and shadow spread-sheet or document, must follow the structured process set by the organisation.

Figures on "time spent on filling in forms" are shady. One reason for this is that the funders of most sales surveys are the very CRM vendors with most to lose from any implication that their wares take too much of a user's time and are largely ineffective. Another is that boundaries are deliberately blurred when it comes to activity studies. Input sales data can be hidden inside a multitude of different tasks, such as general admin, call preparation and even territory management or thrown in with meetings.

In the same mould that aforementioned training and strategy consultancies can put you in their debilitating concrete CRM systems can be just as restrictive, regardless of their salespeople's protestations of simple user-definable structures.

Leaving aside these omnipresent perceptions, the biggest waste of a salesperson's time is undoubtedly coming second and post-sale fire-fighting. Getting to the last two on a bid and not being selected is fatally unsustainable behaviour. The remedial action to prevent this from happening is to institute your victorious process, a process with robust qualification and all the other parts already mentioned.

A salesperson embroiled in any negative issue that occurs after a deal is signed, even if they are an account manager, is also a shockingly stifling abuse of time.

Procedures can be developed as previously explained to prevent this.

Contact Regimes

One specific area of planning that can get overlooked and impact negatively on sustainable sales ambitions addresses how often and who you contact client-side.

Many sellers segment their business base using a function of the number of touches each individual role occupier requires and the amount they buy, or potentially will spend. It is not uncommon to discover that a sales operation can cull the number of names on their sales ledger and become more profitable with more sustainable activity.

The typical treatment is to choose bands of clients (or prospects) and match their contact plans to them – it is common to find pyramids drawn to visualise this. Analysis can then select whichever of email, telephone or face-to-face contact is required, how often and at what frequency. Effort should be better targeted for all concerned as a result.

Communication Breakdown

There may well be external forces seemingly beyond Sales' control whose differing perspective could sink your plans. The most obvious example is Marketing. Serious needs to be applied to how they can buy-in to your plans for process.

Whether it be the type of leads they introduce into the mouth of your funnel, the collateral they produce or campaigns they run, how much do they reinforce the messages and strategy Sales are pushing forward?

Losing momentum down cracks in the pavement is a commonplace delayer. What is in place at the intersection of each functional border? When the baton is passed is the frequent moment when impetus can drop.

Action Tools – Opportunity Assessment

Creating an accurate and complete sales qualification yardstick is a good investment of time and effort. It not only allows you to elect whether to bid or not to bid, but also, as your campaign progresses, it allows you to continually assess the strength of your offering.

The SUSTAIN model is a generalised example, which is relatively straightforward to adapt to your own circumstance. Categories of essential intelligence are shown by the easy to remember mnemonic, SUSTAIN. See figure 8.6:

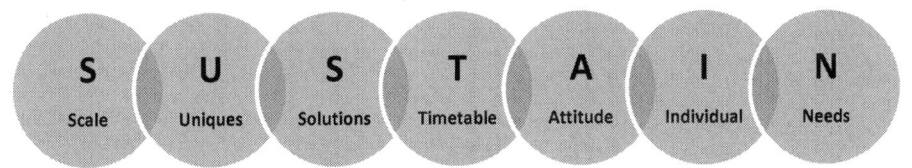

S	U	S	T	A	I	N
Scale	Uniques	Solutions	Timetable	Attitude	Individual	Needs

Figure 8.6 – The SUSTAIN Model

or each dimension of the SUSTAIN model, characteristic, scores are recorded as per the matrix in figure 8.7, and then displayed in graph 8.9 to allow results to be tracked over a number of months or years.

Growing

It is possible to change this acronym by using different headings to signify similar elements. For instance, you can generate an equally valid treatment using the word 'green'. The components here could be; Goals, Roles, Economics, Exclusives, Needs.

Values

In figure 8.7, sample figures have been used as guidance. You should insert your own values. Where italicised answers are in parentheses, it is to show the broad range of possibilities.

Where necessary, columns can be blank, if only one or two values apply. This suits binary choices, two poles where one is desirable the other not.

The Sustainable Business

Dimension	Parameter	Measurement Criterion
Scale	Size	1 - Too small, 2 - Too big, 3 – Borderline, 4 - Second best 5 – Perfect
	Products	1 – Impossible, 2 – Ideal
	Sector	1 - Way off, 2 - Tenuous 3 – Tangential 4 - Close relative, 5 - Sweet spot
	Geography	1 - Far away, 2 – Close
Total		
Uniques	Product Uniques	1 - Only me toos, 2 - Marginal usp, 3 - 3rd best usp, 4 - 2nd best usp 5 - Best usp)
	Company Uniques	1 - Only me toos, 2 - Marginal usp, 3 - 3rd best usp 4 - 2nd best usp, 5 - Best usp
	Product Fit	1 - Heavy, 2 - Bespoke needs, 3 – 'Futures', 4 - Small bespoke, 5 - Minor tailored standard
	References	1 - Poor reference, 2 - No reference, 3 - Good local 4 - Good close, 5 - Fit twin
	How did we get on deal	1 - RFP, ITT, SOR, 2 - Cold call, 3 - Consultant / Seminar 4 - Incoming lead, 5 – Referral
Total		
Solutions	Cost Benefit	1 - Touch and go, 2 – Unknown, 3 – Sought, 4 – Promising 5 - Documented & agreed
	Competition	1 - Strong incumbent, 2 – Unknown, 3 - Won't divulge 4 – None 5 – Logical / Known
	Budget Approval	1 – No, 2 - Blind to process, 3 - Unknown 4 - Involved in process, 5 – Yes
Total		
Timetable	Deal Cycle	1 - >2yrs, 2 - 1 to 2 Years, 3 - 6 to 12 Months, 4 - 3 to 6 Months 5 - Inside 90 days
	Deal stage now	1 – Cold, 2 – Suspect, 3 – Prospect, 4 – Proposal, 5 - Quote closing
	Decision Activity Agreed	1 – No, 3 - to do, 5 – Yes
	Decision Criteria Agreed	1 – No, 3 - to do, 5 – yes
Total		
Attitude	How do we stand	1 - Way out, 2 - +10% Above, 3 – Unknown, 4 – Close, 5 – Within
	Corporate Ownership	1 - USA / other, 2 – Europe, 3 - Far East, 4 – Australasia, 5 – UK

	Reason for project	1 – Unknown, 2 - Cost saving, 3 - New supplier 4 – Breakdown, 5 – Expansion
	Would I Buy?	1 – No, 3 – Maybe, 5 – Yes
	New Tech Ideas	1 – Sceptics, 2 – Conservatives, 3 – Pragmatists, 4 - Visionaries, 5 – Enthusiasts
	Cloud Approach	1 - Low regard, 3 – Traditional, 5 – Progressive
	IT Structure	1 - Non-existent, 2 - Part-time, 3 – Average 4 - Self sufficient, 5 - Very able / 3rd party
Total		
Individual	Is key person access	1 – Difficult, 3 - Average 5 – Easy
	Main Contact	1 - IT Manger, 2 - Network Manger, 3 – CIO, 4 – CFO, 5 – CEO
	Contact Status	1 - Unknown / tyre kicker, 2 - Background Influencer 3 - Key recommender, 4 – Proposer, 5 - Decision maker
	Relationship	1 – Hostile, 2 – Cold, 3 – Average, 4 – Professional, 5 – Warm
Total		
Needs	Project Need	1 - Not accepted, 5 - Agreed & documented
	Need shaped	1 - Documented with competition influence, 5 - Documented with our guidance (SOR, RFP, ITT)
	Futures	1 None, 5 – Plenty
	Company performance	1 - Cutting back, 2 - Newly acquired, 3 - Middling 4 – Profitable, 5 – Growing
Total		

Figure 8.7

Taxonomy

Considerations when constructing your own framework include bringing out a widespread management clarion, "have you spoken to the MAN?" M-a-n in this case refers to the person who has the Money, Authority and Need – See figure 8.8.

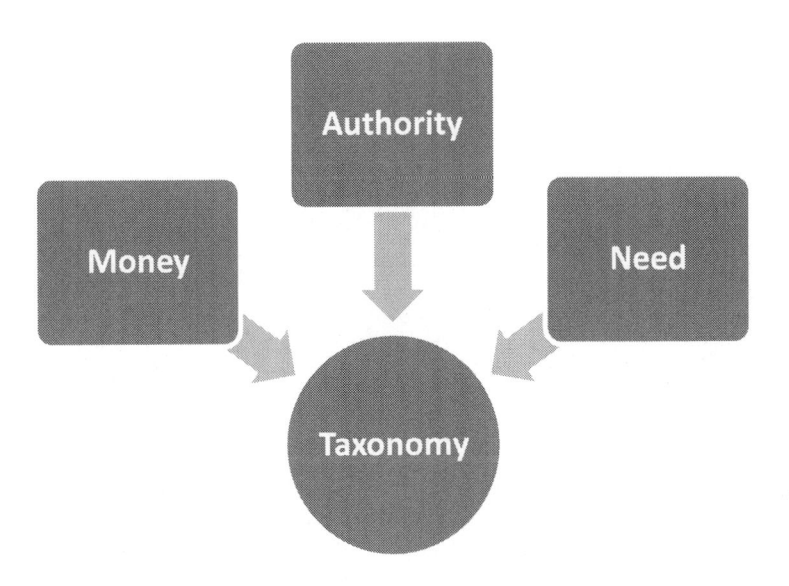

[Diagram: Authority, Money, Need → Taxonomy]

Figure 8.8 MAN Model

Further, consider some kind of measurement of size, scale, scope or numbers is handy, as well as something that denotes your 'fit', in terms of solution. And you should incorporate one part on the personalities, politics, roles and individuals involved in your own classification

Scoring

If you mark each cell that applies to your current opportunity, then if you can see highlighting mainly down the right-hand side, you're hopefully on to a winner. You can add further sophistication if you wish, by utilising the points at the column headings, and even attribute an overall percentage of deal pursuit attraction or current bid security.

Once we have collected the seven totals for each of the Sustain seven elements, we can use this to graphically track the sustainable performance, and to identify areas where the performance is improving or getting worse. Commonly, a radar or spider chart can be used for this, as per graph 8.9:

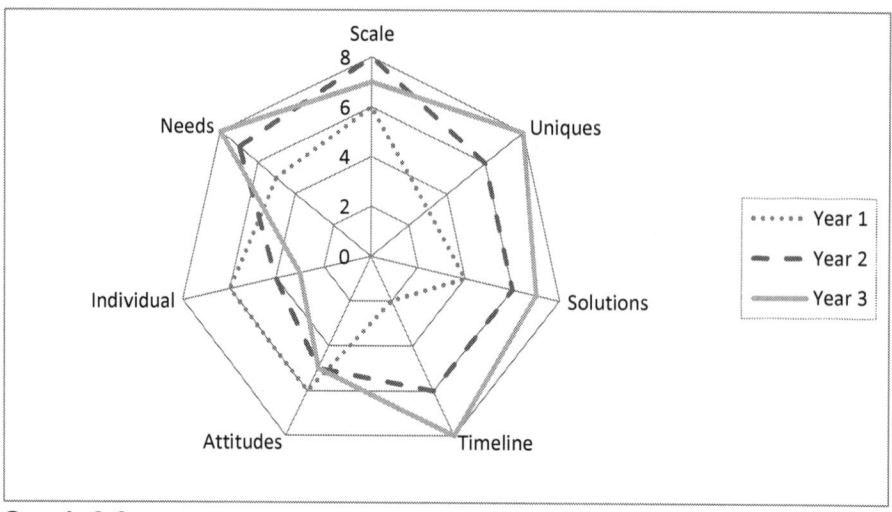

Graph 8.9

Sustainable Process Quickstart

Determining how sustainable your sales process is can be a daunting prospect for the first time. To assist, there is a QuickStart Process analysis model, see figure 8.10.

	12-point Checklist
Headlines	☐ Sales Intent published
	☐ Process/Project named
Balances	☐ Customer Handover procedure
	☐ Target Market defined
	☐ Sequential Process mapped
	☐ Key Process Elements extracted
Numbers	☐ Top line Revenue/Sales
	☐ Bottom line Margin/Profit
	☐ Average Deal length & value
	☐ Target Deal ranges
	☐ Prospect churn rates
	☐ Retention & Attrition rates

Figure 8.10 – 12 Point Sustainable Checklist

Sustainable Canvas 'Green Screen'

The need to measure across *the Sustainable Business* has been clearly documented in chapter 14, and once again it is important that this transparency is maintained throughout the organisation. There are few more externally facing departments than the Sales team, and few with more to lose.

Environmental catastrophes, scandals and mischief are widely reported when they happen; consider oil spillages, children caught working in factories, or production of unsafe products. Examples are plentiful of where organisations have failed in their sustainable responsibility, and the sales have suffered. Consider the impact on BP from the 2010 Deep Water Horizon calamity in the Sea of Mexico, or the fallout from the UK News International phone hacking scandals investigated so deeply in 2011 and 2012.

Whilst it may only be a temporary blip, sales teams need to be aware of their pursuit of "deals" with potentially dangerous side-effects. Any present deal can be mapped for review purposes by filling-in the kind of grid shown previously which may include by way of an example, use of words such as: QUALIFACTION, FORECASTING, SECURITY, PROCESS, ALIGNMENT or HANDOVER.

What is crucial is that the sales team are "on board", recognise the importance of *the Sustainable Business*, and understand the potential impacts on the organisation going forward.

Case Studies – Chapter 8

Study A – Chubb Fire - Changing Course Greenwards

- Chubb manufacture, sell and service fire safety equipment, most notably extinguishers
- UK HQ Sunbury, Surrey, England
- Circa 50 Area Sales Representatives on road plus around 50 more Service Sales Representatives spread
- Sales and Service Representatives allocated across five geographic regions, as well as to dedicated national accounts

A situation occurred in the early 2000s, immediately prior to the mid 2003 United Technologies Corp (UTC) takeover.

The Chubb Fire possessed a leader whose previous teacher training was put to good effect. With an effervescent way of getting his ideas across, he was a natural persuader. He realised that they could no longer try and grow like they had traditionally, the inference was to banish any laziness and dismissive attitude towards the customer. In order to grow, he sensed a change in approach was required. One key metaphor used was of the leaky bucket. In the same way you don't use a bucket with a hole in to carry water, there's folly in working hard to gain customers only to see more leave than were won. They sought a sustainability sales function.

He announced that they would now try something other than to cut costs and put prices up. It was a dynamic statement.

As CEO he saw the future moving away from commoditised product selling towards solutions. He introduced services that offered value such as fire risk assessments and a whole raft of new products like large range public and workplace health and safety signs.

The organisation had an almost military feel at the time. Sales rep basic salary was only around £15,000. Many sellers were former engineers, brought up on tasks such as checking and re-filling fire extinguishers. There was always the whisper that many could allegedly 'sell' by threatening to tip-off the local Fire Officer, if they felt not enough fire extinguishers were taken at a client site.

So to support this shift, a series of workshops using outside sales training expertise took place across the country. At the same time, a large external consultancy devised a sales management system.

The training was however unfortunately tired and isolated. A majority of salespeople were so ingrained with selling 'on the regs' that it was very difficult for them to embrace any new way. Further, the spreadsheet created to manage all aspect of sales activity was so complex appreciation and understanding of it was low.

An experience with halon is a demonstration of how difficult such a change can be. Halon eradication was compulsory within ten years of the 1993 Montreal Protocol on ozone-depleting chemicals. A marketing slogan even chimed, "remember: no action is not an option" - hardly "on-message". Then a senior exec, a man who promoted the new ways with gusto, was caught off guard. A BBC Radio 4 Today news programme interviewer asked why halon systems must be decommissioned. With lots of benefits to lean on and the sustainable slant to evoke, he instead paused and replied simply, "it's the law". Out of character, this certainly went dead set against all he stood for and envisioned, yet shows just how tricky it is in the heat of the pitch furnace to engage your new, green mindset.

Study B – Océ - The Business Window

- Sales division circa 20-strong, dealing with both resellers and clients
- Sell high-speed wide-format digital print systems
- Became part of Canon Group in 2010
- UK Headquarters in Brentwood, Essex, England
- Global HQ Venlo, Netherlands.

As a corporation, Océ now publicly embrace sustainability. In 2011 they quoted CEO, Rokus van Iperen:

> "For many decades it has been normal practice at Océ that economic considerations are always balanced with ecological arguments. These drives are mutually reinforcing."

Océ published a sustainability mission, instituted five focal areas for a sustainability forum (paper, energy, re-use, product responsibility, employer of choice) and conduct activities such as green-orientated new product development and holding annual sustainability weeks.

In the mid-2000s, new products emerged that promoted Océ's green ideals to such an extent that they even released a piece of software (Document Distribution Manager, aka DDM) that sought to help companies print less. At the time particularly radical advice from a printer manufacturer in a sector historically bred to charge per click and thus encourage as much hard copy output as possible.

As Océ progressed to openly broadcast their sustainable goals, the UK's wide format (for paper known as A0, A1 and A2 as opposed to small format A3 and A4) division realised that more such software was coming. A huge fresh opportunity opened up beyond their traditional hardware bias. Their initial move was to discover and latch onto the CSR policies of their prospects.

They thought that producing fewer printouts in a drawing office arena where the likes of architects and designers constantly ran off multiple copies of enormous plans, with its attendant power and materials savings, should surely hold wide appeal.

Through the pioneering work of managers Dave Parford and Ken Welsh they advanced this to construct a sales tactic they called the Business Window. This aimed to map all customer's goals (including financial and sustainable) directly to specific Océ functionality.

Whereas they had traditionally focused on where a prospect might desire, for example a faster machine, the purpose now was to allocate where and how usage of their solutions would help hit business and monetary objectives.

One of their anchor breakthroughs with this new mentality came from Scotland, at the Edinburgh offices of building services support group Arthur McKay. An old proposal that had gone nowhere in February 2005 was revisited the following Autumn. By adopting their Business Window lens they found a new justification to replace a pair of aged machines; an Aarque photocopier and a superseded Océ colour forerunner to the newly chosen Océ kit.

So within a year after a stalled initial proposal, two new placements were achieved with a solid payback of just nine months, bought for £23,000.

Study C – Trend Control Systems – Selling to Sceptics

- Manufacture and sell building management systems
- Case study set in mid-2000s
- Estimated market penetration; one in four of all new projects won across the UK Design
- Circa 20-strong sales department, dealing with both resellers and clients
- Community of approximately 150 resellers, top tier of which are on an exclusive basis
- Later in 2005 became part of Honeywell
- Headquartered in Horsham, Sussex, England

Prior to its becoming part of Honeywell, Trend Controls' sales team had several sustainable ambitions during the 2000s. Yet they encountered what ranged from apathy to hostility in the marketplace, with both buyers and their large number of influencers and recommenders obsessed with lowest price, and ignoring all other considerations. This was particularly frustrating as they felt that despite higher upfront CAPEX costs, when deployed, their systems – which control up to a fifth of all building energy use (in a sector known as HVAC; heating, ventilation and air conditioning) – saved energy and thereby money, and were far more competitive over the product life cycle than the commonly cheaper-up-front competition.

How could they gain growth where purchasers focused on the cost of everything, the value of nothing?

Several innovative measures were undertaken; one in particular involved changing perceived values through focusing on lifetime value debates; and a second introduced a new product with a new mindset.

Why were these chosen and what were the results?

Having lost the account of Birmingham City Plaza shopping precinct around five years earlier, local area manager Mark Stanton was determined to win the business back from rivals Satchwell. The incumbent looked set to remain in place with a bid around 15% lower than Trend, yet he pushed the concept of lifetime value hard. The client accepted that although his solution featured higher day one costs, over the course of operation, greater savings would in fact accrue, with possible lifetime savings in excess of £50,000. This success inspired a new style of communication with the market. They leant on their own findings, documenting where more investment would release more savings, and implemented elements of the 1:5:200 "Evans ratio" thinking alongside Best Value Principles as then promoted by the Government of the day seeking more cost effective procurement.

Furthermore, they also sought to add more peripheral products around its core solutions. This was to both increase the average project till-ring, and change the landscape of each bid to highlight total long-term cost savings.

One particular product range that seemed to have stalled sales-wise was Variable Speed Drives; this product was widely viewed as an unnecessary and expensive add-on. Yet its contribution to improved overall system performance enhancement far outweighing the extra investment, leading instead to demonstrably reduced maintenance and greater efficiency; this was at the heart of the renewed pitch.

By January 2005, two quarters after re-focusing, sales of this line had increased by 183%; in cash terms, around £900,000.

The Sustainable Business

Notes Page | **Page Ref**

The Sustainable Business

Summary Chapter 9
Sustainable Operations

Key Learning Points
- Recognising and maximising value
- Identification of waste
- Achieving value at lowest Total Cost of Sustainable Ownership
- The process of producing in different environments
- The impact of the operating processes on the Supply Chain
- Achievement of "Fit for Purpose" output
- Understanding customer requirements
- ISO process mapping
- Conformity versus Individuality
- Core features of sustainable operations
- Forecasting and ERP modelling
- Service operations
- Use of quality models
- Establishing "Common Cause Management"
- Implementing DMAIC process
- Identifying issues in the operational process
- Developing operational improvements
- Dealing with people in the Operations process
- Use of CAD/CAM technology
- Explanation of the Toyota processes
- Production styles
- House of Toyota
- The elimination of waste

Tool Summary
- Process Cloud
- SIPOC
- Value Chain
- PESTLE
- DMAIC
- TQM
- Six Sigma
- 6Ms Model
- 3E Model

The Sustainable Business

- Job Rotation/Enlargement/Enrichment
- Fishbone diagrams

CIPS Syllabus Reference
- Level 4 Negotiating and Contracting in Procurement and Supply
- Level 4 Managing Contracts and Relationships in Procurement and Supply
- Level 5 Sustainability in Procurement and Supply
- Level 5 Management in Procurement and Supply
- Level 5 Managing Risks in Supply Chains
- Level 5 Operations Management in Supply Chains
- Level 5 Improving the Competitiveness of Supply Chains
- Level 5 Category Management in Procurement and Supply
- Level 6 Leadership in Procurement and Supply
- Level 6 Corporate and Business Strategy
- Level 6 Strategic Supply Chain Management
- Level 6 Supply Chain Diligence

Chapter 9: Sustainable Operations

"Almost all quality improvement comes via simplification of design, manufacturing... layout, processes, and procedures."
– Tom Peters

Operations Management is "the process of doing". This includes all the activities from acquisition of inputs through to final delivery. This can be constructing something, changing the state of a raw material or resolving a customer issue through the delivery of a service. These processes are aligned and structured to help the organisation fulfil the business goals and achieve its vision.

Once again, central to the operational processes are the issues of value and waste. As defined previously, the delivery of value is key to *the Sustainable Business*, to the *Profit Pillar* and to its fulfilment of customer satisfaction. Equally important is the elimination of waste, both to the profitability of *the Sustainable Business*, the *Planet Pillar* and the best use of resources.

The Sustainable Business needs effective and honed processes to help it achieve its *Sustainable Vision*. These processes need to reflect the best use of resources to ensure that *the Three Pillar* principle is upheld and longevity is assured.

When considering Operations Management, the nature of the specific business activity needs to be understood, and delivered recognising the need for flexibility, rapid reaction to changes in customer requirements, and attention to the risk profile of the organisation. Generally, operations fall into four core types:

i) Manufacturing
ii) Delivery of services
iii) Retail operations
iv) Not-For-Profit

Examination of the individual facets and traits of a business process falls outside the scope of this text and remains the domain of the protagonists in that organisation. Common to all organisations however are some generic rules. Whilst each and every business will have a different set of processes, they should all possess a desire to **add maximum customer value at the lowest Total Cost of Ownership**.

> **Rule: Maximum Value & Minimal Waste**

The business processes will sit within the overall Supply Chain – the P in the SIPOC model - utilising the inputs and (hopefully) producing the desired outputs. The collection of processes are often blended, inter-related and utilise common elements. Sharing and coordination of machinery, manpower, capital etc makes eminent business sense and increases the rate of return on the investment made in the business and thus enhancing *the Profit Pillar*. This activity will also reduce the overall risk within *the Sustainable Business* by increasing the business diversity, and allowing more resource - either machinery or manpower - to be interchangeable between functions.

The process cloud represents the bundle of processes commonly seen in an organisation, see figure 9.1, and are normally detailed in the organisation's Process Manual.

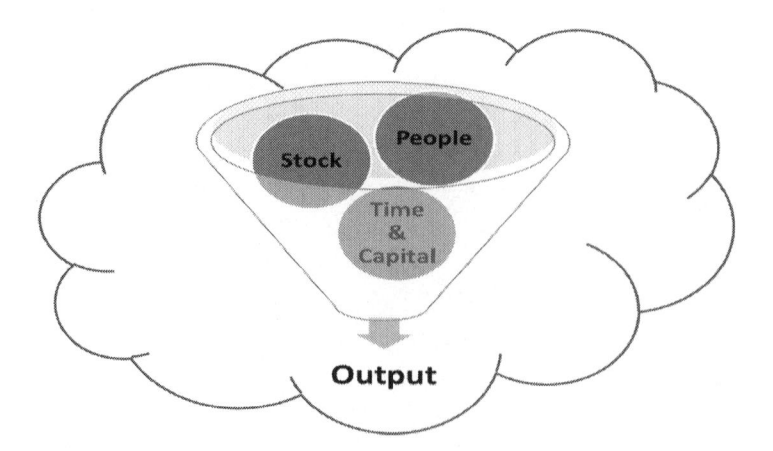

Figure 9.1 – The Process Cloud

Understanding and mapping the processes is an important part of ensuring the processes are consistent, reliable and sustainable, but also helps ensure that investment returns are optimised. Producing and recording these processes is typically the first job when implementing an ISO9000 or equivalent system into an organisation. The production of the Process Manual is to maintain a definitive record of the organisational operating rules and methods, which can then be audited to establish compliance.

Any ISO implementation revolves around this Process Manual and the unwavering compliance of the organisation, its management and all its employees. In most organisations, these processes will have evolved over its life. Few, if any, businesses have started with a set of rules and worked outwards. When organisations attempt to attain ISO accreditation, some implementation consultants try and enforce process changes to match a predefined manual. The incumbent processes were the organisation's arteries; changing those involves metaphorically rewiring the body, and can create potentially fatal problems and internal conflict between people who have developed or become accustomed to the *status quo*.

In other organisations, a template structure and operational procedures – albeit ones which have evolved over time – are set from on high, with regional sites needing to comply. Whilst restricting an operating unit from showing any individuality, this uniformity has benefits, see figure 9.2:

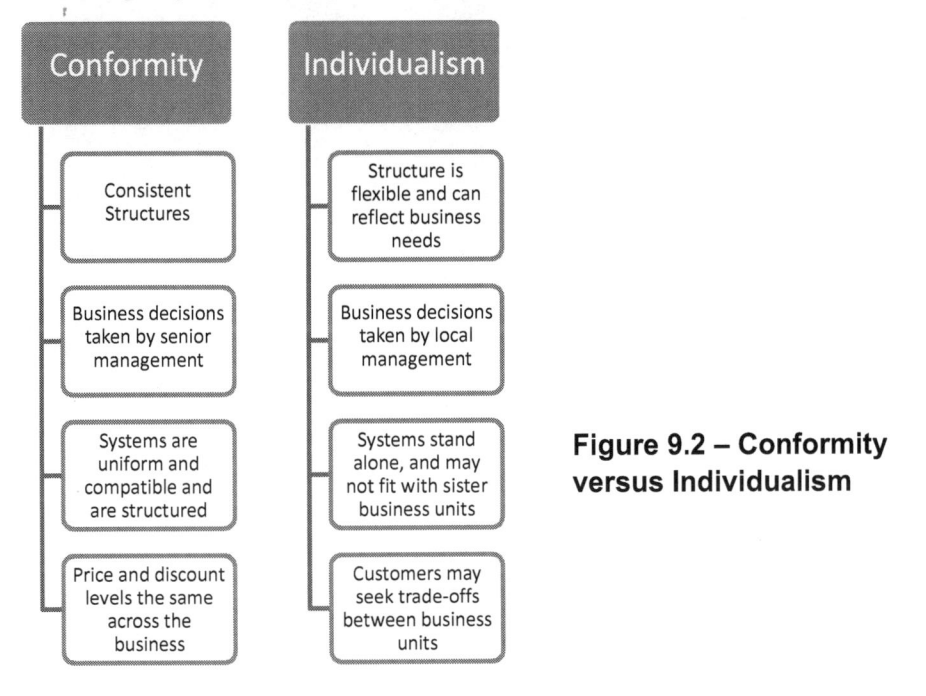

Conformity	Individualism
Consistent Structures	Structure is flexible and can reflect business needs
Business decisions taken by senior management	Business decisions taken by local management
Systems are uniform and compatible and are structured	Systems stand alone, and may not fit with sister business units
Price and discount levels the same across the business	Customers may seek trade-offs between business units

Figure 9.2 – Conformity versus Individualism

Each position has advantages and disadvantages, and across different markets both can be shown to have been successful. However the drive internationally to cement brand into business culture, and the transparency enabled by modern IT, makes the renegade's life far more problematic.

In summary, within *the Sustainable Business* as a whole, what is undeniably needed is clear process, defined structure and robust management – See Figure 9.3.

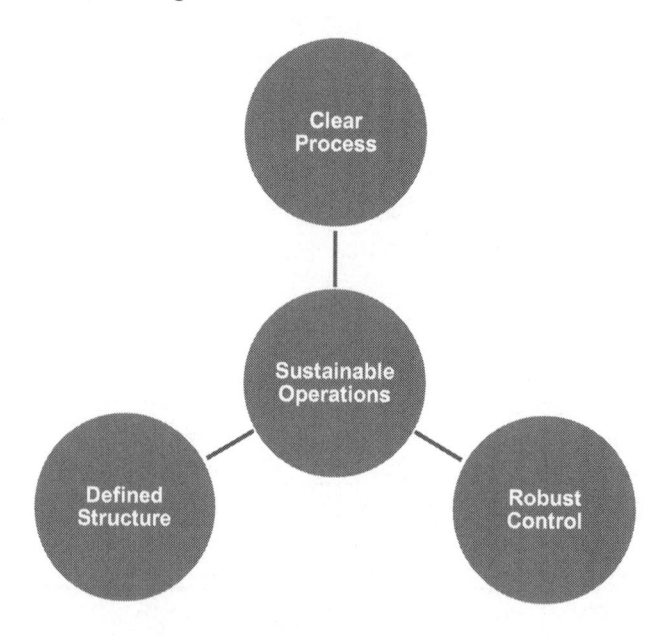

Figure 9.3 -Sustainable Operations

Adopting this approach will ensure:

1. That both the aims of the operation – and thus customer expectations – are fulfilled;
2. That quality, environmental and service level aspirations are consistently delivered;
3. And that the profit and wider commercial needs of the organisation are achieved.

The need to adopt such an approach is the critical issue. Whether the structure of an organisation is decided at a local, national or international level is not as important as the fact that thought and strategy has been applied pursuant to the needs of the customer, the prevailing market and the economic climate. Commonly overlooked, however, is the need to show humility and flexibility when making and reviewing decisions. Changes in conditions may require a fundamental rethink in the approach taken previously, albeit that investment and risk modelling may need to occur to vindicate any stance taken.

When the issue of Sustainability is applied within the Operations Management spectrum however, this position shifts somewhat. Given the issues of logistics, waste and longevity, a local management approach has often to succumb to the bigger and longer term picture. Whilst individual customer issues can be dealt with locally, they increasingly need to reflect a bigger system and processes that sit behind. This could simply be a reliance on a national distribution structure, centralised billing, or global sales management.

Whilst a centralised approach is not directly advocated, a consistent strategy needs to be applied to allow the customer to recognise and relate to the organisation's identity. As mentioned previously, one of the defining traits of organisations like the MacDonalds restaurant chain is that every outlet looks and feels the same. Local management have relatively little say in the look and branding of their outlet, as the wider and global image of the organisation is deemed more important than the aspirations of the local store management. Increasingly, such branding and overarching guidance from "head office" are affecting the way big businesses are run and managed. So where is the entrepreneurial spirit that has long been considered the backbone of a successful and growing economy?

In such a business, there is even more of a need for strong management to oversee a delicate balance between:
- The focus on aspects such as the management of the cost base (for example the number of staff or hours worked)
- And the reduction of waste (for example the cooked food which is then disposed of)

And:
- The delivery of exquisite service (for example satisfaction of demand from or attention to customer demands)

The Sustainable Business

- And the quality of product delivered (for example the temperature of the food or the freshness of product used).

Invariably, decisions taken on processes will have some link to the structure of the organisation as well as how inputs, activity, and outputs are managed. A clear process and flow map will identify and record process and support the overall process manual. Process maps take on many guises however identification of value and waste within each stage is a worthwhile addition, as is highlighting the different layers of customer and supply, see figure 9.4:

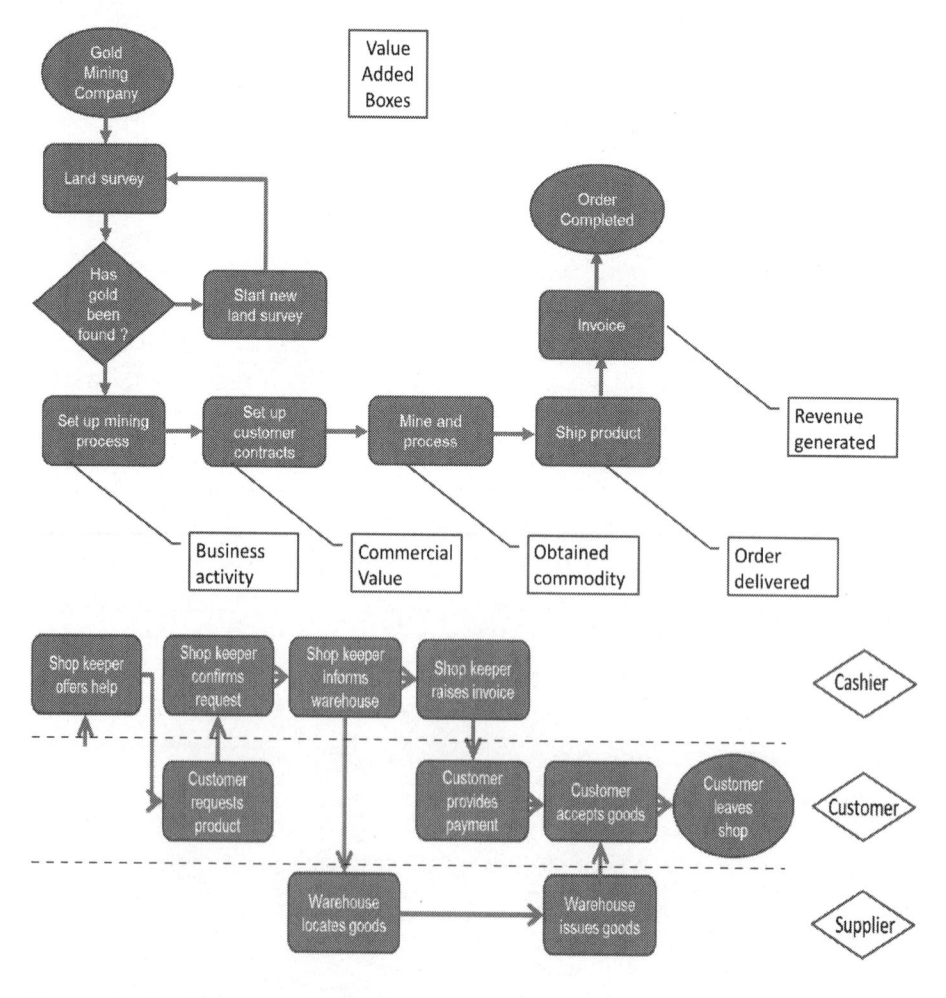

Figure 9.4 – Process Map Examples

Having established an effective and functional structure, as well as an agreed set of processes, the management of the organisation can be undertaken far more easily. Frequent review of the operation is essential to ensure that it remains fit for purpose both for the customer base and for the strategic direction of the organisation. A clear focus on the delivery of value helps maintain the operation, and the management process.

> **Food for Thought**: Consider the impact that the internet boom had on retail organisations globally. As late as 2003, organisations were questioning the long term feasibility of on-line trading, with many suggesting that there would always be a demand for the local shopping centre or high street. At that time, organisations were continuing to invest in their high street portfolio through new store openings, extending retail premises or via acquisition. Whilst there remains a level of demand for the "shopping experience" increasingly these are concentrated at out-of-town shopping malls as opposed to traditional high street or local shops.
>
> But how long can this be sustained? The underpinning cost base of a precinct environment, coupled with long leases and highly competitive services offered by on-line competitors make the longevity of such organisations somewhat bleak, with inner city operations faring equally poorly. The failure to address access, parking and the wider shopping experience makes it an urgent need to reverse the trends.
>
> Organisations which ignored this fundamental change need to adapt to survive; a number of global and local organisations have failed as a result of their inability to recognise the future trends and move with the times.

Forecasting

Whilst mentioned elsewhere in this book, the emphasis on planning and forecasting cannot be over-emphasised. Good planning – possibly using an ERP solution – helps ensure that the correct resources are made available at the right time in the right place to enable the operation to take place. The use of Kanbans such as within the Toyota model helps this to occur; goods are required in a specific half hour timeslot, not before and not after. Each and every delivery and output is forecasted and delivered.

> **Food for Thought**: Local suppliers are often heralded as being greener and more carbon friendly, and indeed this is often the case. True sustainability however requires all three of *the Pillars* to be maintained, with local supply sources sometimes less reliable, more erratic or incompatible with the overall business needs. In such circumstances the lower carbon content of an input could be counteracted with higher Total Cost of Sustainable Ownership, or a higher risk premium.

Forecasting may typically apply to any input or output requirement. This helps the upstream and downstream Supply Chains to react in good time to maintain flow and prevent bottlenecking. Equally, however, forecasting should identify where there is likely to be a shortage of resource or capacity. Highlighting shortages early enough may enable the management to make alternative supply arrangements or amend the output schedules.

Service Operations

Service operations differ considerably from their manufacturing counterparts and need to be managed and controlled in a way that reflects these differences:

- Services are intangible;
- Service needs to be produced at the time it is needed;
- Measurement of quality may be difficult;
- Services cannot be stored and are perishable;
- Service involves people and everyone is different.

Value

Understanding how the organisation adds value is fundamental to the overall achievement of its goals and vision. Establishing the value adding activities can be achieved using the Porter's Value Chain - see figure 7.2. These are what enable the organisation to make a profit, and thus enhance its *Profit Pillar*.

The Value Chain breaks the organisation into both primary activities (those aimed at the main operational objectives) and secondary activities (those activities which support the primary activities). Within each segment, assessment and guidance can be applied, often with reference to many of the models – both traditional and sustainability driven – detailed herein. For example, in any segment, use of the SWOT analysis can help drive departmental strategy, enabling strengths to be exploited, weaknesses protected, opportunities secured and threats mitigated. Equally the PESTLE model could be used to understand the external issues. See figure 9.5.

Whilst profit is invariably the primary benefit and value derived from a commercial relationship, it is worth considering the position from the client's perspective. In many cases the customer is looking for a quality product or service, for something cheaper than the competition, delivery quicker, etc. Pursuant to the longevity mandate, it is therefore the purpose of a sustainable operation to ensure that these aspirations are also fulfilled.

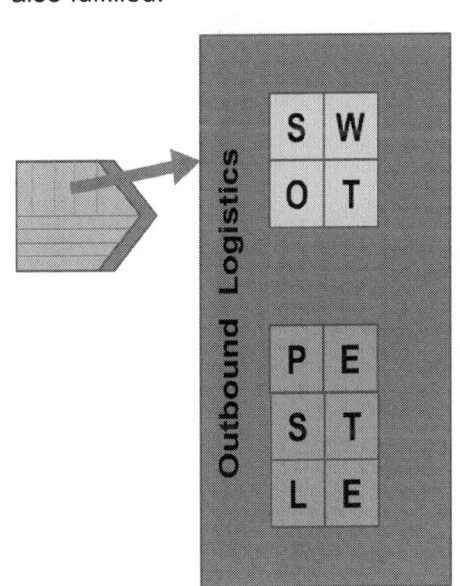

Figure 9.5 – Assessment of Value and Strategy attributed to the Outbound Logistics element of the Value Chain

Quality

Quality is central to the subject of customer service, and vital to *the Sustainable Business'* longevity aspirations. All great and memorable organisations renowned for their customer service will have a quality product or service at its heart. Where such quality exists, the issue of price is often overlooked, especially in an industrial or retail climate where the costs incurred from a faulty or low grade product entering a supply chain is often more than the cost of the product itself.

The first objective in quality management is establishing what the customer *really* wants. Quality is defined as being "fit for purpose", and reflects the needs, objectives and aspirations of the customer or user. There are numerous methods for identifying customer quality requirements however it is essential that the designers, operation, processes and management reflect these needs in the planning. Fishbone diagrams, brainstorming, customer interviews, Voice of the Customer analysis, etc all help *the Sustainable Business* appreciate what the customer is looking for, or for identifying where the quality levels have perhaps failed to meet the desired targets.

Rule: Quality is in the eye of the beholder

Introduced by W E Deming, Total Quality Management (TQM) suggests that the concept of quality should be the responsibility of everyone in the organisation. It states that quality should be considered within everything the organisation does, with its suppliers, and throughout the Supply Chain. With quality inputs, quality design, quality planning, quality processes and quality people, quality will flow through every sinew of the business.

Rule: Quality is everybody's responsibility

Wider, a major strength of TQM is its belief in Kaizen or "continuous improvement". The continual focus on self-improvement helps the organisation develop and strive for better ways of undertaking its processes, yet the impacts are more far reaching. Kaizen instils a philosophy and culture within an organisation where its employees and management search endlessly for utopia, recognising they have an unending journey. Being part of the development of the solution makes the workforce more committed and dedicated to its implementation, thus making any changes lasting and sustainable. This approach also reduces internal conflict and enhances cross functional working.

> **Definition: Common Cause Management – Uniting the workforce in the face of adversity**

Use of "Common Cause Management" is particularly effective when an organisation is under extreme pressure. In such instances, the worst thing that can happen is the metaphorical "abandoning of ship" or the "vote of no confidence". Here, the strength of a dynamic leader becomes invaluable. Military structures and some sporting teams highlight this tendency particularly well. Consider the forthright *screaming of orders* from a Sergeant Major leading his troops into battle, the politician before an election, or the impassioned half-time team talk from a sports captain looking to redress a deficit.

> **Food for Thought**: What makes a great leader? Invariably, great communication is at the top of any list. Communicating the message might be through a rousing speech, a structured devolution of a plan, or through a specially crafted marketing campaign; however a great leader ensures that everyone involved understands exactly what is required of him or her, their contribution and the consequences on the overall outcomes. Equally, as Adizes suggests, leaders and managers have a mix of four different parameters - process, administration, entrepreneurial thrust and implementation - a failure to appreciate these aspects leads inevitably to "mismanagement".

In contrast to the concepts of TQM, the Six Sigma approach explored elsewhere in this text, and examined in case study 9, strives, through similar efforts, to reduce the number of defects produced in a process using a complex mix of models, planning, and statistical analysis: the Six Sigma approach is underpinned with the DMAIC model – See figure 9.6:

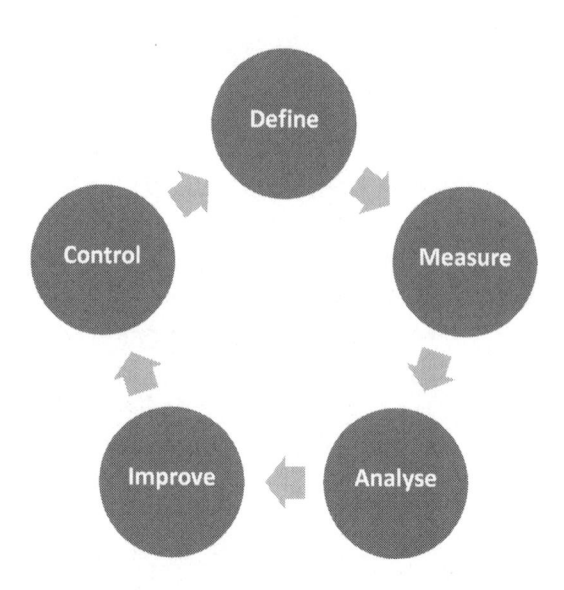

Figure 9.6 – DMAIC Model

Define – Once the quality issue has been identified, the first priority is to define and quantify the problem, setting clear boundaries, listening to stakeholders and most importantly the customer. Setting targets and objectives is core to the success of the project.

Measure – Measurement of the state of the process at the commencement of the project generates a clear record of the as-is status and establishes an agreed and structured approach to the measurement of process and outputs.

Analyse – Assess the collected data to identify cause and effects from within the process. Understand how different inputs and outputs are mapped together, and determine the root causes of the quality issues.

Improve – Establish and implement improvements to the process following the outcome from the data analysis. This may include a pilot scheme, and a project roll-out.

Control – Implement a structured control mechanism that takes the new process into the future, monitoring the new process against boundaries and targets, and managing future changes and management decisions.

Understanding and analysing quality related issues is central to the improvement of operational processes. As illustrated and discussed in chapter 7 (diagram 7.8), the Fishbone diagram can be used to assess quality issues which can generally be reduced to six causal areas: Materials, Man, Method, Machine, Measurement and Mother Nature.

> **Food for Thought**: TQM focuses on ensuring that the processes within the operation are designed to reduce errors within the production of the goods or services, whereas, the Six Sigma approach endeavours to reduce the overall level of defective output to just one part in a million.

Materials

The materials used in both a product manufacturing process, or a service delivery scenario are clearly important to the sustainable delivery of a quality output; the old adage "Garbage In, Garbage Out" remains true.

In both the delivery of services and manufacturing, a failure to use quality products will have a detrimental impact. Consider the differing needs and impact of a contract cleaning company, and a company producing computer circuit boards, see figure 9.7:

Cleaning Contractor

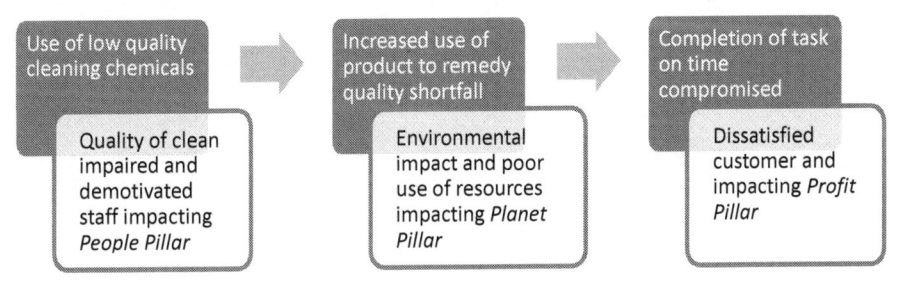

Use of low quality cleaning chemicals → Increased use of product to remedy quality shortfall → Completion of task on time compromised

- Quality of clean impaired and demotivated staff impacting *People Pillar*
- Environmental impact and poor use of resources impacting *Planet Pillar*
- Dissatisfied customer and impacting *Profit Pillar*

Circuit Board Manufacturer

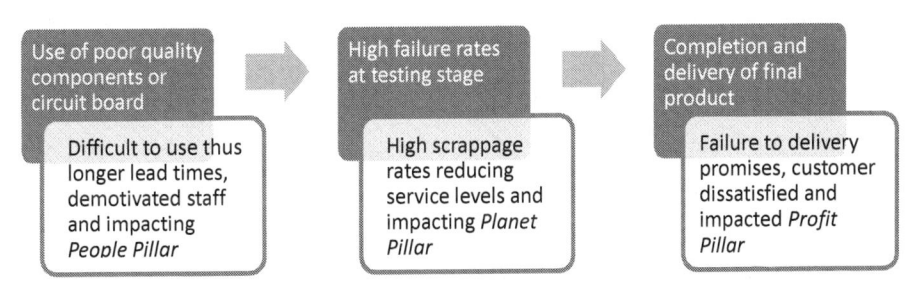

Use of poor quality components or circuit board → High failure rates at testing stage → Completion and delivery of final product

- Difficult to use thus longer lead times, demotivated staff and impacting *People Pillar*
- High scrappage rates reducing service levels and impacting *Planet Pillar*
- Failure to delivery promises, customer dissatisfied and impacted *Profit Pillar*

Figure 9.7 – Impact of the use of poor materials on the customer

Man

Equally, it can be seen how the quality and commitment of the Man element in the processes of both these types of organisation may impact on the quality of the output. In both cases, there is a clear production process which needs to be followed, with Man needing to coordinate the various inputs (including the HR input), reflect on the needs of the customer, and adjust process where necessary. Where there is poor involvement of Man, this can be seen to have a direct impact on quality.

Reflecting an earlier example, the best way for a MacDonalds operative to improve the sales and profitability of their restaurant is through the delivery of great service, an enthusiastic disposition, and an added focus on customer happiness. A strong *People Pillar* is invaluable to the sustainable delivery of process and a quality output.

Method

The methods or processes adopted by an organisation should be generated and documented to ensure on-going compliance and to ensure a co-ordinated approach. In most organisations these evolve over time, steered by numerous factors such as customer demands, personnel, management, resources, cash, etc.

Additionally, there is often some reticence towards change with operatives prone to adopt the "if ain't broke, don't fix it" adage. This leaning to the *Status Quo* can and has for many organisations been seen over the years to prove fatal.

Take for example organisations such as the Borders Bookshop chain which filed for bankruptcy in 2011. With annual sales of over $1bn, this organisation failed to recognise market and technology changes, the arrival of new competitors and the development of new channels such as supermarkets, the internet and organisations for example Amazon, and did not change its business processes to address these developments.

Food for Thought: The Fosbury Effect relates to the development of the "Fosbury Flop" technique in the athletics high jump. The

> traditional scissors technique was the recognised "best approach" yet Fosbury investigated alternative approaches to gain a competitive advantage. Initially, the new jumping technique did not yield the desired improvements, yet perseverance and adaption eventually prevailed.

There is an on-going need for organisations to review their processes, assessing the fitness and efficiency to maintain best use of resources. These processes have a direct impact on the quality of the output and fulfilment of customer satisfaction.

Machine

The choice and maintenance of equipment within a process will naturally impact on the delivery of sustainable quality. Choice of higher quality equipment is at the core of the Toyota manufacturing strategy, and helps ensure both a consistent specification for the output, and a continuity of service. Equally, the choice of machine will also impact on the quality of the output and the amount that can be produced; it will impact on the cost of production, and the cleanliness of the production process. Like the choice of a supplier, the Carter 10C model mentioned in previous chapters can again be used to help guide the purchase decision, albeit at an equipment level as opposed to the supplier level. Choice of the correct piece of production machinery is essential to the success of the process in the short, medium and longer term.

The implementation of maintenance – both reactive and proactive – will improve the efficiency of the machine and the organisation's ability to deliver a product or service which is fit for purpose on an on-going basis. A detailed proactive maintenance will prevent the production of sub-standard items which fail the final inspection, or require rework in, what Six Sigma calls "the hidden factory".

Rework is a waste that is often lost in the overall cost base, and is perceived by some as a way of recovering some of the investment in materials or time prior to the quality failure. Acceptance of rework undermines all *the Sustainable Pillars*: *the Planet Pillar* – as it represents an unacceptable use of resources: *the Profit Pillar* as it increases costs and reduces profitability; *the People Pillar* as it undermines the productivity of the employees, demotivates, and compromises the empowerment of the employee to remedy the situation.

Take for example the simple concept of drilling a hole in a piece of wood. A failure to maintain the sharpness of the drill bit will eventually lead to wear, with holes being drilled which are too small, uneven, or rough. Implementation of a FMEA (Failure Modes Effect Analysis) can help track the performance of a piece of equipment – or in this case a drill bit – to detect any deterioration in quality. "Failure Modes" are real or potential defects or failures within a process, especially those which have a direct impact on the quality of the output or delivery to the customer. Once the "Failure Modes" have been identified, they are then mapped alongside the corresponding "effects" and analysed to determine strategy to alleviate the issue.

Measurement

As detailed in chapter 14, the measurement of a process or system of processes is essential to establish its success, and to enable effective management. In a process, establishing a practical and accurate measurement system becomes central to the success of the measurement – and thus management – function.

Where a quality defect has been identified, one potential reason for the issue may be the suitability of the measurement system. This needs to be verified early on in any assessment; for example having a faulty gas detection meter may provide false readings which create alarm and panic where no problems are actually present.

Mother Nature

Finally, in some processes, quality defects may occur as a result of some genuine outside influence, often referred to as "Mother Nature". This may be due to climatic variations, changes in atmospheric pressure, cultural issues, Force Majeure, etc.

Whilst often used as a catchall for all remaining issues in the assessment, this can act as a catalyst for further team discussion as to what the other influences on the process may be.

Operational Improvement

The broader benefit of the fishbone approach is in helping the organisation establish strategies to overcome their quality and operational shortcomings. Whilst the quality of the machinery, the materials and the measurement approach all have a bearing, these are commonly aspects that the people in the organisation will influence. It is therefore understandable that the focus of any improvement project will necessarily be around two key areas: the people and the process.

In many cases the people element will overshadow any problems with the processes, with the typical organisation more familiar with the management of the personnel and reluctant to amend the processes which will probably have evolved over a number of years. As discussed in chapter 2, the people issues are likely to be influenced by a multitude of complexities, see figure 9.8:

Figure 9.8 – Peo affecting the bus

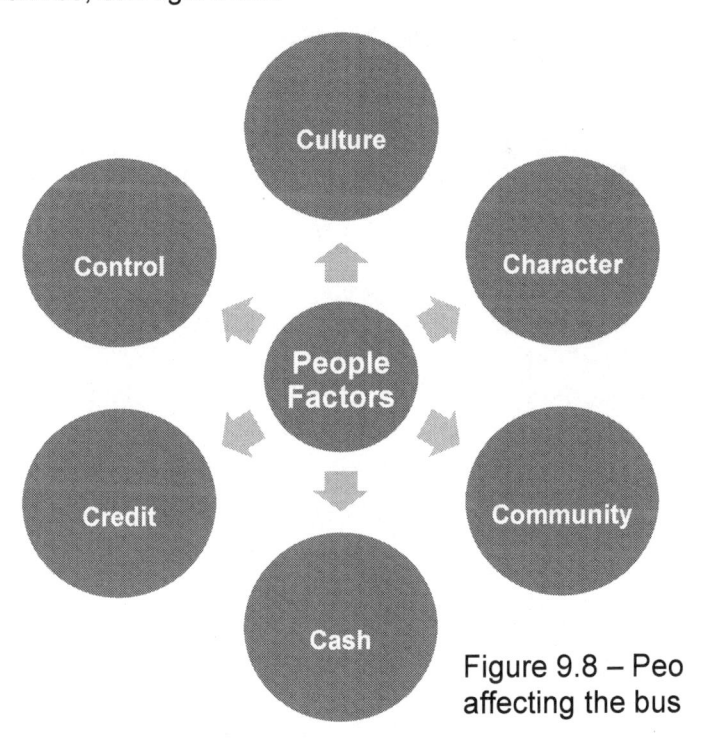

Figure 9.8 –People factors affecting the business operations

These are the core areas which influence a person's motivation and willingness. Aside from the individual's character (which is determined in the interview process) some elements – such as control, giving credit, the working culture and the work community – can be directly influenced by line-side management, however the cash remuneration of the employees must take on a more strategic angle.

The design of the work activities will have a dramatic impact on the motivation, satisfaction of the employee and the strengthening *of the People Pillar*. Historically, techniques such as "job rotation", job enlargement" and "job enrichment" have reflected efforts by occupational psychologists to make the life of the employee more bearable and they remain valid approaches.. Focusing on factory production lines, repetitive work activities can have a profound influence on both the employee and the effectiveness of the operation. Repetitiveness leads to boredom, complacency, a lack of concentration, poor quality and health and safety issues.

Moving employees around the business (Job Rotation), has a number of advantages: it keeps the employees fresher, maintains their concentration, broadens the employee skill set, helps generate stronger work groups, and adds a corporate resilience by ensuring multiple employees can undertake a specific task. Multiskilling has the added advantage of reducing corporate risk and enhances service levels through a reduced likelihood of production ceasing due to an employee related issue.

Equally powerful, expanding the scope (Job Enlargement) of the worker's remit will help the employee better understand the implications of his or her activities and adds a variety of different tasks to the employee's work role.

But concentrating on enriching the life of the employee (Job Enrichment) will typically have the greatest success. Established by Frederick Herzberg, Job Enrichment identifies key areas of a work function which can be addressed to improve the employee's lot, see figure 9.9.

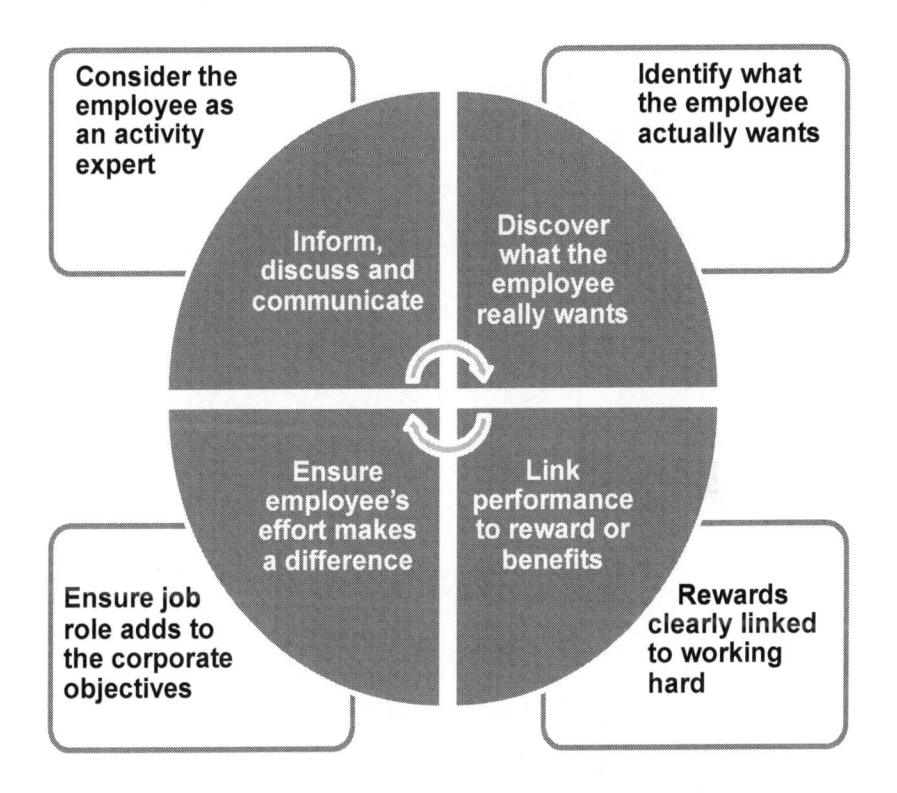

Figure 9.9 – Job Enrichment features

Features shown in diagram:
- Consider the employee as an activity expert
- Identify what the employee actually wants
- Inform, discuss and communicate
- Discover what the employee really wants
- Ensure employee's effort makes a difference
- Link performance to reward or benefits
- Ensure job role adds to the corporate objectives
- Rewards clearly linked to working hard

The layout of the business operation is important for *the Sustainable Business*. The specific nature of the organisation's activity, the facilities and equipment, the building, etc will all have an influence. Each individual operation needs to take time to design a proposed structure, process layout, personnel requirements, etc; IT packages are able to help model a layout and identify bottlenecks, silos, and waste.

Whilst the availability of investment may be limited, the effective design of a work process will have a profound impact on *the Sustainable Business*; wasted materials, best use of time, consistent levels of quality, cost and morale are all functions of an effective process design.

Equally, as mentioned in chapter 14, the use of targets, SMART objectives, and Key Performance Indicators helps the operations management function measure and manage "the Three E's" – Effectiveness, Efficiency and Economy, see figure 9.10 utilising the lighting of a car-park as an example:

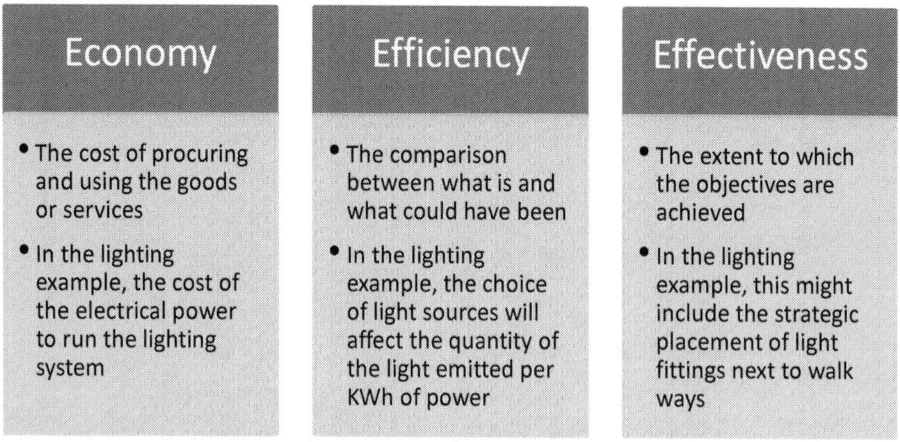

The Sustainable Business

Economy	Efficiency	Effectiveness
• The cost of procuring and using the goods or services	• The comparison between what is and what could have been	• The extent to which the objectives are achieved
• In the lighting example, the cost of the electrical power to run the lighting system	• In the lighting example, the choice of light sources will affect the quantity of the light emitted per KWh of power	• In the lighting example, this might include the strategic placement of light fittings next to walk ways

Figure 9.10 – The 3Es Model

Within the planning process, consideration about the use of resources such as raw material, utilities and labour is paramount and has a major impact on each of *the Three Pillars.* Designing an operation to use less material appears obvious, yet this is not always the case. Take for example, the simple activity of cutting shapes from a large sheet of metal. Until the widespread implementation of CAD (Computer Aided Design) and CAM (Computer Aided Manufacturing) in industry, arranging the shapes to be cut onto a sheet would have been quite arbitrary, thus failing to make best use of the materials and sheet. Each time the sheet was cut a higher than necessary percentage of the sheet would probably have been lost either to scrap or waste recovery, both undesirable costs for the organisation.

This also applies to the use of space in an office, factory or warehouse. Placement of desks, machinery, staff, etc should be carefully considered to give the optimum service, lowest costs, and optimal return per square foot of space. Even the location of the coffee machine can have an influence on the operational performance.

> **Food for Thought**: Consider the issues addressing an office refurbishment: team and personnel layout, furniture size and shape, location of fire escapes, IT, size and needs of a reception, operational aspects, people whims, location of facilities such as toilets or canteen, distance to the print room, and so on.

> In one organisation, the staff members were consulted about what they wanted in the new layout. Answers included: close to the door, not under an air-conditioning unit (the person felt the office was far too cold anyway), back to the window (so nobody could see what was on the individual's computer screen, lots of coffee and water machines, data and telecoms points in every floor box, etc.

And of course this planning process will also affect the use of the personnel resource in the organisation. Inevitably, pessimists will see the reorganisation of a business as another way of saying "redundancies" and this may end up being the case. Organisations may have drifted over a period and introduced a certain amount of corporate fat which can be trimmed during an organisation wide review, in personnel terms this does often mean posts may be consolidated or eliminated. The removal of this fat will often also mean that the remaining employees have to step up to the mark and take over the activities of the departee. This can generate resentment if they are being asked to do more than they did yesterday for the same money or recognition.

Finally, the real strengths of a manufacturing plant comes when alliances are formed which share wastes, capacity or opportunities. Take for example:

- Marmite or Yeast Extract, its core ingredient is a waste product from the brewing industry, and hence why the main Marmite and Vegemite factories are placed next to breweries desperate to dispose of - to them - a waste product;
- Sulphur - mentioned hitherto, the sale to fertilizer manufacturers of Sulphur extracted from oil-fields;
- Recovered heat recycled to generate electricity or deliver some other benefit;

> **Food for Thought**: With the development of heat recovery technology, why are there still air-conditioning units despatching heat into the atmosphere? When using salt water to cool equipment or pipes, why not collect the steam to collect it and with condensation produce fresh clean water. Imagine how much fresh water is lost each year by industrial cooling towers or power stations with steam turbines that let the steam out through large chimneys.

Case Study 9: Toyota

Heralded as one of the founders of many of the modern principles of innovative manufacturing processes, Toyota has long been recognised for its ability to deliver products on time, on budget and to the stated quality – "Right first time, right every time".

The Toyota Production System is founded on six core principles – see below. These are instilled in management and all the operating activities within its manufacturing plants. See figure 9.11:

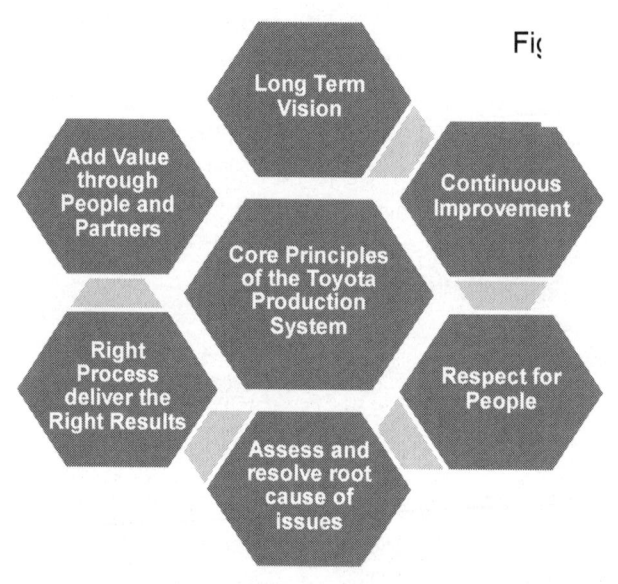

Figure 9.11 The Toyota Production System

The Toyota system focuses on three core areas of waste:

- **Muda** relates to any activity which doesn't add value. This aligns with the "Seven Wastes" mentioned hitherto: unnecessary movement, inventory, waiting etc are all forms of Muda.
- **Mura** relates to the issues caused by having an uneven demand flow. All activities have a specific routine, and must occur in a set and specific period of time. If the fitting of a door takes 36 seconds, and it is done in 38 seconds there may have been a problem which needs to be investigated; equally, if the activity is done in 34 seconds, either the operator has taken a short cut which could compromise the

quality, or the operator has identified a new way of performing the task which needs to be examined and if beneficial implemented for future activity.
- **Muri** relates to overburdening a process or person. Trying to put too much capacity through a machine, or overworking a person will lead to quality and operational issues.

These wastes are then addressed within the Toyota approach with reference to a number of founding principles:

- **Just-In-Time** – The concept of making items when they are required and not for stock. The demand *pulls* the order through the system by raising a "Kanban" or label requesting a part to be generated.
- **Jidoka** – "Automation with human intelligence" allows errors or issues to be detected as part of the process, allowing them to be quickly assessed and resolved. Using the "Detect-Stop-Fix-Preview" mechanism to address issues.
- **Kaizen** – The concept of Continuous Improvement is core to the development and expansion of the business. In theory, Toyota believes that there is one best way of doing a task, but recognises that the "one way" may not have been found.
- **Heijunka** – Addresses "Production Smoothing", fixes work times, manages demand and volume of product.

The system is often referred to as the Toyota House – see figure 9.12:

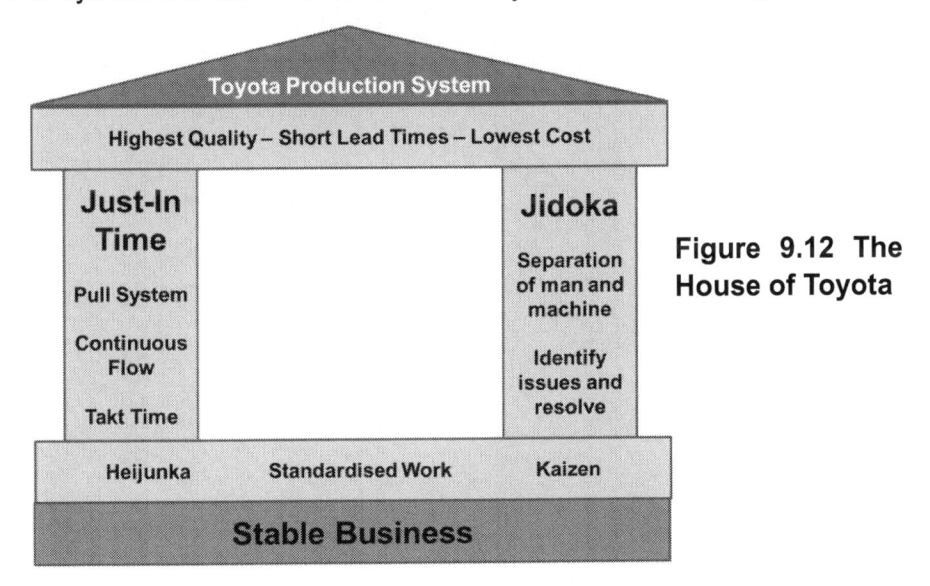

Figure 9.12 The House of Toyota

The Sustainable Business

Notes Page | **Page Ref**

Summary Chapter 10
Sustainable Design & Innovation

Key Learning Points
- The importance and impact of effective design
- Innovation and the development of new products
- The Eighth waste
- Types of design
- Focusing on longevity, reparability and durability of design
- Standardisation, templates and modular designs
- Selection of materials, resources, chemicals and "rare earth metals"
- Managing product afterlife through sustainable responsibility
- Elimination of CO_2, emissions, pollution and fossil fuels
- Clean-up of contaminated land
- Requirements of ISO14000
- Measuring of carbon content
- Material and commodities usage
- Utility Consumption – use of water, electricity, gas, etc
- Choice of fuel sources

Tool Summary
- The 20 Sustainable Paragons
- Activity Based Carbon Distribution
- 3Es Model
- Carbon Impact Mitigation
- Fuel Hierarchy
- Reduce to Produce

CIPS Syllabus Reference
- Level 4 Sourcing in Procurement and Supply
- Level 4 Managing Contracts and Relationships in Procurement and Supply
- Level 5 Sustainability in Supply Chains
- Level 5 Operations Management in Supply Chains
- Level 5 Management in Procurement and Supply
- Level 5 Improving the Competitiveness of Supply Chains
- Level 6 Corporate and Business Strategy

Chapter 10:
Sustainable Design & Innovation

"Design is the fundamental soul of a man-made of a creation"
– Steve Jobs

Managing *the Sustainable Business* involves a conscientious and dedicated approach based on *the Three Pillars* principle. At the outset, organisations need a purpose, a vision or an idea. Sometimes this idea involves a design, innovation and sometimes a patent.

Entrepreneurs and inventors challenge the norms; they seek the illusive *eureka moment* and live in constant pursuit of the next big idea. Equally, many established organisations invest heavily in research and development R&D to drive this process.

Definition: Innovation, the search for that *Eureka Moment*

In whichever way new designs come into existence, there remains a moral and ethical responsibility on the part of the designer to act conscientiously; bringing a new design to market has the potential to make a difference particularly in respect of greenhouse gas emissions, CO_2 capture, contamination and use of diminishing resources.

The extent and breadth of design across all markets and products is too broad to look at the individual facets of any particular design in this book, however the underpinning concepts of environmental responsibility should still prevail and incorporating historic successes and experience is entirely justifiable. Accordingly this chapter will explore ideas intended to drive sustainable design and innovation.

As in other chapters, *the Three Pillar* model applies within the design process. Consideration by the designer will normally be focused on fulfilling the whims and needs of the customer yet the other stakeholders in the organisation need recognition too.

In many companies, there is a significant investment made in research and development activities – for example see figure 1.2 – or the development of patents and designs using external sources, but at its core, making a profit and generating a *Sustainable Vision* must be its goal. *The Profit Pillar*, as we have seen elsewhere in this book, demands strength across its three dimensions: its sales, its service and its strategy.

> **Food for Thought**: Carbon Dioxide is a molecule made up of one Carbon atom, and two Oxygen atoms represented by the chemical equation CO_2 which increases when fossil fuels are burned and is responsible for a significant amount of global warming. In contrast a more unstable molecule is Carbon Monoxide which has only one oxygen molecule.
>
> When considering carbon measures, it is useful to understand the physical size and nature of 1kg of carbon dioxide:
>
> • It is commonly felt that the average person breathes out around 1kg of carbon dioxide per day whereas burning 1kg of fossil fuel generates around 3kg of carbon dioxide.
>
> • 1 kg of CO_2 occupies around ½ cubic metre at room temperature and normal atmospheric pressure.
>
> • China and the USA are the world's largest producers of CO_2.
>
> • Qatar has the highest CO_2 emissions per capita.
>
> Whether new to the organisation or a brand new product to the market, developing new products should be a catalyst to enhance the sales and turnover of the business. A good sales team will usually seize a new product as something to present to the existing customer base in an effort to generate new business, maintain the relationship, or at worse merely as a reason to get a meeting.

The new product needs the support of the sales team to help it flourish. Many a new product has failed due to a lack of support from within the organisation, with other organisations existing purely on the scraps discarded from ideas rich companies, proving the products worth, viewing the product from a different perspective, or targeting a different market.

> **Food for Thought**: Consider Teflon. This was discovered by accident in the 1930s (not by NASA as *legend* would have it), and used initially to coat uranium pipes, yet now it is far more commonly used as a coating for domestic saucepans.

From the Boston Consulting Group model (See chapter 3), a number of new products will start life as a "question mark", with the organisation holding the item which it has developed by accident or outside of any core strategy. This can often come from decoupling the design process from the sales model, or by giving the designer a "free hand".

Recognising the *Eighth Waste* – producing something the customer does not want – for normal organisations it is essential that the sales and design departments work in close cooperation, yet the two departments are rarely comfortable bedfellows. Psychological profiling suggests a completely different skill set for the two roles, and corporate hierarchy often elevates the sales function status way beyond the mere design team, generating a "them and us" culture, with the immortal line "without the sales team, there would be no business"!

> **Rule: Without designs, there would be no sales**

Even in the Belbin model discussed in chapter 2, an effective team needs different types of characters, and these quickly identify designers as needing to be idea generators, with sales people generally falling into other categories such as *Plant* or *Finishers.* In addition, as explored by *Lawson in "How Designers Think" 1980*, great designers think and operate in different ways to other mortals and this needs recognition if the function is to be effectively utilised.

Recognising the individual skills and personal needs of the different people in the company, *the Sustainable Business* will generate an environment that will allow ideas and idea generators to flourish and grow. This may include departure from some of the company norms – such as work hours, dress code, investment authority, etc – which in itself may to lead to resentment by others in the organisation.

It is equally important to recognise the overarching need to give great customer service, and *the Sustainable Business* needs to ensure that the design department recognises the need to fulfil the customer objectives, especially with respect to quality, time and cost. There are instances where designers have been known to design without regard to the underpinning costs, overegging the quality parameters, and failed to hit customer time schedules.

Accordingly, in conjunction with the sales function, clearly identified targets and strategy needs to be established, and more importantly communicated. Communication needs to be clear and regular, with boundaries and targets reaffirmed at regular intervals.

The Designers Impact on the Planet

Nurturing and motivating the designers, recognising the needs of the customer, sales team, and the overall objectives of the business is vital, however the designer's impact is most likely to influence *the Planet Pillar*.

Sustainable design can be split into two clear categories: (1) the design of products that address historical CO_2 or contamination, and (2) designs that address societal requirements but which need to think about resource use and impact going forward.

Remediation Design

Recognising that there has been an historic neglect of the planet which needs to be remedied, some designers have focused on innovations that attempt to reduce pollutants, or designing processes such as carbon capture and storage (where CO_2 emissions are captured and stored either in underground caverns previously containing natural gas, or impregnated into porous rock). Both address the issue of too much carbon in the atmosphere, without confronting the underpinning issue of net production.

Capturing the atmosphere based CO_2 is a major concern, yet simply planting trees can achieve this through the natural process of sequestration. A United States Department of Agriculture research paper identified that hard wood, long living trees represent the most efficient CO_2 sinks. Trees such as hawthorn were especially identified as being the most effective, though a balanced mix of trees is best.

Equally valid as a means of absorbing CO_2, biofuels are becoming a common part of the portfolio of agricultural crops. These crops have the benefit of generating a viable alternative to fossil fuels whilst also taking the CO_2 out of the atmosphere. Yet this CO_2 is returned to the atmosphere as soon as the fuel is used; with demand outstripping supply of biofuel, there is no net capture.

Furthermore, biofuels have a significant disadvantage, they take away valuable land mass which could be used for food production. In a world where the population is thought to have *recently* passed 7 billion, food poverty is already a major issue, and with a warming planet, desertification will increase only further.

However, there are alternatives being developed that look set to form a major part of the fuel sources of the future, Algae fuel. One of the most encouraging and innovative operators in this area is a company called Oilgae. Algae fuels are typically grown and harvested in large salt water ponds. Whilst the CO_2 is released back into the atmosphere once the fuel is used, as the market expands, the cycle of release and capture would develop at worst *carbon equilibrium*. Whilst focused in the short term on biodiesel, this process can be used to produce a wide range of other products, for example ethanol, bio-butanol, methane, jet fuels and so on. But algae harvesting does have an impact on ocean eco-structure.

Furthermore, a significant contribution can also be generated with using surplus or waste bio product. In Brazil, major developments have been made in the production of ethanol bio-fuel – one of the cleanest such fuels in terms of greenhouse gas emissions – from the leaves and husks (called "bagasse") left over from the sugar manufacturing process. This industry which uses nothing but waste material aims to triple production from its 2011 level of $50bn, with a new 10m gallon factory coming on stream in 2012. In addition, Brazil has enough spare land suitable for the production of around a fifth of the world's fuel needs. (See *Financial Times* Report, May 2011)

In terms of alternative carbon reduction innovations, recent discoveries include the production of an artificial leaf which acts in the same way as a real leaf. Artificial photosynthesis uses energy from the sun to fuel the splitting of the water molecule to generate both hydrogen and oxygen. Instead of the chlorophyll in the leaf, organic light sensitive natural dyes are used to absorb the energy from the sun to effect the artificial photosynthesis.

Furthermore, the issue of contaminated land is an issue to *the Sustainable Business* and the wider planet. Contamination can be contained in many cases, but it is a fact of our industrial heritage that land has been contaminated through ignorance or neglect and that land is still being contaminated through industrial spills, accidents, etc. Cleaning up such sites is often fraught with difficulty: however one of the cleanest methods is through effective planting of contaminant hungry plants. Research by the Bangladesh Agricultural Research Institute identified that leafy vegetables such as radishes, Brussels sprouts, etc are one of the best plants to effect the extraction. Equally, some trees such as the Silver Birch have a tendency to perform the same function but take longer to become established.

In conclusion, the impact of technological advances and innovation that can extract the rising levels of CO_2 is of paramount importance to the long term health of the planet. The development of environmental technology and innovation is likely to be at the core of the innovation cycles in the next long wave cycle – see chapter 5.

Product and Service Design

Equally important to remedy past failures is the need to think sustainably when developing new products or services. The breadth of potential products or services that could be discussed is enormous. To help steer thinking, here are twenty guidelines which, if applied, will help move to a more conscientious new product or service strategy.

Twenty Sustainable Paragons

1. Carbon Impact Mitigation – Consideration of the total carbon emitted during the manufacturing or usage enables a new design to be measured and ranked to highlight its impact on the environment, purchaser or user.

When designing a new product or service, designers need to consider the CO_2 produced in the manufacture and usage process. The awareness of how much CO_2 is produced is now better recorded, especially since the introduction of carbon trading, quotas and carbon credits. Assigning value or cost for CO_2 helps raise the profile of CO_2 reduction activities. In some markets CO_2 emission levels are published to heighten the visibility and consciousness with numerous online CO_2 estimators.

As mentioned previously, consider the amount of power and resource needed to produce new aluminium over recycled product. Choice of the materials and utilities are particularly significant to *the Sustainable Business*; recycling reduces the average CO_2 per moment of usage. Even deciding whether to purchase electricity generated from coal, nuclear or hydro power will make a difference.

> **Food for Thought**: Recycled Aluminium uses 95% less energy, creates 95% less air pollution and 97% less water pollution than aluminium extracted from ore.

Equally consider the impact of a 1000 miles travelled in some of the different vehicles commonplace in society – see figure 10.1; deciding which vehicle is most suitable has a significant carbon impact.

Vehicle Type	Carbon Emitted per Passenger
Large Car with 1 Passenger	414kg
Large Car with 4 Passengers	104Kg
Small Car with 1 passenger	206kg
Small Car with 4 passengers	51Kg
Plane	275kg
Train	86kg

Figure 10.1 Carbon Output of travel options
Source *TravelDirect.com*

In *the Sustainable Business*, "Activity Based Carbon Distribution" - See Chapter 14 - can be used to help allocate carbon responsibility to different departments, activities, product, customers, etc, thereby increasing the ownership of the issue and allowing measurement of emissions and emission reduction programmes.

2. Material Makeup – Choice of materials can lead to a significant reduction in scarce or environmentally expensive content.

The decisions a designer takes when selecting the materials and components needed to produce an item is critical to the environmental impact of the product. Choice of "new versus recycled", or second hand material, is one way of limiting or reducing the average CO_2 contained in the production of one *widget*. Equally, use of recycled paper in an office saves trees being cut down, or the capture and consumption of grey water helps ease the demands on clean water, thereby reducing the time and resources used in the preparation of clean water.

Take for example a kitchen designer. The worktops can typically be made out of natural wood, glass, slate, quartz, granite, or a collection of other man-made products. Each has its own design characteristics leading to a different lifecycle, carbon footprint and sustainable impact – see figure 10.2 – a designer has a clear opportunity to reflect these issues in any design.

Worktop Material	Issues
Granite	Very heavy (hence high logistics costs), relatively expensive, fewer colours.
Glass	Expensive, difficult to handle, heavy and can scratch.
Quartz	Heavy, not a natural stone but very hard wearing and robust.
Natural Wood	Natural product, but can deteriorate with stains and burns.
Laminate	Cheap, versatile, but limited lifespan. Some product is not recyclable.
Solid Surface	Versatile but lower durability than granite. Some product is not recyclable.

Figure 10.2 – Kitchen worktop comparison

The designer needs to understand the sustainable impact of any decision taken. Whilst granite may be a relatively abundant natural element, it is difficult and costly to handle, its weight generating a CO_2 transportation cost. Wood is clearly a more natural product and if managed forests are maintained, is replenishable; some of the man-made products inject resin into wood chip fibres making a robust and solid surface, but one that is not necessarily recyclable and will not generally be compostable.

3. Utility Consumption – How much electricity, gas, oil, water, etc is used to make an item.

Within any design, consideration should be paid to the quantity and type of any utilities used in the production process. Measuring such content helps manage the impact of the design on *the Planet Pillar*.

In *the Sustainable Business*, any design should endeavour to, at worst, maintain the "carbon equilibrium" with utilities such as electricity carefully managed for usage and origin. Clearly there is a significant carbon difference between electricity generated from different sources, the fuel hierarchy shown in figure 10.3:

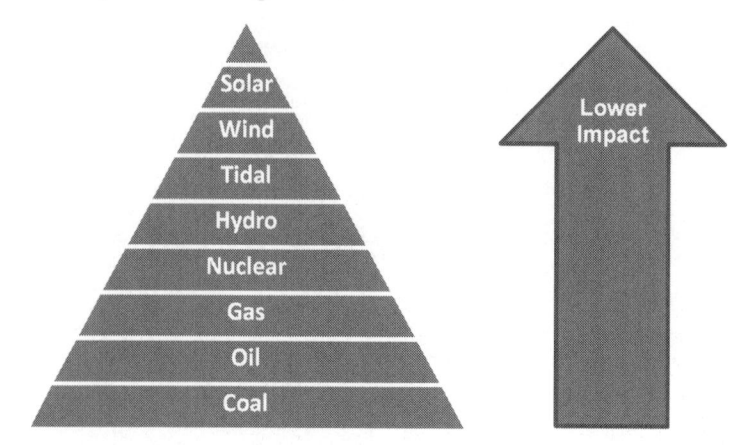

Figure 10.3 – Fuel Hierarchy

Equally important is the reduction of demand for the fuel in the first place. The 3e model – see figure 10.4 - looks at efficiency, effectiveness and economic aspects to drive utility costs lower and one of the consequences of this will be to use less electricity overall.

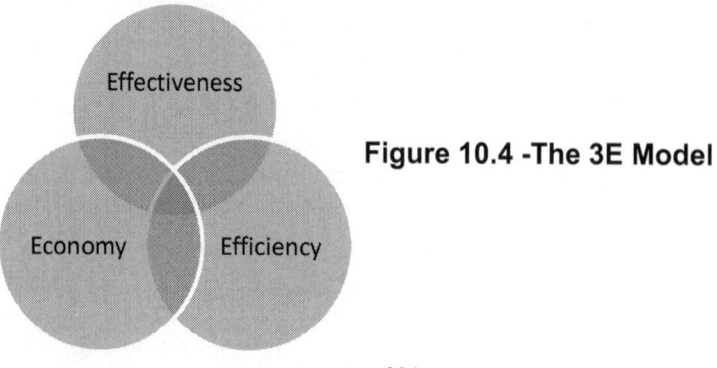

Figure 10.4 - The 3E Model

Take for example electric lighting. Overall net cost for lighting can be improved by doing one of three things:

I. Buying units of power more cheaply (Economy);
II. Getting more benefit (light) from the power consumed (Efficiency);
III. Or using the lighting more strategically to focus the lights on key areas such as corridors, car-parks, etc and use of natural light sources (Effectiveness).

Ideas to help each might include:

a) Selection of power received from a hydro power source;
b) Choice of light source selected (for example consider the difference between incandescent versus compact fluorescent lamps versus the various types of discharge lamps);
c) Focus on lighting key areas using detectors, photocells, and "footfall mapping";
d) Turning lights off when not required, using photocells or timers;
e) Use of natural lighting during the day improved with extra glass, clean windows, roof-lights, light tunnels, etc;
f) Use of mirrors, light walls and surfaces to reflect light internally;
g) Reduce light shades, diffusers, etc;

> **Food for Thought**: Light tunnels can be used to bring natural light to inner rooms along mirrored light tubes

Yet fossil fuel is used in more than just the production of electricity. Consideration of the miles an item travels (use of oil) or of heating types is worthy of attention.

Equally, in many industrial processes, the use of water is significant. In such instances consider using grey water (water that has not undergone the full "ready to drink" cleansing process), or in some circumstances, use of salt water (recall the Gibraltar toilet example).

Water is also used to cool equipment or product, thus extracting heat. Recovery of heat is an invaluable source of energy, yet use of heat recovery equipment – despite numerous tax and grant incentives - is, in reality, rarely seen. Equally, as mentioned previously, where water is used to cool equipment or within power station turbines why is this not captured and condensed as a source of fresh water?

One of the worst culprits are air-conditioning installations which utilise refrigerant to capture internal heat within buildings and transport the heat to externally mounted cooling fins which dissipate the heat into the atmosphere, wasting the energy, and a potential source of value.

Tracking utility consumption is possible with dedicated monitors. Smart metering allows clamps to be applied around live cables to enable an assessment of power usage levels by measuring the strength of the magnetic field. In large users, peaks and troughs can be used to negotiate tariffs with suppliers, or to allow supply balancing with activities such as computer data transfer occurring in the night hours.

> **Food for Thought**: In some countries the power suppliers allow power used at night, when demand is low, to be purchased at a cheaper rate. In Germany there is Niedertarif (night tariff), Malam Tariff in Indonesia, or Economy 7 in the UK.

Equally, in domestic residences, smart meters can now identify appliances being left on, or inefficient equipment within a household, and voltage regulators are now being added to improve the efficiency and longevity of electrical equipment.

> **Food for Thought**: Voltage entering a domestic residence is usually guaranteed across a voltage band for example 220V-250V. Electrical equipment is designed to work across this voltage spread but works most efficiently at the lower level. Voltage regulators receive the voltage from the grid as it enters the property and trims the voltage to this lower limit thereby reducing the power consumed from the network, whilst improving the efficiency and longevity of the items drawing the power.

4. Long Life Cycle – Design of the product to be fit for purpose for a long time, delaying the manufacture of a replacement.

In many countries there is legislation that dictates that a product should last for a reasonable length of time commensurate with the price it is sold for – for example European Directive 1999/44EC, the Uniform Commercial Code in the United States and the UK Sale of Goods Act. Producing products which last longer postpones the need to manufacture a replacement. In contrast, producing disposable items, including the packaging, generates waste even if the materials are recyclable (it still takes energy to recycle).

Society's preoccupation with lowest cost, coupled with the speed of technological changes, increased disposable income, diligent marketing and a modern day obsession for shopping, has reduced the life of many products – especially those helpfully labelled FMCG (Fast Moving Consumer Goods). The competitive nature of markets necessitates that market participants are continually competing for business, with commercial and sales pressures ever present:

> **Rule: In the words of an old sales manager "What you need to do is sell more at a higher margin"!**

To overcome this, manufacturers need to adopt more imaginative solutions such as leasing product, long-life-cycle revenue streams, and so on.

Domestic computer printers are a case in point: Many suppliers would gift the printer to get the revenue generated by unique printer cartridges. Historically this has enabled on-going revenue to offset the loss-leading sale of the printer, however the rise of agents able to refill cartridges scuppered that model. In response, printer suppliers have developed cartridges that prevent the refill process, a move which in itself is not entirely environmentally desirable but clearly illustrates the conflict that can occur between *Profit and Planet Pillars*.

> **Food for Thought**: By way of an example, one particular global manufacturer produces a printer which sells in the UK for £39.99, a colour cartridge in the same store costs £19.99. *(Data as at March 2012)*

Other similar examples might include "free" razors, with the revenue generated from the replacement of blades, or vacuum cleaners that require specialist bags.

> **Food for Thought**: Shaving companies encourage the use of shaving foam to "generate a smoother shave". The shaving foam produces a lather – and of course additional revenue and profit for the supplier - which helps the razor glide, however it also encourages beard growth and makes the whiskers more brittle blunting the blade more quickly and thus increasing replacement blade sales. Stopping use of foam has a short term niggle for the user however quickly hair growth slows and becomes softer, so blades last longer and time is saved not having to shave so regularly. Significant quantities of the foam are supplied in aerosols, and there are chemicals involved in the production. And this does not facilitate our extended life aims.

5. Durability – Design of products using materials that will not quickly wear out.

Within the design process, choice of appropriate manufacturing or service materials is a clear strategic decision. Cheaper production or operational materials will lead to a lower cost of sale and enhanced profits, but may compromise consumer satisfaction, reduce the useful life, and lead to premature failure.

Choice of materials, as with so many choices in business is a balance: a balance between cost, environmental aspects, usability, weight, legislation, ISO directives, and so on.

> **Rule: You get what you pay for!**

For example, there are several thousand recognised forms of steel, a product generated from iron, carbon and other assorted ingredients. Each grade of steel has a different mix of durability, strengths, rust resistance, and how pliable it is. It is imperative that the designer or engineer understands the operational stresses that the steel *widget* will endure as this is what should drive the design selection. This may also impact on the legislative impacts, with food environments demanding a specific stainless steel grade (304), the off-shore petroleum industry specifying another (316).

Where parts are likely to deteriorate – such as blades, drills, bearings, etc – the design should facilitate easy replacement, and the market should sustain the supply of the necessary replacement parts. The automotive parts market is a good example of a supportive supply structure.

> **Food for Thought**: Supplier should be made to fix the price for spare parts to an affordable level to make future repairs viable

6. Cannibalisation – Product has a design that allows serviceable components to be removed easily to allow reuse in other assets.

As mentioned previously, using module components can enable a significant amount of module interchange and reuse. Facilitation of the concept of product cannibalisation enables end-of-life product to be dismantled and its spare parts checked for serviceability and quality.

Recall the earlier example, in the BAE Systems Tornado GR4 and F3 variants, there are numerous common parts. When in 2009, the British Government decided to retire the Tornado F3 fleets, the jets were earmarked for structured disassembly (under the Reduce-to-Produce programme) and core components extracted and reprocessed before being reintroduced back into the Tornado GR4 Supply Chain. This initiative was highly lucrative, yet in contrast, consider the image of a "blue car with a red door": what image does such a view send out?

7. Pollution management – Produce designs that enable pollution to be minimised and contained.

The obvious criterion for a successful design is the satisfaction of the customer and fulfilment of their Critical Success Factors. However, there is a need to think constructively and imaginatively about the issue of pollution.

Understanding the outputs from a process, service or product is essential to identifying the potential pollutants which once identified can be mitigated or contained.

In one project, a UPVC window manufacturer was examined as part of an ISO14000 certification. They had identified waste such as the off-cuts of UPVC (which is a *COSHH [Control Of Substances Hazardous to Health*] substance), the lead from leaded windows, and chemicals used to clean the windows at installation. The assessment identified a need to make remedial changes to the fuel tanks which were not bunded and might create a toxic spill if ruptured. Further and more obscurely, they washed their vehicles with the waste water flowing into the normal storm drains; this *grey* water would undoubtedly have contained oil and other contaminants and thus needed to be treated before release into the environment. Chemicals such as these can easily get into the water table and ultimately cause serious problems. In this instance the organisation designed its vehicle washing process around a specially contained contaminant collector to prevent the issue with previous contamination remedied – see figure 10.5:

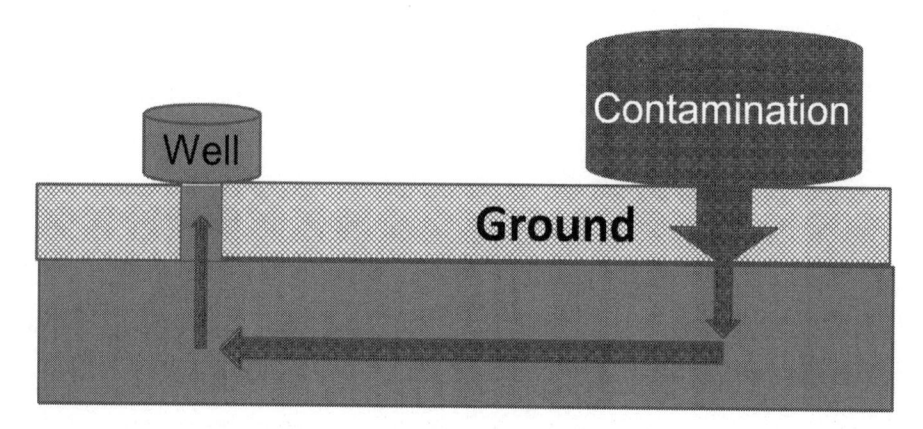

Figure 10.5 – Contamination in the Water Table

In another project on the Westferry Road in London Docklands, excavation of a site revealed high levels of cyanide and arsenic from old metal smelting processes, as well as ground borne asbestos from an old Victorian rope works. Remedy was sought through the "Polluter Pays Principle" clause under European Environmental Law, however none of the historic culprits were still in existence. This left the developer with the responsibility to clean up the contamination which had a very high chance of being released into the high water table (due to the proximity of the River Thames) once the piling and ground excavation had commenced. Ultimately, the design of this project changed to remove the most highly contaminated soil, with the remainder of the site bunded to prevent lateral discharge or leaching.

8. Managed Afterlife – Generating a structured afterlife for the item following its initial usage, and facilitation of the second-hand market to enable a new user to be found to prolong the product's useful life.

In some markets, most notably where products have high ticket prices, the suppliers may work to develop a resale market. The reasons for such a move are however invariably self-focused as opposed to any environmental considerations. Where the initial price is high and a second-hand market exists, sales-people can show that there is a resale opportunity and thus a residual value; this both reduces the net cost to the consumer, whilst also overcoming the issue of how to deal with a surplus item. There is an opinion that in many cases, a sale will be hampered unless the customer can visualise how the existing item can be disposed of.

Take for example the car market. Here ticket prices are usually quite high as a proportion of disposable income. If a car was to cost $30,000 new, but has a two year resale value of $24,000, this could be pitched as a monthly cost of $250, a far less daunting and a more justifiable sum. Offering a part-exchange on the customer's current vehicle helps remove that obstacle from the sale with the second hand-market an outlet for the garage to dispose of it.

Accordingly, whilst having a notable environment benefit, motivation for car companies to support and encourage second-hand markets is clear. This concept also applies to IT equipment, large domestic appliances and so on.

> **Food for Thought**: Consider *car scrappage schemes* used across Europe after the 2009 credit crunch to stimulate automotive demand. Here second hand cars were scrapped in exchange for a voucher for a new car. This had the advantage of stimulating the sale of a new car as well as getting an inefficient beast off the road.

It is also applied in markets such as jet aircraft, where the leading manufacturers (Boeing and Airbus) have a variety of arrangements in place to facilitate the replacement of old stock with new jets, recycling the old jets through a relivery process, and back into periphery or emerging markets. This again has benefits to the supplier, customers (original and emerging) and of course *the planet* at large.

More obscurely, it could be argued that a similar process also occurs within the supply and management of uranium for the nuclear industry. Development of reprocessing plants enables spent fuel rods to be reprocessed, thereby removing a potential hazard, reducing costs for disposal, and extending the useful life of the material

> **Food for Thought**: In many ways, management of materials such as Uranium should be like wringing out a flannel. You can extract a large percentage of the water in a flannel relatively easily, however to obtain the last few drops, the cloth needs to be wrung or twisted to squeeze the remainder out. These last few drops are the environmental "icing on the cake".

In addition to generating a managed aftermarket, the design of a product and the supplier's sales process should enable and encourage onward sale or disposal through other channels designed to prolong the useful life of the product. For example, inclusion of on-line instructions - as per point 9 - help improve the chances of a successful second-hand sale.

Development of Ebay in 1995 generated a formal and easily used way of selling items that were no longer required, albeit often at a nominal cost. Clearly there are now numerous other such websites aimed at facilitating the second-hand markets. The design of a product and the elimination of any reticence from the sales teams helps this process as does the removal of any license restrictions.

Further, the Freecycle™ initiative – see case study 4 – is an invaluable way to prolong the lifecycle of a product, with the key objective of reducing or delaying landfill. Suppliers should recognise the sustainable benefit of such an option, and as Freecycle™ develops further throughout the world, the on-going sustainable benefits will make a huge and lasting benefit.

Of annoyance however is the Microsoft reluctance to allow its Office product to be transferred between machines. This constrains the life of the product – albeit only a software image.

9. Instructions Online – Making any operation, installation and manufacturer instructions available on-line helps develop the aftermarket.

In some markets, suppliers go out of their way to support the second-hand markets with efforts designed to generate goodwill and positive PR. This can include all sorts of support and maintenance, for example ensuring a ready supply of spare parts for a considerable period, access to technical support or repair agents, or simply providing instructions on-line after the product has been discontinued.

An example of this practice can be seen by Mamas & Papas, the Italian based global supplier of baby equipment such as prams. For many, a new baby is a considerable expense, however the sell-on value of the pram or baby item is partially maintained with the availability of instructions on-line and a number of the service-driven sales outlets providing maintenance and repair facilities as an additional service.

Equally, with IT products such as printers, the availability of printer drivers as free downloads, overcomes the issue when years after the purchase of the printer the user buys a new computer and needs to find that illusive CD containing the initial driver software. (Cynically, and recalling the aforementioned revenue stream driven by the printer cartridges, this elongation merely extends the flow of commercial benefit from continual purchase of printer cartridges.)

10. Easily Repairable – Making goods easily repairable elongates the useful life.

In the past, some equipment manufacturers deliberately designed their products to make them difficult for a user to repair. Some needed specialist equipment or tooling (for example special tooling for the oil change on certain makes of cars), others had glued casings to prevent easy access to the inner workings. This was designed to limit the repairs that could be achieved thus reducing the overall usable life of the product; some even had internal batteries that could not be replaced.

Take for example, certain brands of cheaper wrist watches. Some have the aforementioned internal batteries that cannot be replaced others need special tools to remove the back of the watch. This ensures on-going employment for watch repair companies, maintenance of the sales outlet for the supplier, and the continued viability of such business activities. This sort of approach does however lead over time to shorter average life cycles.

> **Food for Thought**: Within the sustainable strategy, there must be a balance between consideration of the *Profit Pillar* and consideration of the *Planet Pillar*.

Good instructions and designs that can be repaired easily with commonplace tooling helps, and effective training of the customer or local agents is also commendable. Suppliers should see this as an extension of their service mandate, and an activity which will have a positive impact on their image going forward.

11. Repair Agents – Developing and maintaining a structured repair network to ensure continued usage.

Where equipment is of a more technical nature, developing a design which can be repaired within a trained network of agents fully equipped and competent to undertake repairs and testing processes, has undoubted sustainable benefits. Take for example organisations such as JCB, ABB Daikin, etc who have dozens of outlets globally.

Designing with structured repairing processes in mind can allow for more elaborate designs, use of difficult materials or higher upfront production investment. This can both assist the functional benefits of the design as well as the value added to the user, whilst improving the length of the product lifecycle, and the effective payback and investment returns. This can be driven with longer or stronger warranty provisions which can also be used as a sales benefit if required.

In broader terms, when highly technical assets are managed in such a structure, service levels can be seen to improve dramatically. This enhancement in service levels helps enhance all of *the Pillars*, and extends the useful life of assets as well as maintaining customer goodwill.

For example, due to the cost and the service levels demanded in conflict, some types of military equipment are maintained using a repair and replace structure. Equipment involved in the aforementioned UK Tornado ATTAC process is coordinated in such a manner. The key modules of the aircraft are managed in cooperation with either the OEM(Original Equipment Manufacturer), or dedicated ex-Ministry of Defence repair organisations. Each organisation is responsible for the management and delivery of the required service, within strict service level criteria based on the on-time availability of serviceable assets, and a set turn-around time on repairs. This approach has been responsible for a dramatic improvement in service provided, asset utilisation and underpinning cost.

Food for Thought: The ATTAC programme is based on several key measurable characteristics, most notable is referred to as AOG – "Aircraft on Ground". The primary objective for a serviceable fleet of jets is available at all times; measuring the unplanned hours that a jet is out of service helps focus attention on this core requirement.

12. Make-to-order – Manufacturers should design product and manufacturing capacity to enable items to be made to order, not for stock.

Whilst inventory is used to sever the supply and demand pressures in an organisation, as detailed on a number of other occasions elsewhere in this book, the general concept of inventory is to be discouraged as it is considered a critical waste in the Supply Chain.

To help reduce the work-in-progress (WIP) and finished goods inventory held by the supplier, design of product should focus on reducing the need to manufacture in batches, adopting instead a "make-to-order" philosophy.

Making goods as they are required necessitates a design focused on much shorter lead times and quick changeover of manufacturing set-ups (as opposed to features or lowest cost). The Toyota SMED (Single Minute Exchange of Die) initiative focused on enabling manufacturing set-ups to be changed extremely quickly. This reduces the down-time in production, lost as a result of the changeover. This single change enables Toyota to produce the exact variant of car to the customer specification with minimal disruption. Clearly, even in this scenario, Toyota would like to have every car the same, with no changeover, however they recognise the importance of the customer getting exactly what they want, taking away *the eighth waste* - the risk of producing something that does not meet the customer expectations.

For a related example, consider the Ford Model T in the early years of car production. As Henry Ford stated "Any customer can have a car painted any colour that he wants so long as it is black". In mass production processing this was an unavoidable reality. As production processes developed, so mechanisms developed to allow paint colours to be switched quickly and easily, without the need to paint in large batches, facilitating exact colour requirements to be factored into the production schedule.

Equally, where products are produced on an order by order basis, enabling the customer to produce a bespoke design builds loyalty and helps ensure that the user will be happy and satisfied with the purchase. See Dell Case Study 7 for specific details on how the Dell customer base uses an online design feature to build a product using generic modular build techniques.

13. Buy-back - Manufacturers should offer to buy back product when the user has finished with it.

Designing and manufacturing product with the intention of receiving it back helps reduce on-going manufacturing costs, reduces the use of resources and materials, and reduces landfill and disposal impact; in some cases there needs to be some control and possible financial recompense for returning the items, typically this is in the form of some kind of deposit or tracking. Furthermore, for the manufacturer there may be environmental inducements or carbon offsetting allowances for such behaviour.

Reuse can come through various mechanisms, some extremely simple. Take for example the now somewhat defunct concept of returning glass milk bottles. In the "olden days" the customer would order milk from the milkman by leaving a note with the empty bottles. The milkman would on a daily basis travel a specific route delivering milk – and latterly other groceries – whilst at the same time collecting the empty bottles (noting if there was any shortfall) for washing and refilling - a very green process we seem to have strayed away from; consider the benefits, see figure 10.6:

In addition, we seem to have forgotten the concept of placing a deposit on an empty bottle. This recovered many a bottle over the years, and significantly reduced the cost of manufacture. Children used to search out old bottles to recover a few extra pennies or cents of pocket money, whilst also reducing the potential of broken glass in parks, forests, etc. Placing bottles into a large bottle bank recycles glass, but the cost of manufacture is lost forever with reprocessing costs and impact added into the overall cost model.

Feature	Benefit
Collect Bottle	Reduced use of glass and other manufacturing resource
Reuse of Bottle	Reduces unnecessary packaging materials
Dedicated Delivery	Reduces need to collect items from supermarket
Reduced Inventory	Daily deliveries reduces need to stock, and reduces milk going sour
Local Suppliers	Invariably, milk deliveries come from local sources rather than having travelled through some elaborate supermarket distribution network meaning it is by definition on average fresher.

Figure 10.6 – Reasons to buy from a milkman

14. Resource Recovery – Item is designed in such a way so as to allow its raw material content to be extracted and recycled.

In a number of areas of the world, there is a legal responsibility for the manufacturer to manage the disposal of electrical items. In many ways this make eminent sense, as they would be in the best position to reuse components, and most likely to have the equipment and resources necessary to manage the handling of dangerous products such as mercury, asbestos or lead, all of which have a structured handling process, but all of which are still permitted to be used in certain applications.

Particularly where products are designed in a modular way, components can be managed in such a way that returning old product to the supplier can lead to the removal and reuse of the components. Invariably, this does lead to quality and inventory obstacles, but in many cases the savings of both operational and environmental costs will outweigh this niggle.

For example, in many cases it is possible to remould car tyres, adding tread and prolonging the useful life; car breakers disassemble cars and sell the reusable car parts for repairs; and returning used printer cartridges enables them to be refilled and used again.

Furthermore, the pending concerns and issues with the production of "rare earths" could prove the subject of war and conflict in the future with China controlling 90%+ of the world's economically viable mining capacity. Yet effective design of product, components and reprocessing activity can recover significant amounts of said elements, thereby reducing costs of infrastructure significantly over time. The 17 rare earth metals in question are shown in figure 10.7:

Chemical Symbol	Chemical Name	Chemical Symbol	Chemical Name
Sc	Scandium	Gd	Gadolinium
Y	Yttrium	Tb	Terbium
La	Lanthanum	Dy	Dysprosium
Ce	Cerium	Ho	Holmium
Pr	Praseodymium	Er	Erbium
Nd	Neodymium	Tm	Thulium
Pm	Promethium	Yb	Ytterbium
Sm	Samarium	Lu	Lutetium
Eu	Europium		

Figure 10.7 Rare Earths

And once again the BAE Systems "Reduce to Produce" process is a shining example of how decommissioned aircraft can be disassembled and the components reintroduced into the Supply Chain for use on other jets, or sold to other nations still flying the plane in question.

15. Restrict Component choice – Designed using common components aids the repair process, minimises replacement component stocks.

Developing design principles that use common components, standardised design parameters and single supplier relationships help ensure more sustainable products and services. The advantages and disadvantages that this brings are as follows – see figure 10.8:

i. Common Components

The decision to use common components helps simplify the design process, but can inhibit the designer's ability to create an innovative and dynamic new product or service: common components can lead to common products.

Action	Advantages	Disadvantages
Common Components	Lower support inventory, and fewer spares for maintenance	Less flexibility or scope for innovative design
Standardisation	Lower support inventory, and fewer spares for maintenance	Less flexibility or scope for innovative design
Sole Supplier	Consistent warranty, servicing, maintenance, training, etc	Less choice of products or components
Existing Inventory	Helps reduce or contain inventory levels	May miss new technology or products
Templates	Generic designs, and can form part of the brand or image	Can lack variety and be perceived as boring
Modular Designs	Products can be disassembled or faulty modules replaced	Can limit designer's scope

Figure 10.8 – Designer constraint issues

IKEA, the Swedish furniture giant focuses on using a common set of fixing, brackets, hinges etc within its flat packed furniture ranges making the supply of spares, the kitting process, and design of new product more concise. It also constrains the breadth of the inventory profile.

ii. Standardisation

Creating standards, setting design norms, generating brand image, common colours, etc, all limit the designer's ability to be flamboyant. Yet from an on-going management of product, equipment, maintenance and service support, having a limited and set range of components helps understand the product and issues better.

Consider the MacDonalds burger chain: wherever you are in the world, a MacDonalds restaurant has the same furniture, the same décor, the same menu, the same promotions and so on. MacDonalds are the masters of standardisation and conformity.

iii. Sole Supplier

Selecting a sole supplier helps support the aims for standardisation and leads towards a restricted component list. However the real benefits of a sole supplier scenario come from the commercial and relationship interests. Assuming there is an attractive turnover or some kudos associated with the client, building a sole supplier relationship leads to loyalty, partnership, exclusivity and lower prices within an all-round stronger bond.

In Toyota in the 1990s and onwards, there was a sole-supplier focus on Telemechanique – see case study 3 – as the highest quality market leader of "motor control gear". Wherever possible, control gear purchases utilised the Telemechanique brand, and the control panels for all equipment bought-in also needed to use Telemechanique, and so on. This meant that the maintenance engineers could be assured of what they would find when opening an electrical circuit.

iv. Existing Inventory

Designing new products using existing inventory is an excellent way of driving inventory levels lower, in effect using up old stock, and limits the pressure to introduce new inventory items.

Yet, designs can be inhibited with a limitation on components, especially where technology is an underpinning feature.

v. Templates

Templates can be used to create alignments in design or to create designs with commonality but with components differing within. The template concept drives similar brand and image, consider how many phone manufacturers have phones which look very similar.

The problem with templates is that the aesthetic features of products can become samey or predictable.

Many of the major telecommunication brands adopt datacentre design templates which can be scaled up or down as required, but which generate facilities which coordinate well, meet consistent parameters and meet the company expectations.

vi. Modular Design

Modular design – as with common components – allows quicker construction, inventory of modules, and no integral components in stock. The main product is assembled rather than manufactured; where a component fails, it can be quickly replaced.

This sort of approach does however lead to a generally higher level of inventory, with money stored for material content as well as labour, overheads and the profit contribution introduced by the module supplier (and that of all other suppliers further down the Supply Chain).

Most modern PCs use modular designs, with items such as power packs, internal processors, hard drives etc, tending to be common modules.

16. Limiting "in-use" emissions – reducing the emissions generated in the production process is one thing, however limiting on-going use related damage should be built into the design.

When designing equipment, careful selection of the operating voltage is required to optimise the power drain. Equally, selecting the wrong transformer could lead to the generation of unnecessary heat and excess wear and tear. And so it is with many areas of design. What we need to consider is what is the environmental impact of using the items?

Even in domestic installations, as mentioned earlier, energy is wasted by both network and appliances as a result of the voltage variances.

In terms of jet aircraft, some suppliers are focused on green issues: they do not overly consider the green impact of manufacturing the plane, but more on the endless miles the jet will fly – See case study 10.

17. Defashioning / Refashioning – Ensuring that the design does not develop a "fashionable" or "iconic" status that renders it "unfashionable" too quickly.

As mentioned hitherto, fashion plays a key role in when and how a product is used and for how long, as market players ensure their own longevity with a strong *Profit Pillar*. Products such as mobile-phones, computer games and electronic products have followed the market for clothes and shoes with the market making frequent and sweeping changes to preserve its on-going revenue stream. Underpinned with effective and targeted marketing to key sectors, the need to have the "latest" is one of the most difficult aspects to address in environmental concern.

> **Food for Thought**: The fashion industry and sustainability will rarely be compatible bedfellows: prolonged use directly conflicts with the underpinning concept of fashion where value is added by frequently updating designs and promoting change.

Commendable, therefore, that there are some organisations and groups that have resurrected old products and refashioned them, dousing them with either nostalgia, mystique or cost benefits. Take for example the revival of the Levi 501 brand in the 1980s on the back of an unusual advertising campaign using a soulful 1950s tune and Nick Kamen in his white boxer shorts washing his jeans in a launderette.

As with previous comments, this again pitches *the Profit and Planet Pillars* into direct conflict.

18. Leasing – Design of product market to make leasing feasible, allowing users to own an asset for as long as they require, and optimise the useful life of the assets in question

Following the recommended approaches to recovery of assets back to the manufacturer for recycling after the product *dies*, the option of leasing has sustainable benefits through an underpinning of *the Profit Pillar*.

Within a leasing plan however there are potentially some conflicting issues. For example, having a leased product for say four years naturally promotes the idea that the user will replace it with a new item. Fortunately, most leasing organisations have a clear outlet for ex-lease machines, so the life of the product is not compromised but indeed is actually often more secure as the product will probably have been maintained to a higher specification than a privately owned equivalent.

Accordingly, when the designer considers a product, it may be useful to perhaps introduce a parallel or sister product that meets the specific requirements of the lease market.

Take for example the issue of leased photocopiers. Here a significant quantity of the market is through leased business so the design of machine may incorporate copy counters, lease related software updates, toner restrictions to enable the leaser to dictate or specify requirements, and so on.

Leasing is a key component of many modern markets which designers and product or service offerings need to accommodate.

19. Use of Chemicals – Avoiding use of dangerous or contaminating chemicals that are not easily disposed of

Industrial processes and services often need to use a variety of chemicals to perform their functions. Choice of process can be a balance between costs, quality and time constraints; but costs should reflect the Total Cost of Sustainable Ownership. Particularly where chemicals are involved, there is a long term legacy that needs to be considered.

In times gone by, some factories took no notice of the impact that their activities was having on the environment. From East to West there are plenty of examples of contamination through industrial neglect: in Bangladesh, there are wetlands which have been all but destroyed through contamination from the textile industries; in the Wolverhampton and Dudley area of the UK there are ex-factory sites that are so contaminated that not even weeds grow; in La Oroya, Peru there is a lead smelter that has been polluting the area since 1922; in Dzerzhinsk in Russia, throughout the Soviet era, neurotoxin and military waste was systematically dumped; and many more – see *Time Magazine* (2007) for a list of their 20 most contaminated places on the planet.

Even in domestic products choice of chemicals is important. Consider the use of sodium laureth sulphate as a surfactant found in domestic shampoos and showering products; in other uses, this chemical is used to strip grease from the floors of industrial factory premises. In some countries this product has been banned, others have taken no action. The Natural Health Information Centre states:

> Far from giving "healthy shining hair" and "beautiful skin", soaps and shampoos containing sodium laureth sulphate can lead to direct damage to the hair follicle, skin damage, permanent eye damage in children and even liver toxicity.

A production process or service needs to consider the sustainable consequences of any chemical or material choice.

20. People motivation – Design and idea generation needs to be nurtured, and occur in the right atmosphere and climate

Selecting the right people, with the right skillsets and installing them with the right resources will be essential for a productive design department. The creation of a specific and detailed goal is required to ensure that the key objectives are communicated and understood.

Further, making the designers aware of their sustainable objectives as part of their fulfilment activities will help guide but hopefully not restrict their thinking towards a responsible design. This coupled with education and motivation is the secret to generating the optimum design function for *the Sustainable Business* over the long term.

Case Study: Aviation Design Innovations

Criticism and debate over the environmental impact of aviation is hardly a new phenomenon. Concern over pollution of the air, noise levels, CO_2 emissions, air-space congestion, and security are well documented. So what have designers done to alleviate some of these issues?

Organisations such as Boeing, Virgin, GE and NASA are high profile investors in aviation research, design and development, yet collaborative institutions such as NACRE (New Aircraft Concepts Research – which is headed by Airbus and 35 partners and part funded by the EU) and SUGAR (Subsonic Ultra Green Aircraft Research) also have a major role to play. As Jill Brady, Virgin Atlantic's Director of HR & External Affairs, once stated:

> "Real progress has been made in many areas, not least in the management of aircraft waste and local air quality, identifying and proving new sustainable fuels, initiatives in air traffic management and airport procedures, and in offering a realistic assessment of the inter-dependencies between noise, carbon and local air quality."

These design organisations focus on both improvements to existing designs and on new innovations and approaches. The focus is often on areas such as:

- Aircraft weight
- Materials used for construction
- Fuel types and passenger to fuel ratio
- Emissions
- Speed and Aircraft "Drag"
- Distance or range
- Noise levels
- Reusability of parts

In design, there is a need to make investment in both people and resources. If sharing of ideas or creating "think-tanks" is implemented, the return on investment can often be increased significantly. Once this investment occurs, targeting, setting goals and driving industry competition can all be seen to have a significant impact on generating new and exciting innovations. For example, in 2010, NASA published its

"N+3 targets" which sought 70% lower fuel burn, 75% lower emissions, and a 71dB noise reduction.

Such activity can be shown to promote innovation. For example, current industry ideas include:

- The MIT D8 Double Bubble Hybrid Wing Body – This new aircraft body is made from low weight composite material and by joining two aircraft fuselages together end to end and powered using three turbofan jet engines on the tail of the aircraft. This has led to prototype benefits which include: a 70% saving in fuel consumed; an 87% reduction in emissions; and a reduction in noise levels.

- The SELECT project run by Northrup Grumman is aimed at aircraft of up to around 120 passengers has led to a reduction of 63.5% in fuel consumption, whilst associated emissions were lowered by over 90%.

- Boeing has focused on the replacement of its 777 class of jets leading to a new prototype 350 passenger jet, delivering a 54% reduction in fuel burn and a reduction in noise levels of over 40%.

- GE have developed a 20 passenger aircraft with almost 70% lower fuel burn, over 70% lower emissions and reduction in noise levels of over 50dB.

- Jets with fuselage blended into a giant wing are being developed by a number of designers. The wing contains the pilot, payload, etc, with engines in the rear. This streamlined design reduces drag, and thus fuel consumption.

- Virgin Atlantic, and others have invested heavily in jets designed to run on biofuels to reduce the dependency on fossil fuels.

- Development of lightweight composite materials are on-going, with the aim of producing sustainable, reusable strong and lightweight materials; reducing the flying weight has an immediate impact on the fuel consumption.

(Reference Institute of Mechanical Engineers)

The Sustainable Business

Notes Page | **Page Ref**

Summary Chapter 11
Sustainable Project Management

Key Learning Points
- The elements of project management
- The Prince2 approach
- Project reporting and log maintenance
- Understanding stakeholder needs
- Producing a project specification and project structure
- Establishing Critical Success Factors
- Robust and sustainable business cases
- Building effective teams
- Team roles and use of specialists
- Avoiding "Group Think"

Tool Summary
- Prince2 Model
- Stakeholder Positioning Model
- Lewin's Freeze Model
- Belbin team roles
- Lessons Learned Logs

CIPS Syllabus Reference
- Level 4 Managing Contracts and Relationships in Procurement and Supply
- Level 4 Contexts of Procurement and Supply
- Level 4 Business Needs in Procurement and Supply
- Level 4 Negotiating and Contracting in Purchasing and Supply
- Level 5 Sustainability in Supply Chains
- Level 5 Operations Management in Supply Chains
- Level 5 Management in Procurement and Supply
- Level 5 Managing Risks in Supply Chains
- Level 5 Improving Competitiveness in Supply Chains
- Level 6 Leadership in Procurement and Supply
- Level 6 Programme and Project Management

Chapter 11: Sustainable Project Management

"There is nothing wrong with change, if it is in the right direction" – Winston Churchill

In organisations, there are people and there are processes, and then comes change. *The Sustainable Business* has a vision, a long term goal, it intends to be in business a long way into the future by focusing on its *Three Pillars*; its people, its profit and the planet. But it will still need to address short term change; it needs to manage its projects.

A project can be defined as a business activity which is outside the normal operation of the business. It is important to the future of the business but has a finite and relatively short term life. The project will be run alongside the normal business processes until the project handover when it will either disappear or merge with the main operational activity of the organisation.

Traditional project management has focused on a number of key elements:

- The stakeholders including the project sponsor and main users
- The project goals and objectives, the clearly defined aims for what the project has been set up to achieve – typically measured by quality, time and cost, or some other relevant metrics;
- The business case clearly showing value and cost expectations
- The project plan which will include a clear list of deliverables including its critical success factors (CSF), budget, timescales and quality aspirations amongst others;
- The project team
- The project after handover
- And risk

Sustainable projects value all of these yet go further. The project must respect the *Three Pillars*, it must have the same core values as the main business including its longevity aspirations.

The project management approach should embrace all of these aspects. Many different project structures and philosophies are available such as MSP (Managing Successful Programmes) or Prince2 (Projects IN Controlled Environments), for example. Each has slightly different focuses or process, however from a sustainability perspective stakeholder satisfaction is the core element of sustainable success. See figure 11.1

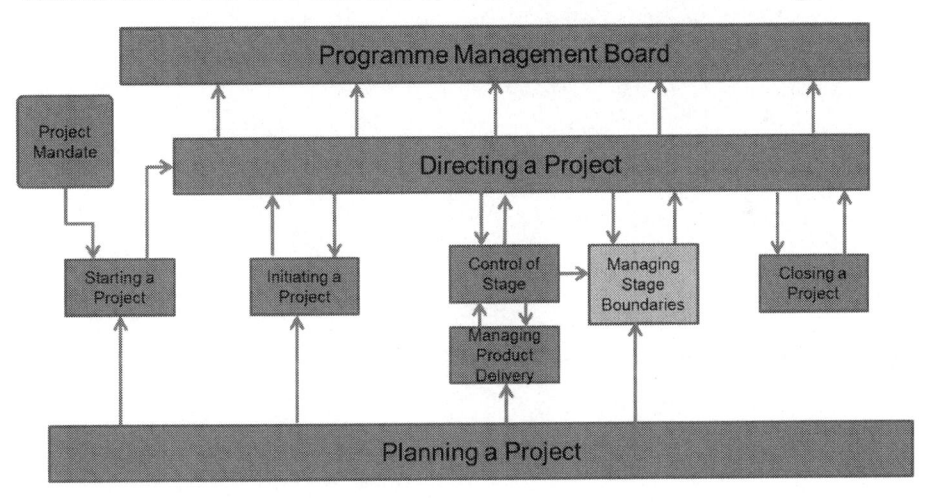

Figure 11.1 – The Prince2 Approach

Vital for all projects are its stakeholders. The stakeholders will include the ultimate users or customers who are key to the success of the project - these stakeholders are of paramount importance when establishing the specification; they will decide if the final product is fit for purpose.

Stakeholders will include a main sponsor, often a board member, financial input, and perhaps operational expertise, designers, sales people, warehousing representatives, amongst others. The stakeholder list may also include other external parties such as the neighbours, local businesses, the town council, government organisations, and so on. It will also include the suppliers to the project.

> **Definition: A user is somebody who tells you what they want the day you give them what they asked for.**

Stakeholders take on many different stances when it comes to a project – see figure 11.2. Many will object to change, others will, to a greater or lesser extent, be positive. Understanding these different views can be critical to the ultimate success and sustainability of the project and the investment.

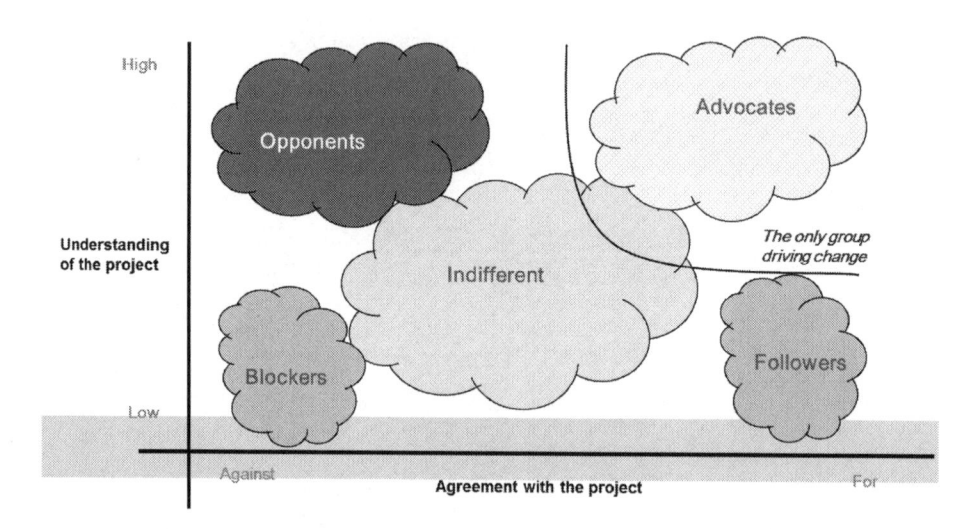

Figure 11.2 – Stakeholder Positioning

Implementing change is a difficult process. Lewin recognised the need to address the status quo as the first objective. The organisational norms, the history and the culture may need to be understood to generate the right environment for the project to occur. Within the start-up phase there will be obvious backers who are ready for change and obvious blockers who will do anything to stand in its way. The unfreezing of this status quo is the first stage in developing an environment which will allow a successful project to succeed. See figure 11.3.

Figure 11.3 – Lewin's Freeze Model

Unfrozen, the change can commence. People's roles, the office layout, activity allocations, or whatever is involved from the "old regime" have a new found flexibility which allows the project manager to go about his work with added freedom until the project is completed, at which point the new roles and processes are imbedded back into the organisational norms for "business as usual"; the refreezing.

The specifics of achieving these three steps are the specialisms of an effective project manager, yet core to the success will be respect, humility and patience. The project manager is often a temporary *resident* in the life of the organisation, many of the employees and stakeholders will remain for a long time after, living the legacy.

Understanding the requirements and aspirations of the stakeholders can be achieved in a number of ways, however once collated, a clear specification and detailed list of requirements should be built into the project charter. The specification should be agreed and cemented as best it can before the work project commences. A fluid specification is to be avoided; this causes issues before, during and long after the project has finished – see case study 11, the Wembley Stadium project.

The specification can of course be amended if required, yet this should be a clear and structured process within the project structure, and not something to be taken lightly. Contract and project amendments are license for the contractor to increase his price, extend the time line, or make additional demands on resources.

Once a specification has been agreed, planning can commence. A project plan will assess the three key deliverables: Quality, Time and Cost (QTC). It will establish the Critical Success Factors (CSFs) pertaining to the project and establish clear method for their fulfilment. These goals, timelines and budgets are essence of the project, and to the sustainability of the final output. *The Sustainable Business* will pay particular attention to ensuring that these fit seamlessly into the long term plans and vision of the organisation.

Equally important is an assessment of affordability, and a robust business case. Understanding what value will flow from the project is essential to determining whether the investment is worthwhile. All activities within an organisation need to add net value, otherwise they should not be undertaken. The business case will validate this mandate.

The business case will clearly show both the value and cost expectations and detail the resource requirements of the project: the finance, the people, the time, the equipment, and so on. These resource needs are important to ensure affordability and feasibility. A project may be required, and may add value, however if it can't be afforded, it should not commence; project momentum should never override prudence.

The project plan will also include a clear list of deliverables including its critical success factors (CSF), budget, timescales and quality aspirations amongst others. This will have flowed from the business case, but will be in considerably more detail. It will identify the project team, the roles and responsibilities and include a detailed time plan, project phasings (in Prince2 called stages), milestones and review points (stage boundaries). These review points are important as a moment to stop and check that the project is on track, and to gain authority from the "Project Board" to continue.

Phasing a project helps maintain focus; focus will help ensure that the final product is fit for purpose, budget has not been exceeded, and that the project has been delivered on time. *The Sustainable Business* – as with any other business – needs to ensure that the business case criteria are met at all times. Going over budget will, for *the Sustainable Business*, impact on its *Profit Pillar*; late delivery will impact on both its *People Pillar* and its *Profit Pillar* through the service component to its customers; using extra resource may affect its *Planet Pillar*, and so on.

The project team, led by the project manager, will deliver the project; it is they who will make the project happen. From a sustainability perspective, these team members need to fully embrace the ethos of the sustainability. They need to focus on the resources, on minimisation of waste, on good service, and positive people management; projects are often stressful times for teams, so the people element needs to be especially recognised.

The formation of a team will also be a key driver of success. As Belbin recognised, different people have different core behavioural characteristics, see figure 11.4. These can be categorised in three distinct groupings: Action, Social and Thinking. A team member will typically fall into one specific category, and will generally feel more comfortable assuming one of the roles therein. Core to the success of a team is creating a balance between behavioural characteristics. All of one type of person can generate what is called "Group Think". This has been shown to generate a skewing of a project focus, and a distortion of the project outcomes, with deliverables invariably compromised. The US decision to attack Cuba in the early 1960s – called the Bay of Pigs incident – is the landmark case, yet the decision to invade Iraq in 2003 might also be considered thus and suggests that politicians have maybe not learnt from past mistakes.

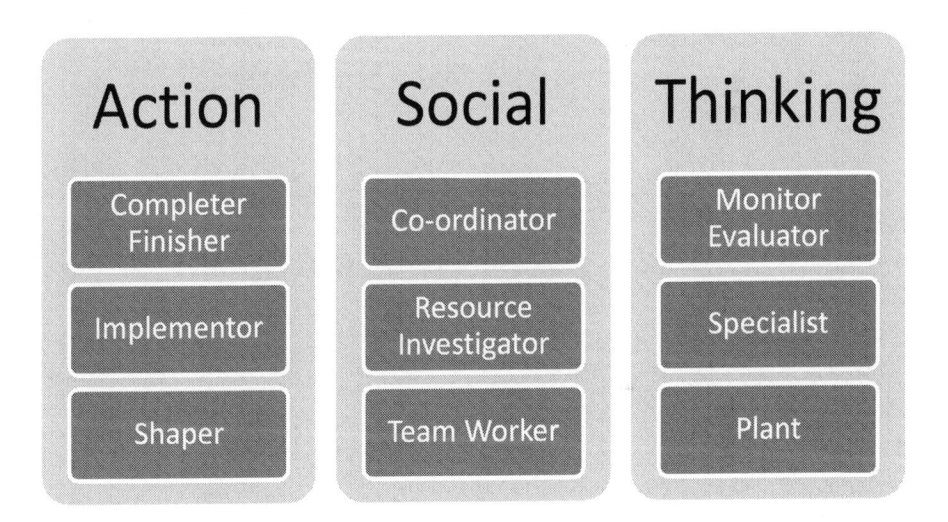

Action	Social	Thinking
Completer Finisher	Co-ordinator	Monitor Evaluator
Implementor	Resource Investigator	Specialist
Shaper	Team Worker	Plant

Figure 11.4 – The Belbin Team roles

Containing too many of one type in a team occurs more readily than one might imagine, with "Halo Theory" suggesting that a team leader, or indeed anyone in a recruitment role, has a tendency to select characters with like thinking. A sustainable team leader should be wary of such leanings, and involve a diverse selection process to avoid such tendencies. A team should also be aware of different management styles and leanings as identified by Adizes and others to ensure that the pitfalls of unbalanced management can be avoided.

In many projects, the need for specialists may be critical to the outcome. In a construction project, for example, you many involve a structural engineer, a ground survey, a builder, a lighting consultant, plumber, roofer, and so on. In such cases, it may not be feasible to involve representation from each skill set, but substitute this with a representative from the main contractor. What is key is a balance of behaviours and tendencies. Recalling again the project structure shown in figure 11.1, an important feature of good project management is the consistent presence of the planning, direction and main project board as validators.

When undertaking a car journey, determining the route, guiding the driver and checking signposts on the way are important to getting where you want to go. And so it is with project management.

> **Food for Thought:** "All project managers face problems on Monday mornings – good project managers are working on next Monday's problems."

Throughout the project, *the Sustainable Business* will have been monitoring progress from the confines of the "Project Board". The long term vision and aspirations of the overall business will have been instilled in the project ethos, but for future facing projects, the alignment of the project and the core business at the project handover will be of paramount importance.

Once completed, a good project manager will ensure that the project is successfully concluded. Documentation, the project log-books, budgets, reports, etc are all completed, signed off and filed. This filing is the ultimate record of what happened, when and why, and will be the main point of reference in years to come.

The life of the project after handover will be assumed into the running of the main business, or in the case of a final project, the project will cease. Either way, recording the project is often a legal responsibility and due care and attention is required. In the project team, the *Finisher Role* is vital at this point.

And finally, *the Sustainable Business* will want to learn from the project experience. Throughout, the project manager should keep a "lessons learned log" detailing issues and observations of aspects that went well, and of those that went badly. Maintaining this log will help future project managers avoid the same mistakes and over time ensure projects within *the Sustainable Business* run more smoothly and deliver improved outcomes.

Case Study: UK Stadia Analysis

"Wembley will be the greatest stadium in the world, and will be a real credit to the nation" – **Sports Minister Richard Caborn**

Success in project management invariably comes down to the relationship between contractor and client. Best results are seen when the undertaking is based on trust and shared values.

Much has been made of the project costs, over-runs, legal disputes and management approach to the construction of the replacement Wembley stadium in 2007, yet nobody has disputed that the project was a disaster from a project and contract management perspective: delivered late, over budget by in excess of £200m, and short of both its initial specification and the high hopes of the sports minister Richard Caborn.

The issue is not just an issue of cost and over-run however, but about net value for money. This is perhaps best highlighted by comparing similar stadia within the UK: The Emirates (Arsenal, London), The Millenium Stadium (Cardiff, National Stadium), Stadium of Light (Sunderland) and Wembley (London, National Stadium), see figure 11.5:

Stadia Name	Location	Capacity	Main Purpose	Cost	Cost per Seat	Comments
Emirates (2006)	London	60,000	Football	£390m	£6400	Delivered ahead of time and inside budget
Millennium (1999)	Cardiff	72,500	All Purpose	£126m	£1700	Delivered on time and budget
Stadium of Light (1997)	Sunderland	49,000	Football	£23m	£470	Delivered on time and budget
Wembley (2007)	London	90,000	Football & Rugby	£757m	£8400	Delivered 1.5 years late £200m over budget

Figure 11.5 – Stadia Analysis

All the stadia have similar characteristics in terms of build, timings, and aspiration, yet the outcomes could not be further in contrast, with contracts in three of the four delivered predominantly on time on budget. So what went wrong with Wembley?

The problem begins with hype and anticipation, and with appalling stakeholder management, but the relationship between client and contractor is where the project succeeds or falls.

The opening statements made by representatives from the FA, government, footballing notoriety and others only compounded the expectation. A failure to clearly decide and fix what was wanted by the various stakeholders, and more importantly what was a reasonable, realistic and affordable budget, were the foundations for the issues that followed.

Wider an often vague and fluid specification only exacerbated proceedings, with contract disputes, failed relationships with the steel provider, an on-site fatality, a sewer collapse, the weather and refinancing just some of the many issues to beset the project.

Yet the core of all the problems was the relationship between client and contractor, and a failure to instil trust. Throughout there was a "them and us" feel to the relationship, with parties working in unison, and focusing more on the contractual terms, the liquidated damages and liability rather than on the delivery of what was supposed to be the greatest stadium on earth, befitting for "the home of football".

Contractual and project conflict only ever leads to financial losses, either as a result of compromise, settlement or costly court battles. In the Wembley case, it has been argued that the contractor simply under-priced the project from the beginning to gain the green light, yet the budgets were approved and overseen by a highly reputable quantity surveyor. So where did the extra £200m+ go?

Whilst footballing enthusiasts and many Londoners may rate Wembley, the neutral and others living outside the capital look on with some scepticism; an acceptable but not world class stadium and poor value for money in light of other similar projects.

In conclusion, surely one of the best value for money stadia in Europe must be the Stadium of Light in Sunderland UK. Built in 1997 and then phase 2 in 2000, this stadium is a 49,000 all-seater stadium (but extendable to 64,000), delivered on time at a cost of only £23m, a cost of under £500 per seat.

The Sustainable Business

Notes Page

Page Ref

Summary Chapter 12
Sustainable Risk

Key Learning Points
- Definition of risk
- Defining risk analysis and risk management
- Identifying types of risk in the organisation
- Understanding the nature of risk
- Building a risk resilient process
- Force Majeure
- Consequences of risk
- Calculating the potential impact of a risk
- Formulating strategic options
- Establishing risk resilient strategy
- Monitoring, reporting and measurement of risk
- Risk in the external business environment
- Risk erosion of the Three Pillars

Tool Summary
- The Sustainable Risk Cycle
- The Risk Equation
- Impact / Probability Model
- Fishbone Diagrams
- Cause & Effect process
- Three Pillars Risk Evaluation Model

CIPS Syllabus Reference
- All units in Level 4, 5 and 6

Chapter 12: Sustainable Risk

The greatest danger for most of us lies not in setting our aim too high and falling short, but in setting our aim too low and achieving out mark. – Michelangelo

Risk is an undisputed fact of life; dealing with risk is part of living. It's about how you deal with the risks, the actions you take to prevent risks, and how you remedy the consequences of the risk once it has occurred.

> **Definition: Risk is the probability of an unwanted outcome happening *(CIPS)***

Risks come in many forms and profiles – see figure 12.1.

Figure 12.1 – Types of Risk

To manage risk we need to understand what the risk entails before determining our risk strategy:

Risk Analysis

- How likely is the risk to occur?
- What are the probable impacts?
- What can I do to prevent the risk?
- How much will it cost me?

Risk Management

- What can I do now to reduce the impact?
- What planning or resources do I need to manage the risk?

Furthermore, it is useful to identify from where the risk has originated. Some risk will come from within the organisation, whilst other risk will be generated from outside.

Take for example a construction company. Some of the risks on a building site will relate to its own activities: it decided when and where the building materials were delivered, and any accidents resulting from this are to a greater or lesser extent of its own making.

Alternatively, a vehicle accident adjacent to the site may have an impact, but may not have anything to do with the organisation itself, albeit that the traffic issues may have ramifications on the project or operation of the company. This is an external risk impacting on the business, it needs to be assessed and actions taken to mitigate the risk.

Additionally, there are Force Majeure – *Acts of God* – risks that may come into play. Earthquakes, weather cycles, drought, famine, etc may all be considered, though Force Majeure in recent times has expanded to include war, terrorism, strikes and other quasi-divine aspects that insurance companies seek to omit from their policy commitments; leaving these out of policy coverage has been the cause of many complaints from persons who failed to read the exclusions criteria, yet is essential to keep insurance premiums affordable.

The risk process is an essential part of sustainability as it is directly related to the organisation's longevity, attainment of its vision, and its future plans. *The Sustainable Business* recognises that risk is based on reliable statistical analysis, a probability dilemma focusing not on the "if", but on the when, where, how much, etc. Its approach to risk has detailed contingency plans based on a pragmatic cost base and a realistic operational code of practice.

The Sustainable Business will plan with risk in mind: for example, it will not build its office next to a river, but on higher ground to avoid flooding; it will avoid extremities of climate; it will seek refuge in balanced and democratic society; it will select solid currency for its transactions; use Forex instruments to offset any fluctuations, and so on.

However, wherever there is risk there is reward. Houses built on flood plains will be cheaper than those built on the hill; ex-pat employees working in dangerous locations do so generally for the extra pay levels on offer; sailing though Somali pirate infested waters is a cheaper short-cut to alternative routes. Risk and reward is about balance and probability.

The Sustainable Business adopts a consistent approach to risk to ensure that its strategic decisions take a due and measured consideration over what the risk is, what it will cost, how likely it is to happen and what the alternatives are. Its process reflects the risk cycle shown in figure 12.2.

Step 1 – Identifying Risk

Risk analysis should start with a simple list of potential risks to the business and gain input from all the key stakeholders as to risks they foresee. It should seek guidance from external sources to determine other hidden factors that may not have become evident. For example, when planning a large corporate event, finding out if there are any other events occurring on the same day may make the difference over attendance and numbers; simply checking hotel availability may reduce the risk of fracturing the group, for example.

This list can form the start of a "Risk Register", an essential business document both for the management of risk, and also for compliance and liability purposes. Typically, legal remedy is governed by who knew and what they did to prevent the occurrence in the first place. Keeping records of risk process will help *the Sustainable Business* combat any unforeseen eventualities as well as combating any "ambulance chasing" chancers trying to make a fast buck at someone else's expense.

Figure 12.2 -The Sustainable Risk Cycle

Equally, use of both the SWOT and PESTLE analysis – first raised in chapter 1 – will help identify risks and indeed opportunities both within the organisation (The SWOT perspective) and in its wider operating environment (The PESTLE perspective).

> **Rule: One man's risk is another man's opportunity**

Step 2 – Understanding each Risk

Once the list is complete, the likelihood of the risk occurring is explored as well as the potential impact of each risk. The risk level relates to just two factors: Probability and the Impact – See figure 12.3 - but both are complex assessments, open to interpretation and opinion.

Calculating the probability can be done in a number of ways and there are several methods and approaches that can be used. Statistical data is often available, and insurance bodies carefully assess this to determine risk premiums but these are aggregated and generic. Understanding the risk will help establish the real likelihood of the event happening to *your* business. Use of probability trees, computer modelling such as "Programme Evaluation and Review Technique" (PERT), "Critical Path Analysis" (CPA), and "Failure Mode and Effect Analysis" (FMEA) can help depending on your approach and investment in risk aversion.

Level of Risk = Impact of Risk × Probability of Risk

Figure 12.3 – The Risk Equation

It is also worth understanding the danger that risk analysis itself can bring to an organisation. Taking a decision over risk will often introduce additional consequential risks.

By way of an example, if an organisation decides to combat the risk of a power failure at its computer facility, it may decide to install a generator situated on the roof to take up the load in the event of a prolonged outage with an Uninterrupted Power Supply (UPS) system to cover the facility for the first few seconds needed to start the generators. This strategic decision is based on the cost of the downtime, the likelihood of the company losing money during this period, and the cost of the generator-UPS installation.

However, deciding to adopt this approach has consequential risks: there is the additional weight on the roof; the risk of craning the generator into place; the fire risk from the diesel fuel tanks and fuel feed provision; the risk related to the UPS battery acid; noise impact on the neighbour when the generator is tested or used; and so on. See Case Study 12 for more on datacentre risk analysis.

Invariably, risks have complex inter-relations, and a portfolio approach can be adopted to soften the impact. If a coffee manufacturer considers the source of its coffee beans as a risk, it may decide to have multiple and diverse supply options. This does not take away the risks associated with its African source for example, it merely adds an alternative sourcing option from say the Caribbean should the need arise. But such decisions come with a cost, see figure 12.4.

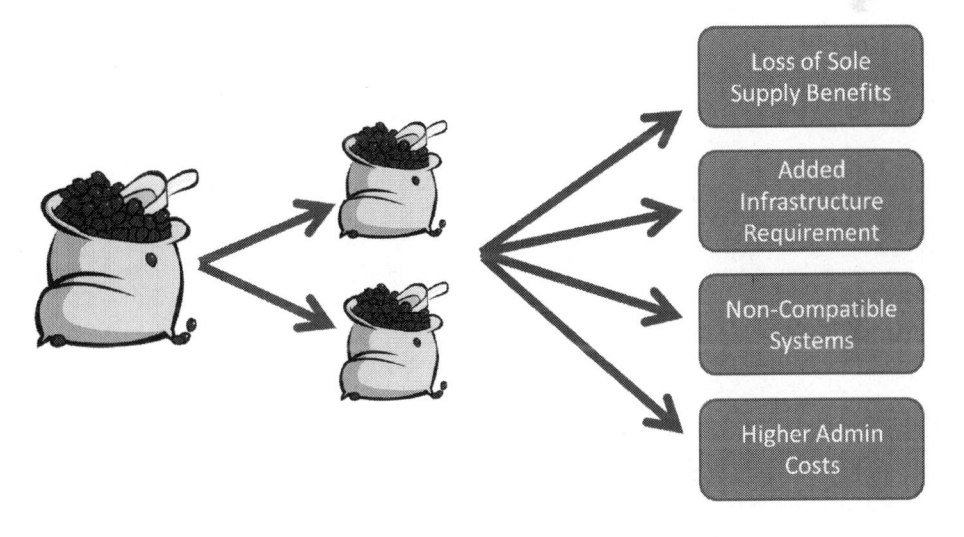

Figure 12.4 – Risk Consequences

One of the more important concerns to the organisation however is the exposure the business has to a particular risk, its Value at Risk (VAR). This is clearly a function of the probability, yet its exposure will determine how much of that probability it needs to consider in its assessment and this invariably drives the business case evaluation. In the earlier computer centre example, the cost of the computer outage can be established by looking at lost sales during the outage, or through customer claims. This is then used to substantiate the business case justification for the investment in the necessary infrastructure to mitigate this eventuality.

Mapping a potential risk has its benefits. Use of an Ishikawa or fishbone diagram can be used to understand the cause and effects of any particular issue. In a production example, these are addressed along each of the six primary fish bones and are related to one of the following: Man, Machine, Materials, Method, Mother Nature or Measurement – see earlier in figure 7.8. For each bone the causes are assessed to confirm or quantify the impact that that sub-element has on the overall impact.

Take for example making a cup of coffee in a coffee shop. What are the risks associated with producing a cup of coffee which is too cold? What are the consequences? See figure 12.5 for a part completed example:

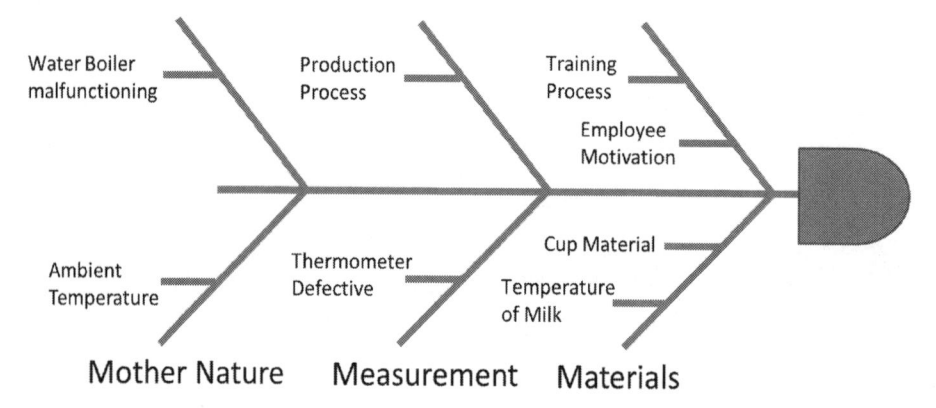

Figure 12.5 – Coffee Shop Fishbone

Potential Root Causes

- Time from making coffee to serving
- External environmental temperature abnormally cold
- Water boiler not heating to 100 degrees
- Milk too cold
- Coffee cup cools down too quickly
- etc

Effects

- Customer rejects the coffee leading to a replacement
- Customer accepts the coffee but withdraws custom
- Cost of reheating

- Bad publicity
- Loss of profits
- etc

Once the potential causes and effects have been established, then the impact analysis and remedy can commence.

Step 3 – Calculating the Impact

The impact can be calculated in a number of different ways, and is a key and complicated strategic decision for the organisation. It may include an assessment of the following:

- Is the cost based on historic costs or replacement costs?
- How is down-time calculated?
- Is it a shared liability or risk?
- What additional CAPEX investments are required?
- What additional OPEX investments are required?
- What are the future reputational costs?
- How long will the issue last?
- What are the alternative options?
- Will consequential costs or damages flow?
- And so on.

This impact evaluation needs to be time bounded and reviewed on a regular basis. Costs change and so do risks. The impact today may not be the impact when the event occurs. This can lead to the addition of an overage or error margin to cover any shortfall. But beware, with insurance policies, this overage inflates the cost of the insurance cover and may even make the policy either unaffordable or uninsurable depending on circumstances.

And impacts may not be merely financial. Reputation, goodwill and other intangibles may be impacted. Determining a cost for such factors is by no means easy and not without its own risks. Breach of accountancy rules, fraud claims, and shareholder rebuke are but a few of the ramifications that an inaccurate assessment may result in. Typically, larger organisations have clear process for such evaluations, smaller organisations can take advice from loss adjusters, accountants and legal firms as to potential assessments.

Step 4 - Formulating Strategy Options

Once the organisation understands its risk, the probability of it occurring and the resulting impact, suitable strategic options can be collated and explored. These different options tend to be circumstance specific and should be considered on a case by case basis involving key stakeholders, sector or technical experts, external resource and management as necessary.

Use of brainstorming, and other idea generation techniques to help facilitate the risk assessment team is valuable. The risk assessment team may be carefully formulated to address a specific risk scenario. In such circumstances however, the team and group dynamics need to be assessed to avoid either the *Group Think* concept or generation of an imbalanced role allocation as identified by Belbin and discussed earlier in chapter 2 figure 2.3.

Step 5 – Selecting the Best Strategy

Numerous models exist to help evaluate potential options. For example, Kraljic's matrix considers the interrelation between the importance of an item with the complexity in the supply of that item; others relate cost with risk, impact with investment, and so on. The interrelation between probability and impact gives us a clear reflection of the Risk Equation shown in figure 12.3. These two parameters can then be plotted to establish a probable strategic direction – see figure 12.6:

Probability of Risk Occurring ↑		
High Probability, Low Impact — Risk management, nominal investment in infrastructure, training so any team member is able to assist with remedy	**High Probability, High Impact** — Investment in duplicate infrastructure, Single Point of Failure Analysis, well drilled contingency plans
Low Probability, Low Impact — Ignore or deal with issue on an ad hoc basis, assign responsibility to a single team member for remedy	**Low Probability, High Impact** — Insurance policy either with an external firm or through a ring-fenced internal war-chest approach

Impact of Risk Occurring →

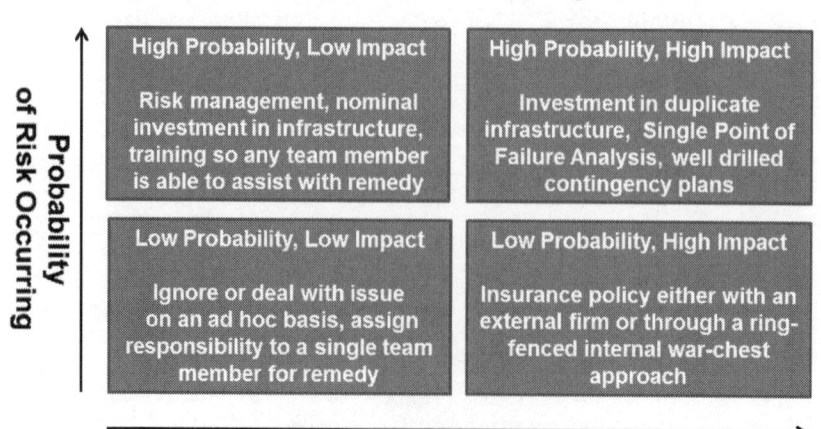

Figure 12.6 – Impact / Probability model

The Sustainable Business

In other circumstances, consideration of different factors may take a heightened role in the assessment, and should be part of the organisation's risk dialogue and process.

From *the Sustainable Business*' perspective, longevity and *the Three Pillars* are the primary focus of any risk assessment and strategy. The preservation of *the Pillars* will form the main driver to determining the strategy. Each *Pillar* should be assessed in isolation taking into account the impact of the risk upon it, considering all of the potential remedial options, whilst addressing any issues that may affect it, see figure 12.7.

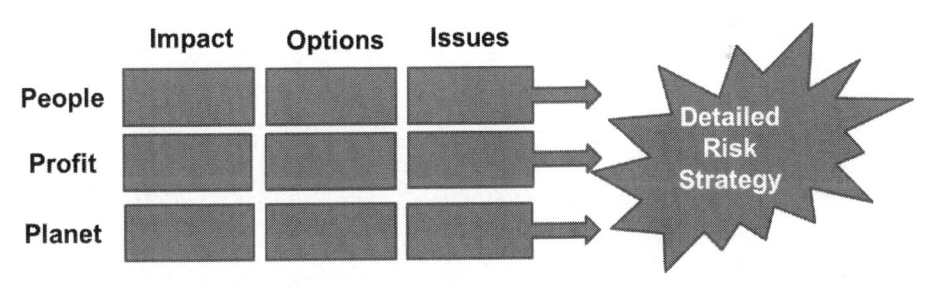

Figure 12.7 – Three Pillars Risk Evaluation Model

The strength of the CSR concept is based on the mutual strength and balance of all *Three Pillars* so whilst assessed individually, the strategy needs to consider them in both their singular and consolidated structure.

Step 6 – Monitoring and Reporting

Once determined, the strategy needs to be implemented and monitored. This monitoring should assess the effectiveness of the strategy in achieving its goals, as well as its continued suitability.

As mentioned on a number of occasions, strategy reflects both the internal and external aspects affecting the business; these aspects are dynamic, they change regularly and so must the strategy and *the Sustainable Business*.

Reporting the changes needs effective communication channels, and managerial support and buy-in. Without the message hitting home at the grass root level, change will be slow and erratic: with risk, possibly more than any other facet of business, this must be avoided. Risk strategy needs rapid deployment, a united front, and strong resolve.

Specific Risks to *the Sustainable Business*

Risk strategies come in many forms from avoidance to combating, from insurance to "hoping". A balanced perspective is essential whilst cost needs to remain a part of the consideration at all times – there is no point in an organisation spending its last dollar on mitigating a risk, if it then goes bankrupt: it has merely changed one risk, the mitigated risk, for another, the risk of bankruptcy.

There are however some specific risks that *the Sustainable Business* needs to consider – see figure 12.8. These apply to most businesses even in a competitive and well regulated economy, and even more so in the modern 21st century, 24 hour, global marketplace, where pace of change is rapid and consequences dire for organisations running behind the game.

These risks can manifest themselves in many ways, attached hereto are some obvious signs.

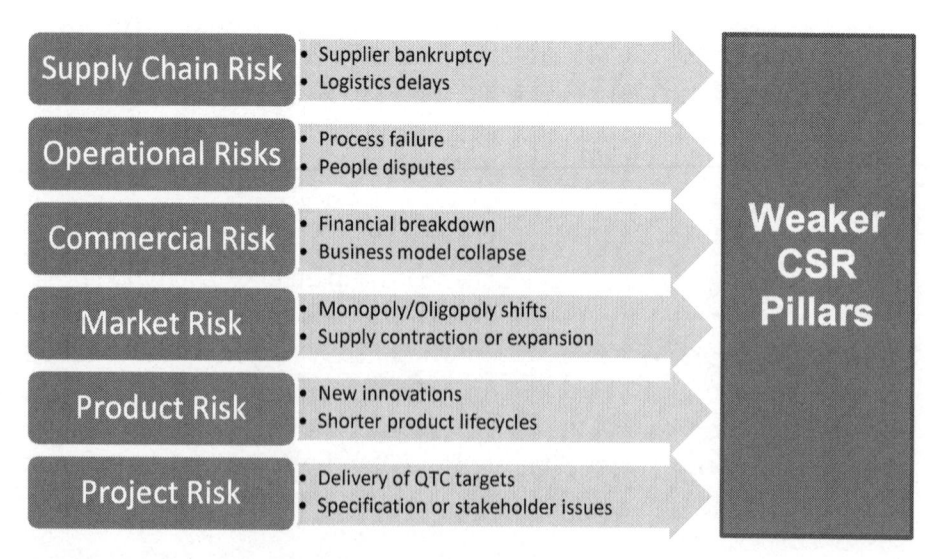

Risk Category	Examples	
Supply Chain Risk	• Supplier bankruptcy • Logistics delays	
Operational Risks	• Process failure • People disputes	
Commercial Risk	• Financial breakdown • Business model collapse	**Weaker CSR Pillars**
Market Risk	• Monopoly/Oligopoly shifts • Supply contraction or expansion	
Product Risk	• New innovations • Shorter product lifecycles	
Project Risk	• Delivery of QTC targets • Specification or stakeholder issues	

Figure 12.8 – Example Risks and Issues

Mitigation of risk need not be a lone challenge however. As seen above, these consequences will be felt by competitors, suppliers and customers of a market alike. Risk can be shared, not on a collusive basis, but in a pragmatic "pulling together at a time of crisis" fashion. This has been seen on many occasions over the years, albeit somewhat sporadic and usually at the eleventh hour.

The financial crash of 2008, the Eurozone crisis which started in 2011, anti-virus software detection, Live Aid in 1985, calamities in space and at sea, fibre optic networks (especially trans-ocean cabling), and drugs companies are all examples where staunch rivals have been seen to work together for the good of the whole, combating issues together and overcoming risks as one.

Risk needs to be addressed and transparent. Prudent organisations audit risks on a regular basis, wary of any change in circumstance. This is particularly prevalent in terms of environment risks where the pace of change is so great. Environmental leadership is both a challenge and an opportunity and is core to many strategic initiatives.

Risk Management is an essential component of *the Sustainable Business*. Where risk forms part of the organisation's vision or core objectives, failure to address issues promptly could jeopardise the organisation's long term future and business continuity ambitions; it will in short compromise its sustainable ambitions.

> **Food for Thought**: In 1912, the Titanic sank with over 1500 people drowning. The ship had a total of 20 lifeboats, capacity to save only a third of the ships passengers and personnel, yet the ship's design exceeded the prevailing legislation which required only 16 lifeboats to be installed.
>
> This case highlights that mere compliance with the necessary standards to address risk is not enough. A broader appreciation of the needs of the situation is essential and must be coupled with a responsible and pragmatic approach to risk, risk assessments and the needs of the user.

Case Study 12: Risk, Fibre Networks and Datacentres

Since the mid-eighties, business continuity has been critical to the thinking of sustainable minded organisations. The thought that *their business* might cease to trade became central to many larger organisation's planning agenda.

Whilst clearly and inextricably linked with the concept of risk – a facet of business which many managers at the time would claim was already addressed – the idea that external issues other than bankruptcy (for example technology, social pressures, corruption, etc) could prevent a business from continuing its daily activities, was a difficult concept to grasp.
The notion prevailing at that time was that good management could address most, if not all, of the possible causes of such an issue.

However, with the advent of Information Technology through to the explosion of the Internet in the Nineties, the mindset and attention of business leaders changed. There existed the notion that a business was utterly dependent on its computer, communication system, and huge, relatively insecure telecommunication networks with downtime directly impinging on the operation of the business, on its ability to earn revenue, and its exposure to client claims for loss of service.

As the internet and mobile telephony developed, so did the fibre-optic networks that form the backbone infrastructure of both. Original "twisted pair copper" cabling became redundant as capacity and demand outgrew the traditional communication mediums, leading to an explosion of fibre production and installation.

> **Food For Thought**: Fibre Optic Cable was invented in 1970 by Maurer, Keck and Schultz who recognised the ability to pass light, and later data through a thread of glass fibre. This revolutionary discovery drives internet, satellite, telecommunications, and phone transmissions across the world. Arguably, this is the Kondratief innovation that drove the investment bubble of the late 1990s and 2000s leading up to the 2008 global financial meltdown. (See Chapter 5)

Organisations involved with fibre networks focused heavily on resilience and contingency as they countered the commercial and litigious risks of network outages. Fibre networks were constructed in a similar way to power networks with the network formed in loops to give alternative routings in the event of a network becoming fractured. These loops contained thousands of spare fibres to future proof the investment, customers confident of the long term sustainability of the network.

Datacentres – or internet hotels as they were initially termed – were constructed at strategic points to both bolster the fibre signal, and form essential junctions for customers and networks to meet, the fibre equivalent of a motorway intersection. These became larger and more complex offering complete end-to-end services for customers looking to manage their virtual business in a secure and reliable location (See for example Global Switch or Telecity).

Datacentres grew at a rapid rate, becoming a critical part of the modern organisation's infrastructure. As 9/11 hit, the focus on security was heightened with rapid introduction of a multitude of security devices such as enhanced fire-walls, retinal scanners, earthquake proof server-cabinets, and so on.

In their design, Datacentres undertook "Single Point Of Failure Analysis" and started to adopt a rigorous N+1 approach to risk. This involves looking at the end-to-end processes within the organisation and where necessary adding extra infrastructure, design or process to manage the risk of failure. These included, for example, having two separate power cables into a data centre from different parts of the grid, running from different sub-stations, and with the cables entering the building at least twelve metres or more apart to prevent the risk of a pneumatic digger severing both cables at the same time.

Air conditioning equipment, power management equipment, fibre cabling, generators, and other essential equipment was also installed using the N+1 approach. If the facility needed four generators, then five (four plus one) were installed, if eight air-conditioning units were required, then nine would be fitted, and so on. This was clearly great news for the manufacturers who benefited from this extra demand, and were able to escalate prices due to the demand for the products at that time. An expensive option, but all in the name of a lower risk profile.

The Sustainable Business

Notes Page

Page Ref

Summary Chapter 13
Sustainable Legal and Finance

Key Learning Points
- The "Legal Mind Map"
- Basic structure of legal processes
- Core contract components
- "Continuous Ethical Responsibility"
- Finance limitations

Tool Summary
- Ten Sustainable Axioms

CIPS Syllabus Reference
- Level 4 Negotiating and Contracting in Procurement and Supply
- Level 4 Managing Contracts and Relationships in Procurement and Supply
- Level 5 Sustainability in Supply Chains
- Level 5 Management in the purchasing function
- Level 6 Legal Aspects in Procurement and Supply
- Level 6 Programme and Project Management

Chapter 13: Sustainable Legal and Finance

"The Sustainable Business should focus in the first instance on 'Continuous Ethical Responsibility'."

Hitherto, chapters have focused on a specific issue or functions within *the Sustainable Business,* yet not all business functions can be addressed in such a fashion and some have thus been omitted or covered as part of other chapters: the legal and finance functions are however outlined in this chapter.

Legal and Compliance

Quite rightly, the issue of sustainability is embraced by existing legislation, policy and direction at global, regional and local levels, yet is being added to all the time as situations develop.

The issue of legality and compliance is both critical to *the Sustainable Business*, yet a vast and complicated minefield – see figure 13.1. Specifics to any geographic location and individual scenario, and numerous differences of opinion, have thus led to this being omitted at this time.

Whilst mentioned at a number of points herein, the need to review each legal issue on its own merit, and in isolation, is a core legal requirement. Recognition of the fundamental principles of contract law is essential for *the Sustainable Business*, yet legal compliance goes way beyond knowing the basic components of a good contract, or the things for which the organisation can be prosecuted.

Accordingly, *the Sustainable Business* should focus in the first instance on its "Continuous Ethical Responsibility". In many cases, acting prudently, responsibly, and taking due care and attention will be enough to ensure that legal issues are not encountered in the first place, or can be addressed with limited concern or cost where necessary. Often, the authorities will recognise endeavour, attitude and intent; *the Sustainable Business* should ensure that these are visible and substantiated traits consistently applied throughout the organisation and recorded for future reference.

> **Food for Thought:** Continuous Ethical Responsibility is the concept of being able to show ongoing commitment to ethical and sustainable activity.

Figure 13.1- The Legal Mind Map

Compliance therefore, coupled with responsible reporting will both help prevent issues from occurring in the first instance and assist in their resolution if subsequently encountered.

> **Rule: "If it seems too good to be true, it probably will be"**

Finance

Equally, the same can be said of finance issues. In the turbulent times when this book was written, financial instruments, policy and strategy are under extreme scrutiny and subject to constant review. Revised policy at national and international level highlights the pitfalls that can occur in this area at any time.

As with the legal function, financial matters are deemed beyond the scope of this book, and should be reviewed and addressed in their own right with specific guidance applied on a case by case basis.

The need to invest or borrow is a fundamental part of business, yet one beset by issues and strewn with examples of error and bad judgement. In the fast moving financial, currency and investment world, comment is often outdated before the ink is dry and thoughts or comment potentially litigious.

Notwithstanding this caution, consideration of the following ten sustainable axioms are however pragmatic and advisable for *the Sustainable Business*, see figure 13.2:

Ten Sustainable Axioms
1. If it seems to be too good to be true, be very careful
2. Ask yourself honestly, does this feel right
3. Is anybody getting disadvantaged or hurt by the activity?
4. Be realistic, set limits, and walk away when they are reached
5. Question offers that are too far from the market rates
6. There is no such thing as a free lunch
7. Ask where the money is coming from – is it ethical?
8. How long will the good times last: Is the offer sustainable?
9. Read the small print
10. In business, respect all, but be cautious about whom you trust

Figure 13.2 – Ten Sustainable Axioms

In accordance with *the Three Pillars* approach, adopting a prudent approach will statistically both preserve the profitability of the organisation, and ensure longevity. Finance and Legal matters involve additional complexity and added risk. Know your limits and seek informed and independent advice where necessary.

Case Study 13: Enron

The need for legal and financial stability in the modern age has never been more important. Whilst rarely excusable, financial and legal shortcuts are at best short-sighted, in a world full of 24-hour media spotlights and IT traceability they could be considered somewhat naive.

In 2009, following the global turbulence felt a year earlier, ABC News in the US reported that the FBI had identified over 500 cases of possible corporate fraud, of which a number were large publically recognised organisations. Many of these cases related directly to sub-prime lending, yet others simply to malpractice, deceit or rash management. This situation was replicated around the world with other agencies facing similar issues, and has been seen throughout history on a number of occasions, for example the South Sea Bubble of 1720.

This situation is not unusual at the end of a period of an economic boom as was seen during the late 1990s and early 2000s. Organisations living on the edge, expenditure sustained by next month's revenue, employee demands exceeding contribution, over-valued real estate, and an underpinning business model incapable of longevity: this was the era of *the Unsustainable Business!*

Yet no circumstance has come close to surpassing the Enron crisis seen in 2001. It employed over 20,000 employees across the globe in multiple sectors from energy, communications, steel, paper, wind turbines, and others, with earlier revenues purported to be in excess of $100-billion.

Analysis of the condition of the organisation's finances at the end of its tenure was damning. On the face of it, Enron was a blossoming organisation with an innovative approach to its business, its markets and its future, yet beneath this glossy exterior were examples of alleged malpractice, misrepresentation, and fraudulent activity.

Whilst the issues that led to Enron's demise can be traced back many years, its foray into the water market is where many believe its problems begin. As early as 1998, some analysts warned of excessive debt levels, and unsubstantiated opulence through the company trading units, with some investment managers recommending selling Enron stock in mid 2001 before the scandal hit.

Following the collapse, reviews showed that a significant volume of the Enron assets and profits were allegedly over inflated or fabricated in a fraudulent manner. Where debt and write-downs were seen, these were commonly understated, not recorded, or "lost" in complicated off-shore funds.

One of the most significant areas of Enron's business empire was in the construction of over 30 power facilities around the world, often in more remote countries – such as Nicaragua, The Dominican Republic, and Guam amongst others – desperate for new infrastructure.

Activities in India were particularly extensive, with Enron going where others had feared to tread Most notable was the Maharashtra state power infrastructure scheme, with this ill-fated project suffering from a change in India's political power, turning it from asset to burden.

Eventually, in late 2001, everything unravelled for Enron as revelations of financial, legal and accounting irregularities came to light. Fraud was muted on numerous occasions and from many diverse sources, and the move to "Chapter 11" made it the world's largest bankruptcy in history.

Use of financial instruments along with off-shore and covert structures typically used for the avoidance of tax and distortion of profitability were unearthed, with company employees on occasions trading for their own personal benefit rather than the wider organisation.

The process entered a spiral, which needed to be furnished with funds and revenue. As the vicious gap widened so did the deception and the fear within the higher management of the organisation, with key executives selling stock whilst outwardly suggesting it would continue to grow.

Such behaviour is unsustainable, with bankruptcy the only conceivable outcome, longevity sacrificed for short-term gains and a fast, but hollow buck.

The Sustainable Business

Notes Page | **Page Ref**

The Sustainable Business

Summary Chapter 14
Measuring Sustainable Performance

Key Learning Points
- "If you can't measure it, you can't manage it"
- Creating a measurement system
- Measuring processes
- Setting objectives
- Different levels of targets – Strategic, Tactical and Operational
- Difference between quantitative and qualitative measures
- Areas and aspects for measurement
- The Toyota measurement system (TMS)
- Measurement of the seven/eight wastes
- ERP/MRP/DRP measurement systems
- Sample business measures
- Planet and green measures
- Supplier measurement pre and post tender
- Measurement of satisfaction
- KPIs and performance targets
- Measurements that strengthen the supplier partnership
- People measurement and a robust HR process

Tool Summary
- Measure-Data-Value
- SMART Targets
- Supply Inputs Model
- Kaizen & Continuous Improvement
- Customer Perspectives Model
- Financial Ratios
- RITUAL Model

CIPS Syllabus Reference
- All modules in level 4,5 and 6

Chapter 14: Measuring Sustainable Performance

Companies should decide what processes and competencies they must excel at and specify measures for each. – **David Norton, CMO Harrahs**

Measuring performance of a business and its various facets is essential to the management process; measurement determines strategy, drives decision making, ensures success and establishes value contribution. Establishing and understanding measures and data is therefore critical to the long term future and success of *the Sustainable Business*.

> **Rule: If you can't measure it you can't manage it**

Creating a measurement system can be central to the operational activity of the organisation. Whether it is as part of the customer process measuring order times, determining delivery schedules, tracking market prices, or part of the production process measuring activity, throughput, or waste, the need to measure is vital.

In order to add validity to the measurement process, we need to be able to collect accurate and representative data easily and without contamination; without irrefutable data, any management process or decisions will immediately lack gravitas.

The measurement process needs to add net value to the organisation. In *the Sustainable Business* all activity must lead to net value being added to the organisation, otherwise it should not be undertaken, see figure 14.1.

So in *the Sustainable Business* what are the key areas that we need to focus on and measure to ensure sustainability for the *People, Profit and Planet*?

Measurement across the organisation can be split into three main areas and these will be explored over the course of this chapter:

1. Measurement of business processes: which can include operations, administration, sales, procurement, finance and investment matters amongst others;

2. Measurement of the suppliers and customers of both goods and services;

3. Measurement of the employees and management in the organisation.

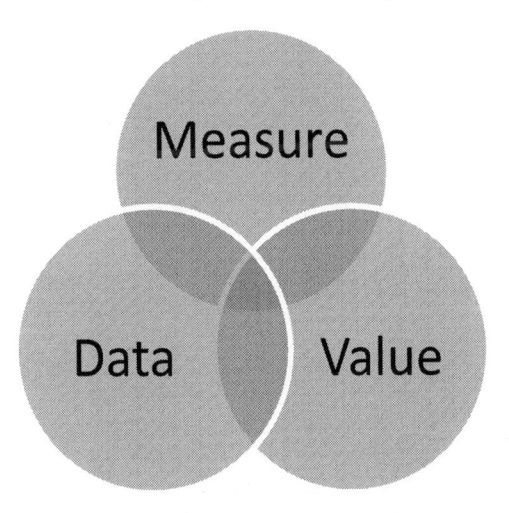

Figure 14.1 – MDV Model

The Sustainable Business however has a wider interest to carefully measure the aspects affecting *the Three Pillars* and their respective dimensions, and these will be examined for suitable measuring process.

Once in place, effective measures can underpin the targeting system, KPI setting, bonus model, statistical analysis and the strategic management of the organisation. It focuses the management on both the strengths and weaknesses of the business allowing strategic decisions to be taken and promoted with confidence.

Objective Setting

The setting of objectives in an organisation can be generally split into three distinct levels: Strategic, Tactical and Operational, as shown in figure 14.2. Each target level and target type is focused on the key overarching objectives of the organisation, whilst supporting the efforts of the level above.

Operational targets may for example reflect the number of components that a line-side worker produces within a business function. The individual may have a target of perhaps 120 fully tested and functional units per day.

Strategic Targets - Long term visions and objectives for senior management

Tactical Targets - Medium term targets and objectives for middle management & supervisor levels feeding into and supporting the Strategic Targets

Operational Targets - Short term process and transaction based objectives or goals, often required over the course of a day or less

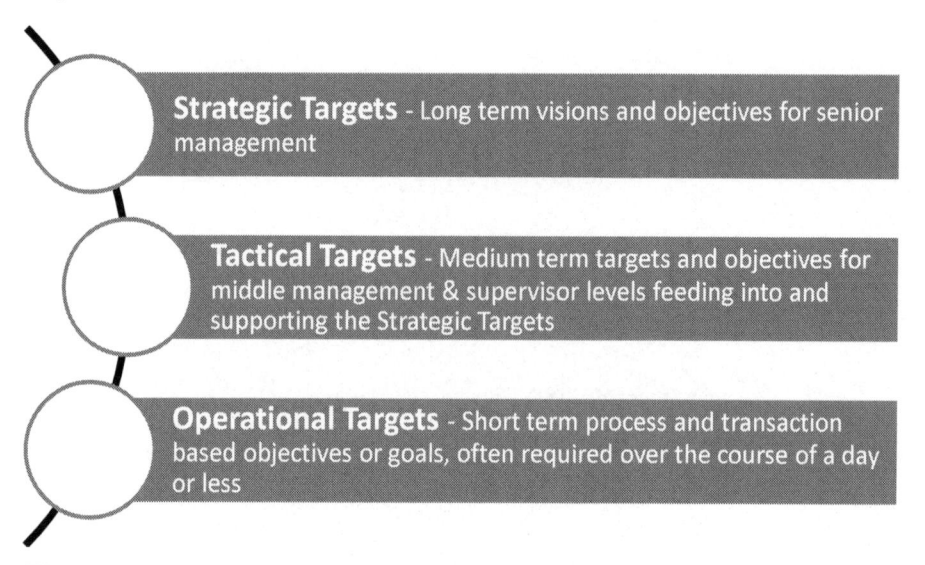

Figure 14.2 – Targeting across the organisation

These components may form part of a wider order to a key new customer who has been targeted with a sales growth or product development over a six month period, for example, the sales function may have a target to raise sales for the SME customer sector by 8% over a three month period; this would be a tactical target.

Similarly, there may be a long term organisational aspiration to become market leader in the business sector or market. This will be achieved by sales and product growth, through the development of new customers, and through the achievement of service levels to those customers. As detailed in chapter 3, sales and profit growth must be underpinned with an ambition for service excellence. In a manufacturing process, delivery of the right quantity of the right quality of product to the right place at the right time at the right price is fundamental to the delivery of that service and the development of a sustainable *Profit Pillar*.

It can be shown how important, if structured correctly, effective targeting is at all levels in the organisation. Targets need to be SMART – as discussed in chapter 5, figure 5.8 – i.e. Specific, Measurable, Achievable, Realistic and Timed. To be measured it is necessary that undisputed data can be sourced economically for the facet being measured, and that the effort of measuring adds net value to the business bottom line.

The design of the measurement system needs to reflect this value assessment. The cost and effort involved in the collection of data must not outweigh any benefit to the business. When developing measures and targeting systems, thought should be spared as to how the data can be obtained. In particular, be aware of issues surrounding qualitative data and its validity.

> **Food for Thought**: A Qualitative measure is one for which the data is subjective, i.e. it is subject to the opinion of the person involved in the action or the data collection. Such measures may include descriptions such as "Good", "Blue", "Heavy" or "Strong". In contrast, Quantitative measures are precise and easily collected. For example, a number, a height, a weight, etc. In the above list, goods could instead be described by more specific references, for example: Blue could be a specific pantone colour number, heavy by a specific weight, strong by a specific force, and so on.

Value has been explored a number of times in earlier chapters, and is surprisingly a commonly overlooked concept in business. Value is the positive contribution that an activity gives to the business bottom-line. No activity should be planned that does not add some net benefit to the organisation though that benefit need not be just fiscal: goodwill, happy staff, positive publicity, etc are all worthy benefits to generate.

Accordingly, as shown in figure 14.1, in order for the measurement system to be effective we need these three components: the measure, effective and reliable data, and some value contribution to make the effort of measuring worthwhile.

Areas for Measurement

As mentioned hitherto, traditionally there are three key areas to consider when implementing a measurement system: Process, Suppliers, Customers and Buyers. Some examples of areas for performance measures are detailed in Figure 14.3:

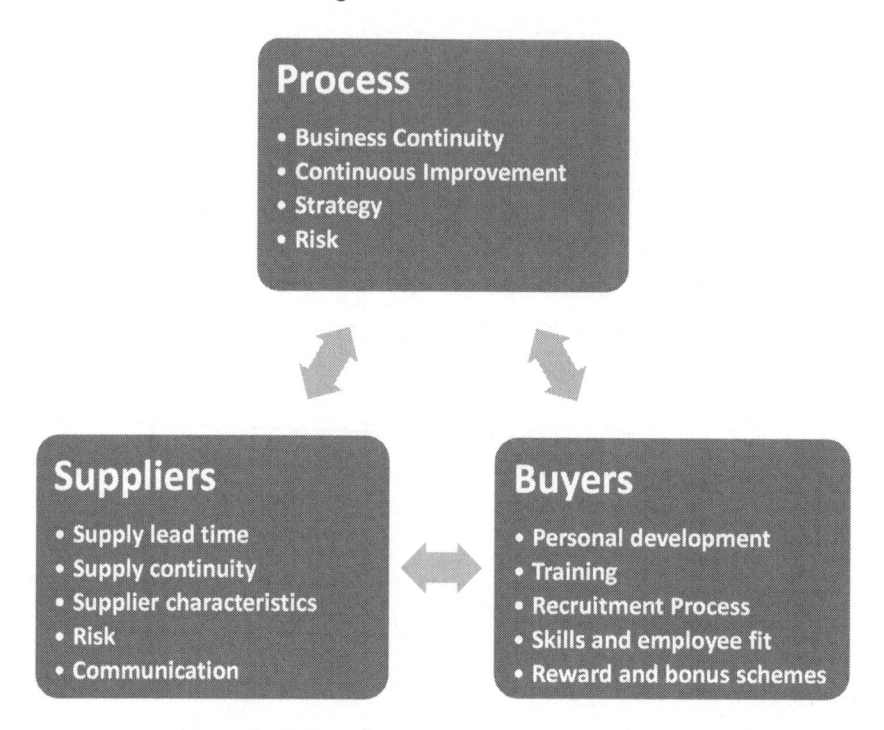

Process
- Business Continuity
- Continuous Improvement
- Strategy
- Risk

Suppliers
- Supply lead time
- Supply continuity
- Supplier characteristics
- Risk
- Communication

Buyers
- Personal development
- Training
- Recruitment Process
- Skills and employee fit
- Reward and bonus schemes

Figure 14.3 – Example Performance Measurement Aspects

Process Measurement

The number of areas within a standard business process that can be measured is huge. Take for example a standard factory production line such as a Toyota car plant see case study 9. Toyota is renowned for its Just-In-Time (JIT) and other business philosophies and particularly when it comes to waste such as Muda (losses in the processing and business activity), Muri (uneven or unbalanced work activity) and Mura (irregular or surprising activities), see figure 14.4. Measures exist throughout the plant and production line to ensure that the process and procedures are followed every time exactly as planned. Attention to detail is considered at every turn if it might shave a second off the production time, or reduce material waste. From a sustainability perspective, the elimination of waste is vital; measuring *Muda, Muri* and *Mura* will help improve the management of the processes across the organisation and enhance its sustainability credentials.

Measures operate using the highly coveted "Toyota Kanban" system to measure and manage inventory. Store areas and inventory are considered an evil and unnecessary waste within the Toyota establishment. To this end, goods are ordered for delivery at a specific time when the maintenance or installation processes require them. There is no "just in case" ordering, with goods generally used within 24 hours. Even manufactured sub-assemblies or components made on site are made in small batches depending on the economics, but to a strict plan so only a minimum of WIP or process stock is in place at any one time.

Muda - Waste in the process — For example, inventory, idle plant time, staff break times

Mura - Irregular activity — For example, unexpected breakdown of equipment

Muri - Uneven Working — For example, customers placing orders at erratic times

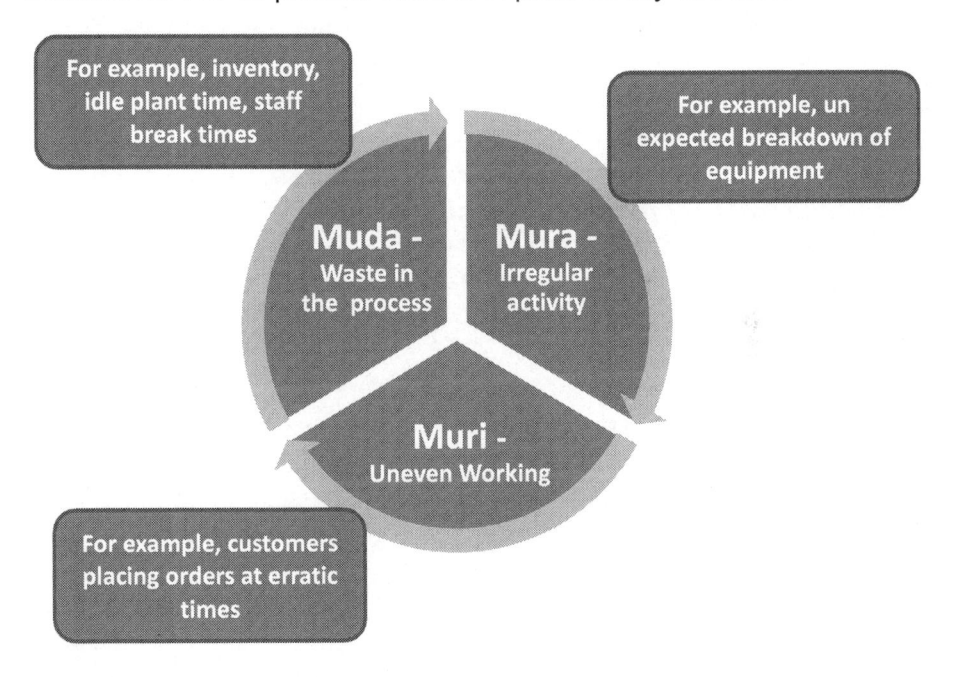

Figure 14.4 – Toyota Production 3Ms

Whilst the hallmark of the Toyota success, the JIT approach has on occasions caused a work-stop at the Toyota plants. For example, the 2011 earthquake in Toyota caused a fracture in the delicate supply chains feeding the Toyota plants. The issue of *Force Majeure* or "Act of God" incidents remain an issue for organisations like Toyota and how it handles such events: from a Toyota perspective, removing single points of failure (SPOF) leads to duplication and waste.

The Sustainable Business

> **Food for Thought**: A "Single Point Of Failure" is a fundamental flaw in a process where a certain circumstance could result in a catastrophic failure. Where a SPOF is identified, risk process should identify a strategy to resolve or counter the weakness.

Detailed material management assessments drive the business and allow purchase decisions to be made with confidence. This is coupled with due consideration of all design, planning, maintenance, etc. Suppliers are chosen for the long term based on proven quality processes. For example, use of Telemechanique products – due to their high quality and reliability - was a core and strategic decision at the outset of the factory design at Burnaston in the UK, and at other plants around the world. The Toyota approach is based on strong, sustainable supplier relationships, long term win-win partnerships (rather than strict mandated win-lose contracts), guaranteed profit margins, and theoretically low cost of servicing the business.

In theory and in line with the Toyota mandate, suppliers into Toyota should "theoretically" embrace the concepts of JIT. In practice however a significant number recognise the lucrative nature of the contract and merely through extra resource at the issues to ensure compliance and maintain the preferential supplier status.

Throughout the business measures track and monitor performance. Waste is a central theme within the Toyota philosophy; taking an extra second on a task, making a mistake, checking previous work has been done correctly, unscheduled toilet breaks, moving stock or materials around the building etc are all frowned upon. Waste is eliminated at all opportunities.

To focus the workforce and management on waste elimination, Toyota produced a list of seven key wastes or Muda which it stringently measures and relentlessly tries to eliminate – see figure 14.5

Transportation	Inventory	Motion	Waiting
Over Production	Over Processing	Defects	

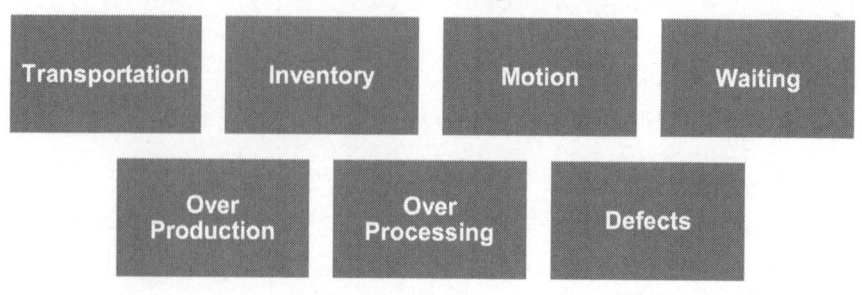

Figure 14.5 Toyota Seven Wastes

> **Food for Thought**: Toyota believe is that if you have a quality system, with quality operators and quality inputs you should not need to check the quality of the output. In summary, each of these wastes adds costs but no value to the process.

- Inventory relates to the unnecessary holding of inventory, including spare parts, work-in-progress not being processed, and excess materials;
  - *Example Measure – Value of inventory, number of items not being processed, quantity of left over material, volume of excess delivery (Toyota strongly objects to having too much delivered, even if it has been sent free of charge).*
- Transportation relates to the unnecessary movement of product where the movement does not have any relation to the processing;
  - *Example measure – Distance between where the item is and where it needs to be.*
- Motion is excess movement of people or machinery that is not necessary to perform the task. Job roles on the production lines need to happen between two marker lines on the floor and taking a set number of footsteps for the operator;
  - *Example Measure – The number of footsteps the operator will take between his activity start point and the activity handover point. In some extreme cases, production lines will alternate left handed and right handed people so they do not "bang elbows" at the interchange point – leaving a gap between one operator finishing and another starting would be deemed a wasted moment; 1 second per car, over say 50,000 vehicles a year = 13 hours of wasted production time.*
- Waiting refers to any item that is queuing to enter the next process step. Work in progress must be moving the whole time towards its completed state;
  - *Example Measure – Number of seconds stationary in the production process, time spent waiting for the change of a process configuration, or a change in operator.*
- Overproduction refers to the manufacture of any item or component before it is needed, in effect this item would become inventory for a short period;
  - *Example Measure – Number of components made for orders but then not used. As defects are not expected or tolerated, if there are 10 cars to be processed, then 10 bumpers will be produced,*

not 9 and not 11. It's a fairly basic concept once the zero defect expectation is understood.
- Over processing identifies areas where poor design characteristics or incorrect use of equipment leads to excess or repeat activity;
  - *Example Measure – number of reprocess activities undertaken and the reason for that occurrence.*
- Defects are the errors, the quality failures and the inspection process. The Toyota philosophy believes that if the inputs are of the right quality, and the process is quality approved, then the output, by definition, will be of the correct quality, rendering inspection as unnecessary and a waste.
  - *Example Measure – Number of quality rejections*

> **Food for Thought**: SMED refers to Single Minute Exchange of Die, i.e. effort was focused on reducing the time taken to change a process over. Consider the time it historically took for other car firms to change a paint run, producing batches of red cars, then batches of blue cars, and so on. This led to a large inventory of finished product, production reliant on the marketing department's ability to project consumer taste and fashion and ability to react dynamically to changes in customer preference.

These represent the original seven wastes, however in recent times there has been an eighth added to the list, that of producing something that does not meet the customer expectations or quality aspirations. This was introduced and explored in depth by Womack and Womack in their work entitled "Lean Thinking".

This focused on vertical integration through the Supply Chain to both maximise service levels whilst reducing inventory. This can only be achieved by truly understanding and reflecting customer needs, and by producing exactly what they want, when they want it. This takes away the stocking of a wide range of periphery products often through the design and development of products that have more flexibility and versatility – see case study 16.

Furthermore, Toyota and companies such as Motorola value the input from their operatives and employees, often through implementing Six Sigma and other similar "Voice of the Customer" programmes. Six

Sigma is explored more fully in chapter 10 but suffice to say, Toyota *et al* recognise the ideas and inputs from its employees, rewarding suggestions as to how to reduce waste in the business.

Understanding the importance of the Supply Chain to *the Sustainable Business* is critical. The Supply Chain is at the core of the business, and fundamental to its *raison d'etre*. The Supply Chain will impinge on almost every operational activity, management activity, and strategic decision, and is therefore central to the fulfilment of its profit delivery aspirations, as well as its ability to invoke its wider People–Profit–Planet ambitions. This importance reiterates the aforementioned motto – *"if you can't measure it, you can't manage it"*.

Wider, the Supply Chain needs to be viewed as a collation of numerous business facets, all complicit in the ultimate goal of the operation. These different elements generally focus on the inputs to a process, for example raw materials, power, people, data, and so on. The typical ERP solution merely tries to map when each input is required to maximise service throughput, minimise waste and ensure on-time delivery. Raw material, for example, should not be delivered until it is needed - the essence of the Just-In-Time concept - and the human element should remain active at all times, finance should reflect the best return on investments, and so on. See Figure 14.6.

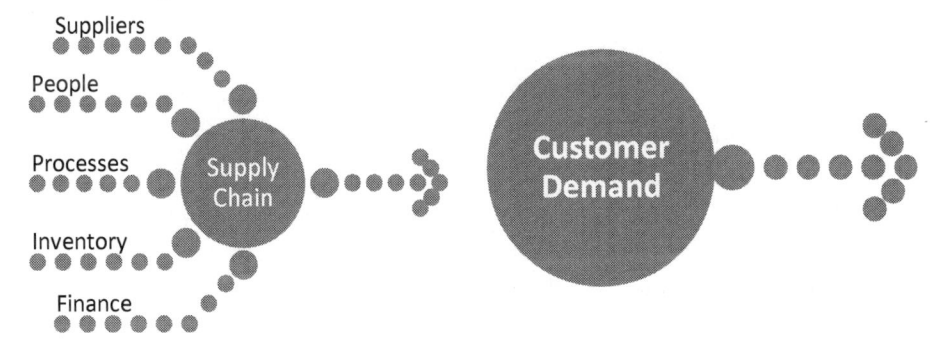

Figure 14.6 – Supply Chain Inputs

Effective measurement across the Supply Chain is now more established in business culture. The developed use of IT solutions (such as ERP products) necessitates the continuous analysis of key business parameters to determine operational activity. Leading Supply Chain IT providers – for example Manugistics, SAP, etc – track minute changes in a wide range of operational parameters, recognising shifts in demand patterns, lead times, customer preferences, trends, and so on.

The ERP system also recognises the need for rest periods for both man and machine. It ensures there is the necessary down-time, maintenance and servicing within the schedule.

Modular systems such as these allow an organisation to create a structured solution aligned to its own business needs whilst minimising IT investment costs. It also allows the system to be implemented over a structured period with financing spread accordingly.

ERP solutions – as well at MRP (Manufacturing Resource Planning) and DRP (Distribution Resource Planning) – manage resources flowing through the organisation. They link different functions to ensure each coordinates at the required moment to enable the right quality of goods or services to be delivered to the customer at the right place and time. Some of these input functions are shown in figure 14.7.

Figure 14.7 – Potential components of an ERP solution

In addition, each module may have numerous sub-functions. For example the Supply Chain module may incorporate a warehousing or logistics module, the finance module may include an accounting or invoicing link, and the customer module may include a sales or marketing link.

The importance of systems configuration and implementation is critical to *the Sustainable Business*. A poorly structured system will hamper the organisation, jeopardising its long term direction and profitability, as well as generating stress and distraction for the employees during the transition. In addition, a poor implementation will irritate even the most loyal of customers.

Notwithstanding the issues of new system integration, the merits of an effective system on the measurement and management of the organisation is undoubted and worth both the pain and strain. Measurements applicable to a specific department will differ depending on both the functional activity and nature of the organisation: See table 14.8.

Department	Example Measures
Sales	<ul><li>Average invoice value</li><li>Profit margin</li><li>Customer churn</li></ul>
Marketing	<ul><li>Promotion success</li><li>Price point analysis</li><li>Product range analysis / Profile gaps</li></ul>
Purchasing	<ul><li>Purchase order value / Order frequency</li><li>Number of suppliers / Number of new suppliers</li><li>Supplier lead times / On-time deliveries</li></ul>
Inventory and Warehousing	<ul><li>Stock turn / Out of stock occurrences / Pick percentages</li><li>Stock losses / Breakages</li><li>Stock accuracy</li></ul>
Administration	<ul><li>Invoice process time</li><li>Bad debt management / Commercial query handling</li><li>Overdue invoices / Average days to pay</li></ul>
Logistics	<ul><li>Mileage per gallon or per day</li><li>Van route analysis /Fleet management</li><li>Tachometer analysis</li></ul>
Finance	<ul><li>Return on Capital Employed</li><li>Current Ratio / Quick Ratio / Yield</li><li>Asset turnover</li></ul>
HR	<ul><li>Staff turnover / Absenteeism</li><li>Staff satisfaction levels</li><li>Male / Female / Ethnic mix</li></ul>

Table 14.8 - Sample business measures

Linking these to the issue of Sustainability and *the Three Pillars* will help drive the sustainability agenda. Many of these example measures can be shown to have a direct impact on the *People* and *Profit Pillars* - both of which are clearly of importance for *the Sustainable Business* - yet few reflect the environment or the *Planet Pillar*. This is clearly an issue with the prevailing concerns over global warming, the extended use of the Earth's resources and the desire for a balanced approach to sustainability.

The imbalanced measurement and management of the relative *Pillars* may be a result of historical tendencies or due to the fact that both profitability and people related facets of a business will have relatively quick and visible manifestations. Either way, *the Sustainable Business* needs to appreciate the *Planet* within its measurement activity. Recalling the previous list, table 14.9 offers some alternative measures to redress the balance:

Department	Example Planet Measures
Sales	• Carbon content of sales proposal • Sales force air-miles flown
Marketing	• Green product mix • Catalogue materials
Purchasing	• Percentage ISO14000 suppliers • Packaging analysis
Inventory and Warehousing	• Product returns percentage • Recycled packaging
Administration	• Quantity of recycled paper used • Percentage electronic invoicing
Logistics	• Number of shared transport shipments • Bio-diesel content
Finance	• Finance from green sources • Impact cost component
HR	• Transport to work mix • Car sharing analysis

Table 14.9 – Planet related measures

The introduction of "green measures" is however only the first step in measuring sustainability across the organisation and measures should be in place to determine the effectiveness of process, people and suppliers at all levels in the organisation.

> **Food for Thought**: What are your current business issues and what on-going measures are *really* in place to track, monitor and guide the strategy to address said problems? Do management respect the findings or is it really *business as usual*?

Measurement in the processes adopted by *the Sustainable Business* will therefore look at a broader remit than merely its green credentials. The analysis of its cost control and sales margins will drive the organisation's ability to make a sustainable profit; the investment in the right plant, machinery, capital and people will determine its ability to deliver a sustainable service; and its ability to accurately measure and manage its business will drive the implementation of an effective strategy,

Particularly in uncertain economic times, *the Sustainable Business* needs to adopt prudent approaches to spending its money. Well publicised are companies' efforts to cut costs with ideas and initiatives broad and varied.

Take for example the decision in the 1960s by Swan Vesta to remove one of the match striking strips from the side of its matchboxes following a suggestion from an employee, or British Airways decision in the 1990s to standardise all uniforms to a single fabric and reduce the number of buttons on each sleeve. Both assessed the value added by the additional features and deemed the extra expenditure unnecessary.

Equally important are environmentally focused initiatives, with such endeavours now stretching beyond turning the lights off in the office. Innovations, IT developments, and design changes have helped organisations across the world develop a better focus on saving costs in their businesses. Hilton Hotels, for example, have assessed their cost and value propositions as part of their LightStay™ programme leading to an extensive range of measurements, benchmarking and value analysis. This initiative reviewed the disposable items placed in hotel rooms, the costs of clean lining in rooms, and incremental costs incurred by each resident.

Further, there has been somewhat of a sea change in the employee take-up of cost control in *their* organisation. In many regions of the world, there has been an historic ambivalence towards helping the company save money, yet now in some quarters it is becoming a crusade to saving the planet. Sustainability officers are becoming commonplace, often at board level, with the sole objective of championing green initiatives and challenging the status quo.

> **Food for Thought:** The Hilton LightStay™ is the Hilton's own dedicated sustainability measurement system. It is designed and focused on "helping improve hotel performance and profitability while effectively managing the company's use of natural resources." In 2009, Hilton Worldwide properties reduced:
> - Energy use by 5 percent
> - Carbon output by 6 percent
> - Waste output by 10 percent
> - Water use by 2.4 percent

As shown in Case Study 2, organisations such as Tengizchevroil are investing significant resources into limiting the natural gas released and burnt off through flaring. Capture of this commodity has not only helped reduce the environmental impact, but also led to a supplementary revenue stream for the business with 9.1 billion cubic metres of natural gas contained during 2010 alone.

Recall the previously identified situation in Gibraltar, where fresh water is at a premium and toilets are flushed using free salt water which is in abundance; in other similar regions use of *grey water* is not unusual to keep utility costs under control.

And organisations such as Virgin Airways are exploring and implementing bio fuel technology as standard. See case study 10.

> **Food for Thought**: The introduction in 2012 of the GHG (Greenhouse Gases) protocol looks at the measurement of carbon impact up and downstream with "scope 3" emissions measured from the supplier's suppliers, and consideration paid to downstream activities such as franchises or leased assets.

From a sustainability and process perspective, this is all encouraging progress, and long may the momentum continue. The Kaizan approach of "Continuous Improvement" will help processes develop; effective measurement across these processes will help sort the good ideas from the bad hopefully driving management strategy and systemic change going forward.

Supplier/Customer Measurement

Whilst measurement and management of *the Sustainable Business'* processes are important, the need to engage and contract with the right suppliers and customers are key ingredients of sustainable success. Accordingly, appropriate attention to the measurement of the selection and performance of such business partners is required.

Any successful business needs a clear and unambiguous strategy that reflects both its internal needs and the external environment in which it operates; these are typically addressed with SWOT and PESTLE analysis respectively and are examined more closely in chapter 1. There is a need however to ensure that a rational and pragmatic approach is taken when it comes to the formation of any supplier or customer strategy to encourage any would-be partners to invest time and effort in any tender or selection process. *The Sustainable Business* has aspirations to exist and grow into the future so any new and existing relationships need to concur with this vision and contribute positively to the on-going business continuity.

The image of *the Sustainable Business* as a reputable organisation with whom a supplier would want to do business is of paramount importance. It is likely that in the first instance they will evaluate and thus measure *your* business to gauge its financial strength, future potential and the mutual compatibility. The degree with which this analysis takes place varies considerably however, especially where such analysis is left to a "process averse" or "target shy" salesperson. A glossy website carefully worded and constructed to give an image of size can shroud a fledgling business; equally a large multi-national, complacent with its status and position, may not invest the due resource in its online persona, though this has changed steadily and has been accelerated since the "dotcom" recovery and the 2008 global slow-down.

Equally important is the compatibility between organisations, an element often overlooked. Like a marriage, two entities need to be compatible to make the relationship work. Globally there are many examples of non-compatibility for a plethora of reasons: historic adversity, geographical differences, language, religion, conflicts and so on are but a few. Such incompatibility might include political conflict, favouritism towards like-minded nations, or anti-Semitic boycotts of Jewish companies.

With supplier and customer, these same tensions exist and the compatibility is vital to the development of a sustainable relationship. Where historic tensions encroach into business life special care needs to be taken in recognising the risk and consequences that might transpire.

Measurement of a sustainable relationship is of course far from easy. As mentioned hitherto, the difficulty of assessing qualitative measures is subjective and far harder than quantitative measures with measurement criteria needing to reflect this difficulty.

The financial assessment of a would-be supplier or customer is however easier to determine. Typically, financial records are accessible for most free-market organisations to some degree, though a clever business person or an efficient accountant can be used to some nominal degree to manipulate the numbers across years with capital purchases, sales projections and investment recovery – see Sandbagging in chapter 8. This activity is however only useful for a finite period and closer evaluation of the numbers invariably sets alarm bells ringing. Increases in debt levels, longer cash collection times, and changes in the Current Ratio or Quick Ratios – discussed later in this chapter – are all useful for this closer scrutiny.

In the immediate term, the relationship between buyer and supplier often starts with some sort of sourcing process. The buying organisation determines a requirement, and must establish possible sources of the goods or services. The processes the procurement department undertakes are explored in more depth in chapter 6, however at the supplier selection stage a clear specification is required with which to approach the market either with a targeted RFI (Request for Information) [alternatively a RFP (Request for Proposal) or RFQ (Request for Quotation) may be used] or an EOI (Expression of Interest).

These approaches may take the form of a formal written approach or merely a telephone call, however once the process has started the buyer and seller should undertake some level of due-diligence to assess the potential of further dialogue. In some instances, from the buyer's side, a PQQ (Pre-Qualification Questionnaire) may be used to obtain more information on the seller, though experience suggests that an effective sales team would seek direct interface rather than filling in such a request; this meeting request is of course part of their own assessment of the buying organisation.

As a form of measure, the range of PQQ and EOIs that are used in the market are vast and somewhat diverse. Many are simple one page surveys asking for low level detail and often of little real use to the buyer; in others the PQQ can run into many pages of complex and detailed information requests that can leave the recipient baffled, bemused and demoralised, such emotions often leading to a failure to complete the exercise and the loss of a potentially desirable business partner.

The secret is in the balance, seeking the important information without causing issues within the selling organisation, without requesting overly sensitive information, whilst promoting an image of a business that is both professional and responsible.

> **Food for Thought**: Completion of a PQQ takes time and effort. Time, as they say, is money. This investment, howsoever it is measured, needs to be built into the seller's business budget. Completing a 20+ page PQQ needs to have a realistic payback and chance of success for the seller to be motivated to respond.

So what sort of information should a PQQ look to assess? This will of course depend to a large extent on the business, the commodity being procured and the risk profile. If the organisation is looking to secure a new kettle for the canteen, then the selection of a supplier will differ greatly to the measurement of a new maintenance contractor for a large factory or the logistics contractor for a global distribution company.

Typically therefore there is a "shopping list" of criteria that may be used to construct such an assessment, reflecting of course the value of the contract which in the previous example may differ from perhaps a one off $10 purchase to many thousands or even millions of dollars over a multi-year period. Such a shopping list may include, though not limited to, any of the following:

- Core competency
- Previous experience
- Physical resources
- Size of organisation
- Geographical location
- Financial strength
- Cost
- Quality of product
- Risk profile

It would be wrong to try and produce a "one list fits all" list as that in itself would undervalue and demean the process. The buying organisation should produce a document that is both bespoke for their needs, and reflective of the facet being procured, though many larger organisations have standardised on a template PQQ for all new suppliers.

> **Food for Thought**: Toyota measure perspective supplier based on just four main criteria:
>
> - The approach to quality management
> - The capability and approach of the management team
> - The quality and investment in production facilities and technology
> - The future development of the organisation reviewing such areas as the investment in research and development, production investment, recruitment, etc.

Furthermore, in certain European and American procurement activity, strict processes are in place to establish fairness and transparency for all organisations within certain markets. The OJEU processes incorporate many of these measures and whilst seen by some as draconian and bureaucratic, they do represent an environment where new entrants can generate an audience. In such circumstances, the criteria set out for any would-be supplier are critical and need to be carefully scripted before producing an OJEU notice of intent.

Once a list of potential suppliers has been produced however, the tender process can commence. Here a detailed assessment of the suitability of any potential supplier can be undertaken using any one of a number of models measuring for example the suppliers ability to deliver on QTC criteria – Quality, Time and Cost – to an assessment of its ability to deliver the Five Rights – Right Quantity, Right Quality, Right Place, Right Time and Right Price – or wider models such as the 9C model: these are explored in chapter 6 where the wider Sustainable Procurement process is discussed more fully.

Equally important however is the use of simple research and review of internet or press representation of historical events, issues and successes. A quick check of most web-sites will show a section entitled "About Us" or some similar title often with a company news-feed link. Alternatively, simply ringing the company and asking for a visit is an invaluable insight into the organisation if time, investment and mutual inclination allows.

Further, external accreditations and benchmarking reports provide an external assessment of the organisation's ability to deliver. If an organisation has obtained an ISO accreditation for example, or in automotive a brand quality recognition – for example Ford Q1, or Jaguar Landrover's "JLR award for quality excellence" – then this can provide an impartial ratification of the supplier's credentials.

A new commercial relationship should however also be considered from the selling organisation's perspective. Many companies – either consciously or unconsciously – pigeon-hole customers based on the relative importance of that business to their sales model – see figure 14.10.

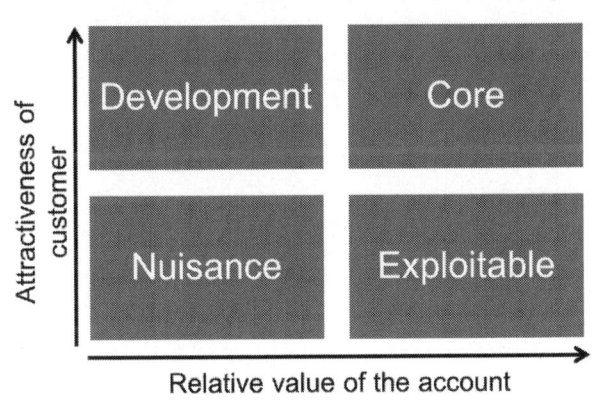

	Attractiveness of customer →	
	Development	Core
	Nuisance	Exploitable

Relative value of the account →

Figure 14.10 Customer Perspectives – from Steele & Court Profitable Purchasing strategies

Some customers are identified for their long term development or their earnings potential, whilst others can be deemed a nuisance. From an on-going management perspective, *the Sustainable Business* should consider its customer mix to generate a balance of customer types. A business based purely on development clients may suffer from their relative low value and higher risk profiles, whereas a business focused purely on the short term exploitable clients may suffer in the longer term from a lack of pipeline customers; neither is overly desirable. Businesses with an abnormal level of nuisance clients may well become swamped with small, low value or query ridden orders and a process of consolidation may be required.

All these measures help both the buyer and the seller determine the suitability of a prospective partner as a would-be "bedfellow", and should be a precursor of any procurement process for *the Sustainable Business.*

Once engaged, all partners need to be measured on an on-going basis to ensure that they remain fit-for-purpose, committed to the relationship and commercially competitive – see figure 14.11.

Figure 14.11 – Sustainable Partnership Characteristics

On-going measures for both parties can be implemented, typically these are either profitability, opportunity or risk focused assessments for the supply side and measures of service, quality and price for the buyer.

From the supplier's perspective, measures may include aspects such as the customer's ability and history of paying on time, and the relative number of invoices either held in query or contested. The administration department of most larger organisations will keep a register of outstanding invoices, commercial queries, payment history and so on to enable these statistics to be modelled into the profitability assessment of each client; this has the benefit of assisting the sales team price future quotations more accurately, as well as enabling trend analysis to forewarn of any impending issues of bankruptcy or exposure.

From a different perspective, a little time measuring the time spent servicing a set of customers can provide an interesting business insight highlighting the effort to reward balance of a customer. In one such exercise, it was shown that the time spent servicing the top three business accounts showed that they were operating at a negative margin, i.e. making a loss. An Activity Based Costing approach focusing on the time and costs to profit would also highlight such deficiencies.

On the buyer's side, Key Performance Indicators (KPIs) and supplier audits may be incorporated into the contractual mechanism to help formally recognise the buyer's needs, and the aforementioned 9C model can be utilised to measure on-going performance of the supplier. Once engaged however the Culture and Clean criteria reduce in importance as both relate to relationship and image issues and less about deliverables. Within a relationship, this can be managed through dialogue, exit being the final option.

Relationships should acknowledge the "win-win" or "win-lose" nature of the engagement. In a Master-Servant scenario, there would have been one dominant and one submissive party. The customer, in such cases, is typically portrayed as having dominance, with the "customer is always right" mantra, yet modern focus on a "win-win" ethos tempers such a stance. Take for example where global giant organisations are suppliers to many relatively small customers, or in an oligopolistic market where suppliers have undue dominance over demand and pricing.

In many of these genuine "win-win" relationships innovative approaches are in place to both develop mutual benefit and encourage the working together concept. Introducing IT solutions such as VMI (Vendor Managed Inventory) – where the supplier has sight of the customer's stockholding and takes a contractual obligation to manage this for the good of the on-going fulfilment of demand for the end or next organisation in the Supply Chain – helps foster closer ties reducing both cost and risk for both parties. Equally, there are organisations – such as BAE Systems – whom operate Gainshare/Painshare approaches with suppliers: where savings can be identified and implemented, both parties benefit, yet in tougher climates, both *tighten their belts* together in unison.

Supplier / Customer visits and audits should also be encouraged to foster better relationships and maintain the relationship. One commonly found shortcoming of Outsourced relationships is a medium and longer term reluctance to make that "journey" especially if it requires investment of time or money; use of Skype or video conferencing is often cited but is commonly a poor substitute for a face-to-face meeting. Where suppliers are based in less desirable locations, interest and motivation to visit can diminish very quickly indeed leaving the relationship based on presumption, an hollow trust and a contractual bond. In the short term this may suffice, though *the Sustainable Business* recognises the longer term risks associated with such an approach. Such visits should be scheduled and diarised in accordance with the criticality of the supply, and the prevailing geographical or supply market volatility; alternatively an ORM (Outsource Relationship Management) specialist should be appointed – for example see www.profittthroughchange.com.

The necessity of a constant assessment of a partner's financial health is also high on the list of measures undertaken by *the Sustainable Business*. Regular review of credit limits, financial accounts, creditor or debtor exposure and other such measures will warn of any impending issue. Measuring the reliance a supplier or customer has on *your* business affects the risk model and associated strategy. Simple financial ratios help address this, see figure 14.12.

By way of an example, the Current and Quick ratios focus on the ability of an organisation to repay its debts by looking at its Current Liabilities (those falling typically within a year) and its Current Assets, the differentiating factor being the consideration of stock as an asset. The Quick Ratio suggests that if stock (termed by accountants as a current asset) has to be realised to pay off a liability, it would normally be either sold at a discount, or take a significant amount of time to sell through. In either of these circumstances the current value of the stock is altered and as such affects the ratio analysis. Equally, measures such as the profit margin recognise the health of the on-going business of that organisation. Producers with a product in demand will generally be able to secure a higher price and thus a higher profit margin in the market. This can be viewed as a general measure of the success or strength of a supplier over the short term.

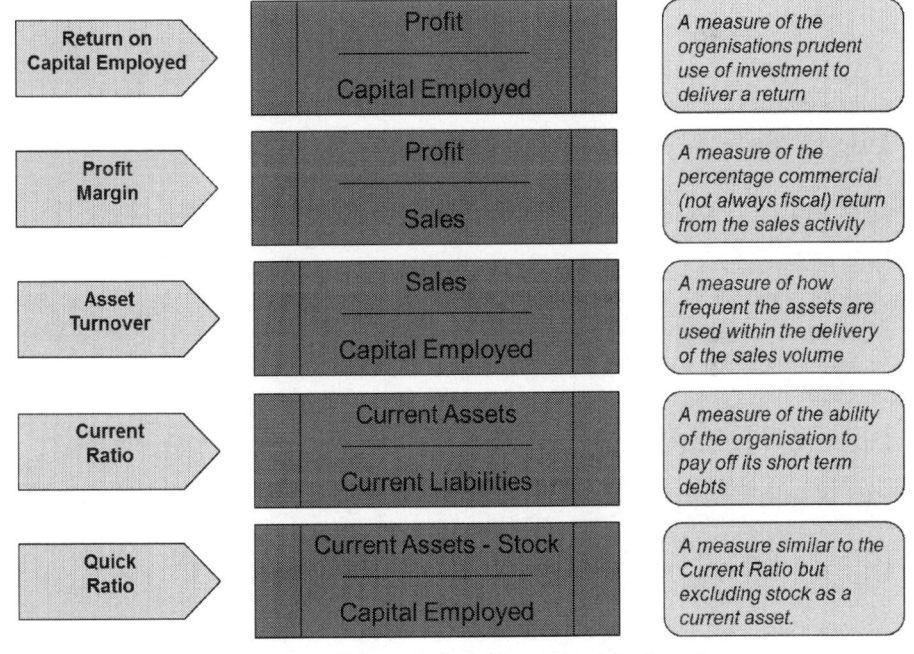

Ratio	Formula	Description
Return on Capital Employed	$\dfrac{\text{Profit}}{\text{Capital Employed}}$	A measure of the organisations prudent use of investment to deliver a return
Profit Margin	$\dfrac{\text{Profit}}{\text{Sales}}$	A measure of the percentage commercial (not always fiscal) return from the sales activity
Asset Turnover	$\dfrac{\text{Sales}}{\text{Capital Employed}}$	A measure of how frequent the assets are used within the delivery of the sales volume
Current Ratio	$\dfrac{\text{Current Assets}}{\text{Current Liabilities}}$	A measure of the ability of the organisation to pay off its short term debts
Quick Ratio	$\dfrac{\text{Current Assets - Stock}}{\text{Capital Employed}}$	A measure similar to the Current Ratio but excluding stock as a current asset.

Figure 14.12 – Common financial ratios used in business

Finally, and often overlooked, is the pressure that the parties in a relationship can bring to bear to invoke change or maintain responsible behaviours, none more important than the approach of both suppliers and buyers to the maintenance of their *Planet Pillars*. A vigilant regard to ethical and green behaviour is important for many reasons not least the long term damage to the planet. Contamination or pollution can have a real short term impact on profitability if a clean-up is ordered; an irresponsible act can have devastating effect on an organisation's image;

and issues such as child labour or funding using unacceptable sources can cause catastrophic ethical fallout.

Rule: Strive for the Win-Win relationships

In summary however, core to the "win-win" relationship remains the underpinning realisation of the need for both partners to add value at all times and any measurement structure needs to recognise this. The sustainability of a business whether supplier or buyer, needs to address these long term health issues, measuring and managing in real time.

Measurement of People Factors

The role of people in an organisation can be the difference between success and failure, between profit and loss. People make the decisions, they run the processes, and they direct the work either manually or through machinery. Measurement of the people inputs into the *Sustainable Business* needs to be measured to enable effective management of this facet of the organisation.

Man is a complex beast with emotions and self-interest at the core of his or her demeanour. From the early analysis undertaken by Taylor, and subsequent work by Maslow and Herzberg among others, we have a picture of man which suggests a complicated, dynamic and bespoke mix of parameters. Each individual seeks different outcomes from work, has different focuses and different motivations.

With this in mind, the need for a clear and dedicated resource within an organisation is essential to best utilise this valuable yet costly resource. The Human Resources or HR department leads this area of the business process, however it is often left to line-side supervisors and managers to implement HR measurements and policy.

As discussed in earlier chapters, stringent recruitment policy will underpin the successful use of the human resource. By developing the RITUAL approach (see figure 2.7) we address the human element from Recruitment through to Leaving, however the issue of measurement should still be incorporated into each element:

- Recruitment – during recruitment we should outline the areas upon which the prospective employee will be measured, reiterating an appraised culture;
- Induction – during the induction the measures should be highlighted so the employee understand what they will be measured on, and the value this adds to the overall process;
- Training – during the training, measures need to be reiterated to highlight their importance and value;
- Utilisation – during the utilisation of the employee, they must appreciate and recognise that they are being monitored;
- Appraisal – during the employee's annual or periodic appraisal, the measures can be discussed with either a focus on the success or shortfall in performance;
- Leaving – and finally measures need to be discussed at the leaving or exit interview to reflect the successes or otherwise of the employee's time with the organisation.

Measurement of the people element can again be both subjective and objective. Employee performance in particular needs to be as clear and unambiguous as possible as this will often be the driver for both reward and disciplinary procedures. A target of "do your best" is uncertain as one person's best may not be the same as another's.

Indeed, even where there are clearly defined numbers involved, weighting of individual elements can again cause consternation.

Effective measurement of people is invaluable *to the Sustainable Business* if channelled effectively and it can strengthen *all Three Pillars* simultaneously. When planning measurement of the people side of business we need to remain cognisant of the issues and conflicts that inaccurate or disputed findings can cause, to ensure that the consequences are wherever possible positive to the overall outcomes of the business.

Employee measures do not necessarily always relate directly to the business operation itself. For example, measurement of staff happiness or time off work is a useful indicator of the state of the Human resource in the business. Measures such as the aforementioned "Bradford Index" (See chapter 2) can be used to determine the sickness pattern and impact of an employee's absence, and analysis of ailments can often show interesting trends, especially where stress or injury is the cause.

Discussion of people measures can occur at any time, yet the frequency of such discussions varies considerably between organisations. In some, dialogue occurs daily as issues arise, in others it will be focused on the classic "annual appraisal". Either way, the need for accurate evidence is clear.

> **Food for Thought:** Recalling an example from chapter one, the sustainable vision of Manchester United, and the longevity of Sir Alex Ferguson's tenure is unquestioned, however the return over that period, and the investment is some way short of other managerial greats particularly in the trophy return from European competition. Whilst contestable, it can be argued that, in terms of trophies won, Sir Alex Ferguson has been successful yet not an overly prolific manager during his many years at the helm with a European trophy on average every sixth year – see below. What is required is a measure of what "success" actually means. Are Sir Alex Ferguson's four European trophies acceptable to a club like Manchester United ? How does this compare with a record like Jose Mourinho's of two Champions League titles and one Runner up, with three different clubs, or with Brian Clough who won back to back European Cups without large numbers of foreign players and on a shoestring budget ?
>
> | Manager | Years as Manager | Trophies Won | Trophies per season | European Trophies | European Average |
> |---|---|---|---|---|---|
> | Sir Alex Ferguson Manchester United | 25 | 35 | 1.4 | 4 | 6.25 Years |
> | Jose Mourinho (Porto/ Chelsea/ Inter Milan) | 15 | 9 | 0.6 | 5 | 3.00 Years |
> | Brian Clough Nottingham Forest | 8 | 8 | 1 | 3 | 2.67 Years |
> | Bob Paisley Liverpool | 9 | 19 | 2.11 | 5 | 1.80 Years |

Where targeting and objective setting is within the organisational culture, measurement takes on an even greater importance. Any contention between findings will lead to a difference of opinion and a consequential conflict in the perceived benefit, invariably considered to be a demotivating impact.

This feeling of reduced worth can hinge on the manager's ability to handle the reaction. The climate in which the review process is conducted then takes on an even greater importance. Reviews held without due planning or consideration are invariably transparent, disorganisation leads to added dissatisfaction, and a vicious spiral of demotivation.

Accordingly, the need to structure, plan, substantiate and deliver appraisals is one of the most important roles of a people manager, yet oft overlooked.

> **Rule: Look after your people, and the profit will look after itself**

Case Study 14: Philips Lighting EcoVision 5

"We believe that big changes start small and that every one of us should contribute to saving our planet. What's more, we are convinced that those companies that combine the principles of economic growth and environmental stewardship will be the winners of the future and offer long term rewards to you, our employees, and to our customers, partners and shareholders." – Gerard Kleisterlee, President and CEO of Philips

Since the early 1990s, Philips Lighting has been at the forefront of organisations promoting a long term environmental and sustainable vision. Their first Ecovision in 1994 clearly spelt out the company's goals and ambition for its sustainable future, in a clear and measureable way.

Each Ecovision statement is published, monitored and managed, underpinning the whole business approach to the environment. The Ecovision 4 statement reads as follows:

> With EcoVision4, Philips have committed to the following by 2012:
> - Generate 30% of total revenues from Green Products
> - Double investment in Green Innovations to a cumulative €1B
> - Improve our operational energy efficiency by 25% and reduce our CO_2 emissions by 25%, all compared with the base year 2007.
>
> Our EcoVision4 environmental action program began in 2007 and will run through 2012, next to our EcoVision 5 programme which runs from 2010 to 2015.

But Philips, as a model sustainable business, are constantly looking forward, planning for the future and striving to go further. Their Ecovision 5 programme asks for more – it reads:

> To deliver on our brand promise of "sense and simplicity" and at the same time provide the company direction for the longer term in this area, we have identified three sustainability leadership key performance indicators where we can bring our competencies to

bear, 'care', 'energy efficiency' and 'materials' including targets for 2015:

- *Bringing care to more than 500 million people*
  - *Target: 500 million lives touched by 2015*
- *Improving energy efficiency of Philips products*
  - *Target: 50% improvement by 2015 (for the average total product portfolio) compared to 2009*
- *Closing the materials loop*
  - *Target: Double global collection, recycling amounts and recycled materials in products by 2015 compared to 2009*

The ambitions set by the Ecovision policies are both challenging and engaging. The inclusion of objective targets, and clear metrics make assessment and success irrefutable, and thus far easier for the organisation to mandate.

But they have a further goal, enrichment of people's lives:

Our aim is to develop our business further by creating products that improve people's lives. At the same time, we believe in improving our own people's lives by creating a fulfilling and exciting work environment.

With clearly stated values, policy and goals, coupled with world-class communication infrastructure, Philips has generated a platform from which it can make a real and sustainable difference to its *Three Pillars* – Its People, its Profit and its impact on the Planet.

Philips, a truly sustainable business.

Reference: www.philips.com

The Sustainable Business

Notes Page   **Page Ref**

Summary Chapter 15
Creating a Sustainable Strategy

Key Learning Points
- The importance of a strategy focus
- Longevity, *the Three Pillars* and the minimisation of risk
- The need to set "Sustainable Success Factors"
- Identifying "Corporate Personality"
- Importance of Internal and External awareness
- The impact of electronic communications and financial controls
- Business types, purpose and strategic organisational structure
- The consequences of market shocks
- Product, Customer and Sales strategy
- Pricing strategies
- Departmental and stakeholder requirements
- The need for corporate environmental strategy

Tool Summary
- Strategy Cascade
- Strategy and Cultural Nucleus
- The Cultural Web
- McKinsey's 7S Model
- PESTLE/SWOT/Value Chain/BCG Matrix
- Ansoff's Product Strategy Model
- Customer Needs Analysis
- Marketing Mix
- Nature and Scope of Change Model
- Lewin Forcefield Analysis
- Objections to Change Model

CIPS Syllabus Reference
- All Modules in level 4, 5 and 6

Chapter 15: Creating a Sustainable Strategy

*"If you want one year of prosperity, plant corn.
If you want ten years of prosperity, plant trees.
If you want one hundred years of prosperity, educate people."* – Chinese proverb

Effective delivery of an organisation's vision requires a clear strategy, based on experience, the prevailing conditions, the organisation's forecasts, and the future expectations of the organisation.

The strategy decides the path the organisation will take into the future; it will determine the decisions it takes from investment to customers, from structure to recruitment. The strategy will embrace every element of the organisation as it wrestles with matching the organisation's resources with its efforts to generate stakeholder value.

Fundamentally, the strategic aims of *the Sustainable Business* will be:
- Longevity;
- The maintenance of *the Three Pillars;*
- To add maximum value;
- The reduction of waste;
- And the minimisation of risk;

Throughout each chapter in this book, strategy has been discussed pertaining to the relevant needs of the organisation as applied through the individual department or facet of the business; each business must therefore have their own overarching functional strategy which reflects their own objectives and needs. The corporate strategy cascades down through the organisational levels to formulate the strategy adopted by the individual business units which in turn generates the strategy adopted by the individual process or functions and thus the employees within the organisation – see figure 15.1.

Understanding what the stakeholders in the organisation perceive as being of value has been discussed on a number of occasions in earlier chapters, but this is central to the formation of a corporate strategy. These values are the essence of the organisation's reason for being, and drive the development of targets, direction and its Critical Success Factors (CSF).

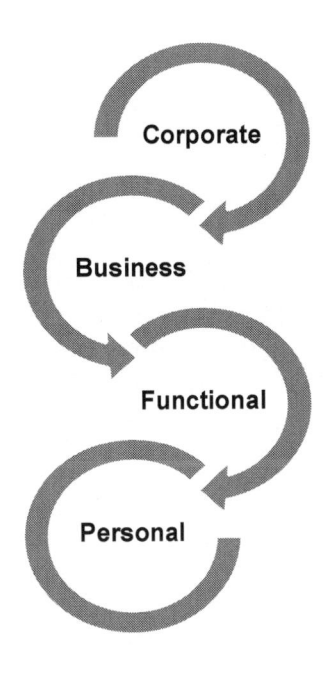

Figure 15.1 – Cascade of Corporate Strategy

Equally, where the strategy being considered is sustainable in nature, introduction of Sustainable Success Factors (SSF) helps *the Sustainable Business* identify the characteristics that illustrate "success".

Furthermore, within each function, the employees will be affected by the cascade of strategy. As discussed previously, the employee and the management of the employee welfare, play an important part in the organisation's sustainable profile. Implementation of a strategy which impacts on the *People Pillar* has inherent risks. Whilst the strategy may be in the best interests of the organisation, it may generate a change in the strategy adopted by the individual employees; the employee's strategy may include working harder, but equally it may lead to the employee considering their long term employment options, or worse lead to a vindictive response through laziness, poor quality work, disruption of the work environment, or even sabotage.

At the start of this book, we defined what constituted a sustainable business:

"A sustainable business has no lasting impact on the global, national or local environment, commits to the rights and contribution

of the employees across the whole supply chain and in the wider community, whilst recognising its own need to generate a robust commercial structure to deliver on-going value to its stakeholders."

This same mandate must therefore drive the formation of a corporate strategy. It recognises the need for *the Sustainable Business* to understand both its internal and external position, allowing it to adapt and blend its people and processes to enable it to generate its core values and achieve its Vision – See figure 15.2. Further, this strategy needs to align itself with the prevailing corporate culture if it is to succeed; a failure to balance the strategy with the culture generates an imbalance which rarely results in success.

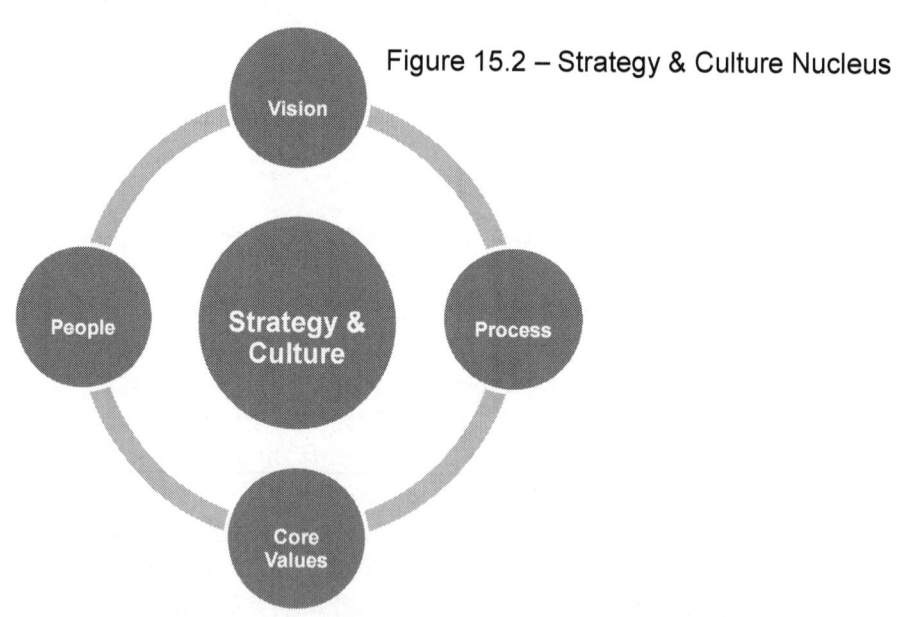

Figure 15.2 – Strategy & Culture Nucleus

- Vision
- People
- Strategy & Culture
- Process
- Core Values

The culture in the organisation is critical to the successful implementation of the strategy, with everyone needing to be in agreement and committed; in modern business there is no room for passengers. But how is a culture formed and managed?

Johnson & Scholes suggested that there six main influences on the way an organisation's culture forms as shown in their Cultural web – see figure 15.3.

Figure 15.3 – The Cultural Web

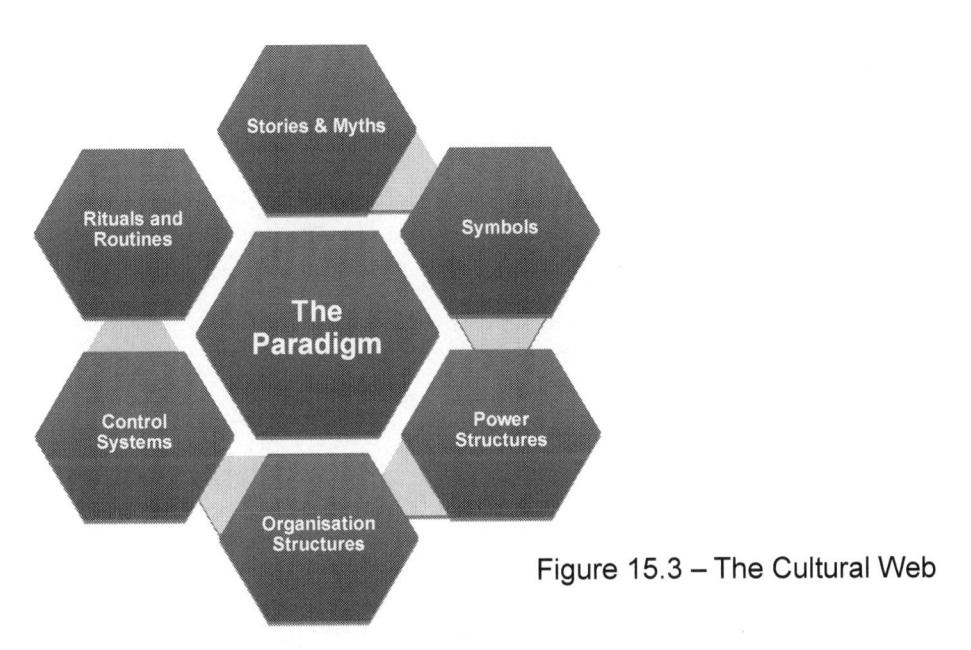

The "Paradigm" or culture that exists is not just stated by the company management, but develops and evolves over time, like a "personality". This corporate "personality" needs to be understood and nurtured to generate the implementation plan for the strategy. If the culture is one that is overtly opposed to risk, the implementation process will be markedly different to a culture that covets challenges and sees opportunity and value from risk taking.

To effectively deliver the strategy, recognising and evaluating the elements of the McKinsey's 7S model is of use – see figure 15.4

This was developed in the 1980s by Peters and Waterman, but remains an excellent model for appraising the organisation's ability to identify its chosen objectives or in this case its strategy. The model highlights seven core areas which are vital for the implementation to be successful, all of which have been discussed hitherto.

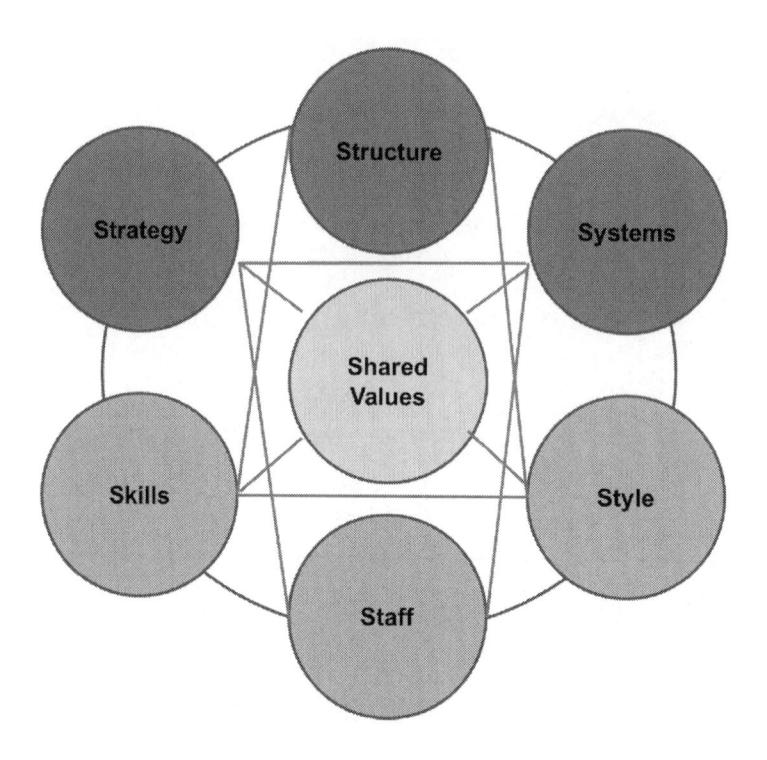

Figure 15.4 – McKinsey 7S model

External Environment

When setting its strategy, *the Sustainable Business* needs to understand the environment in which it is operating. This has been explored in a number of chapters hereto, most notably chapter 5.

Using the PESTLE model, we can see how an understanding of the Political, Economic, Social, Technical, Legislative and Environmental aspects in the geographic or market region will impact upon how the business operates, the decisions it makes and its ultimate success. Once understood, this knowledge should play a major role in dictating strategy, direction and the planning process.

Take for example a political issue such as a change in government. This will often result in a change of policies, particularly when the political party's allegiance swings from left to right or right to left. Each party – even in coalition – maintains their own identity and has their own manifesto driven objectives which may impact on the organisation's stance. Equally, this change in government may affect: the legislative environment and aspects such as taxation changes; the view on inflation which would affect exchange rates and export demand; investment decisions; public sector demand; and so on.

Where political change is rapid or sudden – for example following a *coup d'etat* or revolution – the impact on the sustainable strategy can be extreme. Equally, where softening in a regime's approach occurs, such as with the dismantling of the former Soviet Union, and Perestroika, or more recently the seismic shift in the stance taken by Myanmar (formerly Burma), strategy needs to be both flexible and robust to the unforeseen.

The external environment needs therefore to be closely monitored and the strategy reactive to any changes. Organisations which take a long term forecast have been shown to significantly reduce their exposure. Even the simple act of looking at the weather forecast and taking an umbrella can reduce the risk of getting wet.

Forecasting effort needs to target aspects which specifically affect the organisation's business model. This forecasting activity may be an intuitive stab at "what might be", sometimes it can be based on scientific modelling, and in others based on research or investigation.

In a military jet component supplier which was examined, not surprisingly demand for spare parts was broadly proportional to the number of hours the jets flew. Notwithstanding military confrontations, these flying hours are often forecast by the air-force in question as part of their budgeting process: a close relationship between customer and client in such an instance is invaluable.

More complex forecasting in financial markets or with customer demand can reduce risk. Being closer to the customer helps build an understanding of future order requirements, allowing resources and capacity to be in place to deliver what is required on time. Equally, use of EDI (Electronic Data Interchange) links and VMI (Vendor Managed Inventory) will help ensure that a supplier anticipates orders and can thus deliver product more quickly when required.

The assessment of the external factors will be specific to each organisation with careful consideration of processes, time and resources dedicated to the activity.

Internal Organisation Strategy

The Sustainable Business needs to establish an internal operating strategy as the foundation for other elements of the wider corporate strategy. This internal strategy will involve detailed decisions relating to its vision, its long term plans, its business structure, personnel and the resources it has and those it needs to fulfil its objectives.

A quick and easy assessment of the organisation's capability and risks can be undertaken using both the SWOT and Value Chain models detailed in previous chapters. This helps the management identify core areas of focus and opportunity.

- In the SWOT model, a business strategy would look to exploit its strengths, protect against its weaknesses, explore its opportunities and take action to mitigate its threats.
- In the Value Chain model, understanding where an organisation adds value will help focus the strategy either on exploiting this value generation, or by taking actions to strengthen areas of the business which show weakness or the potential to grow.

The type of business that an organisation undertakes will generally have evolved over time, however occasionally a company may decide to take a sharp change in direction. This may occur as a result of many different factors such as a new CEO, a change in the external operating environment, competitor analysis, consumer trend, locality or demographic of the target customer, etc.

As these differences are identified, so a reactive management team will make strategic decisions for the business. Take for example the situation which occurred in the late 1990s when there was a global shortage of steel due to the developments being undertaken throughout the China and the Asian Sub-continent. This had major ramifications for many of the major steel users as prices soared and demand dried up. Management of major users needed to make strategic decisions to enable their respective businesses to remain competitive.

Equally, following the 2009 credit crunch, the price of some raw materials rose significantly with oil reaching all-time highs as the market feared shortages and supply chain issues. Organisations at this time needed to review their design and commodity requirements, as well as considering their overall reliance on logistical networks to maintain delivery promises.

Depending on the size and reach of an organisation, the managerial structure and location of business activities may feature in a strategic review. As discussed elsewhere in this book, the choice of distribution network is vital to the effective delivery of a quality service.

Further, fleet and distribution modelling software is now commonplace allowing the company to understand the optimum distribution portfolio. This could make a significant improvement to the carbon costs associated with the vehicle use, thus strengthening *the Planet Pillar*.

Finally, the type and skillset of the people employed in the organisation is important to the strategic direction of the business. As described in chapter 2, the management and motivation of the team needs constant attention as does the maintenance of the corporation-wide pool of resource and skill-sets. In organisations that require specific and specialised skills, contingency plans should always be in place. Improving the existing workforce through training and investment strengthens *the People Pillar*, whilst also improving the diversity of the workforce. Equally, there are many other ways of helping nurture a willingness within the workforce: generating a culture that is flexible and accommodating through conscientious management; development of positive people skills to generate goodwill that will help in a time of crisis; allowing flexibility in working hours; time-off in lieu; duvet days; etc

Sustainable Product Strategy

The maintenance of a detailed and structured product strategy is an essential component of the organisation's ability to make a profit, affecting all three of the dimensions of *the Profit Pillar: Sales, Service and*

Strategy. This is clearly different from developing sustainable products which is covered in chapter 10 on Sustainable Design.

The essence of a successful Sales function is having a set of products – goods or services – that are desirable to the potential customers. This product set needs to be maintained and planned so that new products are sought and developed for the future; without this foresight longevity is compromised.

Take for example the demise of Kodak, a household name since 1880. Whilst at the time of writing Kodak are still in administration, few commentators dispute that Kodak had an overreliance on traditional film (old technology) and a business culture reluctant to implement the radical changes needed to compete with its modern adversaries and proponents of digital alternatives. The strategy was embraced at the top level to compete in the new digital arena, however questions have been asked as to whether the organisational culture had changed sufficiently to allow the strategy to work: strategy and culture were not as one.

This misalignment is not uncommon, albeit rescue bids, wholesale restructuring and bank interventions may conceal the true extent of the issue. Over the years, a number of organisations have fallen foul of complacency, over reliance on one product, changes in consumer taste, legislation, technology, staying with the tried and tested methods, and often a reluctance to recognise good and bad business decisions. Other examples might include Blockbuster Video Stores which have struggled to recognise the decline of mediums such as VHS and latterly DVDs, whereas organisations such as Memorex – traditionally a major market player in magnetic media products – have expanded and diversified into other business fields to combat falling demand on its previously core products.

Use of models discussed in earlier chapters can instantly be seen to be of use. In terms of product range management, the Boston Consulting Group Matrix - see chapter 3 - helps identify where in the cycle a specific product sits, enabling an assessment of the strategy that needs to be taken either with the disposal of the product, the development of new product ranges, or the diversification of the company mandate. *The*

Sustainable Business avoids over-reliance on just a few products, and recognises the need to maintain a balanced portfolio of "Question Marks", "Stars" and "Cash Cows", as well as maintaining an open channel for new products to be considered; Dog products, by their very definition are no longer of worth and need to be disposed of in whichever means is deemed the most advantageous.

As important to the organisation is the strategy applied to each product. Ansoff's Matrix – see figure 15.5 – identifies the optimum strategy to adopt for differing product types.

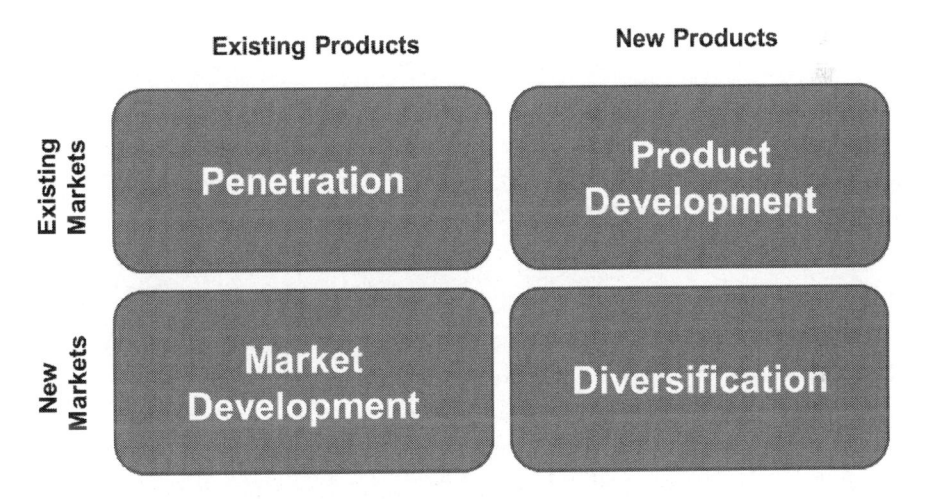

	Existing Products	New Products
Existing Markets	Penetration	Product Development
New Markets	Market Development	Diversification

Figure 15.5 – Ansoff's Product strategy model

Equally, a structured and sustainable product set should have a selection of products to meet different budgets and the specific needs of the target customers. Regular review of factors such as the market, competitor activity, Customer Needs Analysis (see figure 15.6) and price comparisons will ensure that the product offering remains fit for purpose.

The Sustainable Business

Score 1-5 weighed x2 for primary factors and x1 for secondary factors.	Primary Needs			Secondary Needs				Totals
	Cost of "Pen"	Cost of Ink	Quality of production	Flexibility	Leakage	Versatility	Ergonomics	Transportable	
Ball Point Pen	4	4	2	4	4	5	3	4	44
Fountain Pen	1	3	5	4	2	3	4	3	38
Roller Ball Pen	3	4	4	5	4	3	3	3	45
Fibre Tip	4	2	2	3	5	3	2	4	36
Pencil	5	5	1	3	5	3	3	5	44
Feather Quill	1	3	3	1	5	1	1	2	25

Figure 15.6 – Customer Needs Analysis

Within a structured product set, inclusion of complementary products help both add to the sales ticket value, whilst increasing the overall profit margin. In one previous employer, sale of electrical cable would often be sold at cost in order to secure the wider project sale; invariably, the cost of the glands added to each end of the cable would generate more net profit than the cable itself albeit at a fraction of the ticket value. Failure to include some of these peripheral products may in fact have a detrimental effect on the service perception of the organisation, as many customers increasingly look for a "one-stop-shop"; poor service clearly impacting on the profitability, *the Profit Pillar*, and thus the overall sustainability of the organisation.

> **Food for Thought**: In the electrical installation industry, galvanised conduit is often cut by customers. To preserve the integrity of the galvanised protection, customers request paint brushes and tins of galvanising paint to coat the bare steel and thus prevent rust. In one former employer, this was analysed, and an alternative, more effective and greener product solution was found using a spray on paint. This was added to the product portfolio and proved instantly successful as a supplementary purchase.

Finally, taking the time to rank products helps identify the products critical to the overall product strategy. Using Pareto and ranking in terms of volume of sales, by profit contribution, or by percentage of customers using them, will help establish the contribution of a product to the overall strategy of the business.

Sustainable Customer Strategy

Understanding the needs of the customer is of course fundamental to the success of the sales function (explored in chapter 8) and is addressed in dialogue relating to the assessment and management of the market (chapter 3).

Wider, however, is the need of the organisation to maintain and nurture a balance and strategic customer mix. A focus on a single type of customer such as SME (Small & Medium Enterprises) may lead to a higher net margin, and a good spread of risk, but equally may lead to a rise in operational costs as a greater number of individual customers would be required to attain a high level of turnover. In contrast, having a very large dominant customer leads to a higher risk as *your* business fluctuations will start to mirror *his* business activity with *you* powerless to affect *his* business strategy. You are also very vulnerable should *he* change *his* allegiance, or worse should *his* business fail.

Within the Customer Strategy, due care and attention should also be paid to the issue of bad debts and credit risks. As mentioned in previous chapters, regular review of customer credit limits, "time taken to pay", level of commercial queries and market intelligence is essential to contain bad debts; a resilient approach to outstanding debt is fundamental to *the Sustainable Business*.

> **Rule: A sale is a debt until it's paid for**

Determining the most effective customer mix for the business is a difficult challenge. Where there is a large and diverse customer mix, understanding where to focus the organisation's efforts can be essential to maximising *the Sustainable Business'* best use of resources. To achieve this, use of Activity Based Costing (ABC analysis) can help.

Activity Based Costing and similar approaches such as Pareto, look at the business and identify critical areas to the success of the organisation. For example, it could be used to rank customers by:

- Overall profit contribution;
- Time spent to profit generated;
- Investment to profit return;
- Profit to delivery miles;
- Carbon content of customer activity.

Understanding where profit is best achieved leads to a better use of valuable resources and enhances both *the Profit Pillar* and *the Planet Pillar*.

Sustainable Pricing Strategy

Within a business strategy, pricing of products is important to ensuring an optimum balance between sales, service and profit, all fundamental elements of a balanced Sustainable Strategy.

Developing a pricing strategy starts with understanding the prices commonly charged and the strategy taken by other companies in the market. As discussed in chapter 3, the market can be analysed to establish where competitors are placed, and with some intuition a view of the competitor strategy can be gauged. This competitive arena is where *the Sustainable Business* will compete so the pricing strategy needs to reflect the prevailing position.

There are a large number of different pricing strategies used by companies across the planet, and no sooner has the ink dried on, so a new strategy is developed. There are a few core strategies however worthy of note and useful to ensure a strong *Profit Pillar* – see figure 15.7.

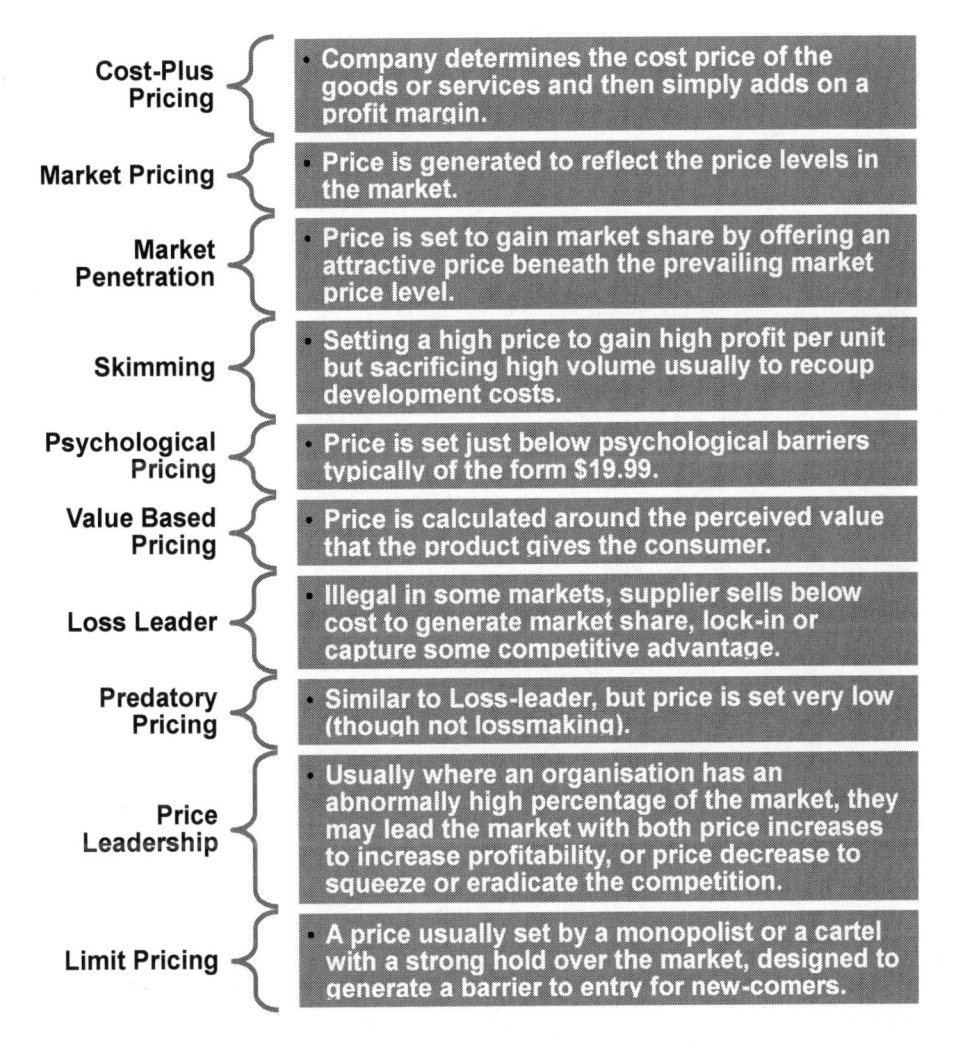

Figure 15.7 – Common pricing strategies

Cost-Plus Pricing	Company determines the cost price of the goods or services and then simply adds on a profit margin.
Market Pricing	Price is generated to reflect the price levels in the market.
Market Penetration	Price is set to gain market share by offering an attractive price beneath the prevailing market price level.
Skimming	Setting a high price to gain high profit per unit but sacrificing high volume usually to recoup development costs.
Psychological Pricing	Price is set just below psychological barriers typically of the form $19.99.
Value Based Pricing	Price is calculated around the perceived value that the product gives the consumer.
Loss Leader	Illegal in some markets, supplier sells below cost to generate market share, lock-in or capture some competitive advantage.
Predatory Pricing	Similar to Loss-leader, but price is set very low (though not lossmaking).
Price Leadership	Usually where an organisation has an abnormally high percentage of the market, they may lead the market with both price increases to increase profitability, or price decrease to squeeze or eradicate the competition.
Limit Pricing	A price usually set by a monopolist or a cartel with a strong hold over the market, designed to generate a barrier to entry for new-comers.

Each of these pricing strategies has a role depending on the wider objectives of the organisation, and the relative fluidity of the market. In elastic markets, demand for a product can be very price sensitive. This can be as a result of a number of factors including:

- The number of suppliers in the market;
- The availability of the core materials;
- Availability of alternative products or solutions;
- Short and medium term risk of shortages;
- Cost

Arguably the most common strategy in Western markets is the Cost-Plus model. Simply, this takes the sum of all the costs for making the product or delivering the service, and adds on the desired margin. This generates a sale price, however this is prone to being uncompetitive in the market as it has taken little or no account of what competitors are charging. In such circumstances, it is not uncommon to see heavy discounting in an effort to realign the price with the market. This action results in the supplier not meeting its profit objectives and thus undermining the associated business case. Organisations that adopt this approach are thus more prone to making a financial loss or ultimately going bankrupt.

In contrast, a Market Pricing approach starts with the price in the market, deducts the desired margin and assesses whether the supplier can produce the goods or service for that cost level. Starting with a price competitive in the market increases the likelihood of the business case assumptions being met and reduces the likelihood of discounting in the first instance.

Some of the pricing strategies recognise the strength of the supplier's position in the market place, be it as a result of being first to the market, a technology advantage or as a result of a perceived market leadership role. Organisations such as Sony and Apple are masters in this approach, with the iphone and other Apple products skimmed with remarkable success, see 15.8 for a pricing strategy summary.

Unfortunately, technological developments designed to reduce carbon emissions such as some solar panel solutions, grey water recovery techniques and wind turbine technology are also being sold at a relatively high price as suppliers look to recoup their investment in a market which is still in a transition phase. This discourages some would-be clients, and in some cases makes the business case unaffordable.

In contrast, other manufacturers have developed a pricing policy aimed at market penetration and generating a large user base as quickly as possible. This is often as a result of a very short product life cycle – for example merchandise relating to large sporting events. Some medical companies reacting to urgent medical needs – such as the AIDS crisis in the 1980s – and technology aimed at disadvantaged regions – such as the wind-up radio – are two cases in point.

> **Food for Thought**: Wind-up radios were invented and patented by an English designer Trevor Baylis in the early 1990s making use of human effort to power a radio and for use in areas where there was no mains power or easy access to batteries.

Skimming	Cost Plus	Penetration
• Good where there is immediate demand or a shortage • Good where the competition may not yet have a product ready to market	• Targets a desired margin based on the underpinning costs of production • Can produce an uncompetitive price level in the market	• Effective where the market is highly price sensitive • Low price discourages competition • Use production methods to give a cost advantage

Figure 15.8 – Summary of three pricing strategies

The need therefore must surely be to clearly establish and maintain a strategy that combines both the target customer mix and a complementary product mix which is competitively priced. This is mirrored with the marketing concept of the 4P's or Marketing Mix (see figure 15.9). This concept demands that for a successful marketing of a product or service, it (1) has to meet customer needs, (2) be competitively priced, (3) must meet an established need (demand) in the marketplace, and (4) the market needs to be aware of the fact that the solution is available. This promotion could be via any one of a number of channels, for example: traditional advertising, word of mouth, retail visibility, legislation, product placement, social media, and so on.

> **Food for Thought**: A business that makes nothing but money is a poor business. - *Henry Ford*

The selection of the most effective channel is often core to the success of a product launch, but should also reflect the demographic being targeted, their linguistic skills and levels of intellect, etc. *The Sustainable Business* needs to clearly identify its target market and its channel to ensure a strong *Profit Pillar*.

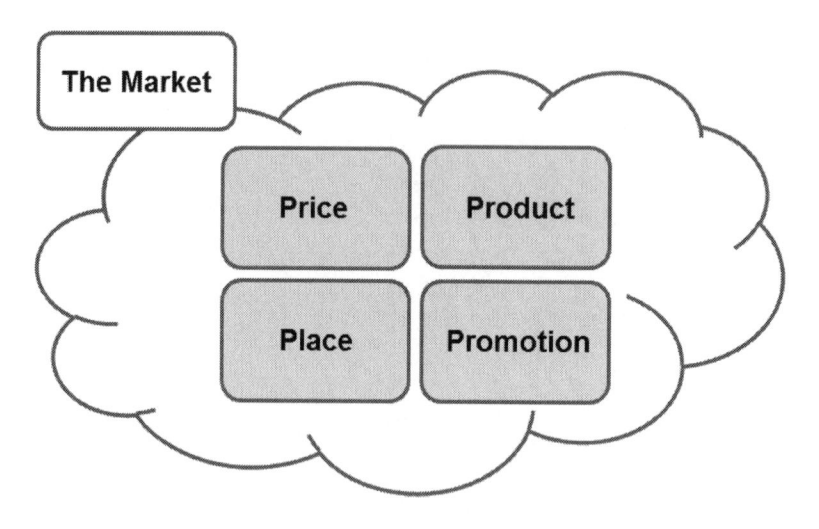

Figure 15.9 – The Marketing Mix

Departmental Overview

Most of the key organisational departments have been covered in one form or another in earlier chapters. Each chapter has explored the department in some depth, however the strategic needs of each department are summarised below:

- Design

The Design Department is arguably one of the most important in *the Sustainable Business*. This department is responsible for the design of new products, services and some organisational facilities, determining the materials used, the on-going operational or maintenance costs, and the impact on *the Three Pillars*.

When developing a strategy for the Design Department, clear and unambiguous directives should be set for the design operatives. This may be demotivating as it restricts the designer's ability to show any artistic flair, and could therefore have a negative impact on the *People*

Pillar, which would need managing.

The design is however at the centre of many of the strategic dilemmas featuring in decisions over product portfolio, target market, manufacturing material, carbon content, price, durability, reparability, modularity, and so on, each of which has been discussed in chapter 10.

To drive effectiveness, clear targeting and performance parameters should be integral to any objectives or projects set. Targeting CO_2 content, water used, recyclability of product and components, projected longevity, durability, etc, is essential to help guide the designer, with this a critical area of focus for *the Sustainable Business* and one which may impact on potentially all of *the Pillars*.

Strategic Goals
- Unambiguous Objectives
- Focus on Lowest TCSO
- Implement the "Twenty Sustainable Paragons"

- Procurement

The Procurement Department plays a significant role in the delivery of sustainability and should be nurtured by *the Sustainable Business*. Effective selection of sustainable and sustainability conscious suppliers is required to underpin the other sustainable activities undertaken and thus strengthen the *Planet Pillar*, effective cost reduction and other value added activities which will help strengthen the *Profit Pillar*.

Strategic decisions such as which supplier to select, length and terms of the contract, type of contract, and analysis of what constitutes best value within the mix of value contributors preoccupy the commercial procurement operatives.

Strategic Goals
- Use "Sustainable Conscious Suppliers"
- Focus on Cost Reduction and Value Added Activities
- Analyse impact of commercial terms

- Supply Chain

The Supply Chain is the engine room of the organisation. It takes input from the supplier, through the production process to ensure that the output meets the customer demand aspirations. Within this cycle is effective use of resources, minimisation of waste and maximum addition of value. Value can be mathematically defined as the price the customer will pay minus the sum of the cost of all the inputs and the profit and overheads.

Strategically, however, decisions can be taken over the route and time taken through the production process (*People, Profit and Planet Pillars*), the value of inventory either in stock or held in silos through the operation as work-in-progress (*Planet and Profit Pillars*) and the waste seen through the process (*Planet and Profit Pillars*). The management of this inventory is balanced between ensuring a prompt, zero lead time supply, versus low cost of inventory but longer lead times. Further, use of assets including whether the organisation decides to buy, rent or lease capital or equipment can help manage the value of capital tied-up in the organisation and related depreciation calculations *(Planet and Profit Pillars)*.

Rule: Decide: Lower Cost or Higher Sales ?

In short, it often comes down to a simple and fundamental decision: the Supply Chain needs to establish whether it wants to be *Lean* and cost conscious or *Agile* and responsive. As stated in earlier chapters: **Profit equals Sales minus Costs**. A *Lean Supply Chain* will have lower costs, an *Agile Supply Chain* should drive higher levels of service.

Strategic Goals
- Manage lead-times
- Focus on reduction of waste
- Delivery of supreme customer service

- Operations Management

The Operations Management function relates to what the organisation "does". From a strategic perspective, the main thrust is on design of the products or services, however there are strategic decisions to be taken in the structure, organisation and management of the production capability.

The operational focus must be on delivering quality products, in the shortest possible time, at the lowest cost, and with as little waste as possible. The strategic set-up and layout of the production processes (*Profit, Planet and People Pillars*), the types of equipment used (*Profit and Planet Pillars*), and the work schedules of the people involved represent very real decisions which have a sustainable impact.

For all processes there must be a *"best way"* – find it and make it mandatory. However always recognise that circumstances change, and be ready to adopt new or amend existing methods.

Rule: Develop "Most Effective Pathways"

In addition, numerous funding and investment decisions will be considered within the Supply Chain with impacts on all *Three Pillars*. The Make-Buy-Lease decision, payback requirements, life-expectations, the decision to Outsource or Insource, the Supply Chain's attitude to risk, and so on.

Strategic Goals
- Consider structure and layout of processes
- Identify best way and implement
- Evaluate Make-Buy-Lease options

- Quality

The Quality Department determines the level of quality delivered to the customer, and the mechanisms that are in place to ensure quality expectations are fulfilled. There are of course costs and benefits for doing this (impacting on the *Profit Pillar*). Where items fail the quality checks, there is an impact on the *Planet Pillar*, as well as on the Sales and Service dimension.

Decisions as to what quality approaches are taken – for example TQM, Six Sigma, etc. – are strategically sensitive, require complete cross platform support, and a fundamental change in the way a company operates (*People, Profit and Planet Pillars*).

Strategic Goals
- Clearly identify quality parameters
- Develop and implement quality process management
- Assign an owner for the output quality

- Technology

The strategic decisions on technology can be broken into two core areas: "If to invest", and "when to invest". These decisions depend themselves on three criteria: how much is the new technology needed, what value will it generate, and how long will it last.

Understanding the impact of technology on *the Sustainable Business* will vary depending on the industry, the profit margins and the culture (some industries are preoccupied with demanding the latest technology. Industries such as IT, telecommunications and medical science typically demand the latest irrespective of other criteria). Having robust process and a clear vision is core with the wider strategic direction of the company central to any decision. Typically, for organisations with a strategy at the extremities (for example as market leader, as cost leader or where the delivery of a supreme service is required) technology leadership will be more critical.

Strategic Goals
- Ensure technology is fit for purpose
- Measure technology impact
- Confirm technology investment is covered by a robust business case

- Sales

A Sales Strategy will have the customer at its core. Understanding and capturing the customer's needs, budgets, quality aspirations, timescales and other issues is vital to ensure on-going customer satisfaction and longevity of the selling relationship or the likelihood of future referrals.

The Sales Strategy will often drive the whole customer-company relationship with the salesperson being the first and sometimes only direct interaction with the customer.

The Sales Strategy will address aspects such as:
- Target margin
- Sales volumes
- Sales cost management
- Target customers
- Sales promotions
- Product of the month
- New markets
- Demographic movements, etc.

Equally, in some organisations, debt recovery, cash collection and service calls may also feature within the sales team's activities and strategy.

The Sales Strategy will however need to liaise closely with numerous other departments: Design so products are available which meet the customer requirements, Warehouse and Despatch to guarantee on time delivery, Manufacturing to enable deadlines to be hit, and so on.

Strategic Goals
- Keep the sales team close to the business
- Maintain a constant focus on the margin
- Consider strategy from each of the Figg 9P Sales Cube perspectives

- Personnel

The selection of the personnel with a business will obviously have a dramatic impact on the organisation's ability to deliver value and its vision, but treating the employees well from interview to exit is also vital to the motivation and image of the company. Where organisations have invested heavily in *People*, personnel costs are often lower through lower levels of staff turnover, lower recruitment costs, and lower levels of cost related to the change (for example customer upheaval, loss of information, continuity, etc).

Strategic Goals
- Develop excellent selection processes
- Focus on training, appraisals and employee retention
- Reward and recognise employee effort

- Marketing

The Marketing Strategy will have a clear understanding and strategy for each of the Ps – Price, Product, Promotion and Place. It will recognise who the customer is and what they are looking for, where they will procure the product or service, and who the key market players are in that market.

The Marketing Strategy will also undertake regular price and competition analysis in the market to enable the Marketing Strategy to reflect competition changes as quickly as possible.

Strategic Goals
- Undertake regular market analysis
- Frequently validate the customer needs
- Allow strategy to change quickly to reflect market needs

- Project Management

A project is a stand-alone activity within the organisation which has a finite timescale. As such the strategy which is adopted in the project scenario may be markedly different from the main organisation.

Notwithstanding this differential, projects need to have a strategy. Focusing on Quality, Time and Cost is key, however incorporating communication, stakeholder management, measurement and reporting into the project plan will help deliver customer satisfaction, increase value, and if managed correctly will strengthen each of *the Three Pillars*.

Rule: Under promise, over deliver

Further, within the Project Strategy and planning, an evaluation of the risks and approach taken to risk is essential.

Strategic Goals
- Focus on Quality, Time and Cost
- Under promise and over deliver
- Provide excellent communication

- Finance

The Finance Department will often be responsible for a number of core strategic parameters and processes which flow through numerous other departments. These include:
- Business Case Criteria
  - Payback duration
  - Discount rates used
  - Investment assessment criteria
  - Models for the determination of cost
- Sources of lending
- Payment and credit terms
- Bad debt process
- Cash holdings and profit retention
- Current Liabilities & Current Assets
- Gearing & debt ratios
- Return of Capital Employed

Many of these are central to the performance of other departments, so to ensure unity and consensus many should be decided at a cross functional board level. All affect *the Three Pillars* in different ways and to varying extents.

Strategic Goals
- Establish clear financial guidelines
- Audit processes and deliverables on a regular basis
- Maintain consistency throughout

- Legal Strategy

A coherent strategy to the contracting and legal management of an organisation will help mitigate risk of litigation or breach of contract. The strategy may include reference to types of contracts used, contract duration, model versus bespoke, and remedy.

The strategy should address the measurement and control of contracts, tracking of any opportunities and payment of any rewards or penalties. Having a single legal point of contact or overseeing authority will help align contracts, drive consistency and cement the strategy.

Strategic Goals {
- Focus on maintaining legal compliance
- Ensure intention can be proven
- Maintain detailed records to support any litigation

- Risk

The Risk Strategy will clearly identify risks and establish how likely the risk is to occur. This may be based on past experience or projections. State initial assumptions and review these assumptions at regular intervals.

The strategy should establish how the impact of a risk is measured, and equally how the cost of any remedy is calculated. Maintain consistency in the measurement process is required, failure to do so is itself a risk.

Further, nominate a risk manager to own the risk register. Set dates to review the Risk Register and the Risk Strategy, organise cross functional input as risk affects all parts of the organisation.

Strategic Goals {
- Appoint risk manager to own risk strategy
- Review risk strategy regularly
- Assign values to all risks

Rule: Sound strategy starts with having the right goal. (Porter)

Implementing strategy

Implementation of change requires three core aspects to be successful:
- A destination or solution which has been designed to blend into the existing business activities;
- A culture which is open to the prospect of change;
- People ready to accept change

Rule: Change is about changing people not organisations – *Balogun*

Effective implementation of a strategy needs to start with stakeholder buy-in which is best generated by, where possible, including the principal stakeholders from the earliest point in the development of the strategy. Use of Cross Functional Teams, ESI (Early Supplier Involvement), ECI (Early Customer Involvement), "Voice of the Customer", Employee Forums, Brainstorming sessions, Quality Circles, etc all help achieve this.

Depending on the strategy in question, the agreement of a strategic approach may not be that easy or politically acceptable and might be problematic to implement. This strategic change can be rapid or slow and it can be a major change or a slow transition, with many strategies evolving over time or mutating from previous versions. Strategy can change in a variety of corporate climates and the approach taken should differ depending on the business climate:

- In a stable state adopting incremental change appears more productive (see Quinn 1980)
- In a crisis, use of rapid or revolutionary change is required and most effective (see Mintzberg 1978, Pettigrew 1987 amongst others)
- In a turbulent condition, use of the Tectonic change model is preferred when the mind-sets of employees need to change – see Reger 1994)

The approach to implementing change and the barriers that prevent change from occurring smoothly was examined by Balogun and Hope-Haley 1999 – see figure 15.10. They suggested that the way in which an organisation approaches change should reflect the scope and nature of the facet being changed.

Embracing change is never particularly popular, and *the Sustainable Business* needs to carefully manage and plan the process. Ensuring that the approach is appropriate can make a huge difference. Consider the reported less than popular 2009 decision to move significant parts of the BBC from London to Manchester. Whilst this could have been done using a Big Bang approach – i.e. closing in London on the Friday, and reopening in Manchester on the Monday – this would have generated huge social and organisational tensions, and would have risked jeopardising the services delivered. Instead, an evolutional approach was used to migrate North. Not without its issues and casualties, this approach did allow services to be continued in the immediate aftermath of the move; only time will tell if this achievement is maintained as several core members of the team objected and resigned accordingly taking up positions with rival broadcasters.

Scope of Change

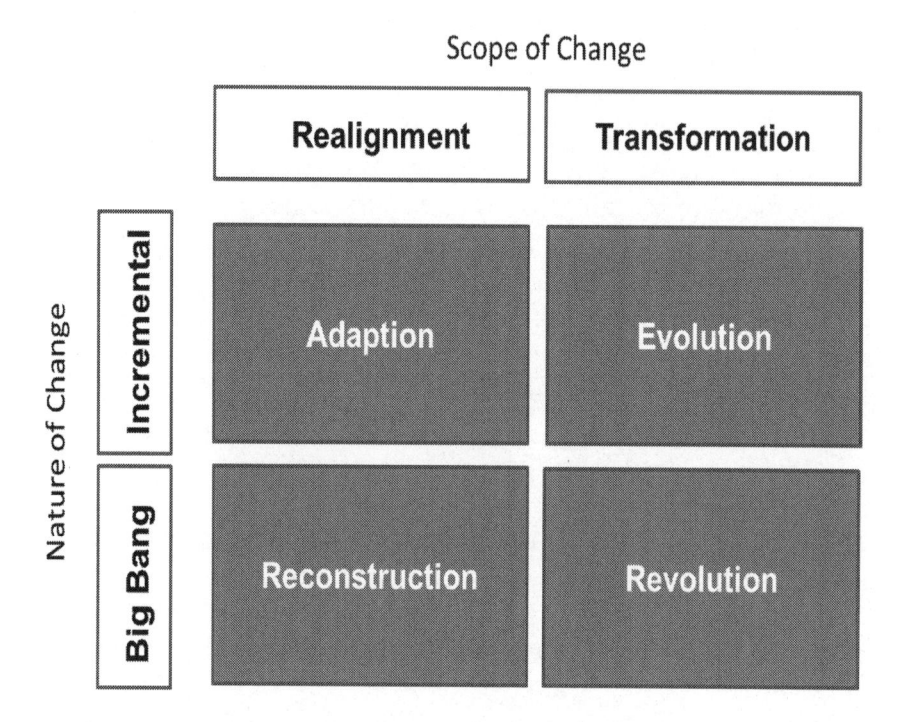

	Realignment	Transformation
Incremental	Adaption	Evolution
Big Bang	Reconstruction	Revolution

Nature of Change

Figure 15.10 – Nature & Scope of Change Model

Equally, consider dissatisfaction against the ruling government at a national state level. On some occasions this can lead to a nation's citizens demanding rapid *Big Bang* transformation in the way the governance of the country is undertaken, leading potentially to a *Coup d'etat*.

As is often seen, various forces emerge during a change process identified by the Kurt & Lewin Force Field model – see figure 15.11:

Further, as stated many times hitherto, from a sustainable perspective, a major theme of any corporate strategy must be:

1) The best use of resources and reducing waste (*Planet Pillar*);
2) Consideration of the employees and their needs (*People Pillar*);

3) The need to make a profit and add value (*Profit Pillar*);
4) The need to plan for the future (*Longevity*)

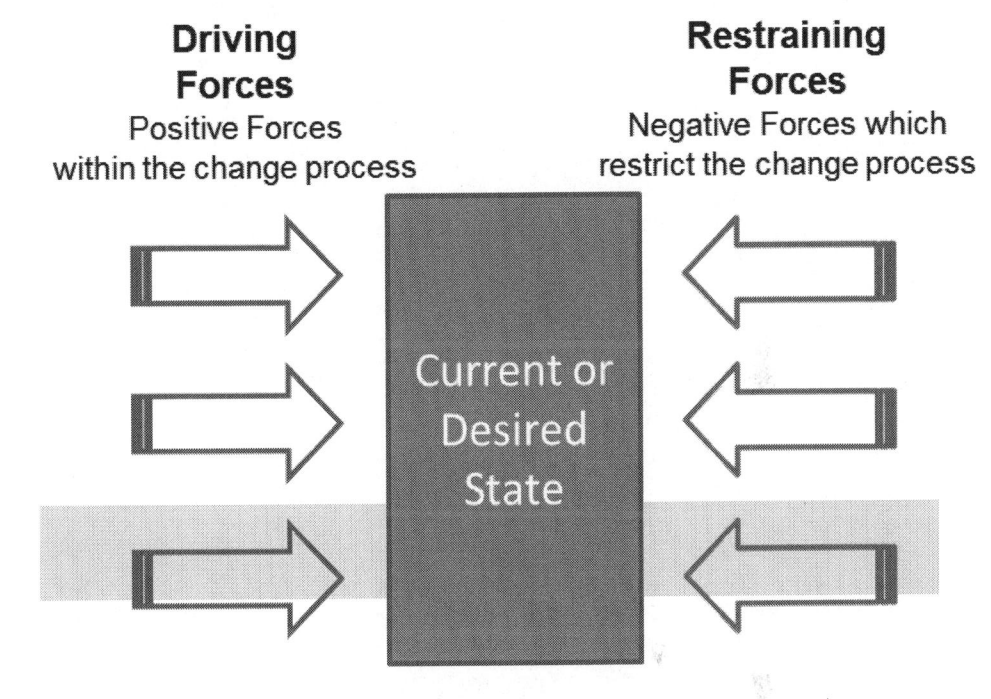

Driving Forces
Positive Forces within the change process

Restraining Forces
Negative Forces which restrict the change process

Current or Desired State

Force Field Analysis – Kurt Lewin

Figure 15.11 Force Field Analysis

Presentation of Strategy

In whichever way the strategy forms, once the strategy has been generated, it needs to be presented at the very least to the organisation. Presentation techniques have been discussed previously (see chapter 3), however choice of presentation media and mode is critical to transmitting the message effectively: choice of language, vocabulary and delivery style needs to emulate the expectations of the target audience.

Inevitably, throughout the organisation there will be different views towards any new strategy. There will be a variety of opinions from very positive to very negative, and it is the responsibility of management to handle these different perspectives. Typically, the areas that generate this consternation can be summarised as shown in figure 15.12:

Objections to Change

1. No clear benefit or value
2. Poor understanding in the nature of the change
3. Poor inter-personnel skills
4. No or poor leadership skills
5. No clear structure for managing the process
6. A lack of defined barriers or clarity of issues
7. Progress not measured or structured
8. Poor communication
9. Low stakeholder buy-in
10. People not involved in developing quick wins
11. Poor Focus
12. Success not defined, measured or recognised

Figure 15.12 – Objections to Change, based on Balogun & Haley

The Contribution of a Sustainable Strategy

Strategy is the mechanism which turns ideas into actions, ambition into results. The delivery of *the Sustainable Business'* vision is reliant on the adoption and implementation of an effective strategy. To this end, the development of a Sustainable Strategy is critical for the corporate management of *the Sustainable Business.*

Aversion to change is often born out of a lack of understanding. This can, in many cases, be overcome with education, information and reasoning, thus any strategy must be supported with effective communication: Regrettably, however a significant number of organisations appear to find it difficult to effectively transmit strategy outside the Boardroom.

Rule: Strategy - Agree, Implement, Communicate

Case Study 15: Unilever

The Compass Strategy - "Making a Big Difference"

Developing a Sustainability Strategy has been a core element of the Unilever Mission Statement for a number of years. Its sustainability activity can be traced into the 1990s evolving into what they call in 2012 their "Compass Strategy".

The core focus of the strategy is the delivery of growth and the longevity of the business, coupled with the improvement of society, whilst continually reducing the organisation's environmental impact. This is perhaps best summed up with the company catch phrase:

"We work to create a better future every day."

The strategy incorporates a wide range of organisational factors, both internal and external, in pursuit of this goal. These include:

- Setting tough sustainability targets which stretch the business, its suppliers, its employees and its partners;
- Consideration and involvement of all the stakeholders in the Supply Chain from Suppliers through to Consumers;
- Measurement and management of the raw materials used within the production process;
- Focused reduction in utility consumption, most notably water, electricity and gas;
- Understanding and managing the impact of the various brands and products that sit within the Unilever portfolio;
- Ensuring sustainability features at the core of its innovation development and research;
- A culture of "Continuous Improvement" throughout the business;
- Appointment of "Sustainability Champions" to initiate, oversee and encourage sustainability initiatives;
- And education of the consumer of the products to help them participate in the sustainability challenge.

The Unilever vision was highlighted with a goal set in the Autumn 2009:

> *"To double the size of the business while reducing our overall environmental impact across our entire value chain."*

Practical evidence of the Unilever efforts to deliver this mandate can be shown with their work to reduce water and utility consumption in their Canadian operations. In that region, there is a huge reliance on water both within the manufacturing and consumption activities as well as within the upstream Supply Chain, where over 60% of raw materials originate from agricultural sources relying on the on-going supply of fresh water.

Accordingly, the preservation and management of water is a major element in the Unilever Risk Plan. To mitigate this risk, the Resdale plant in Ontario took positive actions to combat this risk: they have successfully reduced water consumption by over 45% since 1999, whilst decreasing CO_2 emissions by over 20,000 tonnes, lowering electricity consumption by over 20% and shrinking natural gas usage by over 45%.

Further the *"Brand Imprint"* programme which began in the 1990s, continues to review the PESTLE impact of the organisation's products. It undertakes what Unilever calls:

> *"a 360° scan of the social, economic and environmental impact that their brand has on the world."*

At the strategy's core is education of the consumer. Unilever recognises it cannot do everything itself, however, with its huge consumer base, education and just a small change, Unilever can make *"a big difference"*.

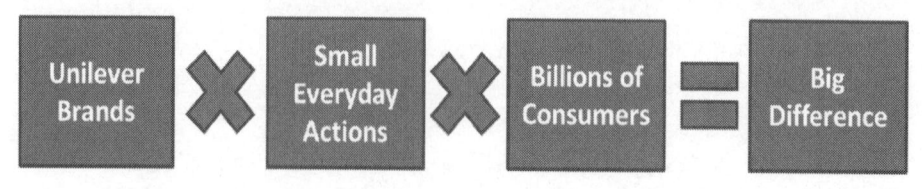

| Unilever Brands | × | Small Everyday Actions | × | Billions of Consumers | = | Big Difference |

In conclusion, therefore, it can be seen how adopting sustainability as a central theme of an organisation's strategy can make a dramatic contribution both to the organisation's success, to the planet and to the stakeholders throughout the Supply Chain. This can be seen to reduce risk, improve profitability and enhance the organisation's image.
See www.unilever.com

The Sustainable Business

Notes Page | Page Ref

The Sustainable Business

Summary Chapter 16 Conclusion

Key Learning Points
- Recap of core areas of sustainability
- Identifying Sustainable Commitment
- The need to pursue the Longevity and The Three Pillar mandates
- Recognition of consequences, impact and responsibility
- Minimisation of waste
- Reduction of staff turnover
- Effective funding & debt management
- Compliance legislation
- Generation of a balanced organisation
- Recognition of GDP, GNP & GSP
- Closed Loop Recycling

Tool Summary
- The Sustainable Impactor Model
- Cultivators/Continuers/Conservers
- Sustainable Balance
- Traffic Light Matrix
- SIPOC
- Mintzberg's 5P Model

Recommended Additional Reading
- All modules in levels 4,5 and 6

Chapter 16: Conclusion

"Obsessive profit growth without a vision is a corporate cancer fed by greed, watered by avarice but starved of legacy."
– Paul Jackson

Throughout this book, the concept of sustainability has concentrated on what scenario would be best for *the Sustainable Business,* and on the structural or strategic changes which would be needed to generate strong *Sustainable Pillars* to enhance the organisation's long term survival and growth.

Any successful organisation needs a strong vision, corporate identity and a set of underpinning values to achieve success; it needs to plan, set goals, drive and motivate its team to fulfil its aspirations whether or not they themselves have any sustainable desires.

It also needs to have belief and commitment to sustainability throughout its management, workforce and wider stakeholders.

> **Rule: Adopt a "can-do" approach**

Within a sustainable remit, there must remain a commitment and recognition of the long term objectives. There is an expression - "Rome wasn't built in a day" – and neither will *the Sustainable Business*. Stakeholder conflict and differences over the relative importance of each of *the Pillars* is likely to occur, with arguments possible over profitability margins, the cost of being *green*, or whether "pandering" to the people is an acceptable cost and a consequential impact on the bottom line.

Such statements remain plausible in certain circumstances, yet the defining merit of *the Three Pillars* approach is its strength in unison, its vulnerability in discord.

For example, a highly profitable but ruthless or wasteful organisation may experience problems maintaining a loyal and consistent workforce, and may find raw materials constrict its development in subsequent years; both features potentially impact on the profitability, the risk profile and the organisation's longevity.

Indeed, though difficult to substantiate with empirical evidence, a "Pillar Equilibrium" would potentially intervene to combat any extremities in organisational behaviour.

For example, if a company were to pay scant attention to its use of resources and waste (a weak *Planet Pillar*), this would have an adverse effect on *the Profit Pillar*. To remedy the fall in profits, the organisation would need to address the use of resources, thus creating a *Pillar Equilibrium* between these two areas; other similar relationships occur between all *the Pillars*.

Rule: Do not exclude any of *the Pillars* from the Strategy

Within our opening definition of *the Sustainable Business*, the concepts of impact and responsibility and a long term focus lie at the core of its sustainable endeavours; these affect the decisions and organisational choices it makes:

> *"A sustainable business has no lasting impact on the global, national or local environment; commits to the rights and contribution of the employees across the whole Supply Chain and in the wider community whilst recognising its own need to generate a robust commercial structure to deliver on-going value to its stakeholders."*

Further, as mentioned throughout this book, *the Three Pillars* are more complex than at first thought, reflecting wider organisational dimensions. Each *Pillar* contains *three core dimensions* and these in turn should form the basis of due consideration by *the Sustainable Business* when taking decisions and forming strategy.

Whilst the sustainable strength of an organisation can be shown using *the Three Pillar* principle, the impact of the various departments within an organisation can be shown to make a significant contribution; these can be split to highlight their individual roles – see figure 16.1.

The Sustainable Business

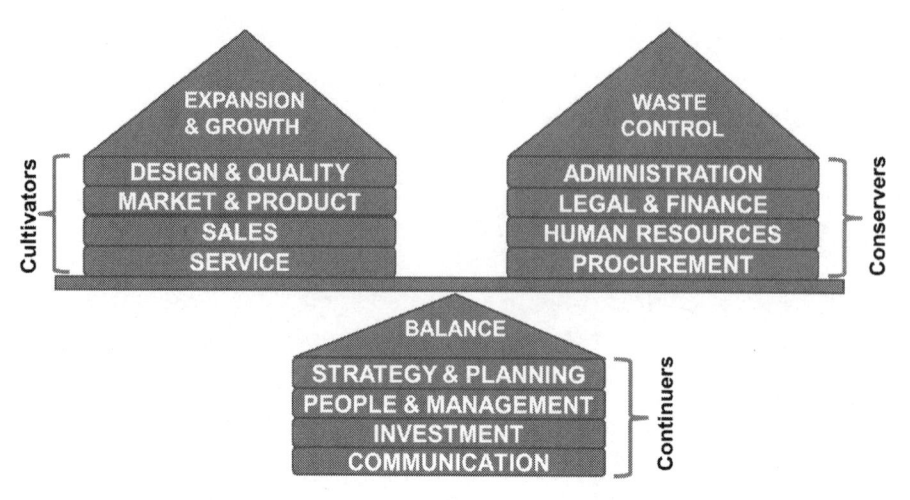

Figure 16.1 – The Sustainable Impactor Model

(Cultivators: EXPANSION & GROWTH – Design & Quality, Market & Product, Sales, Service)
(Conservers: WASTE CONTROL – Administration, Legal & Finance, Human Resources, Procurement)
(Continuers: BALANCE – Strategy & Planning, People & Management, Investment, Communication)

As shown, different functions within the organisation will contribute to the sustainable efforts in different ways. Labelled as "Cultivators", functions such as sales, design, service, etc principally assist in the development and **expansion of shareholder value**; if managed effectively, these will:

- Lead to the growth and development of the organisation;
- Increase sales and profit;
- Develop the product portfolio and customer base;
- And so on.

Equally important are the functions that serve to support the expansion activities, these include effective administration, personnel management, a strong finance function, and effective procurement. These factors are labelled as "Conservers" and have the primary role of **minimising the waste** within the organisation such as:

- Reducing staff turnover;
- Cost reduction;
- Establishment of effective funding arrangements;
- Collection of debts;
- Compliance with legislation
- etc.

The Sustainable Business

> **Food for Thought**: Definition of Cultivators and Conservers
> Cultivators – Factors which **increase the value** of the organisation by increasing the customer facing fulfilment of demand through satisfying customers, giving a, good service or extending the product portfolio and customer base.
> Conservers – Factors which **maintain the value** of the business through preservation of the existing business, protection of the margin, and support of the past activity.
> Continuers – **Generate longevity** through strategy and management decisions.

Collectively the Cultivators and Conservers act to protect the overall "Sustainable Balance" of the business, with expansion and waste reduction improving the wealth of the organisation and contributing to its longevity. Meanwhile, there are other supplementary actions – called "Continuers" – that need to be undertaken to generate the organisation's longevity; these include strategy, planning effective personnel management and communication.

Conversely, where an organisation focuses too heavily on one particular facet of the business, the business can become unstable and lose its "Sustainable Balance" – see figure 16.2.

Figure 16.2 – The Unbalanced Organisation

The Sustainable Business

There are numerous cases over the years where organisations have become obsessed with one facet of the business such as design of new products or more commonly with the delivery of sales objectives, without recognising the need to reinforce other areas of the business; this can arguably be the cause of some of the boom and bust scenarios seen in many economies over the years. The Sustainable Impactor Model assists management identify and quantify where "Sustainable Balance" is lost and where resource is required to recover the situation.

> Take for example the "Wise Acre Frozen Treats company" in Maine, USA (see CBS August 2010). This organisation, in the words of its CEO Jim Picariello, "grew too fast -- and went out of business". Its unprecedented success in sales and expansion were not backed up with the financial support needed to develop production facilities, buy equipment and support the front-end sales push.

Management needs to embrace its responsibility to the long term guidance of the organisation. The measurement of sustainability and the old adage that stated "if you can't measure it, you can't manage it" were introduced and discussed in chapter 14. So how do we measure sustainability?

Using this model we could assess and analyse the status of each element of the matrix- see 16.3. This "traffic light matrix" gives a quick and simple visual which can be reviewed and compared year on year.

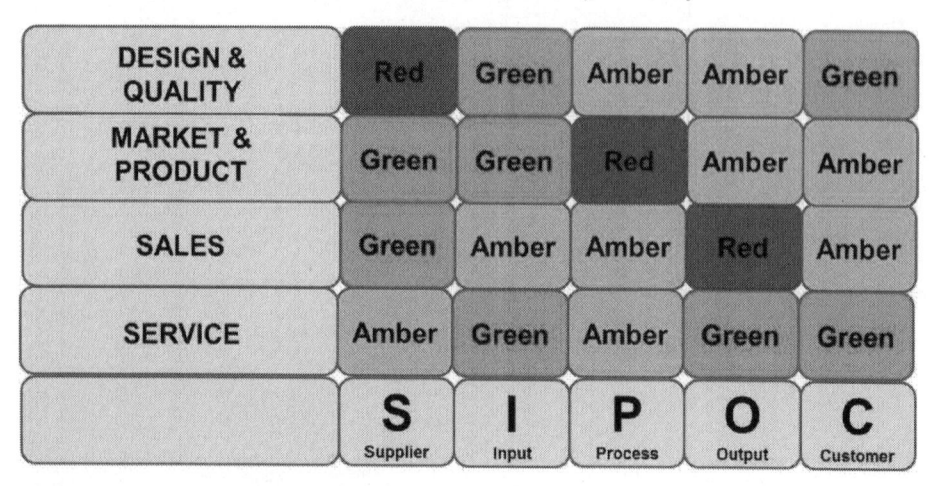

	Supplier (S)	Input (I)	Process (P)	Output (O)	Customer (C)
DESIGN & QUALITY	Red	Green	Amber	Amber	Green
MARKET & PRODUCT	Green	Green	Red	Amber	Amber
SALES	Green	Amber	Amber	Red	Amber
SERVICE	Amber	Green	Amber	Green	Green

Figure 16.3 – Traffic Light Matrix

The Sustainable Business

Departmental activity can be assessed at each stage through the Supply Chain or SIPOC with the issues identified at a micro level and input back into the Sustainable Impactor Model as shown in figure 16.4. Understanding the change in any single component and evaluating the magnitude of this change gives strong management guidance as to where to focus strategic resources.

This and other options to measure the characteristics of each *Pillar*, and the underpinning dimensions have been shown, however what of a broader or more general measure of sustainability? The development of a measure entitled "Gross Sustainable Product" (GSP) attempts to provide this. This measure utilises the traditional Gross Domestic Product (GDP) or Gross National Product (GNP) but deducts from it the value of all the resources which are depleted as a result of the production of the Nation's output.

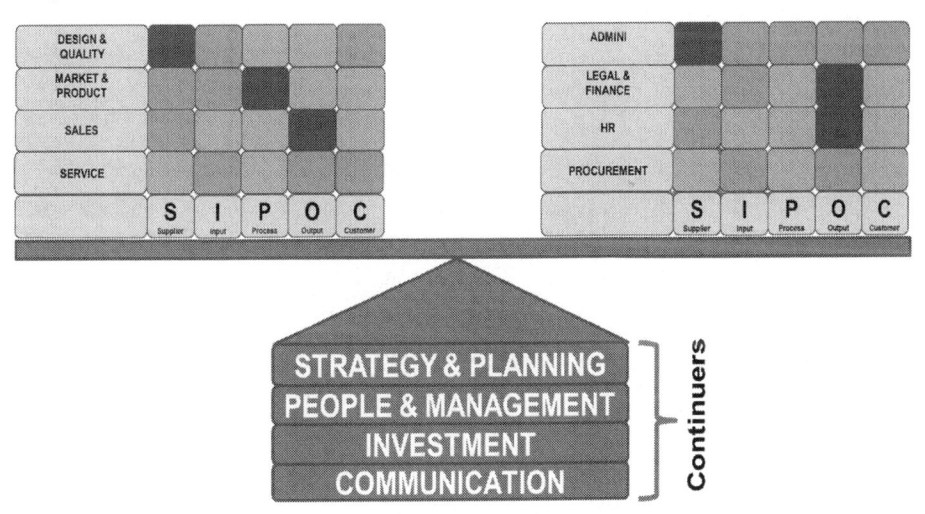

Figure 16.4 – Measured Sustainable Impactor Model

For example, if a Nation relied very heavily on a single commodity extracted from the ground – as is arguably the case with oil and some Middle Eastern economies – the natural assumption is that this resource is finite. As the economy continues to use up the resource, so its sustainable status changes; this is shown in case study 1; whilst there may have been output and production in the early years of Easter Island, there was a depletion of resources that shifted its sustainable status and eventually signalled its demise.

This awareness of the levels and availability of resource leads us back to the issue of the Corporate or Sustainable Strategy. *The Sustainable Business* recognises the need for it to carefully manage its resources. Minzberg identified five areas that are important when setting a strategy - see figure 16.5; and *the Sustainable Business* should consider this when setting strategy.

Planning is critical to the success, but structure, patterns, decisions and a defined stance are required.

Analysing organisations perceived to be great proponents of sustainability, most have a clearly defined and conscious Sustainable Strategy. These organisations plan, have a clear perspective, develop a clear position on important matters and develop strategy and ploys to address major issues. In such organisations, the Sustainable Strategy is usually well publicised and communicated effectively through the business, the market and to all the stakeholders. Further, such organisations make stringent efforts to publish and herald success wherever possible.

Whilst progress is being made, many organisations still fail to publish their Sustainable Strategy, instead relying on a few vague semi-green and somewhat "*Me Too*" statements, this half-hearted approach rewarded accordingly.

Fortunately, examples of organisations who are making successful progress are becoming more plentiful. Take for example Johnson Controls – see www.johnsoncontrols.com. They operate in over 150 different countries worldwide with over 140,000 employees and revenue over $30bn. One of their product lines involves the manufacture and recycling of batteries with global brands which include Varta, Heliar and Optima. Johnson Controls have now incorporated "closed loop recycling" (i.e. use of **all** waste material for the production of other products) in the Lead Acid Accumulator batteries, a chemical and toxin intense product. This, together with publicity and legislation has helped recycled levels exceed 97% of the product, considerably higher than resources such as aluminium, paper and glass. Further, the recycling process contributes significant levels of the raw materials – lead, plastics and chemicals – for new batteries, reducing both impact and cost of manufacture.

Mintzberg's 5P's

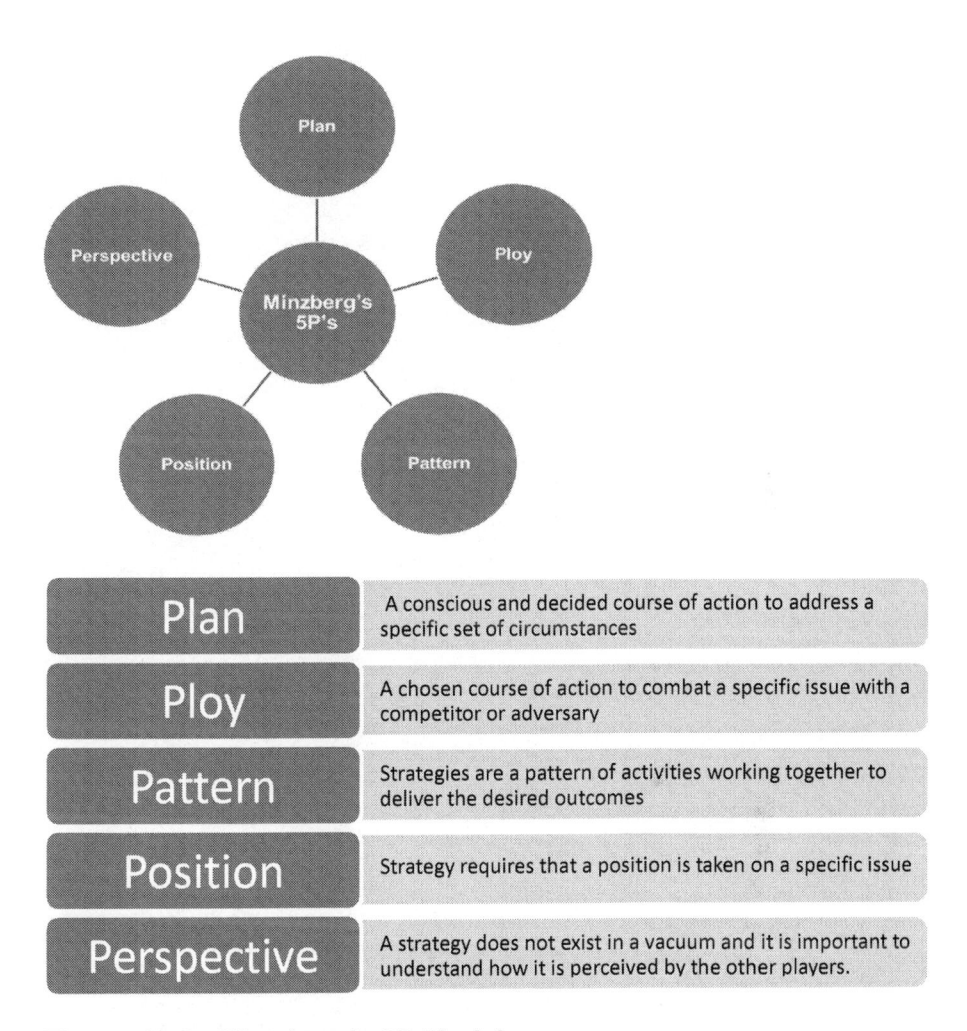

Plan	A conscious and decided course of action to address a specific set of circumstances
Ploy	A chosen course of action to combat a specific issue with a competitor or adversary
Pattern	Strategies are a pattern of activities working together to deliver the desired outcomes
Position	Strategy requires that a position is taken on a specific issue
Perspective	A strategy does not exist in a vacuum and it is important to understand how it is perceived by the other players.

Figure 16.5 –Mintzberg's 5P Model

Equally, organisations such as JLR (Jaguar Landrover), EDF Energy, Carbonomics, Fairtrade and others are worth wider reading as all have made significant inroads into their sustainable impact, delivering policy and actions to make a difference.

What all these – and the numerous other sustainably minded organisations – have in common is management and people dedicated to making a difference, and then willing to devote resources to the effective implementation and communication of *their* plan. These skills are often overlooked, but the difference between a poorly executed and a well-executed plan, is enormous, and can often be attributed to the effectiveness of the management function. It is these skills that can ultimately make the difference between success and failure.

> **Food for Thought**: Sustainable Awareness – A survey by Worcester Research Ltd of companies in Herefordshire in the UK:
> - 87% of those surveyed had acted to reduce their environmental impact, taking actions which included:
>   o Implementation of a waste management plan
>   o Carbon reduction plan
>   o Travel reduction plans
>   o Accreditation such as ISO14000
> - 12% of the employers set targets to reduce energy, waste output, carbon consumption, or fuel usage

In conclusion, therefore, we have shown that sustainability is about more than just going green. It's about building a profitable, low risk, stable and structured organisation that operates with a responsible approach to its inputs, outputs and its people, is conscious of its impact on the environment and community in which it operates, and has management focused on the long game.

Success is possible and is occurring. The more we follow the example set by some of the ground-breaking organisations, the quicker we can reap the rewards of momentum and effort - for our children and future generations.

> *"A journey of a thousand miles begins with a single step."*
> *– Lau-Tu*

Case Study: Wiremold

"Designed to be Better"

The Wiremold Company was established in 1900 by Daniel Hayes Murphy as a metal forming company, and developed steadily over the 20th century and established itself as a market leader in electrical cable management products.

In the 1980s, Wiremold, whilst originally a successful company, had seen growth lagging and recognised a shortfall in its quality processes. Accordingly, it explored and then implemented a number of quality orientated processes including TQM, but then latterly, following the appointment of a new CEO, Art Byrne, Wiremold embraced Lean.

Prior to the change, the organisation manufactured in large batches, it had a very long manufacturing changeover, with some products taking as long as eight weeks from raw materials to finished product. It also had a number of large and very expensive warehouse units stocking product to help ensure customer deliveries.

Following the decision to go Lean, Wiremold focused on getting things right: the right infrastructure; the right resources; the right technology; the right product range; the right distribution systems; and the right workforce. A lean business needs a structured approach to all the components of the organisation, and Wiremold recognised this.

As part of the implementation, Byrne targeted the following:

- Product should be made to order, not for stock;
- A reduction in overall inventory;
- Shorter set-up times allowing specific customer requirements to be made quickly to order;
- Shorter manufacturing lead times;
- Design of product offering features, quality and affordability;
- Improved design of products and components

In addition, Byrne recognised that to be successful, his management style and the implementation process would be critical – so critical in fact that he decided to drive the implementation from the front, leading teams, delivering training, and getting personally involved.

Furthermore, a Kaisan approach was adopted, coupled with employee idea generation. On one occasion, Byrne was helping on the production line where some of the team members were falling behind the production schedule. Upon investigation and discussion, the factory workers suggested that the product design was flawed and was largely responsible for the long process times, and poor quality. Byrne analysed the product and concurred.

The company introduced a QFD (Quality Function Deployment) process to enhance the development of new products. This process draws the customer requirements to the core of the design process, with ECI (Early Customer Involvement), customer workshops and dialogue central to the success.

The Lean concept demands product made to customer orders not for stock. To achieve this product needs to be made from common components, have very quick set-up times and have minimum batch quantities of just one. Product needs to be made using a JIT process, with shipping happening when the order is complete. An in-house and reliable shipping process then ships goods as soon as the order is ready rather than trying to fit the shipment into a courier's schedule. In summary, demand drives the process.

Due to the nature of the product – physical size and heavy weight – efficient down-stream stockists were essential. A new commercial package was developed, designed to encourage the local stockists to invest in service stock to support and underpin the main Wiremold users, creating a partnership between stockist and supplier dedicated to the delivery of service, quality and innovation to the end customer.

Between 1991-95, Wiremold saw its profit treble, and over the course of the Byrne era, turnover doubled with a notably improvement in the reputation of the company and its market recognition.

The success of this project has been heralded in a number of books, for example "Lean Thinking" (Womack & Womack) and "Wiremold – A century of Solutions (Jim H Smith)

The Sustainable Business

Notes Page	Page Ref

The Sustainable Business

Appendix i: List of Illustrations

Figure 1.1	Current Status Model
Figure 1.2	Relative Investment in Research & Development
Figure 1.3	SWOT Analysis
Figure 1.4	Porter's Five Force Model
Figure 1.5	The Product Life Cycle
Figure 1.6	Boston Consulting Group Matrix
Figure 1.7	PESTLE Analysis
Figure 1.8	IMPACT Model
Figure 2.1	The People Pillar
Figure 2.2	People Pillar Dimensions
Figure 2.3	Belbin Roles
Figure 2.4	Tracom Four Styles
Figure 2.5	Tuckman Team Development Cycle
Figure 2.6	The RITE Way
Figure 2.7	RITUAL
Figure 2.8	McGregor & Ouchi Theory X, Theory Y, Theory Z
Figure 2.9	The Five Vulnerabilities of People
Figure 3.1	The Profit Pillar
Figure 3.2	The Profit Pillar Dimensions
Figure 3.3	The Stable Sales Dimension
Figure 3.4	The Global Car Market
Figure 3.5	The VAG Market Offering
Table 3.6	Direct & Indirect Costs
Figure 3.7	Cost Allocation examples
Figure 3.8	Establishing Total Costs
Figure 3.9	Five Rights
Figure 3.10	Quality, Time and Cost
Table 3.11	Competitive advantage and Customer Added Value
Figure 3.12	The POINT Model
Figure 3.13	PREP Model
Figure 3.14	The Seven Steps to Sustainable Service
Figure 4.1	The Planet Pillar
Figure 4.2	The Planet Pillar Dimensions
Figure 4.3	The Total Cost of Sustainable Ownership

Figure 4.4	Avoidance to Disposal
Figure 4.5	Reduce Options
Figure 4.6	Lease Driven Supply Reduction
Figure 4.7	Recycling symbols and corresponding descriptions
Figure 4.8	Recycling rates for UK authorities
Figure 4.9	European recycling rates
Figure 4.10	8R Model of responsible waste treatment
Figure 5.1	The Kondratieff Cycle
Figure 5.2	The Innovation Lag
Figure 5.3	The Impact on Society
Figure 5.4	The Technology Dilemma
Figure 5.5	Centralised vs Decentralised
Figure 5.6	Hierarchical Structure
Figure 5.7	Regional Business structure
Figure 5.8	Matrix structure
Figure 5.9	SMART Targets
Figure 6.1	Functions of Sustainable Procurement
Figure 6.2	The Procurement Cycle
Figure 6.3	Cost Collation
Figure 6.4	Nigerian Corruption graph
Figure 6.5	Carter's 10c Model
Figure 6.6	Components of Win-Win Relationships
Figure 6.7	BAE Reduce to Produce
Figure 6.8	STOP WASTE Model
Figure 6.9	Stakeholder Strategy
Figure 7.1	The flow of value through the Supply Chain.
Figure 7.2	The Value Chain
Figure 7.3	The Three Pillars and associated dimensions
Table 7.4	EdF Operating Companies
Figure 7.5	Southwestern Airlines
Figure 7.6	The sales and profit equation
Figure 7.7	The SIPOC model
Figure 7.8	Fishbone Diagram
Figure 7.9	Example Supply Chain Analysis Models
Figure 7.10	Ansoff Planning Model
Figure 7.11	Specification Presentation

Figure 7.12	Kraljic Matrix
Figure 7.13	The Cost of Poor Quality
Figure 7.14	Costs associated with holding Inventory
Figure 7.15	Standard Deviation
Figure 7.16	Inventory Best Practice Rules
Figure 7.17	Sample Incoterms
Figure 7.18	2011 Incoterms
Figure 7.19	Distribution Structures
Figure 7.20	Goods organised by usage rates
Figure 7.21	Goods organised by product, type or franchise
Figure 7.22	Single In & Out
Figure 8.1	The Sales Eco Cube
Figure 8.2	Pitcher – Pipeline – Planet Intersect
Figure 8.3	The Sales Focus
Figure 8.4	Patron-Purveyor-Pitcher
Figure 8.5	The Third Dimension
Figure 8.6	The SUSTAIN Model
Figure 8.7	Sales Value Measures
Figure 8.8	MAN Model
Graph 8.9	Sustainable Sales Measurement
Figure 8.10	12 Point Checklist
Figure 9.1	The Process Cloud
Figure 9.2	Conformity versus Individualism
Figure 9.3	Sustainable Operations
Figure 9.4	Process Map Examples
Figure 9.5	Assessment of Value and Strategy
Figure 9.6	DMAIC Model
Figure 9.7	Impact of the use of poor materials on the customer
Figure 9.8	People factors affecting the business operations
Figure 9.9	Job Enrichment features
Figure 9.10	The 3Es Model
Figure 9.11	The Toyota Production System
Figure 9.12	The House of Toyoda
Figure 10.1	Carbon Output of travel options
Figure 10.2	Kitchen worktop comparison
Figure 10.3	Fuel Hierarchy

Figure 10.4	The 3e Model
Figure 10.5	Contamination in the Water Table
Figure 10.6	Reasons to buy from a milkman
Figure 10.7	Rare Earths
Figure 10.8	Designer constraint issues
Figure 11.1	The Prince2 Approach
Figure 11.2	Stakeholder Positioning
Figure 11.3	Lewin's Freeze Model
Figure 11.4	The Belbin Team roles
Figure 11.5	Stadia Analysis
Figure 12.1	Types of Risk
Figure 12.2	The Sustainable Risk Cycle
Figure 12.3	The Risk Equation
Figure 12.4	Risk Consequences
Figure 12.5	Coffee Shop Fishbone
Figure 12.6	Impact / Probability model
Figure 12.7	Three Pillars Risk Evaluation Model
Figure 12.8	Example Risks and Issues
Figure 13.1	The Legal Mind Map
Figure 13.2	Ten Sustainable Axioms
Figure 14.1	MDV Model
Figure 14.2	Targeting across the organisation
Figure 14.3	Example Performance Measurement Aspects
Figure 14.4	Toyota Production 3Ms
Figure 14.5	Toyota Seven Wastes
Figure 14.6	Supply Chain Inputs
Figure 14.7	Potential components of an ERP solution
Table 14.8	Sample business measures
Table 14.9	Planet related measures
Figure 14.10	Customer Perspectives
Figure 14.11	Sustainable Partnership Characteristics
Figure 14.12	Common Financial ratios
Figure 15.1	Cascade of Corporate Strategy
Figure 15.2	Strategy & Culture Nucleus

Figure 15.3	The Cultural Web
Figure 15.4	McKinsey 7S model
Figure 15.5	Ansoff's Product strategy model
Figure 15.6	Customer Needs Analysis
Figure 15.7	Common pricing strategies
Figure 15.8	Summary of three pricing strategies
Figure 15.9	The Marketing Mix
Figure 15.10	Nature & Scope of Change Model
Figure 15.11	Force Field Analysis
Figure 15.12	Objections to Change based on Balogun & Haley
Figure 16.1	The Sustainable Impactor Model
Figure 16.2	The Unbalanced Organisation
Figure 16.3	Traffic Light Matrix
Figure 16.4	Measured Sustainable Impactor Model
Figure 16.5	Mintzberg's 5P Model

The Sustainable Business

Appendix ii: List of Abbreviations

Abbreviation	Definition
ABC	Activity Based Costing
ABCD	Activity Based Carbon Distribution
AOG	Aircraft On Ground
AQL	Acceptable Quality Level
ATTAC	Availability Transformation Tornado Aircraft Contract
BARS	Behaviourally Anchored Rating Scales
BATNA	Best Alternative to Negotiated Agreement
BCG	Boston Consulting Group
BOM	Bill Of Materials
BOQ	Bill Of Quantities
BPF	Ball Park Figure
BS	British Standards
CAD	Computer Aided Design
CAM	Computer Aided Manufacturing
CAPEX	Capital Expenditure
CBD	Competitive Bid Document
CFI	Custom Factory Integration
CFR	Cost & Freight
CFT	Cross Functional Teams
CIF	Cost Insurance & Freight
CIP	Carriage & Insurance Paid to Destination
CIPD	Chartered Institute Personnel & Development
CIPS	Chartered Institute Purchasing & Supply
CLAN	Centre Lead Action Network balances
CAN	Critical Needs Analysis
CO_2	Carbon Dioxide
COPQ	Cost of Poor Quality
COSHH	Control Of Substances Hazardous to Health
CPA	Critical Path Analysis
CPO	Chief Purchasing Officer
CPT	Carriage Paid to Destination
CQ	Commercial Queries
CRM	Customer Relationship Management

CSD	Critical Success Drivers
CSF	Critical Success Factors
CSR	Corporate Social Responsibility
DAF	Deliver At Frontier
DAP	Delivery At Port
DCF	Discounted Cash Flow
DDP	Delivery Duty Paid
DDU	Delivery Duty Unpaid
DMAIC	Define-Measure-Analyse-Improve-Check
DRP	Distribution Resource Planning
ECI	Early Customer Involvement
EDI	Electronic Data Interchange
EIS	Executive Information Systems
EN	Euro-Norms
EOI	Expression Of Interest
EOQ	Economic Order Quantities
ERP	Enterprise Resource Planning
ESI	Early Supplier Involvement
EXW	Ex Works
FAS	Free Alongside Ship
FCA	Free Carrier
FCP	Forward Commitment Procurement
FFP	Fit For Purpose
FIFO	First In First Out
FMCG	Fast Moving Consumer Goods
FMEA	Failure Modes Effect Analysis
FOB	Free On Board
GDP	Gross Domestic Product
GNP	Gross National Product
GRP	Glass Reinforced Plastic
GSP	Gross Sustainable Product
HR	Human Resources
HSE	Health, Safety & Environment
HVAC	Heating Ventilation & Air Conditioning
IMPACT	Inputs-Minimise Waste-People-Asset Utilisation-Cash-Time

IP	Internet Protocol
ISO	International Standards Organisation
IT	Information Technology
ITT	Invitation To Tender / Invitation To Treat
JIC	Just In Case
JIT	Just In Time
KPI	Key Performance Indicators
KSO	Key Sales Objectives
LCI	Late Customer Involvement
LDO	Least Desirable Outcome
LED	Light Emitting Diode
LIFO	Last In First Out
LOI	Letter of Interest (or Intent)
LSI	Late Supplier Involvement
LT	Lead Time
MDO	Most Desirable Outcome
MDV	Measure-Data-Value
MIL	Must / Intend / Like
MRO	Maintenance, Repair, Operational items
MRP	Manufacturing Resource Planning
MRS	Management Reporting System
MSP	Managing Successful Programmes
NACRE	New Aircraft Concepts Research
NASA	North American Space Agency
NI	Net Investment
NISO	National Individual Standing Offer
NMSO	National Master Standing Offer
NPV	Net Present Value
NVA	Non Value Added
OEM	Original Equipment Manufacturer
OJEU	Official Journal of the European Union
OPEX	Operational Expenditure
PERT	Programme Evaluation and Review Technique
PEST	Political-Economic-Social-Technological
PESTLE	Political-Economic-Social-Technological-Legislative-Environment

PLC	Product Life Cycle
POINT	PREP-One Page-Interesting-Newsworthy-Three
PONC	Price of Non-conformance
PQQ	Pre Qualification Questionnaire
PR	Public Relations
PREP	Point-Reason-Example-Point
Prince2	Projects IN Controlled Environments
QA	Quality Assurance
QC	Quality Control
QE	Quantitative Easing
QFD	Quality Function Deployment
QTC	Quality, Time & Cost
R&D	Research and Development
RFI	Request For Information
RFP	Request For Proposal
RFQ	Request For Quotation
RFSO	Request For Standing Offer
RITE	Recruit-Induct-Train-Evaluate
RITUAL	Recruit-Induct-Train-Utilise-Analyse-Leaving
RTP	Reduce To Produce
SCAN	Strategically Controlled Action Network
SEGPA	Supplier Engaged Green Product Awareness
SIPOC	Supplier-Input-Process-Output-Customer
SMART	Specific-Measurable-Achievable-Realistic-Timed
SME	Small Medium Enterprises
SMED	Single Minute Exchange of Die
SOAR	Supplier Opportunities Assessment Review
SPC	Statistical Process Control
SPOF	Single Point Of Failure Analysis
SSF	Sustainable Success Factors
SUGAR	Subsonic Ultra Green Aircraft Research
SUSTAIN	Scale-Uniques-Solutions-Timetable-Attitude-Individual-Needs
SWOT	Strengths-Weaknesses-Opportunities-Threats
TAC	Total Acquisition Cost
TBL	Triple Bottom Line

TCO	Total Cost of Ownership
TCSO	Total Cost of Sustainable Ownership
TNA	Training Needs Analysis
TPC	Transactional Process Control
TQM	Total Quality Management
TSD	Tender Submission Document
UNASUR	Union of South American Nations
UPS	Uninterrupted Power Supply
UTC	United Technologies Corp
VA	Value Analysis
VAG	Volkswagen Audi Group
VAR	Value at Risk
VFM	Value for Money
VMI	Vendor Managed Inventory
VOC	Voice of The Customer
VW	Volkswagen
WIP	Work-In-Progress
WMS	Warehouse Management System

// The Sustainable Business

Appendix iii: The Sustainable Rules

- Look after the People, and the Profit Will look after itself
- Sales are Vanity, Profit is Sanity
- Fail to Plan, Plan to fail
- Deal with and clear CQ's inside the first year
- If you can't measure it, you can't manage it!
- Happy Customers come back
- At Air Canada, we are not happy until you are happy.
- Adding extra value is fine if the customer recognises it.
- One man's rubbish is another man's treasure
- Mend the roof while the sun is shining
- What goes up, must come down!
- Know your supply market, track prices and movement
- If total cost is more than the total contribution don't do "it"
- The essence of trust is not in its bind, but in its bond
- Value is the motivation for all the parties, all of the time, and is their motivation for taking risk
- A "Sustainable Stakeholder" is someone who affects or is affected by a sustainable issue
- You get what you pay for!
- Great service is not just about what is delivered, it is as much about value for money and meeting expectation
- Look after the pennies and the pounds will look after themselves
- Under promise and over deliver
- Inventory decisions need to be driven from the heart, not the pocket
- Respect is the best reward
- Time is money, make every second count
- Nurture the pro, counter the anti
- Legendary customer service is the greatest deal closer
- Focus on why you succeeded and do it again!
- Continuous Improvement and learning = Higher sales
- Quality is in the eye of the beholder
- Quality is everybody's responsibility
- Unite the workforce
- Innovation, the search for that *Eureka Moment*
- Without designs, there would be no sales
- In the words of an old sales manager "What you need to do is sell more at a higher margin"!

- Environmental innovation is 1% inspiration, 99% perspiration – *Albert Einstein*
- A user is somebody who tells you what they want the day you give them what they asked for
- One man's risk is another man's opportunity
- If it seems too good to be true, it probably will be
- If you can't measure it you can't manage it
- Strive for the Win-Win relationships
- Look after your people, and the profit will look after itself
- A sale is a debt until its paid for
- A business that makes nothing but money is a poor business – *Henry Ford*
- Decide: Lower Cost or Higher Sales?
- Develop "Most Effective Pathways"
- Under promise, over deliver
- Sound strategy starts with having the right goal. (Porter)
- Change is about changing people not organisations – *Balogun*
- Strategy – Agree, Implement, Communicate
- Adopt a "can-do" approach
- Do not exclude any of *the Pillars* from the Strategy

Bibliography

Title	Author(s)	Date
Balanced Scorecard	Olve & Sjostrand	2006
Blue Ocean Strategy	Chan Kim & Mauborgne	2005
Cut Carbon Grow Profit	Tang & Yeoh	2007
Essentials of Balanced Scorecards	Nar	2004
Excellence in Global Supply Chain Management	Emmett & Crocker	2010
Exploring Corporate Strategy	Johnson & Scholes	2007
Game Theory and Economic Modelling	Kreps	1990
Green Supply Chains	Emmett & Sood	2010
How to Solve the Mismanagement Crisis	Ichak Adizes	1979
Integrated Material Management	Carter & Price	1998
Into the Upwave	Robert Beckman	1988
Lean Thinking	Womack & Jones	1996
Learning Organisations in Practice	Pearn & Mulrooney	1995
Marketing Management	Kotler	1994
Organisational Behaviour	Buchanon & Huczynski	2004
Outsourcing The Human Resource Function	Cook	1998
Practical Procurement	Carter & Kirby	2006
Profex (CIPS) Study Guides	Various Authors	2011
Purchasing Scams	Trevor Kitching	2001
Screw It, Lets Do It	Richard Branson	2007
Six Sigma Course Manual	Capella Associates	2011
Six Sigma for Managers	Bruce	2005
Stores Distribution & Management	Carter, Price & Emmett	2004
Strategy	Harvard Business Essentials	2005
Supply Chain Excellence	Bolstroff	2007
The Constant Economy	Zac Goldsmith	1988

The Journal of Organisational Behaviour	Zahhly & Tosi	1989
The Kondratieff Cycle	Alexander	2001
The Machine that Changed the World	Womack, Jones & Rose	1990
The Performance Prism	Neely, Adams & Kennerley	2002
The Quest: Energy, Security and the Modern World	Yergin	2006
The Relationship Driven Supply Chain	Emmett & Crocker	2009
The Six Sigma Handbook	Pyzdek & Keller	2008
The Sustainable MBA	Weybrecht	2000
The Wiremold Company: A century of solutions	Smith	2001
Tools for the Learning Organisation	Pearn & Mulrooney	2003
Treat People Right	Lawler & Lawler	2011

Periodicals – Numerous Copies of:
Institute of Director's publications
Institute of Mechanical Engineer's publications
National Geographic
Supplier Management Magazine
The Economist
The Financial Times and Supplements
Time Magazine
The World Wide Web - Untold sites, links and blogs

Index

5P Model
 - *see also* Mintzberg 421, 429, 439
8R Model 117, 436
9/11 345

ABB 304
Acceptable Quality Level (AQL) 441
Activity Based Carbon Distribution 27, 73, 285, 292, 441
Activity Based Carbon Distribution (ABCD Costing) 73
Activity Based Costing (ABC) 59, 73, 351, 377, 399, 400, 441
Adding Value 6, 145
Adizes 271, 325
Adjourning 44
African Cup of Nations 53
Airbus 301, 316
Air France 183
Airtel 79
Ajka alumina sludge 25
Amoco Cadiz 25
Angola 53
Ansoff's Matrix 397
Apple 402
Appraisal Process 48
ATTAC 305, 441

BAE Systems 117, 299, 308, 378
Ball Park Figure (BPF) 154, 441
Bangalore 17
Bangladesh Agricultural Research Institute 291
Bay of Pigs 325
BBC 16, 182, 253, 413
Behaviourally Anchored Rating Scales (BARS) 48, 441
Belbin 39, 41, 42, 43, 288, 319, 324, 325, 340, 435, 438
Belgium 116, 183
Best Alternative to Negotiated Agreement (BATNA) 157, 441
Bhopal 25

Birmingham City Plaza 255
Blockbuster Video 396
Boeing 16, 301, 316, 317
Borders Bookshop 274
Boston Consulting Group Matrix 9, 65, 396, 435
BP 25, 251
Bradford Index 50, 52, 381
Brainstorming 173, 188, 189, 221, 413
Branson, Richard 80
Brazil 183, 290
British Airways (BA) 182, 369
Brown, Gordon 125
Bureau of Public Procurement 152
Burger King 79, 80
Burnaston 362
business case 83, 90, 99, 148, 149, 150, 158, 164, 186, 192, 320, 323, 324, 337, 402
business ownership 123
Business Structure 123, 134
Buyers 67, 227, 360

Café Nero 79
Cannibalisation 299
Cape Town
 - see also South Africa World Cup 36
CAPEX 104, 255, 339, 441
carbon costs 395
Carbon Dioxide (CO_2) 74, 89, 97, 101, 107, 109, 150, 285, 286, 287, 289, 290, 291, 292, 293, 316, 384, 405, 418, 441
carbon impact 72, 73, 292, 370
Carbonomics 429
Cascade of Corporate Strategy 389, 438
Caspian Sea 55, 116
Category management 59, 174
Centre Lead Action Network (CLAN) 123, 135, 441
character 253, 278, 288
Character 181
Chartered Institute of Personnel and Development (CIPD) 49, 441
Chartered Institute of Purchasing and Supply (CIPS) 1, 8, 9, 39, 40,

59, 76, 95, 123, 145, 174, 202, 225, 260, 285, 319, 331, 332, 347, 355, 387, 441
Chevron Oil 28, 53, 79, 140
child labour 380
Chile 152
China 79, 112, 141, 169, 182, 183, 209, 287, 308, 394
China Mobile 79
Chubb Fire 252
Closed Loop Recycling 421
coffee 113, 179, 220, 280, 281, 337, 338
Coke 80
Common Cause Management 259, 271
community 1, 16, 23, 24, 25, 27, 28, 31, 34, 35, 36, 39, 40, 53, 54, 55, 56, 102, 119, 120, 147, 181, 217, 278, 390, 423, 430
Compass Strategy 417
Competitive advantage 79, 435
Competitive Bid Document (CBD) 154, 441
complementary products 67, 68, 163, 398
compliance 154, 160, 230, 263, 274, 334, 343, 348, 362
composting 35, 36, 98, 114, 115, 116
Computer Aided Design (CAD)
 - *see also* Computer Aided Manufacturing (CAM) 259, 280, 441
Computer Aided Manufacturing (CAM)
 - *see also* Computer Aided Design (CAD) 259, 280, 441
Conservers 421, 424, 425
consumption 27, 30, 107, 108, 112, 293, 296, 317, 417, 418, 430
Continuers 421, 425
Continuous Ethical Responsibility 347, 348, 349
Continuous Improvement
 - *see also* Kaizen 243, 283, 355, 371, 417, 447
Control Of Substances Hazardous to Health (COSHH) 299, 441
corporate social responsibility 56
Corporate Social Responsibility (CSR) 6, 10, 40, 44, 46, 60, 71, 96, 225, 235, 236, 237, 254, 341, 442
corporate strategy 6, 13, 388, 390, 394, 414
Corporate Sustainability Policy 7
corporate vision 2, 9
corruption 54, 145, 152, 153, 210, 344
cost of poor quality (COPQ) 45, 173, 174, 197, 441

credit crunch 12, 105, 125, 301, 395
Credit Crunch 5, 124, 125
Critical Needs Analysis (CNA) 201
Critical Path Analysis (CPA) 336, 441
Critical Success Factors (CSF) 190, 197, 299, 319, 320, 323, 324, 388, 442
Crop preservation methods 35
Cross Functional Teams 220, 221, 413, 441
Cuba 325
Cultivators 421, 424, 425
Cultural Web 387, 439
Culture Nucleus 438
Current Assets 378, 411
Current Liabilities 378, 411
Current Ratio 367, 372
Current Status Model 9, 14, 435
Customer Added Value 79, 435
Customer Needs Analysis 387, 397, 398, 439
Customer Relationship Management (CRM) 59, 81, 228, 244, 441
customer service 45, 80, 92, 175, 181, 205, 207, 212, 220, 241, 269, 270, 288, 447
customer strategy 371
Custom Factory Integration (CFI) 222, 441
Customs and Excise 204

Datacentres 344, 345
Deepwater Horizon 25
Dell 80, 212, 222, 223, 306
Denmark 152
design department 288, 314
DHL 79, 80
Discount rates 411
Distribution Resource Planning (DRP) 355, 366, 442
DMAIC model 271
Docklands 17, 300
Dog products 397
Dorming 44

Early Customer Involvement (ECI) 413, 432, 442

Early Supplier Involvement (ESI) 195, 413, 442
Easter Island 34, 427
Ebay 110, 117, 302
Ecolabel 74
Ecological Footprint 95, 97, 98
Economic Order Quantities (EOQ) 91, 174, 205, 442
economy 17, 24, 25, 32, 33, 55, 124, 125, 126, 127, 128, 129, 131,
    146, 182, 203, 265, 342, 427
EcoVision
  - *see also* Philips Lighting 384
Edmonton Composting Facility 98
Effectiveness 28, 36, 41, 48, 77, 178, 204, 214, 278, 294, 341, 368,
    405, 430
Efficiency 28, 44, 100, 107, 108, 109, 117, 207, 256, 275, 294, 296,
    384, 385
Eighth Waste 95, 104, 192, 288
Eight Wastes 95
Électricité de France (EDF) 79, 183, 429
Electronic Data Interchange (EDI) 393, 442
Emirates Stadium 327
Employee Forums 413
English Premier League 11
Enron 351, 352
Enterprise Resource Planning (ERP) 174, 179, 219, 259, 267, 355,
    365, 366, 438, 442
Enterprise Zones 17
European Directive 1999/44EC 297
European Environmental Law 300
European Union (EU) 74, 116, 152, 316, 443
Expression of Interest (EOI) 154, 372, 442
External Affected 25, 31
External Environment 392
External Impactors 18, 22
External Related 22, 23, 31
Exxon Valdez 25

Facebook 85
Failure Mode and Effect Analysis (FMEA) 276, 336, 442

Fairtrade 429
Fannie Mae 191
Fast Moving Consumer Goods (FMCG) 105, 109, 297, 442
Federal Bureau of Investigation (FBI) 351
Fedex 79
Ferguso, Sir Alex 382
Ferrari 70
Fibre Networks 344
finance 2, 26, 66, 72, 130, 141, 142, 148, 149, 177, 324, 348, 349, 357, 365, 366, 424
Finisher Role 326
Finland 152
Fishbone 173, 188, 260, 270, 273, 331, 338, 436, 438
fit for purpose 166, 188, 192, 197, 267, 270, 275, 296, 321, 324, 397
Five Rights 59, 77, 375, 435
Five Vulnerabilities of People 39, 50, 435
flaring 56, 109, 370
Force Majeure 276, 331, 333, 361
Forecasting 9, 124, 133, 240, 259, 267, 268, 393
Forex 334
Forward Commitment Procurement (FCP) 195, 442
France 14, 36, 79, 131, 183, 210
Franco, General Franciso 131
Freddie Mac 191
Freecycle 95, 119, 120
FTSE100 239
Fuel Hierarchy 285, 294, 437
funnel 229, 233, 238, 245

G8 152
Gainshare 378
Gearing ratios 411
Germany 14, 116, 152, 182, 183, 296
Gibraltar 218, 295, 370
Glass Reinforced Plastic (GRP) 118, 442
global 11, 17, 23, 28, 30, 54, 69, 70, 79, 81, 97, 98, 101, 103, 108, 124, 125, 130, 131, 140, 167, 169, 182, 209, 212, 217, 239, 265, 267, 287, 297, 303, 342, 344, 348, 351, 368, 371, 373, 377, 385, 389, 394, 423, 428

Glucksberg 235
goal setting 123
Government Environmental Protection Agency 106
Greece 131
Green Point stadium
  - *see also* South Africa World Cup; Cape Town 36
Greenwashing 225, 229
Gross Domestic Product (GDP) 421, 427, 442
Gross National Product (GNP) 421, 427, 442
Gross Sustainable Product (GSP) 421, 427, 442
Group Think 66, 319, 325, 340

halon 253
Halo Theory 325
hawthorn
  - *see also* CO_2 289
Healthcare 141
Heijunka 283
Herzberg 51, 278, 380
Hierarchical Structure 135, 136, 436
Hilton Hotels 369
Hitler, Adolf 131
Honda 79
Hong Kong 168, 169, 182
House of Toyoda 437
Human Resources (HR) 28, 40, 47, 48, 274, 316, 355, 367, 368, 380, 442
Humanure 98
Hungary 25, 183

IKEA 310
IMPACT model 26, 197
Incoterms 173, 174, 210, 211, 437
induction 46, 47, 381
Information Technology (IT) 344, 443
innovation 7, 8, 11, 13, 15, 24, 66, 118, 123, 128, 130, 163, 169, 182, 228, 286, 291, 317, 344, 417, 432, 448
insurance 206, 210, 333, 336, 339, 342
Internal Organisation Strategy 394

inventory 19, 78, 89, 148, 159, 162, 186, 194, 199, 200, 201, 202, 203, 204, 205, 206, 207, 208, 209, 211, 214, 215, 217, 222, 223, 282, 305, 308, 309, 310, 311, 361, 363, 364, 406, 431
Inventory Management 203, 204, 205, 207, 214
investment 6, 8, 12, 14, 15, 18, 21, 44, 47, 52, 53, 56, 62, 65, 66, 79, 87, 89, 99, 105, 111, 112, 113, 128, 130, 138, 141, 151, 152, 166, 186, 198, 199, 214, 217, 232, 237, 245, 256, 262, 263, 265, 275, 279, 286, 288, 304, 316, 322, 323, 336, 337, 340, 344, 345, 350, 352, 357, 366, 369, 372, 373, 374, 375, 378, 382, 384, 388, 393, 395, 402, 407
iphone 402
IP network 218
ISO9000 263
ISO14000 74, 285, 299, 368, 430
ISO accreditation 263, 375
Italy 74, 131, 183

Jaguar Land Rover (JLR) 70, 375, 429
Japan 68, 74, 141, 142
JetBlue 184
Jidoka 283
Job Enlargement 44, 278
Job Enrichment 44, 278, 279, 437
Job Rotation 44, 260, 278
Joint Quarterly Review Meetings 161
Just in Time (JIT) 50, 91, 199, 360, 361, 362, 432, 443
 - see also Kanban 173, 205, 283, 360, 365

Kaizen 270, 283, 355
 - see also Continuous improvement 270, 283, 355
Kanban 205, 206, 283, 361
Kazakhstan 55, 101, 109, 209
Key Performance Indicators (KPIs) 180, 197, 225, 234, 279, 357, 377, 443
Key Sales Objectives (KSO) 225, 234, 443
KFC 79
Kia 68
Kingdom, Geeta 2
Kondratieff 13, 123, 125, 126, 127, 128, 129, 436

Kraljic's matrix 196, 340
Kyoto 6

Laptop Larries 243
lead time 34, 204, 205, 208, 406
Lean Thinking 364, 432
Lease driven supply reduction 95
Least Desirable Outcome (LDO) 157, 443
Legal Strategy 411
Legal Structure 137
Letter of Interest (or Intent) (LOI) 154, 443
Levi 114, 312
Lewin's Freeze Model 319, 322, 438
Liberal party 132
Liberia 183
life cycle 20, 74, 100, 101, 104, 150, 255, 402
logistics 28, 54, 55, 73, 89, 109, 112, 199, 208, 210, 211, 213, 214, 265, 293, 366, 373
longevity 1, 2, 8, 104, 106, 110, 137, 146, 152, 156, 164, 191, 192, 194, 197, 212, 214, 219, 220, 226, 261, 265, 267, 269, 285, 296, 312, 320, 334, 341, 350, 351, 352, 382, 396, 405, 408, 417, 422, 425
Longevity 192, 193, 387, 388, 415, 421
Long Life Cycle 296
Lufthansa 183

MacDonald's 79
MacGregor
  - *see also* Theory X and Y 51
Make-Buy-Lease 407
Make-to-order 305
Malthusian Trap 95, 96
Malthus, Thomas 96
Mamas & Papas 303
Managed Afterlife 301
management 1, 9, 12, 13, 19, 27, 28, 32, 33, 35, 41, 43, 47, 50, 53, 59, 71, 72, 76, 79, 87, 88, 99, 100, 104, 116, 123, 131, 134, 135, 137, 145, 146, 148, 157, 159, 160, 162, 163, 165, 169, 173, 174, 179, 187, 190, 194, 196, 197, 203, 205, 206, 207, 208, 209, 211, 214,

219, 220, 221, 227, 228, 229, 238, 244, 248, 253, 255, 263, 264, 265, 267, 268, 270, 272, 274, 276, 277, 278, 279, 282, 299, 302, 305, 310, 316, 319, 320, 321, 324, 325, 326, 327, 328, 331, 334, 340, 344, 345, 351, 352, 356, 357, 361, 362, 365, 367, 368, 369, 371, 374, 376, 380, 389, 391, 394, 395, 396, 399, 406, 407, 409, 410, 411, 415, 416, 417, 418, 421, 422, 424, 425, 426, 427, 429, 430, 431
Managing Successful Programmes (MSP) 321, 443
Manchester United 12, 382
MAN Model 225, 249, 437
Manufacturing Resource Planning (MRP) 355, 366, 443
Manugistics 366
margin 14, 24, 33, 45, 63, 71, 87, 88, 89, 91, 92, 104, 134, 152, 163, 169, 176, 192, 219, 227, 297, 339, 367, 377, 379, 398, 399, 402, 409, 425, 447
Market Analysis 59
Marketing Mix 387, 403, 404, 439
Marmite 281
Maslow's Hierachy of Needs 51
McKinsey 7S model 392, 439
Measure-Data-Value (MDV) 355, 357, 438, 443
Memorex 396
Mendlow 145, 165
Mercuri 239
Microsoft 16, 302
Millenium Stadium 327
Millennium Dome 36
Mintzberg
 - see also 5P Model 413, 421, 429, 439
Mission 6, 11, 417
MIT D8 Double Bubble Hybrid Wing Body 317
modular designs 223, 285, 311
Monarch 183
Monetarism 124
Most Desirable Outcome (MDO) 157, 443
Mother Nature 95, 96, 98, 99, 115, 118, 188, 273, 276, 338
Motorola 364
MTN 79
Muda 282, 360, 362

Multiskilling 278
Mura 282, 360
Muri 283, 360
Mussolini, Benito 131
Must / Intend / Like (MIL) 443
Myanmar 393

N+1 345
National Geographic 106
National Individual Standing Offer (NISO) 154, 443
National Master Standing Offer (NMSO) 154, 443
Nazarbayev, President 55
Net Present Value (NPV) 90, 443
New Aircraft Concepts Research (NACRE) 316, 443
new entrants 19, 67, 152, 163, 374
New Zealand 152
Nigeria 98, 152, 218
North American Space Agency (NASA) 287, 316, 443
Northrup Grumman
  - *see also* SELECT Project 317
not-for-profit 119

Océ 253, 254
Official Journal of the European Union (OJEU) 152, 154, 195, 374, 443
Oilgae 290
Oldham 128
Olympic villages 36
OPEX 104, 339, 443
Ouchi 50, 435
Outsource Relationship Management (ORM) 378
overheads 72, 75, 76, 149, 311, 406
Overproduction 363

Painshare 378
pantone 359
Paradigms 221
Pareto 207, 214, 399, 400
Patron-Purveyor-Pitcher 225, 437
payback 11, 90, 125, 255, 304, 373, 407

People Pillar 39, 40, 41, 44, 46, 50, 52, 53, 60, 78, 180, 221, 274, 276, 278, 324, 389, 395, 404, 414, 435
Perestroika 393
Performing
 - see also Tuckman 44
PESTLE Analysis 9, 23, 24, 124, 259, 269, 335, 371, 387, 392, 418, 435, 443
Peters and Waterman 391
Philips Lighting
 - see also EcoVision 384
Pillar Equilibrium 423
pipeline 61, 62, 181, 193, 231, 233, 240, 376
Planet Pillar 95, 96, 97, 207, 216, 221, 231, 261, 275, 289, 294, 304, 324, 368, 395, 400, 405, 407, 414, 423, 435
Point-Reason-Example-Point (PREP) 82, 444
Political-Economic-Social-Technological (PEST) 124, 443
Polluter Pays Principle 300
Pollution management 299
Porsche 70
Porter, Michael
 - see also Five Force Mode (Porter's) 18, 19, 59, 67, 129, 152, 169, 185, 268, 412, 435, 448
Preferred Procurement Process 241
PREP-One Page-Interesting-Newsworthy-Three (POINT) 82, 435, 444
Pre Qualification Questionnaire (PQQ) 152, 153, 373, 374, 444
President Goodluck Jonathan 153
Process Cloud 259, 262, 437
Process Manual 262, 263
Process Map 266, 437
Procurement Cycle 145, 436
Product Life Cycle (PLC) 9, 19, 20, 21, 435, 444
Product Mix 59
Profit margin 367
Profit Pillar 59, 60, 61, 65, 67, 68, 71, 85, 90, 146, 151, 175, 178, 181, 185, 193, 194, 206, 214, 217, 220, 221, 226, 261, 262, 268, 275, 287, 304, 312, 313, 324, 358, 395, 398, 400, 404, 405, 407, 415, 423, 435
Programme Evaluation and Review Technique (PERT) 336, 443
Project Board 324, 326

Project Process 242
Projects IN Controlled Environments (Prince2) 319, 321, 324, 438, 444
Project Strategy 410

qualitative measures 355, 372
Quality 11, 59, 76, 79, 173, 174, 188, 197, 198, 199, 269, 270, 323,
    374, 375, 407, 410, 413, 432, 435, 437, 441, 444, 445, 447
Quality Circles 413
Quality Function Deployment (QFD) 432, 444
Quality, Time & Cost (QTC) 59, 76, 323, 375, 444
quantitative measures 234, 355, 372
Question Marks 20, 21, 397
Quick Ratio 367, 379

Recommended Price List (RPL) 154
Recruit-Induct-Train-Evaluate (RITE) 39, 46, 47, 51, 435, 444
Recruit-Induct-Train-Utilise-Analyse-Leaving (RITUAL) 39, 47, 48, 355,
    380, 435, 444
recruitment 39, 46, 49, 137, 325, 374, 380, 381, 388, 409
Reduce-to-Produce programme 299
Reduce to Produce (RTP) 117, 145, 161, 162, 285, 308, 436, 444
Reims 36
Relationships 39, 145, 174, 225, 260, 285, 319, 347, 377, 436
Request for Information (RFI) 154, 372, 444
Request for Proposal (RFP) 154, 247, 248, 372, 444
Request for Quote (RFQ) 154, 372, 444
Request for Standing Offer (RFSO) 154, 444
Research & Development (R&D) 14, 15, 21, 59, 65, 66, 130, 286, 444
Return on Capital Employed 367
Richmond Dam 24
Rima River project 98
Risk 131, 145, 174, 192, 212, 331, 332, 333, 334, 335, 336, 337, 340,
    341, 342, 343, 344, 374, 412, 418, 438, 445
Risk Strategy 412
RITE Way 39, 46, 47, 51, 435
Rivalry 67
Rolls Royce 70
Rough Order of Magnitude (ROM) 154
Ryanair 183, 184

Safety Stock 174, 204, 205
Sale of Goods Act 179, 297
Sales Eco Cube 230, 437
Sales Prevention 235, 236
Sales strategy 239, 387
Sandbagging 225, 227, 372
SAP 366
Sea of Mexico 25, 251
Seasonings 241
security 65, 125, 126, 138, 205, 217, 242, 249, 316, 345
SELECT project
  - see also Northrup Grumman 317
Sheffield 17, 128
Shell 79
Shenzhen 169
Silkair 184
Silver Birch 291
Singapore 152
Single Minute Exchange of Die (SMED)
  - see also Toyota 305, 364, 444
Single Point Of Failure 345, 362, 444
Six Sigma 45, 52, 173, 197, 206, 259, 271, 273, 275, 364, 407
Skype 229, 378
Small Medium Enterprises (SME) 10, 17, 64, 90, 135, 358, 399, 444
Sodexho 11
Somali pirate 334
Sony 402
Sources of lending 411
South Africa 36, 113
South Africa World Cup 36
South Sea Bubble 351
Southwestern Airline 184
Soviet Union 393
Spain 131, 183
Specification 192, 195, 223, 436
Specific-Measurable-Achievable-Realistic-Timed (SMART) 123, 139,
    279, 355, 359, 436, 444
Stable Sales Model 59
Stadium of Light 327, 329

staff turnover 28, 40, 409, 421, 424
stakeholder 28, 30, 83, 84, 86, 165, 192, 319, 321, 328, 387, 388, 410, 413
Standard Deviation 173, 174, 203, 204, 205, 437
Staple Range Model 225
Starbucks 79
Stars 20, 21, 66, 397
Statistical Process Control (SPC) 444
steel 17, 67, 68, 118, 128, 168, 169, 194, 206, 298, 328, 351, 394, 398
Stoke 17, 128
STOPWASTE 145, 164, 165, 186, 223
Strategically Controlled Action Network (SCAN) 123, 135, 444
Strategy 22, 33, 59, 60, 85, 90, 134, 166, 173, 174, 181, 191, 260, 269, 285, 340, 387, 388, 389, 394, 395, 396, 399, 400, 408, 409, 410, 411, 412, 413, 415, 416, 417, 423, 428, 436, 437, 438, 448
Subsonic Ultra Green Aircraft Research (SUGAR) 316, 444
substitutes 19, 152
Supplier Engaged Green Product Awareness (SEGPA) 104, 444
Supplier-Input-Process-Output-Customer (SIPOC) 173, 187, 188, 259, 262, 421, 427, 436, 444
Supplier Opportunities Assessment Review (SOAR) 161, 444
Supply Chain 2, 65, 68, 73, 74, 75, 91, 95, 146, 152, 173, 174, 175, 176, 177, 178, 179, 180, 181, 182, 184, 185, 186, 187, 188, 189, 190, 191, 192, 194, 196, 197, 199, 200, 202, 203, 204, 206, 207, 208, 210, 214, 217, 218, 219, 220, 221, 222, 223, 259, 260, 262, 270, 299, 305, 309, 311, 364, 365, 366, 378, 406, 407, 417, 418, 423, 427, 436, 438
sustainability 1, 2, 3, 5, 6, 8, 10, 26, 27, 29, 30, 40, 49, 55, 60, 66, 90, 96, 99, 100, 101, 102, 119, 123, 142, 164, 180, 206, 226, 231, 236, 237, 252, 253, 254, 268, 269, 312, 321, 322, 323, 324, 334, 345, 348, 356, 360, 361, 368, 370, 371, 380, 384, 398, 405, 417, 418, 421, 422, 426, 427, 428, 430
Sustainable Axioms 347, 350, 438
Sustainable Balance 421, 425, 426
sustainable conviction 41
Sustainable Design 285, 286, 396
Sustainable Destination 31
Sustainable Drivers 10
Sustainable Economy 123, 124

Sustainable Healthcare 141
Sustainable IMPACT 26
Sustainable Impactor Model 421, 424, 426, 427, 439
Sustainable Paragons 285, 291
Sustainable Procurement 39, 95, 145, 146, 147, 149, 151, 152, 157, 158, 159, 160, 161, 163, 164, 165, 166, 167, 186, 375, 436
Sustainable Sales Function 225, 226
Sustainable Success Factors (SSF) 387, 389, 444
Sustainable Supply Chain 173, 175, 192, 197, 199, 220, 221
Sustainable Vision 9, 10, 13, 23, 175, 261, 287
SUSTAIN Model 225, 245, 437
Swan Vesta 369
Sweden 152, 183
SWOT 9, 15, 16, 269, 335, 371, 387, 394, 435, 444

Tachometers 209
Tactical Lip-Service 229
targeting 30, 139, 176, 197, 287, 316, 357, 359, 383, 405
Tata 68, 69, 71
taxation 23, 132, 141, 142, 393
Taxonomy 248
Taylor 380
Team Building 44
Teamwork 39, 49
technology 7, 14, 27, 65, 106, 107, 109, 123, 129, 130, 133, 134, 141, 209, 223, 259, 274, 281, 291, 309, 311, 344, 370, 374, 396, 402, 408, 431
Tectonic change 413
Telecommunications 218
Telemechanique 88, 91, 92, 310, 362
TeliaSonera 108
Tender Submission Document (TSD) 154, 445
Tengizchevroil 55, 56, 109, 370
Tesco 89
The Netherlands 116
Theory X 39, 49, 50, 51, 435
Theory Y 39, 49, 50, 51, 435
Theory Z 39, 50, 435
The Profit Pillar 59, 60, 61, 193, 287, 435

Three Pillar model 39, 286
Three Pillars 40, 145, 146, 151, 175, 180, 200, 219, 230, 231, 234,
    280, 286, 320, 331, 341, 350, 357, 368, 381, 385, 387, 388, 404,
    407, 410, 411, 422, 423, 436, 438
Time Thieves 225, 243
T-Mobile 79
Total Acquisition Cost (TAC) 444
Total Cost of Ownership (TCO) 31, 95, 99, 100, 101, 102, 104, 110,
    145, 147, 151, 164, 186, 222, 259, 268, 313, 435, 445
Total Cost of Sustainable Ownership (TCSO) 31, 95, 99, 100, 101,
    104, 110, 145, 147, 151, 164, 186, 259, 268, 313, 435, 445
Total Quality Management (TQM) 199, 259, 270, 271, 273, 407, 431,
    445
Toyota 50, 67, 68, 79, 91, 173, 179, 186, 205, 206, 259, 267, 275, 282,
    283, 305, 306, 310, 355, 360, 361, 362, 363, 364, 365, 374, 437,
    438
Tracom Four Styles 39, 43, 435
Traditional Behaviours 229
Traffic Light Matrix 421, 426, 439
training 4, 12, 28, 45, 47, 49, 51, 74, 91, 137, 138, 157, 189, 208, 228,
    234, 239, 244, 252, 253, 304, 309, 381, 395, 432
Training Needs Analysis (TNA) 145, 167, 445
Transactional Process Control (TPC) 445
Transparency International 152, 153
Transportation 186, 223, 363
Trend Control Systems 255
Triple Bottom Line 6, 40, 100, 102, 230, 444
truancy 50
Tsunami 68
Tuckman's view 44
Tuckman Team Development Cycle 39, 44, 435
  Forming, Storming, Norming, Performing and Dorming, Adjourning,
    Team Building 44
Turkey 27, 218
Twitter 85, 199

Uniform Commercial Code 297
Unilever 417, 418
Uninterrupted Power Supply (UPS) 336, 337, 445

Union Carbide
 - *see also* Bhopal 25
Union of South American Nations (UNASUR) 154, 445
United States of America (USA) 101, 132, 152, 158, 183, 184, 191, 223, 247, 287, 426
United Technologies Corp (UTC) 252, 445
UPS 79, 336, 337, 445
US Geological Survey 112
US Government Environmental Protection Agency 106
US Navy 113

VAG 70, 71, 79, 435, 445
Value at Risk (VAR) 337, 445
Variable Speed Drives 256
Vendor Managed Inventory (VMI) 208, 378, 393, 445
Viewpoint Rankings 225, 232
Virgin 22, 80, 182, 183, 184, 316, 317, 370
Virgin Atlantic 316, 317
vision 2, 6, 9, 10, 11, 12, 13, 33, 40, 55, 85, 87, 124, 137, 138, 146, 180, 195, 205, 228, 240, 261, 268, 286, 320, 323, 326, 334, 343, 371, 382, 384, 388, 394, 408, 409, 416, 417, 422
Vodafone 79
Voice of the Customer 52, 188, 270, 364, 413
Volkswagen Audi Group (VAG) 70, 71, 79, 445

Walmart 89
Warehouse Management System (WMS) 179, 445
Wembley 323, 327, 328
Whig 132
win-lose 105, 362, 377
win-win 105, 157, 160, 163, 362, 377, 378, 380
Wiremold Company 431
Womack 364, 432
Work-In-Progress (WIP) 305, 361, 445
Wright brothers 130

Zahhly & Tosi 46